D0142538

THIS SACRED TRUST

This Sacred Trust

AMERICAN NATIONALITY

1798–1898

Paul C. Nagel

New York   Oxford University Press   1971

Copyright © 1971 by Oxford University Press, Inc.
Library of Congress Catalogue Card Number: 78-159648

Printed in the United States of America

MOUNT UNION COLLEGE
LIBRARY

917.303
N147t
148344

for ERIC, JEFF, and STEVEN
who must carry on the Trust.

PREFACE

       I have long been intrigued by nineteenth-century American thinking about national meaning. Some of my earlier work convinced me that national self-awareness in the United States has not been properly understood. The familiar rhetoric of affirmation had once seemed to me an accurate representation of American nationality. However, I now believe that clichés about destiny and progress are only deceptive fragments from the Republic's introspection of a century ago.

Consequently, I have tried to assemble and interpret the important elements in America's self-consciousness. The results may startle some readers who will find that their forebears considered American meaning to be complicated and distressing. Nationality had religious, political, social, economic, and literary considerations. They form what I believe was the most significant feature of American thought between the times of John Adams and William McKinley. Involved were agonizing and ecstatic perceptions of the Republic's calling, as well as deep fear that man's weakness would betray the nation.

Today some Americans are struggling anew with the implications of nationality. I hope that this book may contribute to our capacity for dealing frankly with the difficulties of being American.

Two universities have generously helped the creation of this study. The University of Kentucky Research Foundation twice financed research trips. The University of Missouri has given a new faculty member some uninterrupted time for writing. I thank both institutions. I owe special gratitude to two Missouri colleagues, Vernon E. Wilson and Richard S. Kirkendall. For varied assistance and inspiration I thank Robert P. Hay, John H.

DeBerry, John Kleber, Douglas Noble, and Michael Adams, all of whom were once graduate students at the University of Kentucky. Talents of Mrs. Casey Craig, Mrs. Monica Thomas, Mrs. Ida Wolff, and Mrs. Janet Pemberton brought the manuscript from a scrawl to a reality. Once again I am indebted to Sheldon Meyer of the Oxford University Press. Lesser editors would have lost both patience and faith.

Finally, I must turn gratefully to home. Joan and our sons helped in ways that I cannot hope to explain in pages like these. My family's best reward, I suspect, would be that next time I choose a less demanding subject.

P. C. N.
Columbia, Missouri
May 1971

CONTENTS

INTRODUCTION

By 1798 thoughtful American citizens were never far from ideas about national purpose and progress. During the ensuing century these citizens were mindful of what Daniel Webster told a Faneuil Hall audience in Boston mourning the death of Adams and Jefferson. "This lovely land, this glorious liberty, these benign institutions, the dear purchase of our fathers," said Webster, were a "sacred trust" which the present age held for generations both past and to come. From 1798 to 1898 Americans speculated about the nobility of character, loftiness of virtue, and earnestness of religion needed to carry "this sacred trust." Such an outlook became the center of national meaning. Webster was neither the first nor the last to point out that "the world turns hither its solicitous eyes" for "all, all conjure us to act wisely and faithfully, in the relation which we sustain."

This admonition, so characteristic of the century's viewpoint, put America's meaning and fulfillment uneasily between past and future, between man's nature and responsibility, and between the world as it was and as it should be. America's thinking was first widely impressed with the implications of nationality in 1798 when the Republic's supposed danger brought extreme measures for purification and security. From the Alien and Sedition legislation controversy to America's triumph over Spain in 1898, national thought struggled under invocations like those Webster made. It was a confused and confusing intellectual pilgrimage, often tormented and usually clamorous. Beginning with deliberate removal from the European circle and especially from Anglo-Saxon kinship, the century concluded with a strident return to the world and to the venerable comforts of the Anglo-Saxon family.

Students of American thought have begun to recognize nationality's role. Attention has turned to such important considerations as Manifest Destiny, Mission, Liberalism, Race, Character, the Founders, Land, Nature, Loyalty, Abundance, and Union, as well as to certain germane symbols. It is time now for a broader study of America's self-consciousness. Introducing the reader to this venture requires a comment about terminology, organization, and method. The literature treating concepts of national character and purpose has become a babel. Especially confusing are the important words, "nationalism" and "nationality." The varied meanings of "nationalism" suggest a deliberate effort to glory in the spirit, fact, or endeavor of a polity. "Nationalism" regularly has implied a doctrine or a specific form of consciousness conveying superiority or prestige. On the other hand, "nationality" refers to what it meant to be a nation. This word encompasses both the matter of citizenship and the ideology arising from belonging to a polity. Nationality in American thought includes much more than the exultation usually associated with nationalism. To recapture nationality entails reconstructing what being an American implied to citizens of the Republic.

This effort will assume that what Professor David Potter has called multiple loyalties existed within the embrace of American nationality. An analysis of national consciousness needs to mention only obliquely the Southern, or Western, or New England introspective view. While these were fascinating masks for special interests, they drew upon the uneasy spirit in America's nationality.[1]

Nineteenth-century Americans generally agreed that national being was incomplete and unproven. Nationality therefore was something to be achieved. In pondering this, citizens did so in an atmosphere of Christian responsibility. This context is basic, for, as this book will show, Americans thought about their nationality as a Trust and themselves as Stewards. These terms were familiar in the century, as was the word Vineyard in representing America's physical and political settings. Three words, therefore, rich with Biblical implication, are important props for this study.

While Americans exchanged affirmations about their Trust and themselves as Stewards in a remarkable Vineyard, they also displayed much anxiety over the realities of their experience. The Republic never seemed free of great difficulty. Citizens of the time naturally considered this through the Christian language about human frailty. "Mammon" was used to mean the greed and avarice which vexed man. "Passion" represented the emotional instability and excesses which neither divine nor rational power quite let man succeed in mastering. A special adversity was partisanship, which Americans said embodied lust and license, selfishness and pride. In triumph and elegy, anxious Americans used these words in endless talking about their nation.

In tracing such talk, this book is designed on a chronological sequence and is arranged in five chapters. Each of these begins with a short summary of the era and then divides into two major parts. The first section reconstructs the doctrine of nationality as it grew in the period. This involves the affirmations about the Trust which rested upon Stewards toiling in a notable Vineyard, as well as the anxieties expressed over the hazards of mammon, passion, and partisanship. Each chapter's second part listens to the spokesmen who were talking and writing characteristically about what being an American meant. This includes some of the prominent advocates, among them always being the period's chief Stewards who served as President of the United States. Part two also reviews America's broader responses to the concept of a sacred Trust. Some spoke of an assured trusteeship; still more expressed uncertainty; while others despaired that America could be fulfilled.

There is a pattern to national consciousness in the nineteenth century. The first phase, from 1798 to 1815, found America's survival the prime concern. Men wondered if the nation would endure long enough to carry forward the responsibilities placed by Providence. The first chapter begins with the emotional disorders brought by controversy with England and France and closes in the ecstacy prompted by martial victory. Chapter Two traces America's search between 1815 and 1848 for reassuring truth about its character and burden. This chapter also concludes in joy brought by successful war.

Despite a supposed triumph in 1848, American meaning soon raised even more difficult questions. The third chapter extends to 1865 when horrible sacrifices encouraged Americans to talk of their atonement. Thereafter, a fourth chapter examines the national hope which was briefly renewed until mammon showed new capacity to distract the American Steward. This chapter ends in 1876 when the national centennial praised scenes of long before while the scandalous present spoiled the Republic's aspirations. In the final chapter, covering time between 1876 and 1898, national spirit escaped the old Trust. A nation and a world had changed, permitting the concept of America's role to be altered.

In this way nationality dominated nineteenth-century thought in America. It was not surprising that numerous people should observe, as did one in 1836, that "the population of the United States is beyond that of other countries an anxious one." Americans were "an anxious, careworn people." This can be better appreciated if it is recognized that these people considered themselves called to resolve for all coming time the ancient paradox involving freedom and order.

Knowing that they were expected to be model citizens free within a pioneering republican system, Americans instead watched evidence grow of their mortality. Nationality in the United States never came to terms with its most important consideration, human frailty. This fact must modify the emphasis scholars have placed upon the importance to America of lacking a past, or of a pragmatic outlook, or of abundance. The doctrine of Americanism was most dependent upon an awareness of personal and public responsibility and of the tribulations which steadily assailed that responsibility. Prevalence of such an outlook answers Charles A. Beard's inquiry long ago if there was "anything fixed in this flood of feelings" he saw in nineteenth-century American thought. It also replies to another question Beard asked: "Are there any steps in the development of American nationality?" Like so many historians, Beard looked for something "distinctive" about America in its "swirl of ideas and events."

This historical quest has been misled and frustrated by the evidences of liberalism in American thought. These have been examined without recognizing the sense of becoming which Americans understood to be part of their unfulfilled Trust. With recent help from some perceptive students of literature and religion in the United States, historians are now better able to perceive how American consciousness was much more than exclamations about individualism, freedom, progress, destiny, and providential design. In view of the fear and uncertainty, the burden and frustration which were so important in American nationality, it can no longer be asserted that in the nineteenth century the United

States exhibited a "sober faith" or that its norms were so self-evident that its nationality "hardly needed to become articulate." [2]

America's self-awareness grappled with a great contradiction. In advocating democracy, Americans also talked of rescuing individuals from the individual and persons from the people. The fact that nineteenth-century America was a politicized culture chained to a theological post suggests the contrapuntal design of its nationality. It must be understood that while America could not take itself out of the context of republicanism, it still spent a century anxiously condemning the realities of politics, partisanship, and passion. America sought to be a model republic without suffering the infamous results of republicanism. The burden of being an association of free humans brought America to be very cautious about the assumptions of the Enlightenment. Rather than basking in the comfort of certain "givens," America was prodded by knowing that her fulfillment required straightening a circle of paradox long troublesome to mankind.

As Americans watched the strain between republican order and human nature, they were uncomfortably aware of the popular remark that never again would man be granted the chance, as he was at that time in America, to reconcile these ancient foes. All resources were summoned to achieve this reconciliation. Education, religion, literature, and motherhood would lead Americans out of human weakness. Seeking to be in the world but not of it, America followed a difficult path to national triumph. Such fulfillment appeared near in 1898, but not until material triumph had been allowed to claim moral significance over spiritual achievement.

Recapturing American nationality between 1798 and 1898 requires numerous compromises from the historian. It is impossible to read everything which might contain significant expression. However, research can note the regular reappearance of an ideology's content and thus some confirmation of it. As the notes following the Epilogue disclose, the sources for this book include the range of outlook which has come down to the scholar. Orations, sermons, hymns, newspapers, books, magazines, letters, and diaries are familiar stuff for the historian of intellect. They contain the seminal elements of an ideology, dominated as they are by the voice of reflective persons.

A persisting pattern of national consciousness throughout the century indicates the public's willingness to heed its articulate brethren. This should ease the misgiving of those who complain of intellectual history's captivity by written sources. Because there is not much material available that was written by the ordinary person, the historian must learn much from what was offered to the silent community. The public advocates of nationality provided the lore needed in a self-conscious Republic. Furthermore, the intellectual historian makes no guarantees about the viewpoint of the so-called average American. Such a concern need not trouble those seeking only the dynamics of a nation's intellect. The chapters of this book pursue such a search.[3]

THIS SACRED TRUST

CHAPTER ONE

SURVIVAL
1798–1815

Americans began to think about their nationality abruptly. They did so in distressing times. The events and attitudes notable in 1798 inaugurated a century of speculation about national meaning. This awakening discovered issues which dominated American thought until 1898.

When the nation's father, George Washington, was active, his presence had quieted misgiving about America's career. Most persons then had simple concerns. Maintenance of life in its elemental form, both social and physical, was uppermost. Endurance did not require refinement in either polity or culture, as long as America sustained order out of republicanism. Given this, few citizens bothered to pursue the meaning of nationality while Washington presided. In leaving office, the first President did more than sadden the nation. His Farewell Address pointed to approaching specters of responsibility and peril. From Washington's remarks came the first major statement of national purpose, as well as of the difficulties accompanying such stewardship. His words were more like an invocation than a benediction. They would haunt America throughout a century of introspection.[1]

Early in the Farewell, published in September 1796, Washington described his "apprehension of danger." He doubted "the permanency of your felicity as a People," despite a similarity of religion, manners, habits, political principles, and memories of a common cause and triumph. All of this, Washington feared, would be lost on a citizenry deluded by "cunning, ambitious, and unprincipled men." This misgiving prompted the President's candor about the threat to America's experiment in republicanism. He considered "The Spirit of Party" to be the carrier for strong passions inevitably raging in the human mind. Nothing should keep the nation from "a just estimate of that love of power, and proneness to abuse it, which predominates in the human heart."

Washington's admonition about human nature brought an appropriate corollary, one which was not forgotten in the following century: "Of all the dispositions and habits which lead to political prosperity, Religion and morality are indispensable supports." No patriot "should labour to subvert these great Pillars of human happiness, these firmest props of the duties of Men and citizens." Lest his countrymen miss this implication about their frailty, Washington emphasized that a capable public could be sustained only with religion. The President joined the doubters of intellect by saying, with barely constrained sarcasm: "Whatever may be conceded to the influence of refined education on minds of peculiar structure, reason and experience both forbid us to expect that National morality can prevail in exclusion of religious principle." He repeatedly admonished his countrymen to beware of "mere speculation" about the nation's design.

Obviously warming to the association of morality with nationality, Washington spoke of stewardship. "It will be worthy of a free, enlightened, and at no distant period, a great Nation, to give to mankind the magnanimous and too novel example of a People always guided by an exalted justice and benevolence." To this he added the note of uncertainty which would linger. "Can it be, that Providence has not connected the permanent felicity of a Nation with its virtue? The experiment, at least, is recommended by every sentiment which ennobles human Nature. Alas! is it rendered impossible by its vices?" Alas, indeed! Here Washington met the crucial issue in America's struggle to be worthy of its calling. If national well-being resulted from the moral vigor of its citizens, then America's experiment in republicanism was a task of awesome proportions.

The first President had few illusions about the challenge confronting the American role, in both its national and citizen spheres. He doubted frankly that his message would help "controul the usual current of the passions, or prevent our Nation from running the course which has hitherto marked the Destiny of Nations." Having seen so much of men, Washington said he was content to hope that his words "may now and then recur to moderate the fury of party spirit, to warn against the mischiefs of foreign Intrigue, to guard against the Impostures of pretended patriotism." If only America could have time enough actually to become a nation. First it needed a period "to settle and mature its yet recent institutions," and to develop "a degree of strength and consistency, which is necessary to give it, humanly speaking, the command of its own future." For Washington, America's significance was wrapped in survival. He told his countrymen that the worthiness of human nature and of the national design both remained to be proven.

For the next two decades America faced the question raised in Washington's departing words. Would the nation survive even long enough to begin discharging its Trust? Events between 1798 and 1815 seemed to threaten to topple the Republic. Neither citizen nor Republic showed promise, except that both somehow did survive. The period began with the United States entering an undeclared war against France, an old ally. Throughout the country disorder appeared to spread. In desperation the nation's leadership sought to control dissenting individuals and their evil abstractions by the Alien and Sedition Acts of 1798.

Thus, when Washington died at Mount Vernon in 1799, the nation had already given sign of fatal weakness. Some men were going to prison for views adjudged dangerous to the Republic. Others were said to plot anarchy, that awful kinsman of freedom, as in Pennsylvania's Fries uprising of 1799. Partisanship dominated the approaching presidential choice. A month before Washington died, he spoke of watching the nation with "an anxious and painful eye." America appeared "to be moving by hasty strides to some awful crisis," whose result "that Being, who sees, forsees, and directs all things, alone can tell." The most comfort Washington found at the time of his death was that "The vessel is afloat, or very nearly so." [2]

With a new century, the nation moved deeper into the shadows of partisanship, passion, and foreign intrigue. The conflict with France was followed by the disgraceful problem of the Barbary pirates. In the new federal capital, blessed with the father's name, party representatives talked openly of the candidates who were battling for a supposedly aloof Presidency. The triumph of the Jeffersonian movement wore thin during February 1801 when the House of Representatives let connivance and emotion control the choosing of a president. Consequently a hope born of desperation brought many to repeat Jefferson's inaugural paraphrase of Washington, that all were Republicans, all were Federalists. Even so, Jefferson was barely able to keep his followers united as new issues troubled the nation.

Continental expansion, fiscal policy, the role of the judiciary, local challenge to federal power, and even the question of national loyalty were some of the challenges both to the reason and the virtue of citizens. The spectacle appeared of a former vice president on trial for treason. In New England some men viewed Union as an unsuccessful experiment. Then, after an unnerving presidential canvass in 1808, America turned to seek dignity from the field of diplomacy. Again there was misfortune but no relief. The extraordinary venture into statesmanship represented by the Embargo and subsequent legislation brought a succession of disgraces overseas, and deeper discord and even hatred within the Republic. Passion and partisanship flourished. Elections to Congress produced new voices calling for vengeance abroad and expansion at home.

Split over who was the external foe and over internal policy, the nation went to war against Great Britain. If reason would not guide the Republic to safety, perhaps the new spirit expected from war would ensure survival. Such hopes were vain. The War of 1812 brought only more heartbreak. Disasters abounded in military tactics and leadership; the fiscal policy of the government was inadequate; the citizenry was more divided than ever. How much could republican hopes endure? The seat of government, despite its proud name, was left to the enemy for burning, while brethren in the northeast planned a secret convention to extort changes in the Republic's design. Worst of all, the citizen body, so vital to national dignity, appeared distracted by emotion and a new enemy, avarice.

Eighteen-fourteen ended grimly. Beset by disgrace and dissension, America seemed to be unsuccesful in its striving for morality and freedom. Republican survival appeared so dubious that men considered miraculous the intelligence of a peace treaty and Andrew Jackson's great victory at New Orleans. News of both prompted scenes of unaccustomed jubilation during February 1815. Suddenly a new phase opened in the development of America's nationality. Providential intervention at

Ghent and New Orleans had rescued the Republic, despite the failings of reason and morality and the triumphs of passion and partisanship. The men of the next era would seek to know what had been spared, and to what end. They would not soon escape the memory of the time when the nation's survival was doubted.

DOCTRINE

American nationality was tainted by uncertainty throughout the nineteenth century. Questions about existence were soon superseded by considerations of capacity. As Howard Mumford Jones once observed, America rejected Europe only to establish a doctrine of republican culture which "rested upon a group of confused and confusing ideas." In America these ideas were preoccupied with the future, the young nation's chief concern. This was hardly new. Colonial times had enjoyed contemplating "Ye *unborn Inhabitants of America!*" Men in centuries ahead should know "that in *Anno Domini 1758, we dream'd of your times.*" America meant for John Adams in 1765, "the opening of a grand scene and design in Providence" whose end must be to banish ignorance and despotism "all over the earth." But in view of events between 1798 and 1815, thoughtful men doubted that the nation would even be delivered to the future's people and their ministration. The emerging doctrine of national purpose reflected their misgiving.[3]

I: Affirmations   The American Revolution may have pointed men toward the future, but the young nation's steps seemed to falter. Swiftly the national responsibility came to be considered the preservation of past values as a Trust for the future. At stake were such vague treasures as equality and liberty. Their protection required God's aid, for the perils of the 1790's had a sobering effect upon America's outlook. Most contemporaries would agree when Jefferson called 1798 "that gloomy period," although not all for the same reason. However, all observers reacted by apotheosizing the past and affirming America's alliance with Providence.[4]

1

Acknowledging a providential Trust quickly produced a highly conservative stance in national thought. Surely neither God nor

Providence would award America its unique role without imparting guides and practices for an imperfect citizenry to follow. Public compliance was needed to sustain the nation's Trust. It became a popular affirmation that Americans were to be dutiful guardians against any mad effort to alter the nation's essence. America was a "high undertaking" watched by "the special care of its Divine Providence." The nation would survive for its purpose only if the American people continued to serve the established precepts deposited in the Constitution.[5]

The talk about the nation as being providentially called relied upon ambiguity to offset uneasiness. This was less advantageous to those who were attracted to more explicit topics, especially liberty and republicanism. These cherished concepts, normally linked, were considered a heavy assignment for America. The usual response was to denounce any tinkering with what was often called "rational liberty" and the "enjoyment of property." There was very little room in early national doctrine for dissent. Most persons agreed with the sentiment: "Away then, Americans, with every sentiment that is not in unison with the public weal. Let our private concerns yield to the calls of our Country."

Preservation of the republican Trust was said to require reflection, not emotion. Such rational behavior could not depend upon human impulse. This helped explain differences between America and Europe. Europe's limitations kept man from reasoning and so he had mistaken ideas about the rights of humanity. Federalists especially chose to deplore the "miscreants" who brought Europe's unfortunate views to thwart America's republican responsibilities. To survive, America must rise above the prejudice and rancor raised by argument. Argument would produce anarchy or despotism like that in Europe, a constant threat as the nation sought to be republicanism's "last, her only asylum." A prudent, conservative course would cause the floods to abate "and liberty may go abroad upon the land to return no more." It would be necessary for each citizen to recognize that only through exercising civic responsibility could natural liberty be endured.[6]

It was plausible that talk of the republican Trust portrayed the national venture as a great experiment, wherein Americans had "opened a new road to ourselves, and are traveling on it without knowing, to a certainty, what dangers may await us by the way." To view the American condition as more than a state of probation was absurd, ran this familiar affirmation. The nation must not feel satisfied about republicanism with no more to show than a constitution laid upon parchment. American testing still faced the hazards of foreign temptation, internal vice and dissension, and numerous "profanations." Consequently, many trustees yearned for the reappearance of a great mentor. Only someone like Washington, said Francis Blake in the anguish of 1812, could teach the children to kneel "in humble adoration" at the "lofty vestibule" of Freedom's shrine, which was the temple of "NATIONAL GLORY."

Although the years after 1798 were near the time of the Fathers and were often dominated by men who themselves had been Fathers, the cry arose that America was undone lest it exhume the Founders' spirit. This became the plausible outlet for the sense of responsibility. Guard the Fathers' work. "Shall we riot in luxury, in philosophy, and faction, and forget the heroes and the patriots" who had made the nation? Only the same spirit "which originated, can alone preserve our independence." From this came the special importance of the Fourth of July. It was to be a day of national solemnity, taking all citizens back to national principles. These considered the American essence to be a reservoir for the Founders' beliefs. Youthful though the present generation was, its role according to prevailing doctrine was not to create but to conserve.

Holding the past in trust made a compelling concept, permitting exponents to point out that America's splendor was in its start. Other nations had to stumble through the evils of antiquity, but "Columbians" could "look back to their political birth with a placid countenance." The charge was to sustain these early precepts through emulation, not mere profession. Accordingly, the citizens should be immersed in "the holy spirit of our ancestors." Only then could America "cultivate a national character" and "become only AMERICANS!" As the American situation became more hazardous it was comforting to consider nationality an awesome "patrimony of our common ancestors." Only the past was certain, the present was insufferable, and the road to an impatient future was treacherous. With survival at

stake, men of all factions were drawn less to the essentials of the
Trust than to the lurid dangers facing America. These were, in
the times of Adams, Jefferson, and Madison, considered decid-
edly internal with the external menace assailed largely for encouraging inner tumult. America's doctrine thus praised an
attitude, usually called "the unconquerable spirit of the forefathers." [7]

Talk about the Fathers concentrated on their legendary accord. They left no embarrassing memories of divergent sentiment
or enforced conformity. The lesson was obvious. A nation worthy
of its Trust must cultivate unanimity. Jefferson's First Inaugural
Address, like Washington's Farewell, came from a man embarrassed because he had to urge upon a new generation practices
from his own time, so recently passed. Joseph Hopkinson's song,
"Hail, Columbia," composed in the crisis hours of 1798, saluted
the Founders as a "heaven-born band!" The song pleaded that
renewed unity for liberty would be required to keep the Founders' spirit near. Hopkinson's concern over internal disaffections
was widely shared. Initiation of American endeavor was thus
often said to await the creation of domestic accord. Many Americans explained their calling by saying they should be a peaceful
contrast to the brawling larger world. In the tumult within and
beyond the nation, calm at home became such an important goal
that the means momentarily represented national purpose.

An able affirmation of this doctrine was heard in Roxbury,
New Jersey, in 1807. After a sidelong glance at the nation's commercial prospects and its responsibility for liberty, John D. Gardiner wondered why there was so much discord and doubt in the
national outlook. It mocked the talk of defending national
honor. Gardiner concluded that there was inadequate dedication
in America to the noble principles of virtue and freedom. The
unity of the nation was crucial, for, as he said, "split on the
rocks of division, our ruin will be inevitable. . . . A house divided against itself cannot stand, a country divided will fall in
ruins." This refrain, which became familiar by 1860, pleaded
that America evolve into a family in order to fulfill its expectations. As a band of brothers who blended liberty with patriotism,
"then shall we have nothing to fear from within and without,
then shall America flourish like the Garden of Eden, and become a name and praise in the whole earth." [8]

Regardless of local or partisan intent, this idea was common-place throughout the nation. The national Trust, whether for the past, for republicanism, or for Providence, could not even be shouldered properly unless America itself were reverent, united, and virtuous. The dismaying absence of these traits captured much national attention. It was contended that the guile of prosperity was distracting the public from its responsibility. "We are growing rich and great too fast," was one assessment. Others worried over "a fatal delusion" concerning human capacity and reason. This was called folly. America's existence itself proved it was "Emmanuel's land, in which he has planted his Church, and maintained his cause, by a series of signal interpositions." National progress required more faith in God and enlarged education.

Many citizens were incredulous at the miracles of 1815, so desperate had been the nation's plight. Human frailty and republican miscarriage had been so evident since 1798 that Americans of 1815 generally accepted the marvelous turn of events as a mystical bequest of renewed opportunity. One cautious pamphleteer said, America might now be a better guard at "the fountain of justice." It must never "permit the source to be polluted, because too soon the poison will be diffused to the remotest streams, and then the blood of our fathers will have flowed without effect, and we shall have lived in vain." [9]

2

So uneasy were the early years in which Americans thought about national meaning that talk of human aberrations was commonplace. National doctrine concentrated in this era on the Steward who carried American responsibility. This topic involved not only ancient questions about the citizen and society but also the mysterious issue of national character. Whether men urged equalitarianism or elitism, all spoke in a language which mixed religious, moral, naturalist, and rationalist terms. This augmented the confusion and ambiguity in American thinking about nationality.

America's religious revival was especially important for the developing national doctrine. Thoughtful commentators, especially Professor Alan Heimert, have suggested that the Awakening of 1800–1801 not only brought an Americanization of theology but also reflected social discontent and political aspiration. It made democracy more than an abstraction when it encouraged a patriotism arising from fraternal affection. This idea helped to establish personal virtue as the Republic's core. It also aided the Jeffersonian effort to make the public will more important than social contract as the idea central to the national process. The behavior of society was as important as the demeanor of the individual. American doctrine had them both kneeling before the Republic's God. Assuming divine patience, men saw America becoming an invisible church consisting of Christians who loved both God and country. A consequent spirit of forebearance was the basis of Jeffersonian appeals. Agriculture and commerce were to be a national fellowship. Theology, morality, and nation combined to demand what the affirmations of nationality called stewardship.[10]

The American doctrine certainly agreed that the citizen had not yet completed his assignment. Most observers found little reason to exalt the natural man. By 1798 the Republic's ideology had little if any affection for man in his primal state. It was recognized that Stewards obviously needed inspiration and even indoctrination if they were to keep pace in the nation's pilgrimage. The Federalists did not monopolize concern over human passion, ignorance, godlessness, avarice, and poverty. General anxieties were soothed by portraying society as an organic entity whose majesty and selectivity could smooth the ragged edge of individual conduct. Revivalism's wish for men to come to God intended also that they stay closer to the republican circle. If the nation were to thrive with free mortals, these mortals must somehow be taught not to sin while also being indoctrinated in the rightful claims of the nation.

There were few affirmations before 1815 that the individual Steward would thrive. The frail design in all men was widely appreciated, encouraging talk of the need to control the human self. "Consider *that* man an enemy who attempts to make you believe mankind are not depraved." Such terms as "the natural rectitude of man" and "the moral dignity of human nature" were called meaningless by most spokesmen. Many variations of this doctrine were heard, but all urged candor about mankind. "Poor human nature; this world is thy trial, here self denial and

restraint, mortification and disappointment, are thy lot." Most
of the American opinions expressed in the beginning of the nineteenth century agreed that experience outweighed the easy talk
of liberty and equality. Man might conquer his nature only
through learning, with religion as a partner. Consequently, the
best American must "be religious," for "the relation of politics
and religion is like that of the body and the soul." Until religion
was more prevalent, the virtues of the Fathers would remain
"our reproach." [11]

For the more secular minded, a successful American Steward
had to be cautious about confusing "licentiousness with liberty."
Anarchy and tyranny were equally ominous foes. Although it
was possible that Americans had the potential for good, they
were not "imaginary creatures" who needed no governing. They
were beings "selfish, though social, devoured by a cruel egotism,
subject to vices, to weaknesses, and infirmities, which have ever
defied the powers of human intellect." A Dartmouth College
senior suggested that patriotism's highest attainment would be
the noble citizen who readily admitted that there were others
more worthy of public office than himself. Such awareness would
unite all citizens in a selfless pursuit of public good. "May every
American clearly perceive his true interests, and their connexion
with those of his fellow men." The American female was herself
often portrayed as a Stewardess. She would open her arms only
to those dedicated to republican liberty. Cupid, in turn, would
send no arrows save those pointed "with the affections of a patriotic American."

The result was a concept of good citizenship through "heroic
self-denial." The "enlightened Citizen" would surrender himself
to the nation, contemplating only the "universal good" and disregarding "petty personal, or local interests." From the beginning, therefore, the citizen's role, according to predominate
American doctrine, was one of sublimation. The baser instincts
were to be crushed, the pursuit of selfish goals halted, and dedication to the nation made complete. Affirmations about group
stewardship were especially important. Given the ominous hour
and the newness of America, it was plausible that American attention had to be drawn more to society's attributes than to the
old and dingy story of the individual's nature. The most cursory

reading of speeches, sermons, newspapers, and letters originating during the time that Adams, Jefferson, and Madison were president reveals a general unease over the citizen's innate selfishness and an acclaim for individual will's capitulation to national achievement. Such an outcome was usually said to require God's encouragement.

The Almighty was often given an agent, education, for directing stewardship. Society needed aid and education was the means of enhancing civic worth. This was an earnest sentiment in an age when the national culture was dominated by the professional classes, notably lawyers and clergymen. These two groups, eager to retain an intimacy between power and intellect, were prone to proclaim the importance of enduring principle rather than casual opinion. This introduced some important questions to affirmations about stewardship. Was the national outlook, drawn from free men in the American Vineyard, a passive thing, to be admonished and exhorted by a class of taskmasters? Or was this outlook a voluntary association of free minds who were themselves the elements of national will? Generally, of course, the Federal bloc took the former, holistic position, whereas the Jeffersonians adopted the more atomistic concept. The debate between their philosophies drew inspiration from and contributed to the concerns inherent in American nationality.[12]

Since corporate stewardship was deemed necessary for national fulfillment, it encouraged in public rhetoric the use of such abstractions as virtue, fraternity, and selflessness. These verities, ably expounded by Washington's Farewell and by Jefferson's First Inaugural Address, suffered their own agony because of persisting factionalism and unreason. In the nation's earliest moments, society appeared to default its role. Human desire seemed uncooperative as a force for national well-being. The response, however, was limited to more talk of spirit, brotherhood, and surrender to a lofty good. There was no feasible alternative to using the example of the first patriots. Like them "we too must devote life to country's service." Let the sons of freedom renew their ancestors' vows: "Individual liberty depends on the preservation of national independence," and the latter could endure only in total support of *"one government."* American citizenry "were not to be deceived by hurried villainy, or the artful hypocrisy of designing knavery." The more the uneasiness, the more the affirmation about "the whole American family."

A decade of unremitting national distress encouraged this concept of stewardship through surrender. A typical Fourth of July orator urged his hearers to avoid belief in reason or any widespread human capacity. American society's only hope was in concerted patriotic conduct. Indeed, every citizen had the choice "to regard his country more than his own will, or his own will more than his country." The latter decision would render a man "unfit to be a member of a free state." America, then, would be fulfilled only through brotherhood built on "one soul–one spirit." This belief had governed the Fathers. Completed nationality would wait until all Americans "in one blest league of brotherhood were join'd." Anything else would produce a destructive "political paroxysm." Alternatives were usually referred to as any ideology which "detached multitudes from a proper adherence," bringing the nation down from its "erect position" to "cringing meanness of slaves." In other words, the doctrine for a stewardship of survival called for citizens to "sink down into one formidable whole." Those who refused the call of brotherhood and oneness "are not the less our enemies, because they walk in our streets."

Some Jeffersonians preferred saying that national brotherhood arose instinctively and voluntarily from the citizen breast. These affirmed that the "American mind" was thoroughly instructed in "the great and essential principles" which imbued the nation. According to this rather circular reasoning, vital principles leapt from "the only legitimate source on earth—the people." Accordingly, the American "genius" did "utterly forbid that the interest of any individual should be consulted in preference to the good of the Community." President Jefferson contended that the larger the American brotherhood, the less likely would it be shaken by local passion. Albert Gallatin suggested, futilely, that such nationalist theory was both doubtful and "too generally expressed." Nevertheless it was hardly a time when America could afford other than the broadest affirmation. As John Haywood, treasurer of North Carolina, observed in 1802, the nation could expect "a refulgent Noon, that in place of distrust we shall have confidence" only through "urbanity and friendly intercourse." [13]

According to such doctrine no citizenry on earth could feel the attachment to a nation that Americans should. This adherence produced the prudent approach to liberty which was the hope for national fulfillment. Proper thinking was thus the nation's chief tool. "Let the feelings of the people be as they should, and then will be found among them intelligence enough to cherish and protect their best interests." The wisdom of old Nathaniel Macon could not resist qualifying this concept. "We are placed in such a situation that we ought to love each other, and we always should, did not our mad passions sometimes run away with us." More explicitly stated, the majority and minority should acknowledge the importance of fusion. This was a favorite theme of state legislatures in replying to the Virginia and Kentucky Resolutions. According to the Pennsylvania House of Representatives: "Our country's dearest interest demands everywhere unanimity and harmony in our councils, and . . . confidence in the wise and honest labours of those in whose hands is reposed the sacred charge of preserving here peace and independence." Later, when the Embargo was challenging stewardship, the Delaware House resolved: "We have the fullest confidence that the patriotism of the good people of the United States will induce them to submit to unwise and arbitrary laws, rather than resort to violence."

This doctrine of the corporate nation was sometimes challenged. Near the close of the 1812 war, a New Yorker said: "Gentlemen talk of this General Government as if it were a self-supported superior being; some abstract and independent power; some cloud-enthroned Hercules." Nevertheless, the concept generally thrived while a frail nation clearly needed a stewardship of mass fidelity. "Such a glorious land as ours, so inexpressibly favoured by heaven, is entitled to our most sincere and solemn vows, in its support." Even this was too cautious an admonition for some. During the war there was demand for similarity of manner and habit. Sameness of view on all issues should be the national goal. The American citizenry, said one commentator, ought to be "homogeneous, and not a variegated composition." [14]

A close companion to this affirmation was the invocation of national character, a cherished goal. Despite naturalization standards and Jefferson's famous insistence that all were Federalists, all Republicans, most observers saw national character as being beyond reach. Its distant realization was considered to mark the triumphant close of the nation's pilgrimage. Philip Freneau thought that this achievement among the Stewards would absorb several centuries. Others started eagerly at evidence of any "characteristick traits and features" in America. This nascent character, which was usually limited to the virtuous and learned citizenry, was to be held aloft to the masses of Americans still in ignorance and stupor, menaced by vice and cunning. The most sanguine viewpoint predicted an emergent national character would contain elements of originality which might assist America to survive.

Events early in 1815 helped reduce concern over the identity of the Steward. The prevailing sense of relief sustained a poem by Cambridge's Henry Ware. His lines combined several elements in American doctrine.

> Hail, hail, the distant beauty of our land,
> That hope has pictured with a glowing hand!
> Roll on, ye happy years, in rapture roll,
> Pour all your promise on the impatient soul.

If all of this came to pass, Ware predicted:

> The public good on private virtue built
> Shall stand unmoved by vice, unstained by guilt,
> There guided by the wisdom from above,
> We all shall harmonize in perfect love;
> Shall cast the trophies of our wars away,
> And nobler honors to the world display.[15]

3

American talk about itself often turned to consider the setting where republicanism was to be proved. Two locales or Vineyards claimed attention. One was a New World, often seen as a great bequest from nature or God. This version soon encountered difficulty as men struggled between preserving America's lovely setting and seeking to draw from it material abundance. It was awkward being both caretaker and exploiter. Similarly appealing and controvertible was the other Vineyard, best described as an inspired polity. America's overwhelmingly political consciousness made the traditions of government, and more especially the federal Constitution, the place for transacting national destiny. A political structure produced by Founders who quickly moved beyond reproach easily was made to seem a setting for national fulfillment.

The matter of survival affected thinking about the Vineyard. Fortunately, both the Constitution and American geography were highly visible and extensive, capable of embracing many toilers of conflicting pursuits. Additional comfort came in knowing that both the New World and the American polity carried divine superintendence. None of this, however, discouraged controversy as Americans sought to establish their thoughts about the Vineyard, whether natural or political. For instance, nature's importance for national endeavor intrigued men of Adams and Jefferson's time. It was frequently argued that America's magnificent setting would have an elevating influence on those who labored there. Americans dismissed the charge of Buffon and Diderot that natural development in the New World was too primitive to serve as inspiration for men. In fact, the national venture was considered both a reflection of and contribution to the unfolding of nature. Whether this process entailed growth and change for the Republic itself constituted an important part of doctrinal dispute.

From the outset, American thought responded simply by accepting paradox as necessary for national fulfillment. The American Steward must function as modifier of divine nature. He must prayerfully develop a polity whose essence was inviolable. Although America's Trust was often described as an exalted experiment, it was also taken to mean dedication to inspired principle and practice. This contradiction would trouble the affirmations about nationality until the end of the nineteenth century. The effort to pursue America's Trust seemed invariably to entail a physical and political change.

The natural Vineyard's size brought various responses. One insisted that no matter where in the broad expanse a Steward might toil, "while he exults in the name of American," he would somehow "regard as his brother every one who has a title to that proud distinction." Mystical feeling could foster a brotherhood among Americans, "whether on this or the other side of the Chesapeake, whether on the banks of the Mississippi, or the borders of the Atlantic." The difficulty in cultivating such a fraternity encouraged others to condemn size. For them, the Louisiana Purchase hampered already fearful tasks in the Vineyard. A characteristic view pleaded first for isolation, "to support the true American character," and then for containment within the garden of the Fathers. Even now the Stewards were "by far too much dispersed." This controversy persisted, making republicans themselves disagree. Congressman Peter B. Porter claimed that "this very diversity of interest will, if skillfully managed, be the means of producing a close and more intimate union of the States." John Randolph, on the other hand, spoke eloquently for those believing in rigorous limits upon the size of any republic. The thinking of both Porter and Randolph was dictated by the Vineyard's enormity.[16]

Another advantage of America's location was that there was solitude. Only the supreme Architect could have been responsible for launching the American Trust thousands of miles from the intrigues of the Old World. New surroundings were the only hope for an undertaking of such great difficulty. There was a paradox here, too. Some observers feared the strain of isolation might hasten the Republic toward despotism for security. Others saw in the American "asylum" a place remote enough that "every prejudice and every prepossession" threatening national achievement might "be buried in the earth." Still others talked of a second Eden, a theme which would fascinate American thought long after Jefferson's day. In an inspiring natural setting Americans were, according to doctrine, to find "a sense of primaeval liberty" while man's mind assumed its "natal dignity." There was small comfort, whatever the viewpoint about the natural Vineyard, when discord and evil persisted in "this American Canaan."

Those who looked to an inspired polity as America's proving ground found even less assurance. Political design offered fewer certainties than did nature about the likelihood of national fulfillment. A political Vineyard, no matter how nobly wrought, could not be considered apart from human caprice. This was troublesome for a second generation of Stewards facing brilliant ancestral achievement. To preserve a Godly kingdom in the manner of the previous generation demanded deeds of awesome magnitude. It also raised a major philosophical point. If the American government was so handsomely wrought, could such creation be organic and susceptible to change? The dilemma differed little from the question whether nature was made for man's use and alteration, or for his worship.

Although men might have agreed that the American polity was an inspiration, they found nothing else generally evident. The Stewards fell to quarreling. They talked of a neighbor's, or another state's, infidelity to national purpose. Distress at debasement and mutilation of the political Vineyard induced the stern rebuke from the Virginia and Kentucky legislatures in 1798 and 1799. The famous resolutions denounced efforts at political transformation and called for "brethren of the other States" to join in "the most scrupulous fidelity to that Constitution, which is the pledge of mutual friendship, and the instrument of mutual happiness." The polity must stand unimpaired. As one person said, national fruitfulness was threatened by the "metaphysic knights in the science of civil policy" who casually contrived changes. The Steward must be surrounded by steadfast government and religion. Faithfulness to the political design which "the wonderful interposition of Divine Providence" wrought was America's best chance to elude the disaster mankind usually suffered from its lusts. The problem was to get Americans to settle on one design.

The Jeffersonian years saw little relaxation of this broadly appealing insistence on the importance of a stable political Vineyard. Opponents of the Louisiana Purchase challenged it as subverting America's polity, a "sublime spectacle" on which national hopes depended. Republicans usually stressed reverence more than did the Federalists. Pleading for political accord, one Jeffersonian said in 1808 that "the interests of the Americans are the same, *all uniting* in order, peace, virtue, prosperity, and happiness." This sequence of exhortation was not accidental for the times seemed to require total commitment if the nation was to endure to make its Vineyard flourish. Here was "the beginning —*here the end* of genuine patriotism." Such affirmation imposed a devotional act on Stewards, venerating a plan and place for national deliverance. It was plausible only because the political Vineyard "was organized by the hand of divine wisdom; its officers instructed from the oracle of ETERNAL TRUTH."

Nevertheless the era of Adams and Jefferson failed to muster general veneration for the polity. Mood, interest, and events

forced continued quarreling over who had the proper fidelity.
Not even the war's end convinced everyone that the polity would
endure. After all, the "limited powers of the human mind" had
always been unable to promote the internal affairs of a large
nation. America's "arrangement" also might have to be set aside.
The fruitfulness of the political Vineyard "is yet to be proved."
American thought thus acknowledged that man was still mer-
curial, his personal intent bent upon change. Here was the most
dismaying element in the ideology of nationality. Reality forced
the affirmations to become anxieties, as the nation struggled toward its calling.[17]

II: Anxieties   The difficulties experienced by the nation's trusteeship forced America to live with
change. It was so rapid that custom proved to be meager help in
the decisions facing active Stewards. Nationality had no choice
but to keep anxiously seeking more understanding about how it
operated. This in turn centered attention on the hazards afflicting the national venture. There were essentially two dangers,
mammon and passion. Both led to what many considered the
national curse, the rage of party. George Washington's advice
was often repeated in an age worried about republican survival.

4

America was confused about its labor. Would national enterprise
succeed as a dynamic process? Or could it thrive only as a guard-
ianship, an effort to preserve the first nobility of America? Clarifi-
cation required determining whether the nation's Trust was to
conserve or to radicalize.

This issue quickly became a tormenting feature of national
ideology. During the Revolution, men could be more selective
about the past. By 1798 the options available were dwindling,
owing to the haste with which troubled Americans had canonized
their history. During John Adams' reign, the American endeavor
seemed so precarious that all attention went to securing the
nation. Little thought was wasted on interpreting goals. So new
and human a thing as the American community was safest as a
collection of abstractions, of homilies about virtue. Since circumstance placed the Republic near disaster and disgrace, nationality was attentive to how Americans were meant to function.

The view of life and society as growing and changing had limited appeal to early Americans. By 1805, it had become customary to make the Fourth of July a day of warning to audiences caught in the rush of affairs. This required refreshing the memory of heritage and enlarging an appreciation of national precepts. Most orators feared contemporary tumult was distorting the national perspective. Progress and growth were condemned as inappropriate for America's outlook. During the uncertain years between 1798 and 1815, few spokesmen agreed with a Massachusetts orator in 1806 who said that the Fathers had merely been instruments for an "extraordinary impulse." Gripped by benign process, the Founders "seemed to speak and move, while under the operation of a superior power." This minority view argued that Providence had deposited a long-cherished essence in American hearts, there alone to flourish and grow. The national toil would move majestically along.

Henry Wheaton, the distinguished editor, was one of the ardent few who promulgated this doctrine. For him America's task as harbinger of liberty implied that "man walks forth in the original majesty of his nature." Surely, said Wheaton, this was a spectacle so edifying as to cleanse every American bosom of wrong feeling and prejudice, and there "to purify and exalt the instinct of patriotism." Wheaton believed that the 1812 war helped liberty in America. He called for a passionate stewardship, strengthened through blood-letting. It was, said Wheaton, "in war that the best faculties of man have been developed, his noble virtues invigorated, and that undefined principle of honour kept alive in his bosom." Although Wheaton would not be the last to argue that war regenerated America's character, it was a scarcely heard contention during President Madison's anxious times.[18]

More solace came with talk of preserving a perfected design. A profound conflict in American thought arose between Wheaton's doctrine of inexorable process and the argument for conservation. It pitted the domination of law against the primacy of will. National ideology would seek to permit these to coexist with Protestantism's aid. Since it was the future that counted, religion was used less as a means of placating deity and more for aiding the American Stewards in their national travail. Through faith, men might live with progress by seeing it as a confirmation.

This required that the successful Steward would labor amid paradox. The American was free in his pilgrimage, but piety must keep his mind on truth.

It was widely claimed that the nation was established not on abstraction but upon the sober lesson of experience. This doctrine sought to defend America's established wisdom. The point of most diatribes against Jefferson was that he had pushed America "into all the mazes of modern philosophies." The national endeavor could carry on only in the way inspired experience had designed and only if American leadership had unquestioning confidence from the body of citizen-toilers. A favorite assault on the Jeffersonians, "those sons of debauchery and infidelity," pictured them as agents of the great American foe "Innovation." For many, the true American tradition for guiding national toil slept with the Fathers. Unless virtue called forth that tradition, one uneasy Steward predicted, the bread of Americans "is to be taken and given to the dogs."

These traditions readily formed a prescription for successful stewardship. It stressed a dedication to duty; a recognition of the evil inherent in man; an adherence to government and the governors; and a constant guard against the wiles of those who promised happy change. Republicans and Federalists alike adopted this comforting doctrine for their purposes. The Jeffersonians used it skillfully in the tempestuous months of 1812, as when Dr. Edward Durrell Smith wrapped the war in tradition. It was "a second time for our Independence," making the prime question: "Shall we fear to tread in the paths, which were made by our revered progenitors?" Dr. Smith was mindful, unusual in the time's extreme filiopietism, that even the Fathers had been vexed with domestic traitors, the faithless of that day. In Madison's crisis, the call to labor had to "be actuated by one spirit, a spirit of union, of obedience to the laws." Stewardship therefore meant preserving a way of life and outlook. The alternatives to this sacred legacy were the dreaded perversions, despotism, or anarchy.[19]

5

If successful labors in America's Vineyard could not depend upon instinct or reason, but preferred obedience, then national doctrine had to confront the facts of human nature. The chief hindrance to American success was recognized as the evil in man. A special anxiety, of course, accompanied knowledge that, in America's venture, liberty for the first time begat power. This made all the more distressing the undoubted capacities of mammon and passion. The former brought destructive avarice, the latter invited the awful specter of demagoguery. In the days of a primitive Republic, however, America was less troubled by the possibility that greed might deter its stewardship. Anxiety came mostly from reminders of man's passions. His unreason, his vulnerability to flattery, his venality, his fear, and his earthiness, these were materials for perverting America's cause. One of the Fathers, Charles Carroll, considered the masses easily roused to pillage. Religion and law were therefore national mainstays. "Without morals a republic cannot subsist any length of time," Carroll wrote. Freedom without Christianity was unthinkable. A good Steward was consecrated to the nation by reverence for order.[20]

Some expression was calm, contending that American hearts inherently loved liberty, a capacity inherited by each generation. Even so, the citizenry was still susceptible to folly, to partisan appeal, and to delusion. The response to this was praise for education. "Knowledge is the birthright of every class of citizens, and truths moral and divine are taught to all." Others were less assured, noting first the Jacobin and later the Godwinian threats to national practice. It was not uncommon to hear Americans condemn the view that all human regeneration was possible. As Benjamin Silliman put it, God's finger was pointing America's attention to the bloody sins of those nations which had shown faith in human nature. Let America flee "while there is yet hope" to that mountain of safety made of "SOCIAL HABITS, YOUR GOVERNMENT AND YOUR RELIGION."

Numerous voices deplored the prevalence of this emphasis on impending disaster. They did so, not from certainty over national success, but usually from distress lest such pessimism arouse the passions of an uneasy citizenry. The literature of fear in Jefferson's time was enormous. Men were uneasy with thoughts of what free Stewards might do in their toil, despite the Fathers' legacy. Anxiety dominated the Fourth of July spirit in this period. Verse from one occasion was typical:

> Now let each passion be subdued
> And ev'ry virt'ous art pursued,
>   To regulate our life.
> Then shall our peace like rivers flow,
> And by our conduct plainly show
>   That we are void of strife.[21]

The need to offset human deficiencies through various artifices was widely recognized. It was sometimes observed that national survival depended on a cultivated sentiment. A vital spirit must surround the labors of Americans. The Revolution succeeded because of a sensation which "like the electrick fluid, diffused itself through the continent." If a rekindling of this spark occurred, said one person, "the national character will emerge from the cloud which obscures its lustre." Such yearning for a spiritual suffusion of the Stewards entered the era's hymns. One chanted:

> In vain the busy sons of hell
> Still new rebellions try;
> Their souls shall pine with envious rage
> And vex away and die.
>
> Almighty grace defends our land
> From their malicious power,
> Then let us with united songs
> Almighty grace adore.

Another was less hopeful:

> Lord has thou cast the nation off?
> Must we forever mourn?
> Wilt thou indulge immortal wrath?
> Shall mercy ne'er return?
> . . . .
> Our Zion trembles at thy stroke
> And dreads thy lifted hand!
> O, heal the people thou hast broke,
> And save the sinking land.[22]

Realities attending American passions, as well as the endeavors to use or transcend these, had another implication. It was normal

to forecast national division and disintegration. Of all the likely
results of unbounded emotion within America, including despotism and anarchy, none was more frequently predicted or more
ardently feared than disunion. As early as 1803 George Clinton
marveled that the nation should so constantly be menaced with
this agitation. It was a mischievous toying with national feeling,
he said. Others seemed so distressed at the prospect of disunion
that they welcomed war because it would "generate patriotic
love" in calling forth "the energies of character" and the "manly
virtues." In 1814, a Georgia congressman said that only an alliance of interest and fear would defeat frenzy over separation.
This combination had produced a love of Union greater than
any passion raised by the sacrilegious ruffians abroad in the
nation.

Beyond man's vulnerability to social and intellectual evil, an
additional cause for anxiety was his lust for material gain. It
threatened to distract men's thoughts from the elevating ideas
about the American purpose. A Philadelphia physician called it
"the narrowness of grovelling self." As an antidote he prescribed
more numerous patriotic occasions. These would rouse the American soul "from cold indifference," making it "more keenly alive"
to the Stewards' obligations. In the opinion of many observers
such an antidote was urgently needed, for "patriotism and good
faith seem to be lost in self-interest." An embittered follower of
John Adams condemned the reward principle which controlled
even the nation's management. It was certain to "call up, and
keep in perpetual activity, all the evil spirits of the nation."
Americans seemed very mindful of their grossness. There was no
end to anxious reminders that the nation never must mistake
good fortune for merit. To do so would ruin the Republic by
"exuberant passion and puny intellect." [23]

6

The agent of such disaster was the faction or party. Its presence,
for the early Republic, substantiated the worst fears about man's
capacity and discouraged those who hoped for America's survival.
No portion of Washington's Farewell was so copied and repeated
as that on the blight of faction. Not only had Washington said
it, but Americans saw vivid evidence everywhere of this national
frailty.

Intestine faction, as it often was called, seemingly roamed at will with a "destructive hand." So anxious were some that they welcomed war, despite its irony. Richard Rush gave the Fourth of July address in the federal House of Representatives shortly after hostilities began in 1812. He predicted that war would be capable of allaying party spirit. Even the prospect of battle would bring "a willing, a joyful immolation of all selfish passions on the altar of a common country." Ignoring fourteen years of discord, doubt, and dismay, Rush predicted that after war's exuberance, the "excitement of the national mind" would carry "a roused intellect" and a patriotic spirit willing to rejoice in "whatever can gild the American name." At Yale, President Theodore Dwight was neither so hopeful nor prone to accept violence as a means for eluding human shortcoming. Dwight noted that even in the grim light of 1812 the American citizen saw his nation merely as a residence of parties.[24]

The political party from the start was considered the serpent in America's Garden. Because of faction, the doctrine of nationality had to provide for the contention that the Stewards might capitulate to the impulses of political and economic greed. Amidst talk of disunion, civil war, and corruption, words such as those of President Dwight were repeated more than were the blandishments of Richard Rush. The admonitions of these two notable Americans exhibit the tension within the doctrine of nationality. Between the need for affirmation and the justification for anxiety, American consciousness followed a path which led only further into uncomfortable thickets. Those who spoke along the route did not hide their distress.

SPOKESMEN

National purpose and attainment were concerns never far from American thought, dominating the expression of notable advocates and the broad response to their admonitions. Attention went mostly to the frailness of republicanism and to the uncertainty of America's capacity for discharging the sacred responsibilities entrusted to it. From presidents to parishioners, the outlook usually found despair blighting the tender shoots of hope.

III: Advocates   Few voices were better placed both to shape and reflect the spirit of nationality than those of the presidents of the United States. Their expression never escaped the influence of the first President's Farewell. Washington's parting remarks were preface to their own enduring status. It was certainly a lingering farewell. Adams, Jefferson, and Madison presided over events which seemed to make Washington a greater prophet than president. The fact meant no solace and much anguish for America's pursuit of fulfillment.

7

A revealing expression of national concern passed between the luckless John Adams and Congress. It contained unease and hope about the Trust; desperation and optimism over the capacity and intent of the Stewards; and misgiving over the struggles in the American Vineyard. In March 1798, President Adams advised the nation to confess its sin, to fast, and to renew its pilgrimage. It was a Proclamation worthy of succeeding Washington's Farewell. Insisting on the availability of truth, Adams acknowledged that American purpose and hope were in God's hand. National acceptance of this fact was necessary to develop "that morality and piety" required for American well-being.

Adams readily made his own confession. The nation was sorely afflicted, he said. It had sinned mightily, both privately and wholly. Let this be acknowledged before God, and the humiliation might foster renewed kinship among the citizens. By December 1798, Adams seemed more cheerful. He recommended thankfulness to the "Supreme Being" for having granted America a "manly sense of national honor, dignity, and independence." Glancing toward the vital future, Adams urged that this "sense" serve as basis for constructing the nation's well-being. The Senate and House responded by echoing the President's relief that God had inspired a "noble spirit of patriotism." At this Adams felt constrained to reply. Clearly the Trust would be more secure now that Congress had chosen to be steadfast in protecting the American treasure of independence and liberty. Adams said that all Stewards of "sound understanding," all "faithful" Americans would surely applaud Congress.

By March 1799, John Adams had to insist upon another day

of national supplication and debasement. Evil principles were afoot among the citizenry, subverting those crucial "religious, moral and social obligations" which were America's foundation. Adams pleaded that the Stewards find their role by the one sure means, transcending the self. All men righteously inclined should gather to revere "momentous truths" in a great act of national obeisance. Only through such nationwide humility, proclaimed the President, could America hope to be preserved from the hard-pressing threats of "unreasonable discontent," as well as from faction, sedition, and violence.

Later, in answering further presidential exhortations, the Representatives marveled that Americans could misconstrue the national interest and welfare. Nevertheless, violence was desecrating the Vineyard, leaving Congress to "lament the depravity" inducing such disobedience. As additional woe, Congress discovered a new menace to the Trust, a "love of ease." This joined other forces to create not only upheaval but a surely "fatal" and thus "criminal" carelessness about the future destinies "of our growing Republic." Agreeing completely, Adams told America to implore the "Supreme Ruler of the Universe." Thereby, in the new Capitol would appear the virtues needed for the nation's labor—piety, constance, and self-discipline. From this appropriate setting might "simple manners, pure morals, and true religion flourish forever!" [25]

Although he approached the national Trust with more hope, Thomas Jefferson's outlook was similar to John Adams'. Their common premise, one generally essential to the spirit of nationality, was that America stood between a glittering past and an uncertain but challenging future. Like Adams, Jefferson knew that national spirit and attainment had not yet satisfied the requisites of past and future. However, the third President tried to be optimistic. His first inaugural remarks seemed awed by the fact of a "rising nation" and overwhelmed by the implications carried by the honor, happiness, and hopes of "this beloved country." It was a challenge requiring that all Stewards "arrange themselves under the will of the law, and unite in common efforts for the common good." Invoking a national unity of "one heart and one mind," Jefferson said that throughout America there could be no disagreement in principle. Since all were Federalists, all were Republicans, Jefferson called for faith in republicanism.

The latter was actually the American Trust, making the nation "the world's best hope."

Anticipations were the best that Jefferson could muster. His first inaugural message contained a beautiful distillation of the blessed Vineyard, luckily separated from the "exterminating havoc" elsewhere. Ready for thousands of generations, the national setting showed a Providence willing to cooperate in assuring man's future happiness. America's duty was to sustain within the Vineyard a polity both wise and frugal. For this the President proposed nothing novel, rejoicing rather in those principles which had once prevailed to guide the nation's early steps. After his inauguration Jefferson remained reserved about the essences of nationality. He predicted that with time would come enlargement of the Vineyard and the numbers of Stewards who would be "educated in the love of order" and "habituated to self-government." His second inaugural remarks even suggested that an extended nation would be less vulnerable to the passions roused in any one area. Ultimately, all the dissident Stewards would be persuaded. Truth, reason, and interest would contrive, Jefferson said, to "complete that entire union of opinion" vital for national attainment.

When he left the Presidency, Jefferson was uneasy. Like Adams, his associate in founding the Republic, Jefferson could not escape yearning for some token of America's immediate fulfillment. But if the nation were called to prove certain political principles, then Jefferson's own administration showed how premature were his expectations. Belief in America's responsibility to politicize humane ideals had emerged as the fundamental quality of nationality. Jefferson's era was left to discover the difficulty of such a Trust. In departing the White House, Jefferson spoke ruefully of the "extraordinary character of the time"; attention must be fixed "unremittingly" upon the nation's safety. This required more than spiritual accord over man and his future. Jefferson's realism even overcame his detached pacificism. Abandoning general platitudes, he announced that an armed militia, well organized, was the best security for the nation. With this, Thomas Jefferson departed, a markedly subdued spokesman for nationality.[26]

President Madison quickly restored to the "Almighty Being" a role in sustaining "this rising Republic." The description of a nation emerging was Madison's favorite, and he also stressed that such a nation had to be alert against "that collusive prostitution of it by individuals unworthy of the American name." Days of public humiliation and prayer were used by Madison in the hope that the Universal Sovereign might "take the American people under His peculiar care and protection" and "animate their patriotism." Madison called the War of 1812 necessary if America was to escape degradation to renew "the virtuous struggles of our fathers" in behalf of "the magnificent legacy which we hold in trust for future generations." Only the war, he observed in his second inaugural message, kept the nation from "destroying all confidence in itself and in its political institutions." Thus, the conflict was clearly "necessary and noble in its objects." As a result of desperate peering ahead, Madison claimed to see "presaging flashes of heroic enterprise" which promised more ardent labors in the Vineyard. Surely forthcoming would be appropriate "discipline and habits."

The balance of Madison's executive utterance usually spoke for the past and the future. The war was required under "the sacred obligation of transmitting entire to future generations that precious patrimony . . . held in trust by the present from the goodness of Divine Providence." He regularly advised national humiliation to encourage the elusive "fraternal affections" and "mutual confidence" so badly needed among the Stewards. Paradoxically, Madison also urged days of national thanksgiving, these to display gratitude for opportunity afforded by "the Great Disposer of Events," rather than for any pretended success. Even after the close of the war, Madison still sought means of inspiring "liberal sentiments" and "congenial manners," all needed if there was to be national success.[27]

Meanwhile John Adams and Thomas Jefferson in retirement shared their doubts about America surviving long enough to show fruitful stewardship. Adams was especially eager to talk of the great Trust bestowed by Providence. Wholly aware of human shortcoming, Adams also believed in man's predisposition toward good. It was just that the Stewards were so easily dissuaded or distracted. Mankind, meaning well, did so feebly. Weakness, not depravity, was for Adams the curse of humanity. Here was the national handicap, threatening the fulfillment of America's awesome responsibility. Like Washington, Adams hoped to see the Republic led by wise, strong men who could best direct the decent intentions of the many Stewards. Wisdom for Adams meant a knowledge of history. It was certain to show how often liberty had proven disastrous through inexperience and enfeebled understanding.

The longer he lived, however, the more Adams became chagrined and discomfited. He found ambition and avarice dominating the nation, creating baseness, unscrupulousness, faction, and greed. After 1808 he despaired. Luxury, greed, cowardice, and corruption threatened the nation with self-destruction. In his exchange with Jefferson, Adams recalled those who had once dreamed of human nature's perfectibility. Where now was this expectation, as well as ones about the progress of the human mind and the augmentation of human comfort? For Adams, the more germane inquiry in 1813 was: "When? Where? and how? is the present Chaos to be arranged into Order?" The close of the war only increased Adams' doubt about America's likely success. The eighteenth century had honored human nature and witnessed extraordinary improvement. "But, what are we to say now?" Adams thought it likely that the nineteenth century would extinguish all the lights of the preceding age.[28]

Thomas Jefferson agreed that America might never fulfill its calling. Back in 1798, Jefferson considered no more than a sincere wish his yearning that men in America might somehow learn accommodation. He told John Taylor that man's nature would inevitably introduce discord into a free society. This ought to be frankly admitted. The struggle for national success would be easier if America acknowledged that "an association of men who will not quarrel with one another is a thing which never yet existed." Jefferson continued to hope that a spiritual bond would hold America intact to prove, not mere nationhood, but the importance of human rights and representative government. From this alone would emerge American attainment. His comparatively calm rejoinders to Adams conceded the presence of apostasy, a great moral retreat. But the American Trust, which must halt this regression, might yet be carried out. Such was possible, said Jefferson, only because individuals in America had a material stake in "the support of law and order." The natural Vineyard, then, gave hope that the Republic might survive to carry forward its responsibility. Humane attainment was possible through America's peculiar setting and was presumably limited thereto.[29]

8

During the dark days after 1798 some spokesmen slipped into despair over the nation's prospects. The despondency of three of these men, Dr. Benjamin Rush, Noah Webster, and Joel Barlow, shows how burdensome the meaning ascribed to America could be. They were at times indignant that America was expected to prove that God, republicanism, and human nature were allies. Benjamin Rush saw many threats to the delicate Republic. He pleaded that American youth first be well grounded in religion. Then they must be taught "to love and admire" only the federal Constitution, recognizing that "with its destruction will perish the remains of all the liberty in the world." Yet Rush so often despaired of national maturity that he forecast triumph for America's fools, knaves, and madmen. He finally lost a battle to retain hope kindled during his participation in the Continental Congress and the signing of the Declaration. For Rush, the power of both mammon and passion weighed heavily against national survival. He told President Jefferson in 1804 that there was no longer happiness and usefulness in public station. How different had been the feelings in the 1770's, and how fruitful the words "country" and "liberty" then seemed. Rush informed John Adams that there were few true Americans left, because no national character had emerged.

By 1806, Rush felt only Christianity could save the situation. Liberty brought only "the dread of future evils" which "bites us like a serpent." When war became possible, Rush wondered what the nation would fight for. Both polity and leaders were abhorred by most citizens, he said, leaving not even material interest to arouse the nation. As one of Dr. Rush's aged patients said to him, America now was comprised of idolators who worshipped one god, "but that god was GOD DOLLARS." With his old patient, Rush turned to memories for consolation. The hereafter might bring reward, but this world would not.

Rush was inconsolable in 1810, seeing the Fathers rising from their graves on July fourth to ask for news of the nation. When hearing only of "degeneracy and depravity" they hastened eagerly back to tombs which kept them from seeing "the base and in-

glorious conduct . . . of all their posterity." Rush roundly condemned all Stewards for being deluded about virtue. He begged
John Adams to address the entire nation on the truth that since
only religion could support morals, it alone might save America.
By the time war began, Rush considered America was beyond
even the redemptive power of religion. The nation, he contended, was not even worth a war, so corrupted had it become
by avarice. He suggested that it would have been more honest
if Congress had placed as an advertisement in European newspapers:

For *Sale*
to the highest bidder,
The United States of America.

Matters had only worsened in 1813 when Rush died. In his
judgment, the Trust given America had become an imposition.[30]
   Watching the same events that so subdued Benjamin Rush
was the editor, author, and ardent nationalist, Noah Webster.
He, too, had once been hopeful of uniting the youthful national
mind. When partisanship proved a serious affliction to the
nation, Noah Webster's·distress began. He found man's dedication to his nation wholly different from addiction to self-seeking
party. By 1798 Webster withdrew from New York journalism,
disgusted with the human personality and with Federalist pettiness and bungling. He left behind an early optimism about the
American Trust when he moved to New Haven, where he became
an orator in order to promulgate his mature conclusions about
the meaning of American nationality. Nothing in the next forty-
five years would alter his outlook.
   First, Webster conceded that feast days in America were vital.
Otherwise the national ardor would surely be extinguished as
citizens pursued personal ends. However, he hurriedly called
for only a proper ardor. Everything about America disclosed
providential work. The outline of national purpose and meaning required that present and future generations preserve an
inspired polity. The fact that the nation was threatened by upheaval, by experimenters, and worst of all, by "bullies and ruffians" alarmed Webster. "Our business is to love our country,
and to maintain its independence." Thus, experience was the

only guide, and novelty a dangerous lure. Webster was convinced that America had been granted its institutions. The highest deed of patriotism was therefore one of preservation.

In 1814 Webster spoke in Amherst, Massachusetts, like a beaten man. He anticipated disaster and disunion. Webster blamed Constitutional imperfections for national faltering. These must be eliminated if virtue was to have a chance to claim America. Abandoning preservation, Webster talked bleakly of raising the age limit in Congress and of provision for longer tenure. Meantime, he acknowledged that a "dark cloud" encompassed America. Wisdom and property, pillars of national fulfillment, tottered, while the passions of the unlettered citizenry ruled. Like Jefferson, Webster hoped that America's physical size might subdue the wretched Jacobinical spirit. But now the rage for gain was bringing Stewards up from dunghills without the crucial respect for learning and ability. To slow the race for equality, he suggested that no one vote until age forty-five, nor hold office until age fifty. The passions, especially that of ambition, had to cool before a man could be a successful Steward. America depended upon an enlightened and selfless patriotism.[31]

The poet of American republicanism, Joel Barlow, had once been called "a rude, insulting, dogmatical egotist" by Noah Webster. Barlow survived both this and Jacobinism to receive a dinner tribute by New Haven citizens in 1805. His few remarks for the occasion carried the gospel of the sacred Trust. America was both the depository and guardian of mankind's best interests, and Barlow hoped the nation would be "duly sensible of the importance of this sacred deposit." National calling required an ardent patriotism, yet one partaking "of the broad and peaceful character of genuine philanthropy." Specifically Barlow had in mind a project with which Noah Webster, Washington, Madison, and many others agreed. He urged a great national institution where American youth could be educated for the Trust.

Joel Barlow had no trouble identifying the wiles menacing the nation. Calling it a "great national sin," Barlow assailed the "inordinate and universal pursuit of wealth as a means of distinction." He envisioned the tragic day when Americans would tell their children "that merit consists in oppressing mankind and not serving them." Soon the poet planted his mature ideas by revising *The Vision of Columbus*. The new version, *The*

Columbiad, had an exalting concept of national responsibility. America had to develop noble Stewards for the Vineyard. Nations must be educated, requiring more time and more teachers than did the child. As a good Steward, Barlow saw a distant moral and political goal, the "future and permanent meliorations in the condition of human nature." Through its natural and political settings, America must become so forceful an example as to "settle the storms of the world."

In 1809, Barlow delivered the official Fourth of July oration in Washington. Clearly touched by the era's uneasiness, the old Jeffersonian's ardency had disappeared leaving him to stress the nation's inadequacy before its assignment. Americans needed thorough training, for Barlow now turned away from the charms of natural man. His oration rang with the rhetoric of the Trust. "Though as a nation we are yet in the morning of life," said the venerable poet, America could at least recognize "the height we have to climb, and the commanding station we must gain, in order to fulfill the destinies to which we are called, and perform the duties that the cause of human happiness requires at our hands." The American situation was awesome, but a remote and vast natural splendor suggested that a republican citizenry of peaceful and diligent ways might survive. Needed was a new human character. Each American toiler must accept a personal responsibility in behalf of the Trust.

Beyond indoctrinating the citizenry through education, Barlow suggested another inducement for steadfast stewardship. He recommended internal improvements, so that the nation's crucial physical benefits could be more immediately important to the people. Barely disguising his distrust of the general populace, Barlow observed that "the people must become habituated to enjoy a visible, palpable, incontestible good." From these sources of inspiration and training the American Steward might begin to sense that he labored for one great community and for a time long beyond the moment at hand. Each citizen needed to realize he was "an integral member of the sovereignty." This seemed now a vain hope. Neatly, Barlow summarized America's plight: "As a nation, we are not up to our circumstance." The national purpose "in the abstract" was admirable, said the poet-orator. The tragedy was that "the practical tone and tension of our minds do not well correspond with these principles." [32]

Barlow's capacity to tolerate the discrepancy between the actual and the ideal in American achievement pushed him beyond the morbid gloom of Noah Webster and Benjamin Rush. Clearly more hopeful were three men who spoke for the "Rising Generation," Daniel Webster, Henry Clay, and Andrew Jackson. Their sense of national meaning was more expectant than that of the older generation, but it was scarcely one of bumptious conviction. In their youthful days, these spokesmen found comfort in anticipation. America for them could easily be a matter of tomorrow. Typical was the view of seventeen-year-old Daniel Webster, Dartmouth junior. By 1800 Webster's lifetime philosophy was developed, well before he became the high priest of American nationality. The young student admonished a Hanover audience to be mindful of the Fathers' labors, the preciousness of the national institutions and principles, the superiority of the American polity and populace, and the vast responsibility all this placed on the nation. These articles of faith were to be maintained in the face of demagoguery and partisanship. In short, Webster made duty the burden of all Americans. They alone could avert a disgrace of lineage and a shameful disclaimer of "the legacy bequeathed us."

Webster's oration set the national Trust with its cherished traditions in a Vineyard constituting nature's best setting. It seemed "designed to be inhabited by a nobler race of men." Thus did the youthful orator bear down upon the future. Abandoning the present was easier for Daniel than it was for Noah Webster. Daniel Webster called upon the American citizenry, surrounded by the aid of nature and the precepts exemplified by Washington, to rise above current passion. Let the search be made for "principles that may direct us in a path which leads not into the mazes of Opinion." The responsibility of stewardship was to find and follow that path. It was the only way to national fulfillment.

Two years later, Webster brought his message to the district of Maine, where he took up some matters cautiously treated in 1800. Two versions of this oration are extant. One stressed dedication to morality and religion if the nation was to survive the "tumultuous passions of the human heart." Such dedication was crucial for the "grand" experiment which America was. The second version stressed the importance of laws in the face of man's limitation. Even American humans shared "men's mis-fortunes." Said Webster, "Man in all countries resembles man. Wherever you find him, you find human nature in him and human frailties about him." America could only hope to learn from the imprudence of others. Meanwhile Stewards must pre-serve the Constitution with its inspired content. Those who wished to touch this "purity" were either "weak or wicked." Either type "cannot be a friend of his Country," said Webster. Once commotion began in America, "then Farewell to the pros-pect, the bright, the charming, the fascinating prospect of Liberty and Republicanism."

Webster was blunt. Despite the advantages of nature and the blessing of Providence, he asserted that the American venture could fail. The Stewards must wrap much religion and principle about them, for even now there was abroad a counterfeit patriot-ism which sought to delude them. So skillfully were the absurdi-ties of Rousseau and Godwin being circulated that Webster conceded even genuine patriotism had to be studied carefully to discern it from the spurious. "The rage for being patriots hath really so much of the ridiculous in it that it is difficult to treat it seriously." Soon, however, he spoke of a new threat to national fulfillment, the temptations of mammon. Webster wrote in 1804 that the "love of money" had become America's "ruling passion," one so deeply rooted that it was likely "America will produce few great characters." Insisting that Stewards seek capacities only in good morals and habits, Webster asserted that America was lost if its public mind became "thoroughly vitiated and depraved." Said he, "Every nation, as well as every man, hath its ruling pas-sion." The point was, of course, that "national pursuits deter-mine national character."

Between 1807 and 1809, Daniel Webster seemed to despair. He wrote that corruption overwhelmed America and "the course towards total depravity is swift." Rescue was unlikely as the "minds of men are flying from all steadfast principles, like an arrow from the bow." Back on the Dartmouth campus in the summer of 1809 to deliver the Phi Beta Kappa lecture, Webster lamented that America's honorable ancestry was being demeaned by the "inordinate ambition" for wealth. The love of gold was still America's "ruling passion." Let chief Stewards arise—men of letters who alone might develop a proper sense of duty to the nation. Then the most arresting comment of all from this young orator whose election to national activity was yet several years off: "The strife of politics never made a great, or a good man." [33]

Another youthful spokesman, Henry Clay, seemed concerned about the supineness of American character. In 1806 Clay suggested that war could be useful to evoke at least a display of citizens' interest in their rights and situation. At his level of perception and expression, Clay too saw the menace of mammon and passion for the evolving national character. In an 1808 newspaper essay he expounded on the "melancholy truth" that in the American polity were seen "the shafts of malice and detraction." This was part of the vicious practice which sought to poison the minds of the citizenry. All Stewards then were urged to keep constant watch, so that appeals to passion might be "detected and detested."

In the United States Senate, Clay proclaimed war's benefits to the Republic's character. He pointed to the danger that the nation was becoming enervated because of the ruling power of "avarice." With the generation of the Founders passing, war was desirable not only for cleansing the American spirit but for producing "the presence and living example of a new race of heroes." When war did come, Clay prayed for success through the appearance of a new spirit in the citizenry, and especially a common sentiment. To survive, America must be united. Consequently, Clay was obviously pleased by the events of 1815 and his role in them. On being acclaimed in 1815 by the officials of Washington, Clay stressed a conviction he later repeated: "A great object of the war has been attained in the firm establishment of the national character." In Clay's view, America's pilgrimage faced easier paths.[34]

The production of national spirit was even more a concern of Clay's Tennessee neighbor, Andrew Jackson. Long before his providential role in the New Orleans miracle, Jackson was alarmed about American nationality. He emphasized that America's essence was a matter of public virtue. This usually became a question of private merit. How human capacity developed in America would establish national fulfillment. As early as 1798, after brief service as congressman and senator, Jackson yearned to see the "American mind" somehow "awakened from its lethargy" so that it might comprehend the nation's "true interest."

Already Jackson was fond of putting citizens into two groups: Stewards who were true friends of "Liberty," the national concern; or those who sought to establish despotism.

Despite this division, Jackson continued his advocacy of "one voice." He spoke freely of "our national character" as a readiness to defend "our national dignity and liberties." Through the war itself, Jackson spoke repeatedly of establishing, or re-establishing, or retrieving, or rescuing national character. He saw in wholesome action, especially the invigorating bloodiness of war, the means of eliciting the long-awaited righteousness in national outlook. Always proclaiming his own enslavement to this cause and to this character, Jackson talked especially about purging the nation of treasonous wrong.

Jackson expressed fear in 1807 that America lacked nerve to cleanse itself. He regretted any calmness in national outlook, for it led to a dangerous lethargy in attitude. If a few towns were burned, then perhaps "the Spirit of 76 may again rise." Consequently, prospects in 1812 obviously encouraged Jackson who began talking of national vengeance upon American foes. War was "for the reestablishment of our national character," misunderstood and vilified at home and abroad. Just as the Fathers had purchased national character "with so much blood," now America must similarly recapture her honor. There was no longer room for "inglorious sloth," and the Tennessean called all Stewards in his hearing to the "honorable toil of carrying the republican standard to the heights of Abraham." Jackson predicted American fulfillment must involve bloody work. He advised all citizens to welcome death if it would advance the nation's legacy of political, civil, and religious liberty. No worthy Steward would prefer haughty lords to burial in the nation's ruins. Thus, news of disaffection in parts of America by 1814 angered Jackson. America's name had once been proud—"we must retrieve that character" now "so foully stained!" [35]

Jackson, Clay, and Daniel Webster spoke in behalf of America's second generation's hope that the Republic might survive long enough to give new Stewards a chance to toil. National attainment lay far ahead. It was agreed that much labor was needed before the American Vineyard, whether natural or political, might behold a Trust fulfilled. Sentiment expressed across the struggling Republic shared in this agreement.

IV: Responses   Another kind of spokesman for nationality was the chorus of expression arising in America. From journals and letters and from speeches from the pulpit and the stump came reflection of the doctrine of national calling. There were those who felt that the hope expressed might produce national fulfillment. Others pretended that exhortation would compensate for weak stewardship. Additional voices dropped in quiet confession, praying that somehow the American Trust might be preserved for new days and new labors. To these outlooks the astonishing reprieve afforded in 1815 was more than consolation. It meant that the faithful had endured and that survival invited a search for the national self.

9

Some Americans found a litany of assurance comforting while the national Trust was obscure and even dubious. There seemed to be in this expression a belief that republican valor would be heightened through verbal reiteration. A characteristic 1798 orator beheld a resurgence of strength in the dangerous hour. Weakness, timidity, partisanship, all would recede. The present generation was "animated with the same pure valor and manly intrepidity" which had appeared twenty years before. Eight years later, when news of the *Leopard* affair arrived, the same earnest hope was still being lifted. In Charleston, John Fauchereaud Grimke called for the courage of the Fathers, for this alone assured a quickened "national spirit," one which would "be invincible but by death." It was logical that this litany of nationality relied on prediction. Time must bring an all-encompassing national spirit, one emulating the Fathers' outlook. A Maryland Congressman summed it up: "When the moment arrives, there will be but one heart and one hand. . . . All will be Americans."

Others were further encouraged by insisting that Americans would let this spiritual revival lead to a selflessness so necessary for national fulfillment. A Frankfort, Kentucky, speaker, for instance, in 1804 rejoiced over man's capacity. He predicted that Americans would surrender to country. Self-interest could and would bend to public interest. A differing view saw the love of liberty as the great "cohesion," an affection certain to bring success regardless of who led the polity. In freedom alone "we shall preserve the sun of our national glory in its vertical noon-day lustre." So ran the chant, leaving only an off-hand fashion for such voices to mention current troubles. One orator gloried in the fact that America had fellowship through kin and interest, having been given unity in patriotism by oppression. Somehow this would take the nation beyond the "harsh invective of party spirit" whose prevalence meant certain destruction.

With the war, assurances of selflessness became fewer, and chagrin over the "alarming stupor" afflicting national sentiment grew louder. The "dastardly miscreant" who stayed the emergence of this national spirit belonged among the "reptiles." A fit punishment for the recalcitrant had classic proportions. All women, matrons and young, were bidden to spurn men who failed to aid America. "Your arms shall never enfold him who declines . . . your bosoms shall never be pillows on which a *traitor* or an *enemy* to his country shall recline." Those who spoke gladly about American endeavor relied heavily on war as both an inspiration for the elusive spirit and a source of purification. As early as 1804, comments such as Henry Rutledge's were typical. He recalled enviously that when Americans had first entered "upon the work of their emancipation," virtue, talent, heroic courage, and purity had prevailed. Now men must live up to that high example whereby lay national repute. War would be an appropriate sacrifice to this national character, exemplified by Washington. From battle would come "the dignity and independence of the American people."

Variants on this theme were numerous as many locales were hopeful that crisis would establish fresh character in America. Gulian C. Verplanck in New York City saw a "very peculiar character" built upon an emerging "good sense." It permitted Verplanck to say that America "now seems chosen as the sanctuary in which the models of republican institutions may be preserved and perfected." Others who agreed usually tied fulfillment to the persistence of those "imperishable lessons of political truth" which the Founders had left behind. During the war dissent was unmasked as "party delusion" or as an impotent voice from citizens incapable of "national sentiments." Behold instead, said the response of hope, the "nation rises with renovated fame. Its destiny is great. Imperishable be its glory!" This required separating those willing to "degrade our national character" from men who "have *honest principles,* or *American feelings.*" No matter how

ardently men spoke, the uncertainties of this era discouraged any
unqualified assurance.[36]

10

The difficulties of national confidence made a doubtful response
easy. This sentiment, as well as the despair which often followed,
fed upon the danger seen within and without the nation. Lyman
Beecher, who fought valiantly for the Christian posture, recalled
late in life the gravity of the age of survival. Had the Lord
left the nation's side, it would have been overwhelmed. The special menace was the brooding presence of the citizenry's passion.
Beecher said that men learned in the days of Adams and Jefferson
to discard the delusion that "human nature in our nation was
incapable of the violence manifested in other nations." He conceded that a miracle had spared America. "God interposed and
took off the pressure." The fearful storm withdrew, if temporarily.

This era was a solemn season, fit for making the stump more
like a pulpit. Harrison Gray Otis set much of the tone for expressions in most regions when he paused in eulogizing Alexander
Hamilton to say: "We behold the republics of Europe march in
procession to the funeral of their own liberties, by the lurid light
of the revolutionary torch." Those preaching nationality in this
era usually took as a text the grave danger facing republicanism.
Robert Walsh's *The American Review of History and Politics*
began its difficult two-year career in 1811 with this thought uppermost. Walsh especially emphasized America's need for sound
authority. The moment's only satisfaction for him was the fact
that at least principle had once beaten Jacobinism in America,
even though again America's "dissolution be near at hand."

Perhaps the best available avowal of the crisis facing America's
republican Trust was by Jeremiah Evarts in 1812. He conceded
that the premise of American nationality had not changed; it still
assumed that man could make choices dispassionately. Yet the
selfishness, anger, and falsehood raging in the nation suggested a
principle betrayed. Thus God well might convert America "into
a single instrument of Divine vengeance, as a punishment for national ingratitude and corruption." Abandon the demagogues,
Evarts preached, and restore the nation into the hands "of such
men as composed the old Congress." America had once known virtuous republican rule. Now, falling from the Fathers' ways meant

certain and shameful national degeneration. To men like Evarts the moment of choice had come, putting "hope and death, liberty and slavery" before America's Stewards. Their determination would disclose either the folly of republicanism and the power of passion, or bring national regeneration. If the present generation chose wisely, ages to come would call it blessed.

Expression in such times took God's wrath upon an impenitent and wayward nation to be very real and imminent. Pastors like Lyman Beecher knew they addressed a worried people and they made the most of it. For them the nation needed few theological subtleties, but an awareness that Stewards could either sin or avoid sin. America's hope was to have a group of regenerate moral agents as citizens, thus denying total corruption of human nature. Both an embattled faith and a hard-pressed national Trust could profit from this outlook. Religion and republicanism moved closer together. Faith and nationality both wished that men would surrender to righteousness.

President Timothy Dwight told his flock at Yale in 1798 that the duty of Americans in the "Present Crisis" was Godliness. Let the nation humble itself before God, as had the Fathers. Only this, ran one testimony, would let America abandon waywardness, passion, and partisanship for the path of "dignified, practical wisdom." Despite the lingering radiance of the Enlightenment, American thought respected deities and devils, heavens and hells.

No one, however, surpassed the Reverend Lyman Beecher's exhortations for national union with God, on God's terms. On Long Island, in 1806, he preached of a nation defiled, warning that the more America's Vineyard seemed to flourish, "the greater is the guilt of our rebellion, and the more certain, swift, and awful will be our calamity." In New Haven during 1812, Beecher reviewed national morals. His theme was itself the spirit of nationality in crisis: "Our vices are digging the grave of our liberties, and preparing to entomb our glory. . . . We are becoming another people." Human depravity now had no principled opposition in America. "No people are more fitted for destruction, if they go to destruction, than we ourselves." Moral restraint no longer guided American enterprise, leaving the nation defying God in the presence of awesome crisis. Beecher concluded with what must have been one of the great rhetorical inquiries of the age: "Is this a time to throw away the shield of faith . . . ?" [37]

11

Faced by early crisis, many Americans sank in despair before the "awful question" posed by their Trust. John Marshall was certain that "real Americanism was on the wane." The republican process was producing leadership by "odious reptiles," leaving true love of country *to stalk about* like shadows." When war came, there were predictions that Providence was determined to have "another era of Gothic darkness," leaving mankind everywhere to abhor an America destroyed by baseness. This often simply meant avarice and selfishness, favorite topics for the despairing attitude. America must choose the pursuit of ambition and luxury, or self-discipline and a shunning of greed. One observer considered Providence's physical blessing as an ironic prosperity corrupting patriotic devotion. Consequently, "Like the other chosen people of the most High, we began to run after strange deities, the idols of other nations." The point often stressed was that leaders and citizens alike were not discerning properly between selfishness and profligacy and the American responsibility and need.

Amid war, confession of national sin was a fashionable response among a stricken body of Stewards, whether they saw godlessness, avarice, passion, or sheer folly as the sin or the error. Whatever the flaw, the American nation was said to have abandoned its Trust, its Vineyards had been desecrated, and it had fallen like any other people before the blandishments of the flesh. Typically voicing this despair was a New Jersey orator, Daniel A. Clark. In 1814 he admonished the nation to renew its appreciation of God's vast physical blessing. The Vineyard was fertile, beautiful, and healthful. The entire American story was, in fact, "but one continued, affecting account of God's care." He called the nation's degeneracy since the days of the Fathers open rebellion against God. For Clark the sins of American Stewards were: loss of prayer and family discipline, wild youth, Sabbath-breaking, drunkenness, profaneness, and the ultimate evil, factionalism. The career of partisanship in America, said Clark, "proves us a vicious race." [38]

For spokesmen like Clark, salvation for the debased nation would be difficult. It required confession of national sins and surrender to the high principles bought with the blood of the Fathers. The wide despair in 1814 agreed that only a miracle, proof of providential mercy, would preserve the nation for another season of stewardship. The Trust was awesome, the Stewards weak, and the Vineyard unavailing. At least so the national plight appeared to most of those who grappled with the doctrine of American meaning. Then, just as the era entered what appeared to be the deepest gloom, God intervened at New Orleans.

CHAPTER TWO　　SEARCH
1815–1848

The Republic did survive. Ghent and New Orleans signaled fresh pursuit of national fulfillment. The ideology of nationality drew comfort simply from America's preservation. However, early struggles with the Trust had left their marks, as a speech by Richard H. Dana showed. Dana acknowledged that his generation had once believed the American venture was intended "to work an universal change in the condition and character of man." In earlier days, mused Dana, Americans felt called to lead the world into "the beauty and freshness of Eden," where man was suddenly as sinless as Adam. Now it was clear that human nature had proven no different in America, where cunning and violence were as prevalent as they were anywhere else. Accordingly, said Dana, America had a new Trust. It was to find the path back to the old precepts, "the good way in which we once walked." Such a search would skirt the fallen idols of "unrestrained liberty, equality, and perfectibility." [1]

Survival did launch the Republic's quest for understanding, both of its calling and of means for fulfilling that Trust. An immediacy about such attainment lingered until events in the early 1830's brought disillusion. Most of those who had begun talking of "our rising greatness" retreated to the ambiguity of "our rising nation." The interval between wars with Britain and Mexico persuaded few Americans that their work was nearly done. Nor was agreement reached about the Trust imposed upon America, although two matters were clarified. The intent of nationality would have to be carried out later, and the world watched the undertaking. Beyond these, American thought remained divided and uneasy in its affirmations about itself.

Events between 1815 and 1848 produced such a physical transformation that some contemporaries decided America's proper labor was process or simply motion itself. One commentator recently has said: "Within the lifetime of a single generation, a rustic and in large part wild landscape was transformed into the site of the world's most productive industrial machine." Yet the American character seemed on the brink of failure, "dirtied or tempted by a host of vices." Such default represented a breach of the republican Trust in morals and manners set by God or the Fathers. In departing the White House in 1829, John Quincy Adams and the nation stared at the wreckage of anticipations arising a decade before. James Madison's return to Virginia in 1817 had been amid talk of eliminating parties and of a rising unity throughout America. Accordingly, President Monroe and President Adams practiced the politics of optimism in the face of rising dispute over matters like slavery, tariffs, and transportation. By 1829, the curse of party seemed almost overpowering, and national unification had been superseded by the challenge of deliberate dissonance. Thereafter, until the Mexican War, circumstance did little to ease the nation's unremitting difficulty in meeting the challenge of its own peculiar being.[2]

In Andrew Jackson's era, the search for America's meaning became more irksome. The pursuit was troubled by such issues as Negro slavery, tariffs, money, internal improvements, constitutional interpretation, and public land policy. In fact, they seemed to invite two alarming departures from national propriety. These were luxuriance in the passions of party politics and talk of a broken Union. The presidencies of Jackson and Van Buren saw mammon incite the nation to feverish economic exultation. It was soon followed by despair. These vicissitudes were enough for some to argue that youthful America would merely re-enact the classic struggle between economic groups. The presidential canvass of 1840 heightened apprehension over what individual and public passion might do to harm the Republic.

After 1840, American thought seemed especially concerned with national character. An earlier generation foresaw America's spirit arising from the eagerly awaited national literature. However, the new electioneering used in 1840 convinced many persons that it was premature to depict the nation's character or to predict the appearance of national culture. Instead, respectful attention went to James Russell Lowell's contention that genuine culture must await matured national values. Consequently, the eras of John Tyler and James K. Polk featured wider discussion of the nature of man and society. There were varied responses from working men, partisans, abolitionists, Unionists, slaveholders, clergymen, and merchants. From such vantages not only was the American Trust's identity debatable, its attainment seemed doubtful.

Some assurance came by merging growth and foreign policy. Jefferson once had seen national expansion as a balm for discontent. The issues of Texas, Oregon, and California raised shouts of an evident destiny, proving an outlet for troubled spirits. Much of America joined Polk in resting its search for national meaning while revelations came from physical settings and acts. Momentarily forgotten was the struggle in America of reason and religion against passion and selfishness. But not for long. Intoxication with geography afforded merely temporary relief, just as 1815's events only briefly had provided hope that the sins of man and society would diminish. Thus, if geographical fulfillment could not satisfy America's search for successful meaning, new certitudes would have to be sought. The debate over national fate was quickly renewed, since physical demonstrations of American meaning were to become a series of ironical delusions, especially between 1820 and 1854.

A contributor to the ideology of nationality in both Jefferson's and Polk's times was Albert Gallatin. In the 1840's the retired statesman and once-feared Jacobin was a sedate New York banker and ethnologist. At eighty-two, Gallatin was the past incarnate when he addressed the New-York Historical Society in February 1843. He first praised America's comparatively calm pilgrimage toward freedom: in contrast to republicanism's experience in Europe, said Gallatin, "America justly became, for all liberal minds a subject of exultation . . . everywhere the hope of mankind." This was providential and required the present generation to see "that they are bound by the most solemn duty, by the most sacred obligation to their Country and to their God, to preserve and transmit, unimpaired, to posterity, the invaluable inheritance they have received from their ancestors." Gallatin's cautious view of the future was significant. It represented the furthest that hope generally took America in the 1840's. Little evidence supports the familiar contention that this era, when America turned to size for reassurance, was one of "glorious optimism" or exhibited "romantic assumptions of human virtue and social perfectibility at their apogee."

Actually, the nation's headlong growth since 1815 had brought such vicissitudes as to reinforce for many the misgivings over national and citizen capacity so familiar in John Adams' days. Men in Polk's time yearned for a successful transfer of the Trust described by Gallatin. But they could not forget that political tumult, urban riots, material lust, and private corruption suggested America was clearly vulnerable to mammon and passion. Consequently, uncertainty about the present generation's capacity brought much speculation and controversy in the middle period's thought. It is difficult to accept the contention of one historian that the "liberal" outlook of the time created in American thought a benign unanimity. More characteristic was the tone of Nathan Lord's eulogy of John Quincy Adams in 1848. He offered the only plausible benediction upon a generation whose search for the essentials of American nationality had faltered: "Our country is still a problem. Who will solve it?" [3]

DOCTRINE

Events in 1815 dictated that careful attention be given to the theory of Americanism, something impossible until survival was evident. Reconstructing this emerging doctrine leaves one impression. The search to know the Trust, the demands it made of citizens, and the implications of a continental Vineyard brought no more than the comforts of abstract and largely undefined immutables. Even the virtues of the primitive Republic grew less explicit as they became more charming. The issues raised by inquiry into American significance pointed to the past as armament for the future. Searchers for America had to be content in 1848 with either a sense of mystery or a feeling of anticipation. Both left the American Trust, as Nathan Lord said, a problem.

I: Affirmations   The three explanations of America's Trust, dimly apparent after 1798, grew distinct in the era concluded by the Mexican War. Partnership with Providence or God became both an awesome asset and a torment for the nation. Agency for freedom and republicanism brought stronger challenges of expectancy or preservation. Anticipations both from the past and the future challenged America's perspective. Men sought earnestly to know how and when the Republic's kingdom might come to pass. In one respect there was accord. Accepting America as a Trust made the present intolerable. Overcoming it reinforced the call for men to surrender themselves anew. Some persons agreed with an 1831 publication, nicely entitled *The Spirit of the Pilgrims,* which insisted that only a religious spirit "can unite the local, jarring interests of this great nation, and constitute us benevolently one." Others searched for more complex answers.

1

In reflecting upon national responsibility, American thought exhibited a broad range of emotion. A mind like the Reverend Lyman Beecher's, for instance, nourished ambivalences ranging from an ecstatic view of the American prospect to a sullen resentment of the repeated defeats experienced because of national shortcoming. Always there was a cry for persisting American endeavor. Beecher said it was needed in the world's pursuit of Christ. Others entertained the same spirit, only the words and symbols varied. Nationality never performed outside a moral drama. As one historian has suggested, the faith of the middle period was not so simple as some might think. Nor could doctrine entailing charges from both God and freedom be comforting for very long.[4]

This was evident in an 1823 address at Union College by New York governor DeWitt Clinton. He stressed the evolutionary character of national development; he rejoiced in republicanism; he saw a universal struggle at hand between power and freedom; he worried that men took responsibility when passion rather than reason might predominate; and he acknowledged the American Trust was awesome and certainly unfulfilled. Said Clinton: "Let us not deceive ourselves by the delusions of overweening confidence, and the chimeras of impregnable security, and fondly suppose that we are to rise superior to the calamities of other nations." Clinton spied the old foes of faction and greed ahead. Even so, God had charged America and given it a "sublime" Vineyard. Would the Trust extract from the Stewards a proper response?

Since Clinton's outlook combined God and man, materialism and spirit, hope and misgiving, it showed discomfort even in the relatively confident time of 1823. Almost twenty years later at Yale, Rufus Putman Cutler resumed the thread left by Clinton. He saw the same paradoxes and made the customary rejection of the present, but then he offered a new touch. Cutler said that the search for understanding nationality had created expectations for both self and nation which were "too grand for present feeble conception." He displayed a frustration and resentment common to America in 1839. Despite its noble responsibility, America had wasted its energies on material and political development. National fulfillment could begin, said Cutler, only when "the intellectual energies of the nation will turn from the outward and material" to develop "a new intellectual life." American national meaning could not be formulated until a capacity for thought had emerged.

During the era in which Clinton and Cutler lived, discoveries about the nation's essence created an uncomfortably awesome role for the citizen. The expectations of God or the Fathers or the future were difficult yokes. In 1815, Americans pictured Providence presenting a bumbling nation with a second chance to carry out a grand assignment. One typical affirmation conceded that until recently America had wallowed in folly. Then Providence spoke in the war's roar. Its scourge "like the thunder's gust" restored to America "the springs of health and animation." Some said that thereafter Providence would be appeased only through the nation's dutiful pursuit of economic independence. America's responsibility was to make its Vineyards literally fruitful. A benign Providence had richly blessed the nation. It solemnly awaited America's earnest use of its endowment. Now secure from interference, America must not be its own barrier to what one speaker called the enjoyment "of those blessings, which our maker intended as a birthright to the whole human family." [5]

Although Providence was the favorite intellectual device of those advocating growth and materialism as the Trust, it was also useful as the key to the critical future. American self-appraisal found it difficult to take solace solely from the past.

Lewis Cass demonstrated this in speaking as first president in 1836 of the American Historical Society then formed in Washington. Cass refused to linger entirely in the past, despite its story of Anglo-Saxon achievement. Debatable though the future was, its potential was appetizing. "How wonderful are the destinies committed to that future! How vast are our own interests, which are involved in it." Providence, acknowledged Cass, had carried America to the present. "Let us hope that He will protect us in our maturity, till, in his own good season, his design shall have been consummated." Providence proved a congenial companion in the age of search. For many Americans, providential agency was in the Union, creating around it a secular religion. The Union was Providence incarnate as American doctrine looked to future attainment.

God was less companionable. His record was too clear, just as was His call for man's total surrender. Not only would this save man from his corrupt self and thereby spare a nation from otherwise certain disaster, but it was the secret of the Trust. American nationality was for many persons a doctrine of capitulation to God, thereby bringing ultimate glory to God and assured well-being to the nation. The influential divine, Nathaniel W. Taylor, told the Connecticut legislature in 1823 of his deep fear of secularism. Taylor asked "for those provisions of law, and that patronage from every member of the community in behalf of a common Christianity." This was only justly due the faith which was "a nation's strength and a nation's glory." Affirmations of theocracy as America's goal were very powerful in America's introspection in the era after 1815. Only through God, said this doctrine, could the nation escape sinfulness to demonstrate fulfillment. But sin persisted, which brought warnings of retribution. Events seemed to enlarge the distance between God's expectation and "a people incorrigibly wicked."

The affirmations that God's kingdom was America's meaning demanded in Monroe's administration that the Fourth of July observance become one of religious meditation and solemn patriotic rededication. America's search was poorly served when the Fourth seemed bent on becoming a setting for sinful indulgence and excess. It forced a redoubling of such rhetorical affirmations as "What, my brethren, could have kept the ship of State so long and so securely at her moorings but the hand of

God moving by the wisdom he inspires." God had launched "the bark of our national power." He alone could outfit it for unruffled seas and for "the sweeping blast." There were calls for religiously guided reason, but these diminished during the trials of Jackson's time. Simpler ways were sometimes used to advocate that America's meaning was in being God's country. "Jesus Christ was a Patriot" and therefore "every Christian should be a patriot." [6]

In settling for national purpose under Divine superintendence, many voices strove to have Christ and freedom sharing the mystery of American meaning. Generally an agency for either freedom or republicanism seemed to mean the preservation of a constraining but cherished primitivistic order, usually called the old Republic. This portrayal of the national intent had the dubious advantage of being highly descriptive in an age of change. Americans apparently enjoyed thinking about the calm virtues ascribed to past republicanism rather than those implied by liberty or freedom.

As a result, national doctrine tended to consider freedom as a package, neatly wrapped by the Fathers. Much attention was paid to the historical enigma, was freedom present and growing in America long before the moment of truth in 1776? Was it not also correct that the Fathers had with their blood completed the growth of this precious element? There was little inclination in 1820 to recall any differing opinion among the Founders. Instead, men preferred an instantaneous to an evolutionary appearance of perfect freedom. When Adams and Jefferson died in 1826, their departure separated dramatically the Revolutionary supermen from mortals searching for America's true meaning. Liberty and freedom came to be established national features, not to be criticized. This produced a Trust from the wondrous men of '76. The liberty they won should be cherished inviolate.

Debating freedom's ultimate meaning in the life of a fearfully dynamic nation or recalling variances of sentiment the Fathers might have held was neither necessary nor prudent. Jackson's generation scourged the foes of freedom in the name of a historic liberty requiring preservation. The Trust thus necessitated guarding a truism during an era when the relationship between freedom and order rarely entered discussion of American meaning. Many Americans were willing to accept freedom as a mystical legacy and had no need to talk of its further growth or of any internal complexity. Freedom's Trust required only broad spaces and devoted Stewards. Affirmations about nationality often overflowed with description of "this infant people" struggling for "the success of this last experiment to learn whether man can be virtuous and happy while he is free." Liberty was an "important treasure" granted "to our trust." Such "peculiar responsibilities" must be made evident to all Stewards.

Not every American could leave this concept unalloyed. Freedom's Trust for them meant uncomfortable terrain and burdens. Consequently, nationality often sought some relief from virtual enslavement to liberty by substituting a Trust in behalf of republicanism. Here were institutional qualities and matters of practice which the abstraction of liberty did not afford. In fact, true republicanism's immediacy seemed to invite swift action, and therefore much controversy among the Stewards. One element within the Jeffersonian movement represented itself as defending the ancient and pure republic. It urged Americans to recognize their role as restoring and perpetuating this primitive republicanism. Such appeal added glorious connotations to the otherwise drab business of defending strict interpretation of the federal Constitution.

These ideas first became widespread during the 1824 presidential campaign. Calls became commonplace for recapture of true republicanism. This conservative theme remained important after 1824. John C. Calhoun used it skillfully, emphasizing during the critical days of the early 1830's that Americans were "eminently Republican in their character and feelings." How woeful that the Democratic party should make perverted use of this venerable tradition. Calhoun called it "pseudo-Republicanism." Stewards faithful to this view of the republican Trust would find in the Virginia and Kentucky Resolutions their sacred writings.

Others preferred the republican Trust as interpreted in William H. Seward's 1844 oration, "The True Greatness of Our Country." Everywhere he spoke, Seward recommended a conservatism that was less restrictive. This was to maintain a nation undefiled in its astounding nature, "so simple in principle, yet so complex in organization, and resting so much on consent." He mused over the impact which growth might have upon fundamental republicanism, conceding that before America's fulfillment was complete, rising cities in the far west might make Union's separation necessary. Comfortable with growth, Seward could "discern no cause why the motives of nationality should be weaker than now." Should disruption come, let it be peaceable. This would be the ultimate act of stewardship for republicanism, said Seward. Long habits of discipline and mutual affection could bring a harmonious dismemberment, enabling "the American people to add another and final essay on the excellence of republics—that of dividing without violence and reconstructing without loss of liberty."

Still others argued that republican obligations meant simply keeping America dynamic. This required no more careful thought than was evident in Parke Godwin's 1846 advice to President Polk: "The question of war and slavery are only incidental ones, which can easily be put aside, but the question of extending *constitutional republican institutions* over this whole continent is one of the broadest, noblest, and most important that was ever presented to any nation." Godwin's comments took refuge in the limitless and thus reassuring future which the continent's geographical size seemed to guarantee, just as Calhoun's view of republicanism capitalized on the highly usable past. Both vantages showed the nation's tendency to accept a Trust definable only in terms of either the past or the future.[7]

With the simultaneous deaths of Adams and Jefferson, the past seemed ready at last, its contents prepared to be a model. Earlier practices were to be cherished under terms of America's Trust. Yet as the past grew more compelling, it became more ambiguous. Though the first textbooks tried to equate patriotism with unstinted loyalty to establishment, the question was loyalty to what? For many, the answer was the Union. It embodied national salvation, carrying ancient virtues through the troubled present to the wondrous future. "The Union of these States is the production of the spirit of harmony and compromise. Do we remember how much our fathers surrendered to compose, and shall we refuse to surrender any thing to preserve it?" A "common affection and forbearance" was necessary if the legacy from the past would survive the hands bequeathing it.

However, in this era affirmations from the South began to differ from the general doctrine. Men like Robert Turnbull rejected the cant over Union as useless jargon, unless it was a "proper Union." Facing a need after 1825 to perpetuate an acceptable order, the South's voice alone in America concentrated on the present. John C. Calhoun led these affirmations. He described how the South recalled with joy the shared origin and achievements of the rest of America, as well as "the common greatness and glory that seems to await us." These were planted in the soil of existing order and liberty. Should national endeavor be attracted to future development, Calhoun said for the South, "We will then be compelled to turn our eyes on ourselves."

Speaking in 1846 for a new generation of Southerners, Congressman Jefferson Davis reaffirmed Calhoun's doctrine by openly contending that nationality had been fulfilled. Davis insisted that the one true nation was evident. Talk of further Trusts produced envy and strife, both "eating like rust in the bonds our fathers expected to bind us." Recalling such places as Concord, Lexington, Yorktown, and New Orleans, Davis suggested that restless Stewards "retrace the fountain of our years and stand beside its source." He obviously hoped this purification would wash away the hour's malignant impatience with the nobler understanding born of the Fathers' time. Davis left most Americans unconvinced, making them seek a more feasible bond between belief and actuality. Eventually, scourging the South of her national philosophy became the nation's act of atonement expected to ensure general fulfillment.[8]

Except for the Southern view, Stewards largely used the past as a handy storehouse of devices by which the unacceptable present would be outwitted as men sought the promised future. Toward this end, amid "novel circumstances" and "threatening tumults," it was widely affirmed that the Stewards "must go in the armour of our experience and principles." This was the theme of an 1844 Thanksgiving sermon which included a fervent distillation of the Trust: "In all that you do for your country or yourselves, THINK OF YOUR FATHERS! THINK OF YOUR POSTERITY!" There had been an entire year of this during 1824–25, when Lafayette traveled America in triumph, hailed as the goal of a nation's search. This meant he was embodiment of the virtues emerging from the past to aid the future. Better use of the principles vouchsafed by the Founders was now anticipated, America having seen "so perfect a model" of the past's "pure and ennobling virtues."

Yet even after 1846, during a war for national completion, America still was not sure about the elusive future. Samuel G.

Goodrich, who wrote the famous Peter Parley history books for common schools, phrased this outlook: "What a glorious prospect for our country," but he added numerous qualifications. "If the people become indolent, or if they become wicked, ruin and desolation will visit this land." The Steward must select wise leaders in the pilgrimage, for "careless, ignorant, or faithless rulers would bring poverty and vice."

Similar speculations had shaped national doctrine at the close of the 1812 war. While the sustaining element in nationality was the "anticipation of the future grandeur of United America," a time when the nation would be "the wonder and example of mankind," there was need for caution. "Our character is not yet fully formed; it will take fifty years, perhaps, or at least another generation *entirely* to cause the American people to believe and act [as] if they belonged to and had a country for *themselves*." [9]

Circumstances between the two wars made affirmations about a Trust for the future become considerably more complex. These of course took note of the economic and communication changes under way. Both laymen and clergy insisted that those Americans "who think themselves secure, take heed lest they fall." A good illustration of America's effort to find intellectual sustenance by mixing hope and doubt was Gulian C. Verplanck's address at Union College in 1836. Its theme was "We can scarcely be said to have a present—certainly we have none for mere indolent enjoyment. We are all pressing and hastening forward to some better future." For Verplanck, one of the time's prominent intellectuals, this situation explained America's Trust: "The character, knowledge and happiness of that future and distant multitude are now in our hands. They are to be moulded by our beneficent labors, our example, our studies, our philanthropic enterprise." Its proper discharge was threatened by "the rail-road noise and rapidity of this work-day world of America." These must not disenchant America's men of thought, Verplanck warned, sensing a "complacent disgust" was weakening men of intellect.

Verplanck's generation often tried to solve this problem by making the future an outcome of a benign process. The swirl of activity in a transforming nation suggested such an irresistibly dynamic quality in human endeavor that many observers took optimism on faith. One thoughtful person said: "The exciting condition of things in a new and changing community like ours impels us forward. We have no time to reflect. . . . Go ahead is the motto. . . ." Consequently, talk of attaining a glorious future by treasuring sacred precepts often was lost in the drama of sheer development. The difficulty was that such drama assumed the Stewards would not fail the assignment. It left American doctrine uncomfortable, for most observers could never quite forget that, as Congressman Edward Baker put it in 1845, America's future would be fulfilled, unless undone "by our own folly."

The future's uncertainties fostered speculation about the universal import of national fulfillment. After 1815, Americans often agreed that the nation must serve as world exemplar. This assignment grew so weighty that help was found in merging with the broader mission of the Anglo-Saxon race. Ill-formed and tentative before 1848, this concept already had the features which would make it so useful late in the century when America abandoned her traditional loneliness. In Jackson's time, however, lines between Anglo-Saxonism and America's world responsibility were not distinct. Edward Everett showed this in proclaiming a world brotherhood of free people. They were to be taught by America whose Anglo-Saxon origins gave her the best of Europe's traits. America could not retreat, "for the great exemplar must stand." To fail meant "we blast the hopes of the friends of liberty . . . throughout the world, to the end of time."

This global future was especially pleasing to Christians in America. During this era both home and foreign missions began flourishing careers in American Protestantism, a zeal with strong secular overtones. The promptings of national purpose led to calls for a stewardship with nothing less than God's guidance. The American Home Mission Society did not have to elaborate when it asserted in 1842: "Patriotism should constrain us to evangelize this nation." A theme widely repeated in this era was that God expected to see America, through its own redemption, elevate all of the Heavenly Father's children. World salvation was the ultimate impact of the righteousness attained by the American Steward. The burden this posed was staggering, bringing one person to say, "our national character being of such unutterable importance to the world, it may be questioned whether a generation ever lived on whose fidelity so much depended."

Affirmations in this era were rarely content to accept a future role with the simple reminder that America was "freighted with the hopes of humanity" and that it was "the last mighty stake in this wide world in the great experiment of self-government." The emphasis was usually forced to add that America's failure would bring joy to evil despotism everywhere. The New York *Herald* insisted in 1845 that with each day the American mind must come more to realize "that the civilization of the earth—the reform of the governments of the ancient world—the emancipation of the whole race" rested with American endeavor. The more this was stressed, the more Americans seemed constrained to speak of faltering and failure. As orators and editors of the time often said, the nation's role required sleepless vigilance. No longer was America to be threatened "by hostile fleets and armies. It is from among ourselves, we must hereafter look for its most dangerous enemies." This misgiving brought many, like Bronson Alcott, to shelve the stirring sentiments of world salvation. America's fulfillment, whatever the Trust, first required the triumph of human talent and genius.[10]

2

American doctrine found itself increasingly intrigued in this era by speculation about the American citizen. For those who agreed that the citizen was responsible for national fulfillment, the period after 1815 seemed especially important for training this Steward. The ideals required by the Trust had to be established. Thereafter the schooling of the Steward could be redoubled, for it was usually acknowledged that innocence and instinct were not reliable. It is important to recall that the era of Jackson was also the era of Horace Mann. Education in the time of search was less concerned with knowledge than with virtue. A frail, impressionable mortal, each American needed to be made aware of both self and righteousness. Pursuit of national completion would be held up, therefore, until a worthy American character or spirit could be identified and developed.

Discovering the able Steward was an uncertain venture after 1815, especially because of an old paradox. The capable American must be able to shun environment with its devilish distractions and yet to rule the things of this world. The Steward needed to marshal worldly attainment without sacrificing Christian morality and the precepts of the Fathers. The problem was to produce citizens powerful in will and worldly attainment while continuing pure in heart. On the one hand beckoned the enormous physical process which for many was America's essence; on the other towered the ineluctable religious-moral system basic to American thinking. Republican virtue and evangelical protestantism struggled to remain in step during an era aware that the American was still incomplete. Occasionally, the crucial moral education of Stewards seemed to abandon a theological framework. This was owing less to rationalism's influence than to the standards of God being more explicit and demanding than some architects of American nationality could bear.

It was sometimes affirmed that the nation's responsibility was to produce and then rely upon a noble man. Many believed this would happen. Orestes Brownson, for instance, wrote in 1834 that America was turning toward deeper matters than mere "physical well-being." Men were recognizing that "Providence, in the peculiar circumstance in which it has placed us, in the free institutions it has given us, has made it our duty to bring out the ideal man." Thus would humanity be shown what it might do if it had the freedom to develop its faculties. National consciousness cherished this view. Whether in the rhetoric of a temperance meeting or of an affair of state, the prayer was often raised that man might so develop in America as to disclose to the world "the moral force of *personal* virtue" under republicanism.

Idealization of the virtuous Steward was evident in textbooks. They were filled with villains and heroes for the American youth to consider, and invariably virtue was rewarded and vice punished. Right behavior was to be learned, for man was not by nature ethically sound. The texts also simplified the story of the nation's past and the prospect of its future. American fulfillment awaited the appearance of an incredible nobility of public character. The early issues of the *Youth's Companion* endorsed this doctrine in addressing the rising Stewards. Like the schoolbooks of the time, this journal mirrored the nation's eagerness to ensure that children conformed to the high standard established for and by the American Trust.

In some of the era's adult literature the ideal American was more realistically portrayed. Presentations of the Yankee as a sly rustic or a shrewd figure never bested in worldly affairs suggested that the American outlook sought to endure the mixed

blessing of the contemporary Steward's character while determining that posterity emerge with unalloyed virtue. Usually,
however, patience with citizen shortcoming wore thin. The
result was more clamor for indoctrination, for popular conformity to national moral standards. The American was indeed to be
a common man by sharing one character. An interpretation made
to students at the College of New Jersey in 1831 was typical.
"Patriotism, linked almost from moral necessity with a sisterhood
of virtues is irreconcilably and everlastingly hostile to sloth of
mind or degeneracy of action. You cannot sincerely feel the
sentiment, and yet be idle. You cannot pretend to it, and yet be
bad."

The 1840's showed little progress toward such exalted manhood. A second line of defense thus became necessary. It employed affirmations about stewardship concentrating on the
group mind rather than on individual outlook. The nation's
salvation was said to depend upon the masses becoming *Ameri-
canized.*" Middle-period thought was increasingly comfortable
with the idea that American stewardship required a society bound
to live by ancient verities and dedicated to the perpetual adjustment of individual impulse to national well-being. Since this
outlook was not natural, assistance was needed to create a vital
coherence rising from virtuous self-denial.

Important in this undertaking was D. Macauley's popular *The
Patriot's Catechism; Or, The Duties of Rulers and Ruled,* published in Washington during 1843. The volume exhibited endorsements from such dignitaries as Thomas Hart Benton and
John C. Calhoun. Macauley told of many persons who wished to
distribute the *Catechism* among the youth of their neighbor-
hoods. Patriotism, these youth would read, meant surrendering to
the nation, as God's law decreed. National well-being had but
one objective, the glory of God. Preaching that the good citizen
could have only one desire, "the happiness of a nation," Macauley deplored a stewardship selfishly striving after wealth. His
prescription for a dedicated national outlook was for individuals
to obey leadership from virtuous men. These statesmen in turn
required a profound Christian faith.

Whether religious or secular in tone, calls like Macauley's had
gone forth from the moment that the miracles of 1815 had occurred. America needed "a character which will reach future

ages," one that could develop only out of a "union of sentiment
and feeling." This demanded that youth be imbued with "American modes and habits of thinking and acting." Some claimed
that this corporate nature must await the mystical appearance
of national literature, which according to this argument was the
only means by which "to expand our patriotism, and elevate our
national pride." Others spoke of stewardly association depending
upon a vigorous national industry. Economic maturity would
provide a "natural" impulse for American character, in contrast
to artificial indoctrination by letters.[11]

With a national character difficult to perceive, many found it
tempting to talk of a universal temperament. While P. T. Bar-
num worried over a "sheep-like docility" in the American public, others said that this was stewardship by accommodation, an
interpretation that was especially popular after the disputes of
1820 when men first acclaimed a spirit of compromise. It was
said that to such spirit the nation owed its "solid national glory."
The outlook was all the more vital because it was "truly Wash-
ingtonian" and thus would sustain the *moral feeling* of the nation." During the campaign of 1824, candidates vied to display
the most national outlook. For instance, supporters of Henry
Clay insisted he pursued "no anti-national policy" but exhibited
spirit "that soars far beyond those grovelling notions" which
limited the vision of some men.

Unity of sentiment was an easier norm for proper stewardship than was national character. Concerted public endeavor
was the only guarantee for what one spokesman called the good
things "laid up for us by Providence in past years." Such a
"spirit of self-sacrifice" was the sole source of salvation for the
Republic, according to many. In the 1840's, this mystique of feeling moved to even more exalted levels. One person asserted that
without a dream America would falter and perish. "The people
must have a 'vision.' " Others even argued that there was no nation beyond the "Spirit Republic." The political design might
alter, but the national mind was permanent.

For those unwilling to rely on Stewards being impelled
through spiritual accord, there were affirmations about American
participation in a vast racial progression. Jackson's generation
began taking refuge in Anglo-Saxon supremacy. Historians who
dismiss this as simply "a matter of emotion, of Fourth of July

oratory," overlook the distressed quality of American nationality. America's ways became so troubled that thought of marching
with an international force cheered some citizens. As one orator
said in 1834, within the Anglo-Saxon saga "flowed the purest
blood of the civilized world." Here was a race which would
never be in servitude. For others "that SAXON BLOOD which
fills our veins" was the unifying force sure to lead America to
"her future glory." By 1848 it was often heard that American
responsibility could not be discharged without, as one person
said, "a bond of cordial, and, I trust, imperishable love" between the United States and England. According to this doctrine, hope for truth, freedom, and Christianity rested with
America and England. If the natural spirit of brotherly love
thrived among these two countries, the coveted new order for
humanity would arise.[12]

3

After 1815, America's Vineyard continued to be seen as either a
natural physical endowment or a remarkable political setting.
The tendency in this phase of national doctrine was to make
America's undeniable physical growth proof of moral progress.
In both the natural and political locales, mere process itself became reassuring in the face of the Republic's awesome charge.
At the same time, there was diminishing expectation that America's wondrous physical setting would be an inspiration for national endeavor. Belief in an American eden faltered before the
imposing presence of the machine. It left the great natural Vineyard even more vague and abstracted.

While thoughtful observers such as Emerson, Melville, Whitman, and Hawthorne doubted that even an edenic Vineyard
could foster a wholly good man, others, including Clay and
Webster, began telling America that its natural gift demanded
wise usage. Such use, or exploitation, meant improvement of an
ironic literalness. Consequently, the natural Vineyard assumed
drastically different roles for the various schools of American
thought. One role was that of a theoretical environ, the only
place where the universal truths which America had to put into
practice might flourish. The other was of nature developing the
material unity needed for America's fulfillment.

An 1818 pamphlet published in Brooklyn aptly affirmed the

rising doctrine that the Vineyard was a challenge for technocracy. A vital link prevailed between commercial success and national triumph. The document raised what would become the familiar chant about "ties of interest" and "social ties" being sole requisites for "an enlightened and powerful people." For this view, the Vineyard of nature was only a beginning. No sense of preservation was needed: "Our mountains must be politically annihilated. Our sectional barriers must be swept away by a moral arm, whose power is resistless." A commercial spirit would arise, bringing the crucial "settled, uniform, and consistent" aspect to the nation. With this concept of a developing Vineyard, the nation could be comfortably preoccupied with the future. The materialist had a special meaning when he announced: "We are yet a young nation and have scarcely begun to act on the high theatre of empires." [13]

At the other extreme the concept of America's natural setting was considered an inspiration for distant and mystical greatness. George Ticknor realized this after contemplating the two hundredth observance of the landing at Plymouth Rock. America's surroundings must be a source of spiritual exhilaration. Things like "the blessed rock" would afford vital and lively "feelings" that could come only from "associations of place." According to men like Ticknor, America's setting could offer as much of this vital feeling as Westminster Abbey, or the Alps, could. John Quincy Adams was another who agreed on the natural basis for patriotism—"that instinctive and mysterious connexion between man and physical nature which binds the first perceptions of childhood in a chain of sympathy with the last gasp of expiring age, and the spot of our nativity."

All of the claims for the nation's setting considered the Vineyard as incomplete, a place for meeting an obligation for the future. Young Francis Parkman was one of those who saw advantage in combining the approaches. He said that national inspiration came from noble environment and from man's additions to that grandeur. While the "rugged landscapes" recalled the struggles of the past, American fulfillment needed more than a setting dominated by "the succession of the seasons." Man's deeds and fancies had to inspire a nation which was described by Parkman in 1844 as "half a world consecrated to the operations of Nature."

Whereas the natural Vineyard seemed to invite human practical endeavor and ingenuity, the concept of a political Vineyard tended in this era to become an exalting abstraction. Mention of the Union permitted both traditionalists and defenders of growth momentarily to agree. A preservation of political unity promised national fulfillment. But what was to be preserved, and how was it to be done? Could the frail Steward labor successfully in a political Vineyard where there were conflicts over what was to be preserved and what might need process or change?

Having survived the rude shocks so widely predicted in 1798, America's polity needed definition and demarcation. Presidents, jurists, pamphleteers, editors, orators, citizens, all joined in this effort. An early prescription was that familiarity and neighborliness be encouraged. One comment in 1817 was that "the better we become acquainted the more we shall like each other; the less willing we shall ever be to see a national barrier rise up between us and sever the bonds of our Union." An ardent early believer in this was John C. Calhoun. Yet events soon forced him to a very different interpretation of political nationality. "To be too national has, indeed, been considered by many, even of my friends, my greatest political fault." The antidote was a reversal of design. The nation would achieve its intent only so long as "the sacred distribution" of powers among the physical areas was preserved. Sustaining the true polity was the key to American fulfillment. It required a stewardship, as Robert Y. Hayne said, of "firm, manly, and steady resistance against usurpation." [14]

Others, however, demanded a less inhibited future for the nation in its political garden. Such was the view of the historian and public man, John G. Palfrey. For him, America's polity was an engine for liberty's march. Constitutional limitations and geographical niceties were useless concerns in a polity where Stewards labored using only "knowledge and virtue, intellectual and moral power" as guides for "a discerning patriotism." There were also the Fathers' principles, which were now occasionally given a new dynamic character. Had it not become clear, fifty years after the Declaration had entombed them, that "the pure, simple, and sublime truths, into which Americans have resolved the Science of Government and which address themselves so forcibly to all enlightened minds, will continue to spread, until like the sun in the firmament, they shall have illumined the remotest regions of the world"?

By the 1830's the political Vineyard was being accepted by some as a theater for a relentless development in which the nation and its helpless though faithful citizens were swept along. This developmental quality of America's polity was possibly the most comforting discovery made in the search for national meaning after 1826. Politics rivaled nature in becoming endurable and durable through the concept of inevitable growth. Even though it was possible that the nation's fulfillment was still distant, a growing number of observers believed triumph was assured by the order of things.

There was some awareness of the philosophical price paid for this impersonal dynamism. A speaker told the Union Literary Society in 1839 that knowledge of momentum was one thing and that the ability of knowledge to affect that progression was quite another. Stewards should take comfort in recognizing what was happening, even if they could not influence the process. America was asked to concede that there was "in the essence of human events, a sovereign and irrevocable necessity superior to all earthly power. Of what avail will be our puny arm in rolling back the torrent of intellectual ideas and human progress, scooping their way along the steep of centuries?" The American polity was therefore a setting for the performance of "the mysterious instinct of a futurity."

Such affirmations were routine by the mid-1840's. The working out of a political process explained American meaning. The American Revolution was thus the beginning of an age of growth within the wondrous political Vineyard. As one believer said, it was left for men simply to know "that time, with his ever-wasting but improving hand, should one day present to the eyes of mankind one vast Republic." Soon, however, most thoughtful Americans discovered the difficulty of accepting this benign outlook in view of new issues and events.[15]

II: Anxieties   In spite of the shouts about Manifest Destiny, national expectancy became more confused. Man's capriciousness appeared to increase with America's awesome momentum. The affirmations accompanying nationality were often contested by the realities of Jackson's time. Assaults by mammon and passion and the resurgence of more virulent partisanship required greater ingenuity if an optimistic view of America's stewardship was to be taken. Jackson's generation seemed to expect much tribulation before the Republic and especially republicanism would triumph.

4

The celebrations of 1815 were soon quieted by cautious advice. Typical was the view voiced during the uncomfortable summer of 1819. It was now time "we had done with much exultation," for it "suits neither our condition nor our character." America must pause and reflect: "Our growth will be rapid enough; let it rather be our care to make it sound than sudden." Successful Stewards must be known for "their disregard of present evil and anxious provision for the future." Supreme Court Justice Joseph Story was fond of saying "We must serve in the hard school of discipline; we must invigorate our powers by the studies of other times." America's venture could fail, especially with "the great mass of the people" confused in the presence of "so many political demagogues." Story explained his own rising anxiety: "I know not how it is, but somehow it is a fact that, upon political questions, men are blind, and deaf, and dumb, when you attempt to disabuse them of their prejudices and mistakes."

After 1837's depression, more Americans seemed willing to face the problem of a nation seeking its fulfillment while deterred by a faltering people. This plight claimed young Horace Bushnell's thoughts when he appeared at Yale in 1837 to deliver the Phi Beta Kappa oration. He said that the nation's institutions were sound. The current economic ills he predicted would check "the impetuosity and increasing recklessness of our people . . . compelling them to know the worth of principles and of wise and judicious leaders." Bushnell's interpretation of the national travail was widely shared. The nation had been granted "an interregnum of sobriety and reason, in which truth may find a place to interpose her counsels." Bushnell's tactic seemed at first to stress America's part in universal process, glorying in its Saxon design and in the natural Vineyard. From these would "form a people of vast conceptions" and thereafter a national character of "spiritual vastness." Only meanness and sensuality could endanger American completion. Here was the central point of

Bushnell's argument. The nation was an entity whose principles were dangerously mean and low. These could be elevated by two faiths—one religious, the other filiopietistic. "Piety to God, piety to ancestors, are the only force which can impart an organic unity and vitality to a state. Torn from the past and from God, government is but a dead and brute machine."

At this point Bushnell's message became confusing. Abandoning any rejoicing in process, principle, and tradition, the orator appeared to lose confidence in ordained national triumph. He admitted shrinking at the very thought of America's future— "Oh! I blush," said he, for a nation which asked only "questions of loss and gain." Crass inclination had diverted the best citizens in America from the crucial task of training all of the people for the burden of republicanism. America's Trust required creating a "distinct" nation and a deliberate stewardship. In contrast with his earlier organic affirmations, Bushnell closed by portraying the present as simply a time for moral regeneration. America was not yet ready to prove that "LIBERTY IS JUSTICE SE-CURED." With "a chastened but good spirit," America must seek to be "happy, orderly, brave, and just" so that the world might recognize this "true example of greatness in a people." Thus, Bushnell embraced both change and tradition, certainty and doubt. He offered a conclusion characteristic of America's confused outlook. The nation must select the proper truths and leaders; follow these and the Trust might thus be fulfilled.[16]

Warnings about the menace from human senses did not disappear with prosperity's return. There was discomfiture in America's amazing physical and political development. It was widely insisted that esteem for the physical would engender an irreverent spirit, producing Stewards "who have no other idea of national well-being than richness and greatness." Generally the national experience encouraged the call for a moral and intellectual revival. The latter, according to this reasoning, could be devised by educated men who alone might sustain America a little longer in her stewardship. Let the people be taught both duty and truth by men who themselves would shun the office craved by demagogues. This would be possible, of course, only through a Christian outlook, which one anxious voice called the sole basis for "pure morals and true national well-being."

Those who watched America toil during this era certainly shared at least one important concern. They recognized the need to shelter freedom by establishing human self-control through reverence for principle. Few commentators acclaimed man's favorable predispositions. The more men searched for reassuring meaning in America's ambiguous endeavors, the more preoccupied they became with somehow sustaining a burden imposed by God and humanity. This uneasiness was not lulled by talk of certainty in organic process or of innate goodness in the individual republican. Somehow, inspiration must capture the Stewards, keeping them faithful to their charge, undeterred by the call of passion or avarice.

America's disconcerting behavior persisted, however, so that some observers had no choice but to say the nation's meaning was in development. Its unfolding might be watched with either faith or apprehension. John Effingham observed in Cooper's perceptive *Home as Found*, "It is getting to be a predominant feeling in the American nature, I fear, to love change." Cooper himself deplored the difficulty of seeing America beyond the moment. Albert Gallatin let history offer the basis for hope. Surely a nation whose character had been formed and modified in the glorious early years could slowly mature into a triumph for popular freedom. Gradually the idea spread that America's undertaking was in the hands of time. While this explanation found comfort in the past and patterns in the present, there was little sign of the qualities of character needed to signal a fulfilled Trust. Despite the knowledge that the nation was in motion, there still was "no national feeling, no national manners, not even a national costume." America seemed "a mere abstraction."

Most Americans therefore had to wonder how the national becoming so easily talked of would avert a disgraceful triumph of greed over spirit. Anxious observers found little lofty character arising amid the enormous material temptations in America. Deference to the doctrine of process seemed simply to encourage a relaxation amidst the pursuit of luxury. America's uneasiness was in large part a concern over how dangerously long it might take Stewards to see that "they are born not for themselves alone, but for their country and the world." [17]

5

Try though America might to interpret its endeavor through predestination, it had to re-examine the issue of man's limitation. Both passion and mammon seemed to find America easy prey. Material lust especially caused rising concern, since it taught Stewards to let advantage smother principle. The latter was still the anchor for the frail republican craft. In the ecstatic days after 1815 this ship had seemed beyond the shoals of selfishness. America's leading editor, Hezekiah Niles, kept pointing to indications of an emergent "high spirit" that would carry men beyond their personal needs. By 1834, however, the aging journalist had to ask: "Does it not appear that the character of our people has suffered a considerable change for the worse?" Niles conceded that "the moral sense of right and wrong has been rendered less sensitive than it was."

Avarice certainly grew more alarming for nationality. An 1829 editorial in *The Ladies' Magazine* expressed the view of many that America's problems now stemmed from "the vanity and extravagance of the people." It was "thoughtlessness and pride" that beset the nation. This observer, probably Mrs. Sarah J. Hale, asserted: "There is no ambition so mischievous in our Republic as that of personal display." Like many of her contemporaries, Mrs. Hale preached triumph for America through simplicity. Let men cease pretending to be rich, and instead pursue attainment of the mind. From this would come men "ambitious of doing something to advance the prosperity, the happiness, or the glory of his country."

Such advice seemed to fall unheeded. An 1832 observer, in regretting the absence of public virtue in America, said: "We are growing rich, and begin to feel that influence of wealth, which we are told makes it difficult for a rich man to enter into the Kingdom of Heaven." James Fenimore Cooper described his creation, Aristabulus Bragg, as the epitome of a large number of Americans, by saying that Bragg was "ready to turn not only his hand, but his heart and his principles, to anything that offers an advantage." As a result, in America "money has got to be so completely the end of life, that few think of it as a means." Never had a nation been "so absolutely under this malign influence. . . . All principles are swallowed up in the absorbing desires for gain—national honor . . . and anything that is usually so dear to men, are forgotten, or are perverted in order to sustain this unnatural condition of things." Bronson Alcott spoke for those who believed that material lust had overthrown the soul in America. "How doth a man degrade himself to a drudge—a thing among things!" Anxiety over "the love of and devotion to Mammon," as Thomas Corwin put it, was widely evident.

The depression after 1837 was a time for recalling how the Fathers had recognized avarice as a yoke padded with silk, with fetters made of gold. The nation's captivity by scheming, cunning, and fraudulent concerns was said to be destroying its foundations, man's moral and intellectual strength. The nation had lost its way in a "general delirium." Clearly America was being tested, not by adversity, but by prosperity. James Russell Lowell announced that "commerce, trade, and stocks are our religion." Their buildings "are the temples we erect to Mammon, our God." [18]

A nation thus described seemed far indeed from carrying out a divine Trust for humanity. Other observers found the passionate nature of the American remained a serious feature. This brought new appeals that America must stay with God or be lost. Such anxiety took many forms, including the charge that the "spurious patriotism" abroad in the land took heart from whiskey, not God. When God was forgotten, man's hopes were doomed. Others of a practical bent made the school assist the Almighty in saving America from "a gradual and unperceived decline of moral sentiment and moral purpose."

These misgivings grew with the rising awareness after 1815 that the Founders were disappearing. A betrayal of the nation's responsibility would now be wholly the fault of a second generation of Stewards. There was desperate urgency in an assertion heard in Albany that Americans had entered the time "when the living lights that warned and encouraged us, have gone out silently one by one, and we are left to uphold the experiment so gloriously begun." Somehow "lofty virtue" must be rediscovered by America, for without it the citizenry would rush "to despotism itself, as a refuge from their own weakness and licentiousness." Few doubted that in seeking a proper security, Americans must more appreciate that "the *permanent* health of a nation must lie in its *moral* constitution."

Even so, America's vulnerability appeared to be increasing. Despair brought rebuke for those who had "the vanity to think that you can do anything to oppose or correct the prevailing madness." Optimists, however, called for hand-to-hand combat with human nature. "It is ourselves we have reason to fear," said one person, adding, "It is the loss or the want of virtue and integrity in our own hearts. . . . It is the silent working of wrong principles—the gradual corruption of the people." Only with education might the American still come to "feel the responsibilities of his position." Here was continuing sustenance in the wearing pursuit of national assurance.

Horace Mann made the point seem very clear. He said the issue was America triumphant through education or destroyed without it. Unless men were separated from their passions by indoctrination in righteousness, "licentiousness shall be the liberty; and violence and chicanery shall be the law." Writing in 1848, Mann saw the coming generation as America's last hope. "It may be an easy thing to make a Republic; but it is a very laborious thing to make Republicans; and woe to the republic that rests upon no better foundation than ignorance, selfishness, and passion." No matter how promising or aspiring, any republic could come "to an ignominious end" if appetite was not controlled.

No one put more succinctly than Mann an increasingly prevalent view. "Moral education is a primal necessity of social existence. The unrestrained passions of man are not only homicidal, but suicidal; and a community without a conscience would soon extinguish itself." No matter what Americans might believe they had done to contain wrong, "yet the great ocean of vice and crime overleaps every embankment, pours down upon our heads, saps the foundation under our feet, and sweeps away the securities of social order, or property, liberty, and life."

For those sharing Mann's view there was but one way to meet American responsibility. Moral education must be brought fully to bear upon the young. As Mann had warned, the youthful citizen had always been overlooked until too late. This doctrine responded to American anxiety by calling for a new character in the citizenry through indoctrination. From this alone would emanate the fruitful and secure American Republic. It also allowed the present to shift some responsibility onto the future.[19]

6

The ideology of the time never succeeded in separating good and evil passion. Some pleas for a national outlook frankly took their stance with sheer emotion. Mann's fellow Bostonian, George Hilliard, asserted that overwhelming love of country was ennobling and good. "It has its origin in the strength, not the weakness of our nature. It is good for us to feel strongly, if we also feel justly." However, the outlet most national feeling took in this era, partisanship, was by wide agreement fatal to just and powerful feeling. In fact, partisan designs were blamed for the tragic dwarfing of elevated sentiment in America.

For a season after 1815 there were hopes, presided over by James Monroe himself, that America might outgrow petty partisanship. Men swore to embrace "the purest patriotism" and to "rise superior to that ignoble jealousy which weighs all political questions. . . . We would feel as Americans." In 1820 there was virtual but deceptive unanimity in the selection of Monroe for a second presidential term. Claims were commonplace that a national view prevailed, and that parties would disappear along with the pettiness and localism which had engendered them. It was not to be, and "violent" politics rising from "questions of selfish security and cautious expediencey" returned. The campaign of 1824 ended the dream that the nation was abandoning party zeal as it hastened toward fulfillment. Vice President Calhoun gently reviewed the situation in 1828 in a letter to Monroe, concluding with the remarkable understatement that the prospects "render doubtful the beautiful idea, which you cherished so fondly, that our system might under its natural action sustain itself without exciting party feelings."

Soon after Calhoun wrote, it was generally agreed that the word "country" had been replaced by "party" in the language of America. Politics had become a trade, it was said, and the national spirit had been traduced. Little occurred to sustain those hoping that this national curse would be lifted. In 1844 a discouraged Millard Fillmore could see in Clay's defeat that the urge of party was bringing citizens to abandon all principle. Said Fillmore: "A cloud of gloom hangs over the future. May God save the country; for it is evident the people will not." Whether in victory or loss, men rarely disagreed that corruption and demagoguery had left America's character degraded, her Trust unfulfilled. "The Republic is daily sinking," said Justice Joseph Story, "I am in utter despair. . . . I can see little or no ground of hope for our country."

For most Americans there was ample reason to join in the
anxious lines of a Presbyterian hymn published in 1843:

> Oh, be thou still our guardian God,
> Preserve these States from every foe,
> From party rage, from scenes of blood,
> From sin and every cause of woe.[20]

SPOKESMEN

There was ample expression of the frustra-
tions America met in searching for the full meaning of its Trust.
All spokesmen agreed that American character and achievement
both rested in the future. This became distressingly more remote
as the momentary bliss of 1815's events receded before a persisting
deficiency in human nature. Historical fantasy helped the rising
uneasiness, for it permitted many spokesmen to begin demanding
a stewardship of preservation. American fulfillment was said to
depend upon individual surrender to a compelling blend of institutions and majestic events. National goals seemed more remote
in 1848 than in 1815. The era of search concluded in the doubtful comfort of a paradox involving freedom and determinism, as
well as upheaval and institutions.

III: Advocates   The extremes of
thought accompanying the search for America's self-understand-
ing matched the nation's gigantic size and increasing complexity.
This breadth can be appreciated by listening first to Samuel L.
Knapp, who was optimistic about American nature and expecta-
tion. In contrast were the views privately exchanged between two
Fathers doomed to live in this troubled era of search, Thomas
Jefferson and John Adams.

A popular orator until his death in 1838, Samuel Knapp was
also a biographer of Daniel Webster. He published a volume of
lectures in 1829 that was intended to foster reverence for national
character in America. Knapp insisted that education must persuade America's youth to love the nation. The nation lacked self-
respect because it was too conscious of the future: Knapp saw

men on all sides endeavoring "to show what we shall be in a century or two to come." Instead, Knapp believed, Americans should acknowledge the present and rejoice that everything they possessed had "grown from their own sagacity, industry, and perseverance." It meant that Americans "have been blessed by a kind providence, in their basket and their store." In this wondrous setting God walked with man, offering him the nourishing fruit of knowledge. Man in America was left to carry on labors instructively begun by inspired Fathers.

Despite his own admonitions, Knapp proved unable to tolerate contemporary America even with succor from the past. His ardent spirit fell victim to the uneasiness endemic in the search. Knapp peeped cautiously at the future, something which he had earlier condemned. The glimpse beyond suddenly undid both premises and conclusions implicit in the three hundred previous pages of his lectures. "We must not be too impatient for greatness," cautioned Knapp, who was happy that the nation had already attained more than most. He detected evolutionary forces at work, whose mark on American development should be calmly observed. Knapp closed by surrendering to mysticism. The American citizenry was guided by "impulses" and its "settled determination is fate."

Knapp's significant capitulation conflicted with his insistence in many speeches that true Americanism was ancestor worship. Yet both interpretations were optimistic about national achievement, agreeing that the present generation was simply an agent for process or for traditional values. On one occasion, in 1826, Knapp argued that Americans had no choice but to imitate ancestors. "The light shining on one ancient grave will reach to another, until their commingled radiance will form a pillar of fire to guide posterity through every night of danger that may come upon our nation." It was a comforting theme for troubled times. Knapp recommended faith in what had been done in America and thus "what we may hereafter do." Let "the visions of glory that come flitting before us . . . bring us out in the exercise of those virtues which secure national prosperity and happiness." At other times Knapp was vulnerable to the uncertainty which man's nature injected into America's venture. Late in life, he conceded that the nation could "go back to ignorance and anarchy." Knapp wondered if it might "be said in after ages, that avarice and vulgar ambition had seized upon and corroded the heart, and destroyed the life-blood of the republic." [21]

Long before Knapp's jubilation faltered, two of the men he revered had ceased even to speculate about America's purpose and prospects. Both Jefferson and the elder Adams by 1816 had recognized the frailty of national virtue. As Adams observed, though the national traits posed questions "too deep and wide for my capacity to answer," it was apparent that human reason and conscience were no match "for human Passions." Adams considered patriotism among the most dangerous of emotions since it encouraged egocentrism. When, mused the old man, "will all Men and all Nations do as they would be done by"? Jefferson struggled to retain more favorable anticipations. For him America's responsibility was to show the world a moral emancipation. This was a necessary companion to the physical liberty already achieved. Such moral independence was still beyond America, where "the inquisition of public opinion overwhelms in practice the freedom asserted by the laws in theory."

While Jefferson still thought of the future of liberty, so lamely led by America, Adams threw up his hands. American endeavor had become a matter of "perpetual chicanery" with the relations among the citizenry "all a caprice." Jefferson was more willing to give Americans more time to develop public morality. But even he succumbed to despair. "I regret that I am now to die in the belief, that the useless sacrifice of themselves by the generation of 1776, to acquire self-government and happiness to their country, is to be thrown away by the unwise and unworthy passions of their sons." [22]

7

Between the extremes of Knapp's confused ebullience and the dying Founders' gloom fell the official ideas of the presidents. James Madison left office predicting America might well become so dedicated to liberty that it could gratify "the most noble of all ambitions," promoting "peace on earth and good will to man." James Monroe quickly snatched this thread of optimism, announcing at his inauguration that "we find abundant cause to felicitate ourselves in the excellence of our institutions." It was an achievement due to public wisdom which in turn depended upon America surpassing ignorance and corruption. The President stressed the need to inform and arrange the popular mind. "National honor is national property of the highest value. The sentiment in the mind of every citizen is national strength. It ought therefore to be cherished."

This theme remained attractive for Monroe. America's wonderful opportunities under a government which was nearing perfection, required preserving the virtue and enlightening the mind of the citizen. Once this was assured, he said, "we cannot fail, under the favor of a gracious Providence, to attain the high destiny which seems to await us." Monroe saw two polities in America, a central leadership and an association of local units. The two, of course, complemented each other and were to be preserved for national fulfillment. In doing so, the citizenry would be emulating the Founders. Thus the political Trust would "soon attain the highest degree of perfection of which human institutions are capable." Later Monroe abandoned the preservation position for the argument that national continuity depended upon expansion, but he was unsure about the possibility of external threat to America. In December 1823 his famous doctrine spoke fearfully of Europe's intimidation; in December 1824 he said the nation was safe from European influence.

Monroe's reflections on nationality adopted a consistent theme in his final message. "There is no object which as a people we can desire which we do not possess or which is not within our reach." This happy circumstance stemmed from the nation's extraodinary polity. Thus, the American Trust "is to preserve these blessings, and to hand them down to the latest posterity." The progress of civilization, Monroe affirmed, depended on the success of American institutions. Therefore, "on their preservation and in their utmost purity everything will depend." [23]

This joyous approach to the nation's status and prospect was carried forward by John Quincy Adams. He considered America to be a legacy which the present generation must convey "unimpaired to the succeeding generation." The future of this legacy gratified Adams, who seemed to disregard anything he might have known about his father's disappointment. The second Adams publically insisted that "the great result of this experiment upon the theory of human rights has at the close of that generation by which it was formed been crowned with success equal to the most sanguine expectations of its founders." Looking both to the past and the future, Adams suggested that the nation might at once "indulge in grateful exultation and in cheering hope."

Adams' inaugural message contained some of the most cogent talk about impending national fulfillment. He saw a Trust nearing fulfillment. The old issues and misgivings were vanishing. Men could revere what once they had challenged and disputed, the efficacy of federal republicanism. America being freed of international entanglements and dangers, "there still remains one effort of magnanimity, one sacrifice of prejudice and passion" among the people, Adams told the nation. "It is that of discarding every remnant of rancor against each other, of embracing as countrymen and friends." Adams predicted the furling of party standards. In spite of the unhappy fate of this prophecy, Adams continued to repeat only conventional sentiment about America's responsibility, stressing especially universal knowledge and public improvement. The one unique note was Adams' designation of Washington's Farewell advice as appropriate for vanished circumstances. Never once did Adams publicly acknowledge any lessening of the prospect for national attainment. Outside the White House, however, men were once again deploring the swirl of passion, avarice, and revived partisanship.[24]

These distressing aspects of stewardship did not escape President Andrew Jackson. His official assertions gradually resumed misgiving over national capacity and purpose. In 1829, Jackson spoke of "mutual gratulation and devout thanks" for the nation's well-being. America had all things needed for "national strength." He even offered the hand of fellowship to England. "Everything in the condition and history of the two nations is calculated to inspire sentiments of mutual respect," Jackson told Congress in 1829. He called England a nation "distinguished in peace and war." Meantime, he saw a steady improvement in "the genius and laws of our extended Republic." Any discord ultimately would serve to "foster the spirit of conciliation and patriotism" which Jackson called crucial if the American Union should prove to be "imperishable."

By 1832, Jackson acknowledged that he was deeply troubled. Some comfort came from knowing that Providence would give the Republic peculiar care. "Through *His* abundant goodness and

their patriotic devotion our liberty and Union will be preserved."
Loath to leave it at this, Jackson advised America that its evils
were caused by departure from original principles. He called it
time to review those precepts, so that men might revive "that devoted patriotism and spirit of compromise which distinguished
the sages of the Revolution and the father of our Union." Until
that transpired, Jackson turned his office and the nation over to
the supernatural. He closed his proclamation about South Carolina by saying: "May the Great Ruler of Nations grant that the
signal blessings with which He has favored ours may not, by the
madness of party or personal ambition, be disregarded and lost."

In his Second Inaugural Message, Jackson returned to the concept of a Trust. "The eyes of all nations are fixed on our Republic," he said. "Great is the stake placed in our hands; great is the
responsibility which must rest upon the people of the United
States." After the nullification crisis subsided, Jackson kept
prompting the nation: "It is to our own conduct we must look for
the preservation of those causes on which depend the excellence
and the duration of our happy system of government."

By 1837 crisis made necessary another farewell admonition.
Like the first President, Jackson reminded the nation of its astounding history and its astonishing blessing. In the absence of
external foes, Jackson was free to concentrate on the ultimate
threat to American success, human failings. These he listed as
"cupidity," "corruption," "disappointed ambition," and "inordinate thirst for power." He also spoke of "the highest of human
trusts" committed to America's care. "Providence has . . . chosen
you as the guardians of freedom, to preserve it for the benefit of
the human race." The national polity was clearly proven after
fifty years. What remained to be revealed was the citizenry's capacity for its obligation. Jackson's advice here grew vague: "If
you are true to yourselves nothing can impede your march to the
highest point of national prosperity." Whereupon the President
turned to God to make the American Steward "worthy of the fa-
vors He has bestowed and enable you, with pure hearts and pure
hands and sleepless vigilance, to guard and defend to the end of
time the great charge He has committed to your keeping." [25]

Martin Van Buren loyally continued this executive attention
to public shortcoming and weakness. Using himself as an example,
Van Buren announced that a post-Revolutionary generation now

was fully responsible for the nation's attainment. In Van Buren's judgment meeting this challenge required a conservative posture. Stewardship meant upholding "those political institutions that were wisely and deliberately formed with reference to every circumstance that could preserve or might endanger the blessings we enjoy." Repeating Jackson's theme, "The perpetuity of our institutions depends upon ourselves," Van Buren urged faith in the past. "America will present to every friend of mankind the cheering proof that a popular government, wisely formed, is wanting in no element of endurance or strength." In Van Buren's inaugural speech, human dedication was the nation's remaining need. It was a dedication to America's "true form, character and spirit." But about these Van Buren was no more precise.

Ensuing economic travail forced Van Buren to cheer the Stewards with thoughts about the evils of wealth and luxury, and the sound Americanness of frugality and simple life. By joining self-denial with patriotism, Van Buren pounced on the specter of mammon. Speculation and extravagance would destroy in Americans the manly virtues so crucial to a successful national venture. Man was finished as a useful republican, Van Buren warned, if he succumbed to cravings for luxury and enjoyment, leaving him with "a sickly appetite for effeminate indulgence and in imitation of that reckless extravagance which impoverished and enslaved the industrious people of foreign lands." [26]

William Henry Harrison's inaugural message renewed this theme of self-denial and self-control. Special attention went to avarice, materialism, and partisanship, which Harrison called the natural foes of republicanism. Consequently America was gravely menaced. Harrison saw everywhere a partisan zeal so bent upon the aggrandizement of a few that it would destroy national interests. Harrison's successor, John Tyler, enlarged this idea with considerable imagination, establishing a national will whose testament was the Constitution. This was the real America. Tyler warned that the nation's character could be twisted and destroyed by majorities in Congress. He offered the service of the President as defender of the true America as defined by the Constitution.

Before he had left office, Tyler discovered a new mandate. Suddenly forgetting inner peril, he talked of America's role as tutor to Mexico. In fact Tyler grew suddenly ecstatic about the fruitfulness of national endeavor. He took delight in that "great moral spectacle," America's presidential canvass where Stewards displayed their love of order and their obedience to law. Domestic matters seemed so favorable for success in the "great experiment" that Tyler left the Presidency predicting foreign jealousy alone could undermine national well-being. "It may be most devoutly hoped that the good sense of the American people will ever be ready to repel all such attempts should they ever be made." [27]

Near the end of his administration, circumstances prompted James K. Polk to lecture the Republic upon nationality in a way reminiscent of Monroe. Polk's final messages illustrate how America's search since 1815 for meaning and assurance had come to rely upon conventional admonition. His 1848 remarks on the peace treaty suggested that the embodiment of nationality, the Union, was beyond analysis and calculation. It was a model "to all the world, and is the star of hope and haven of rest to the oppressed of every clime." By the act of "preservation," Americans had grown in power and happiness. Surely now, said Polk, America would not be so foolish as to launch inner dissension. Narrow constitutional interpretation was the best precaution. By massive self-restraint in the act of preserving an inspired polity, America would safely grow and gloriously flourish.

Later, Polk's message on the Oregon Territory used the same theme, laced with praise for the vital spirit of compromise as the national essence. "We have now become an example for imitation to the whole world," said the President with an eye on Europe's new convulsions. Surely America would not "peril all our blessings by despising the lessons of experience and refusing to tread in the footsteps which our fathers have trodden." Polk's final address preached this gospel of caution. In the face of foreign tumult, he said, "we may congratulate ourselves that we are the most favored people on the face of the earth"—most favored as a result of the "rich inheritance from our fathers" which subdued "force and violence," always nearby, by the restraints of constitutional majoritarianism.

Renewed blessing and prospect of "national greatness" came with geographical expansion. Polk was horrified at the possibility that the "irrational" could seize America through the slavery issue. Such considerations were "trivial" to the world and to posterity in comparison with "the preservation of this Union." Polk's admonition was clear. Proper stewardship in America meant conserving a sublime legacy. "How solemn, therefore, is the duty, how impressive the call upon us" to cherish "a patriotic spirit of harmony, of compromise and mutual concession." Nothing save "a disregard for the experience of the past and a recurrence to an unwise public policy" would keep America from what Polk called "the first rank among nations." He listed simplicity, frugality, and strict interpretation as means of conserving what the Fathers intended America to be, namely, "a plain, cheap, and simple confederation of States."

The era of search closed as it began, with a President calling for perpetuating the past as the only means for entering into the wondrous kingdom of the future. The wondrous kingdom would be near, provided the proven spirit and policy of the sainted Founders were maintained. The Presidents had generally decreed that only this prostration of all conflicting desire through fidelity to the nation's past could constrain passion, greed, and partisanship in the name of American fulfillment.[28]

8

The leading personalities in this era shared a stubborn but largely unyielding pursuit of national meaning and assurance. Except for a few younger searchers, all spokesmen looked to the fantasy world in which vast material change was glorious while the nation's political and spiritual elements were cherished unaltered.

Among the most cautious advocates were Philip Hone and Noah Webster. These men saw in the nation's endeavors a series of revelations about the essential depravity of man. They wanted to restore the Old Republic. For Hone and Webster national spirit had to come out of past virtue. They would not have been surprised if the American venture failed. God alone sustained any hope the nation might nurture concerning its faithful labor. Hone was a courtly and thoughtful New York City businessman and gentleman. His views were frankly Whiggish, although he deplored the persistence of "party violence." Throughout his diary Hone battled passion, prejudice, demagoguery, and partisanship. He liked to remark: "Reflecting men who love their country and would preserve its institutions are full of alarm and serious forebodings." Social upheaval suggested that "the devil is in the people." America's disorder by 1838 made Hone conclude: "Now is the critical moment of our country's fate." He discovered the re-vival of Jacobinism, bringing near the time "when this noble country of ours will be subject to all the horrors of civil war; our republican institutions, theoretically so beautiful, but relying unfortunately too much upon the virtue and intelligence of the people, will be broken into pieces."

Hone traveled around the nation to talk to the economic and conservative leaders. He was feted by Daniel Webster. Hone car-ried to his diary the deep misgiving over America's capacity for its role, an uncertainty which bothered the professional and wealthy elements of the nation. At the same time, Hone regretted how "money-seeking" kept America from pondering adequately its grave problems. A favorable election in 1840 afforded only a temporary and modest reprieve. Hone still wished to exchange the prevalence "of bastard politics, of selfish views, and simulated patriotism" for the outlook of Adams' and Jay's days. Then "the people's good was consulted, not their prejudices, and the incense of truth was administered to the popular will free from the nauseous alloy of flattery."

By 1843 Hone had lost hope. "Public virtue is the only founda-tion of a republican form of government, and that is utterly swept away. The edifice must fall." Polk's election made Hone "pray that the Almighty will avert from the country the evils which, from present appearances, the people have brought upon themselves." Hone's reverence for the past grew, as he saw its legacy "sunk like water in the sand." Marshall's death appeared to him an even greater calamity than Washington's had been. In short, Hone expected America to default upon its glorious assign-ment through "the depravity of our morals." For him the bells of the Fourth pealed in a mocking and empty way. Even the old Yankee character of New England seemed corroded by the malig-nant influence of cotton mills and railroads. Hone's diary thus remarkably bespoke the fear widespread in national thought that America was disregarding the precious guides left for her as her national treasure and meaning.[29]

Noah Webster's disgust is worth noting. While more unreason-ing than Hone, Webster was another person who considered the Trust far beyond the capacity of the Stewards. By 1835 Noah Webster pronounced republican hopes crushed by passion and partisanship. Only true Christianity might aid America as it aimlessly floated in "a licentious world." In his long "Marcellus" tract of 1837, Webster expanded his views on man's depravity. He took the unique step of rebuking the always perfect Founders by contending that many of them had been "visionary enthusiasts who had read history without profit." History, as Noah Webster perceived it, was filled with "a melancholy truth" about human limitation. The American challenge, then, was to devise a way in which men might be protected against themselves.

Webster was as vague about the solution as he was explicit about America's need. His *History of the United States,* published in 1832, offered as national salvation a true Christianity which "enjoins humility, piety, and benevolence." Consequently, education in America should make its chief aim "to exterminate our popular vices." Meantime, Webster could only moan: "We deserve all our public evils. We are a degenerate and wicked people." Although contemporaries often said Noah Webster was renewing old Federalism, there was no wide dissent from his definition of the problem.[30]

A challenge to the unqualified gloom of spokesmen like Hone and Webster logically should have been the views of Andrew Jackson, whom conservative thought considered the demon who thrived on the aroused passions of the citizenry. Yet neither Jackson's public nor private voice exhibited assurance about American meaning and attainment. Instead Old Hickory pleaded that Stewards somehow restore the simple virtues. For Jackson, men were either very good or very evil, and society was always wavering between governance or bloody chaos. In time, Jackson equated his own view with that of the Republic's best outlook and made his intent consonant with the nation's fulfillment.

Convinced that his interest was identical with national well-being, Jackson's world filled with conspiracy. He considered a few kindred souls to be the group who would thwart evil and save America. Stewardship in Jackson's outlook was to destroy one's own opponents, for these were also the loathsome menace to the Republic's triumph. Old Hickory's grasp of nationality illustrates the extent of paranoia in much of America's consciousness.

Jackson's sense of nationality revealed a skepticism about man. During days of controversy General Jackson had assured President Monroe that the loudest shouts of patriotism came from men who had less than their country's interest at heart. At the same time he advised his wife's nephew to distrust most men, who were usually busy setting snares for each other. Young Andrew Donelson was told to mix only "with the better class of society, whose characters are well established for their virtue, and upright conduct." By 1820 Jackson spoke of evil's mastery in the nation. Demagoguery and greed predominated. The best advice Jackson could offer friends was to learn the true facts about human nature, so often the center of vileness and deceit. Perpetual suspicion was needed in a republic. While he felt some confidence in the general populace, Jackson told Calhoun in 1823 that evidence showed the citizens "have become degenerate and demoralized."

The 1824 canvass made Jackson more convinced of the Republic's threat from evil men. Gradually he came to see the hapless public as having a potentially righteous disposition which intriguers toyed with. His letter resigning as United States senator in 1825 suggested limiting the discretion of Americans in office. Jackson brooded over the imminent possibility of public corruption overwhelming the Republic. "We know human nature to be prone to evil. We are early taught to pray that we not be led into temptation." Brief repose came with his triumph in 1828. Speaking warmly of "the virtue" of a great majority of Americans, Jackson said: "The republic is safe, its main pillars virtue, religion, and morality will be fostered by a majority of the people." Thus would the demagogue and corruptor be undone.

By 1832, the power of evil seemed resurgent to Jackson. South Carolinians were obviously deluded by men ambitious and unprincipled. The President's views were fed by his confidants. Joel Poinsett, for instance, wrote from South Carolina that "bad men" deliberately sought "to ruin this once glorious Republic." Nullification offered Jackson fresh perspective on national meaning. As he told Van Buren on Christmas Day 1832, "The preservation of the Union is the supreme law." Simple national endurance suddenly dominated Andrew Jackson's understanding. Once again, stewardship became the act of conservation, and alternatives meant "blood and destruction." Meantime, advisers like Amos Kendall revealed new plots to corrupt the people through appeals to avarice. It seemed so bad by 1833 that Jackson feared American citizens "do not know where to find their political principles and friends." The time was at hand to separate "true men" from "ambitious men."

Jackson soon began describing the American responsibility in universal terms. Future generations everywhere depended on righteousness now. Yet corruption seemed triumphant, and Jackson confessed to loathing human nature. His friend, Hugh Lawson White, tried to comfort the President with the news that men were really no worse than ever. It was simply that he and Jackson had come to know humanity better. With this in mind, Jackson warmed to a stewardship of restoration. America would be fulfilled by reviving its "primitive simplicity and purity." Only this would destroy the growing menace of venality. In discussing his Farewell Message with Chief Justice Taney, Jackson insisted on warning the people that they were surrounded by "mischievous and intriguing individuals."

The events following Jackson's retirement were, as the old man put it, "truly strange to me." He had hoped that simple decency in America would be sustained and republican purity restored, so that he was chagrined by the election in 1840. He began to shout in his letters that America was undone by a vileness worse than in "the most corrupt days of ancient Rome." His view had become reminiscent of the outlook of his critic, Philip Hone. Despite fleeting joy at the providential removal of Harrison, the old hero lingered to brood over the American venture. Chief Justice Taney spared his old chief very little, as he reported new evidence to shake any lingering confidence "in the virtue and intelligence of the people." He described the "fearful inroads" being made upon American morals by the "desire of growing rich suddenly."

Mammon, passion, partisanship, all of these taunted an unhappy Jackson, who once had sought to persuade himself and his followers that a virtuous and triumphant nation might be restored. It was, however, an America vaguely peopled by a mass citizenry influenced either by the powers of evil or good. Jackson's own view of America rarely beheld a dynamic community. For him, and many like him, a vibrant good or awesome evil would shape the dimensions of American nationality, as a potter with his wheel and clay. This Jacksonian portrayal was still blurred and inconclusive at the end of this era. Its appeal would come later.[31]

More influential in shaping the nation's grasp of its meaning and attainment after 1815 were Daniel Webster and Henry Clay. Where Jackson seemed determined to restrain the present, Webster and Clay preferred to speak prophetically of a transcendent triumph awaiting America. This destiny wavered between the spiritual and material. It required a tortuous journey through ideological quicksand.

More than any other spokesman, Daniel Webster helped his countrymen remember that America meant an awesome responsibility. Webster's grasp of what this implied was, however, as embattled as the views of most thoughtful compatriots. He described magnificently a nation called for special purpose and endowed with wondrous principles. Yet Webster was also acutely aware that Americans were human beings. This left him—and the nation—in the plight of crusaders standing helpless before holy walls while awaiting reason and religion's triumph over passion and selfishness. Conscious of the possibility that emotion and avarice might thwart American nationality, Webster made an important contribution by counseling patience. The national design was supreme. Men must steadfastly strive to meet its mandate.

This dilemma Webster early confronted. He spoke both of the glorious principle that was America and of the frailty of those called to sustain it. In 1816, he wrote in *North American Review* about the "deep anxiety" which accompanied the nation's "goodly prospect." After all, American institutions were "still human," so that evil men might seize upon laxness in those who guarded national well-being. Such carelessness, warned Webster, was usually born of greed or partisanship. His popular 1820 address on the bicentenary of the Pilgrim landing cast brighter light on nationality's challenge. It arose from America's origin as a deliberate act which had employed the finest in intelligence, liberty, and religion. Instant nationhood was far more desirable, Webster contended, than an origin buried in history's mists and fables. This portrait of America's founders as men of inspiring virtue and wisdom so moved George Ticknor, freshly returned from Europe and from conversation with Talleyrand, that he reported being overcome. "I thought my temples would burst with the gush of blood."

Having made America a responsibility to the past, Webster

enlarged the national meaning in 1825 with remarks on its universal implications. One of these was the need for virtue's immediate ascendency in America. Webster here took a difficult theme. America's Trust was to show a nobility in popular character. This meant that "in America, a new era commences in human affairs!" It also seemed to propel Webster by 1830 toward the deepening pessimism which was attracting others. "We are fallen on evil times . . . when public men seek low objects, and when the tone of public morals and public feeling is depressed and debased." The flavor of a New York public dinner for Webster in 1831 was seasoned with talk of the grave challenge facing American character. The grand experiment might indeed fall, said the honored guest, grievously disappointing the hopes of mankind. Such defalcation would come only from "the effects of our own rashness and our own folly." Beneath the shadow of nullification, Webster's gospel had to accept a national design of immutable construction. Only human iniquity could befoul it.

Throughout the rest of the decade Webster proclaimed this doctrine. America's Trust for the future of liberty and republicanism required that every generation maintain unaltered the noble ideas and institutions of the Fathers. Patriotism became devotion to patrimony. The Founders had left the contemporary generation "nothing to achieve; we had only to preserve unimpaired what they had achieved for us." The "sacred trust" carried the virtue of the Republic, still referred to by Webster as an experiment. Thus, "our dangers are from within." The events during and after 1837, of course, brought Webster's increased emphasis on this "inner enemy." The latter's evil work enticed the nation from the immutable principles established by the inspired Fathers. Instead, the precepts deserved from succeeding generations a protracted rite of preservation. Only this would sustain national integrity.

The gloom Webster privately expressed by 1842 about human failing—"the present darkness is thick and palpable"—entered his second Bunker Hill Address in 1843. Here he reviewed the Trust as a repository of principles and pleaded for an elevation in American morality. The ambiguity of this address appears almost painful. Webster tried to seem assured about both character and destiny in America, but his obvious concern over human failure undid him. Later that year, Webster escaped this

dilemma by discovering the relative insignificance of the citizen
and the transcendent importance of the national interest. This
required talking of a broad, overwhelming national spirit, one
great heart, soul, and mind, which would make all men determined through life and death "to be fully American, American
altogether." The common interest in national existence was so
commanding that Webster in 1844 was saying "in my esteem,
men are nothing, or next to nothing. In this country of twenty
millions of people, what is any individual? . . . Principles are
everything." The presidential campaign found this deepened conservatism dominating Webster's gospel. American nationality was
a divine miracle requiring the surrender of all men. This miracle's embodiment was clearly discernible in the federal Constitution and existing national boundaries.

Although he still talked in 1848 of America as an "experiment
of republican liberty," Webster was militant against change in
either the political or natural Vineyard. His search had found
America's meaning in her stability. Webster's depiction of nationality as preservation assumed proportions totally at variance
with the dynamic character of the era. The nation's success required forgetting time, place, and man in a worship of institutions. The good Steward would stand guard. This notion of duty
had a dangerous irony. Americans were given no basis for self-
respect in Webster's doctrine except through capitulating to a
system which denied man initiative or capacity for further development. Sentinel duty was what American nationality meant for
man in the mature Websterian concept.[32]

Henry Clay's search for the meaning of America reached a
similar conclusion, but from a different path. His concept of
America moved with difficulty beyond the immediate and mundane, suggesting how American concerns in this era differed little
from those of earlier days. Fundamental needs had produced
America, and Henry Clay was unusually candid in keeping national values in this materialist setting. Physical well-being was
the American goal, one well worth the compromise and contriv-
ance required of all citizens. Thus, from the Clay perspective,
"accommodation" was a better word than "preservation" in defining the duty of stewardship. Unfortunately for Clay, events
seemed to thwart his plan for America. Much of his testimony
about American purpose was fulmination against such challenges

to the health of accommodation as Jacksonian tyranny, Van Buren's mistakes, and Tyler's faithlessness. In his own way, Clay developed a mistrust of his surroundings that rivaled Andrew Jackson's. His outlook upon American nature and responsibility usually produced a discourse on what was supposed to have happened. Stressing what should have occurred kept Clay moving from factional diatribe to pleas that partisanship be abandoned.

Clay returned from Ghent determined to preach anew the gospel of national self-sufficiency. This would require that all America be interested in preserving the nation. Nationality in Clay's judgment must use its physical charms. These would prevent evil men, unfriendly to liberty, from seducing an America that was otherwise rootless. Until Jackson's presidency, therefore, Clay talked of national growth and of America's unfolding. He often portrayed the nation as a youth occupied by development and exciting motion. This made Clay especially concerned that a material coherence become the basis of nationality, once the appeal of youthful novelty had cooled. Therefore, in the 1820's Clay's primer of national meaning taught an active, dynamic stewardship, one comfortable with change. What worried Clay was America's likely attitude when growth was finished.

To ensure a tranquil response, Clay made physical interdependence the prime goal of stewardship. "Moral causes have a powerful operation," he conceded in his great House speech on internal improvements in 1818, but "depend upon it, when society is settled down, as it will before long be, these moral causes will lose their effect." Then must trade and communication take their stead, said Clay. The present hour, which he called "this infant period of our republic," was less important than the time when the intoxication of change had worn off. America must prepare itself to be what Clay called "an affair of mutual concession." The past, glorious though it was, would be useless. There was no mysticism in Clay's rejection of colonial ways and spirit, and in recommending the "solid foundation of the national prosperity."

A thoughtful early statement of Clay's nationality appeared in a letter of 1823. Having pulled the nation through several crises of sectional discord, Clay insisted that America's physical design made a common outlook plausible. From the fact that some Stewards "must cultivate, some fabricate" would come the essence of nationality. This material Americanness accepted a variety of needs and aspirations but would always keep "an eye to the welfare of the whole." National fulfillment for Clay would be marked "by balancing the countervailing interests." This was Clay's doctrine in the 1824 campaign. America's total need must become the first concern of each American, an outlook which Clay insisted must recognize the changing character of the nation.

He liked to say that "a new world has come into being since the Constitution was adopted." Consequently, America should not confine its perspective to the "narrow limited necessities" of the old nation, but must glimpse the future through the glass of empiricism. Cordial to agriculture, Clay nevertheless sought room for the machine in national fulfillment. Manufacturing and power, said he, made a difference among nations equal to that between a keelboat and a steamboat. The latter moved easily past the former, "laden with the riches of all quarters of the world," and with a gay and cheerful crowd. Nature herself was awestruck and submissive before "Fulton's immortal genius!"

While at this time Clay started to mention destiny, the world's eyes, and duty to posterity, he clearly preferred to put America in the context of common interest. National policy thus must be a systematic augmentation of American interdependence. Genuine stewardship was, in 1830, that "which develops, improves, and perfects the capabilities of our common country, and enables us to avail ourselves of all the resources with which Providence has blessed us." America had been amply endowed; it was man's cleverness which national fulfillment now required. From this stemmed Clay's "bond of affection and interest."

The Kentuckian clung to this view until 1833. In the tariff debate his philosophy was at its most attractive. Using material measurements for national meaning and achievement, Clay advocated nine years of economic calm and development. Such an interval would offer final assurance to posterity. In fact, Clay contended that the stewardship of materialism should leave the arena of politics. But with this, Clay revealed how his own conviction was faltering. His scorn for "the agitating politics of the country" was evident.

Clay's optimism began to diminish, although lasting beyond the expectations of men like Webster and Jackson. After 1833, Clay kept calling for patriotism over party, urging men to keep hope in the Republic and to surrender before national interests. He recoiled "with horror" at the anarchy, violence, and despotism which might stalk America. By 1842, Clay had adopted the general view of America's grave peril. He told his neighbors in Kentucky that "no one can discern any termination of this sad state of things, nor see in the future any glimpse of light or hope." Betrayed by empiricism and materialism, Clay deplored the sad lack of principle in American national meaning. "We are as much afloat at sea as the day when the Constitution went into operation."

As the era of search closed, Clay advised restraint. He talked openly of human frailty, of the dubious outcome of republicanism's venture, and of the likelihood of national suffering. His preference now was to let the future remain in the hands of "the merciful Providence" and of posterity. An aging Clay's disappointed capitulation to a mystical future was balanced by the fact that some of his youthful followers retained explicit expectations. One of these was Abraham Lincoln, who, along with Ralph Waldo Emerson, represented the posterity for whom Clay feared he had labored in vain.[33]

In 1838, Abraham Lincoln addressed the Young Men's Lyceum in Springfield. Given the prevailing uneasy nationality, his remarks are less extraordinary than some historians contend. In discussing the perpetuation of American political institutions, Lincoln showed he shared the general apprehension over man's capacities. Americans had a wondrous legacy left by noble ancestors which now faced internal danger. "If destruction be our lot, we must ourselves be its author and finisher." This was likely, as Lincoln spoke of a citizenry increasingly consumed by "the wild and furious passions." Men committed outrages everywhere, "from New England to Louisiana." Violence and emotion were "common to the whole country." The way was open for ruthless, ambitious men, who would "overturn that fair fabric, which for the last half century, has been the fondest hope, of the lovers of freedom, throughout the world." National survival and progress, said Lincoln, required that every citizen "swear by the blood of the Revolution" to revere law. Such obedience must "become the *political religion* of the nation."

Lincoln then returned to the vexatious matter of human desire. Earlier generations had found satisfaction in establishing the

nation. Now, what could a new generation do to "seek the grati-
fication of their ruling passions"? No longer did enmity of England claim emotions. Would some men turn to tearing down
what others had built? Talking of spiritual bankruptcy, Lincoln
asserted, "Passion has helped us, but can do so no more. It will
in future be our enemy. Reason, cold, calculating, unimpassioned
reason, must furnish all the materials for our future support and
defence." Thus, America's fulfillment demanded that an acquies-
cent stewardship embrace sound morality and reverence for law.
A year later, Lincoln announced further retreat in America. Perhaps with some Whig benefit in mind, he informed his neighbors
that the "lava of political corruption" belched forth from Washington across the land. Pledging to save his nation, Lincoln
seemed like a youthful partisan drawing delicious pleasure from
the genuine gloom of the hour.

In heeding the Clay gospel, Lincoln maintained a preoccupation with human frailty. Here was the challenge of America's
future. It was one his generation of Stewards must meet. "Happy
day, when all appetites controled, all passions subdued, all matters subjected, *mind,* all conquering *mind,* shall live and move
the monarch of the world. Glorious consummation! Hail fall of
Fury! Reign of Reason, all hail!" Distinguished indeed, said Lincoln, would be the people that brought to maturity "both the
political and moral freedom of their species." [34]

Another youthful prophet was Ralph Waldo Emerson. He
dedicated part of his *Journal* for 1822 to the spirit of America,
"who yet counts the tardy years of childhood, but who is increasing unawares in the twilight, and swelling into strength, until
the hour when he shall break the cloud, to shew his colossal
youth, and cover the firmament with the shadow of his wings."
However, Emerson did not anticipate an unvexed growth nor an
easy fulfillment, for he too mused on the feebleness of man. To a
close friend he wrote: "I feel myself a little prone to croaking of
late, partly because my books warn me of the instability of human greatness." America was disturbingly indifferent over
whether men were good or bad, especially in public life. "I think
we Yankees have marched on since the Revolution, to strength,
to honour, and at last to ennui."

Evident public corruption forced Emerson to face the question: "Will it not be dreadful to discover that this experiment

made by America, to ascertain if men can govern themselves—
does not succeed? That too much knowledge, and too much liberty makes them mad?" Orators a century hence might well "drop
our famed figure of *anticipation*," and be doomed to rejoice only
in the past. With astonishing insight for the time, Emerson admitted that "by a kind of instinct, for the poor purposes of glean-
ing relief to fear, I obey the propensity of my nation and rake
praises out of futurity." The years made Emerson no happier,
prone as he was to reflect on the fact that nations were often
misled by leaders and precepts. "We too have taken our places
in the immeasurable train. . . . Is there no venerable tradition
whose genuineness and authority we can establish, or must we
too hurry onward inglorious in ignorance and misery we know
not whence, we know not whither."

Emerson told his brother in 1829, "we are fallen on evil days.
That word Country must make us blush or lament." Indeed, "the
word is now to hope against hope." In 1840 Emerson admitted
to being faintly Whiggish, hoping that someone like Harrison
"could carry into Washington one impulse of patriotism." However, he fully expected the Whigs to continue the scramble for
place, "and then I shall be glad to turn them out four years
later." All of which brought Emerson's lamentation: "Beautiful
Country! Honourable Nation!" These would be hollow invocations until such "preaching will arrive at practice." Talk would
do little for America: "it will not touch the state until it has
built an individual." In his *Journal* Emerson deplored the nation's preoccupation with materialism and gain, which left su-
perficiality to guide patriotism and religion.

Frequently after 1840 in Boston Emerson spoke on public considerations. During 1842 and 1843 *The Dial* printed his "Lectures on the Times." In them he renewed a concern of twenty-
five years earlier. "I think men never loved life less. I question
whether care and doubt ever wrote their names so legibly on the
faces of any population. This *Ennui,* for which we Saxons had
no name, this word of France has got a terrific significance. . . .
Old age begins in the nursery." America's fearful conservatism
was being perpetuated in the schools, he said. Education was
employed to control the people lest they "upset the fair pageant
of Judicature, and perhaps lay a hand on the sacred muniments
of wealth itself, and new distribute the land. Religion is taught

in the same spirit." This last point seemed especially painful to
Emerson because he blamed the feeble American outlook on its
financial leadership, which turned religious institutions into
"conservators of property." Lecturing on the Transcendentalists,
Emerson deplored the nation's captivity by stocks, dress, houses,
and all "things."

Emerson's view was the conventional misgiving over nationality. With Lincoln and countless others, Emerson used the future for sustenance. His lecture "The Young American" was appropriate for the final issue of *The Dial* in 1844. Part of the lecture predicted that American youth would see a narrowing gap
between the culture they grasped and the work asked of them.
Slowly "an American sentiment" was recognizing the enormity of
national being and opportunity. Emerson, of course, wanted
America's great natural surroundings to inspire national thought
and "inflame the patriotism." For him the presence of the great,
untouched West could save America. From it might come "a
new and continental element into the national mind." It was a
familiar doctrine. Emerson's threadworn plea for a national genius, literature, and culture was another call for difference from
Europe. Equally commonplace was his hope that land might
serve to nourish such a prospective spirit.

The Dial essay had a conventional close: "America is the Country of the Future. . . . it is a country of beginnings, of projects,
of vast designs, and expectations. It has no past: all has an onward and prospective look." Emerson foresaw a benign destiny
or "Genius" saving men from their "narrow and selfish" selves.
This vast impulse was working in behalf of the nation, said Emerson, who thus awarded America to a cheering determinism which
avoided the individual for the general. This "friendly Power" received Emerson's repeated attention as the assurance of national
fulfillment. Man was feeble, but the over-all design had an irresistible and benign tendency.

Zest for a dashing future amid a disquieting present produced
murky talk from Emerson and many others of his generation.
American nationality used both a predestinarian scheme and a
promising youth, while regretting the Republic's reverence only
for "the conventional virtues." These ingredients baffled even
Emerson. He could construct no meaningful bridge between his
challenge to youth, his invocation of process, and the imprison-

ment of nationality by "the love of gain." Man's affairs were "pitiful and most unworthy," and the wondrous future simply had to await a mystical redress of man's shortcomings. Thus, Emerson contended that what progress America had made was due not to man but "the blessed course of events." The latter, along with the human situation, preceded the Republic. Consequently, America's Trust was to witness and support a "new order" between the individual and the universe, something Lincoln and others were discovering.

Emerson had his own handsome way of portraying this national mission. "If only the men are well employed in conspiring with the design of the Spirit who led us hither, and is leading us still, we shall quickly enough advance out of all hearing of others' censures, out of all regrets of our own, into a new and more excellent social state than history has recorded." Privately, however, Emerson eyed this conditional future with misgiving. He told Margaret Fuller in 1847 that America was "listless, dumb, lifeless." It had "not a blush on her cheek, not a morning hymn, not a dream of a noble future—nothing has chanced to make the social state less sordid or to open man's eye to the prodigalities of Nature." Emerson and Lincoln shared hope that process and revelation would sweep away the moment's faltering stewardship.[35]

9

A more active force in this era, magazine expression had its own measure of distress in seeking the means of national triumph. Here was the same blend of hope, of misgiving, and even occasionally of capitulation. In advocating nationality, the magazines displayed the confusion and ambiguity which characterized the thoughts of major figures. Three clusters of journals dominated this period. One was led by *North American Review*, with such important colleagues as *Whig Review, Knickerbocker, New York Review*, and *New England Magazine*. This group was the most cautious in discussing America's prospects. More hopeful were the journals identified with *Democratic Review*. Among these were *Boston Post, The Age*, and *Union*. Thanks to a markedly religious attitude, a third set of magazines had the most fruitful search. This sizable collection included *National Preacher, Brownson's Quarterly Review, Ladies Companion,*

Ladies' Repository and Gatherings of the West, and Hunt's
Merchant's Magazine. Regardless of position, all important periodicals spurred the search for national meaning. They were
eager to know both national ends and means.

North American Review undertook to reconcile the nation's
body and mind. This required that it blend the outlook of Clay's
materialism and Webster's mysticism, so that nationality might
comfortably await the universal process to complete itself. *North
American Review*'s contributors seemed especially aware of human frailties. They emphasized the need for national character
and its companion, cultural independence. Awaiting this American character was precarious. From 1815 to 1830, *North American Review* seemed dubious that a national character could develop, given the smothering presence of England and Europe.
The chief spokesman here was William Ellery Channing, who
urged the cultivation of American peculiarities as a first step
toward intellectual independence. Until this happened, America
was an inconclusive human drama. Only "simple folk," Channing said, would say at the time that America was great. It
suffered from a cowardly intellect. Joined by William Cullen
Bryant and others, Channing made the exhortation for indige-
nous ideals a revealing part of nationality.

By 1821, *North American Review* turned to other issues. American fulfillment rested in the hands of the present generation.
Civilization depended upon what happened now and stewardship had to be conscious of that. It exasperated contributors like
Wendell Phillips that America's outlook failed to sense the implication of the Republic's Trust, leaving its viewpoint "ordinary
and tame." Worse was to come. In 1830 a new edition of *North
American Review* announced that duty and religion seemed replaced in the national outlook by "corrupt or low and narrow
views." Alexander H. Everett warned America that its values
were growing dangerously distorted owing to "a too urgent pursuit of worldly gain." The corrective was rigorous enforcement
of the Sabbath. Everett contended that this would lift American
thoughts above the mundane.

As it emphasized nationality through moral order, *North
American Review* stopped campaigning for a unique American
culture. It became concerned with balancing a fear of mammon
and passion with faith in the likely course of events. Edward

Everett said that only the prospect of gradual improvement made endurable the existing signs of man's degeneracy. Any favorable outcome of national development, which could take as much as ten centuries, depended entirely on "the conservative and Christian patriot" who apparently could understand the process at work. After 1836 the *Review* lost its struggle with this familiar paradox, leaving nationality caught between Christian determinism and "worldliness, and anarchy, and irreligion." By the mid-1840's, its contributors had traveled full circle, calling for ties between Great Britain and America, so that the latter might outgrow a "petty nationality of spirit." *148344*

Much of *North American Review*'s advocacy in the 1840's was voiced through Charles Francis Adams and Edwin Percy Whipple. Adams took the theme that America's divinely framed polity was perfect. The question remaining was the fitness of man for the system. Adams believed that discussion of the abstract excellence of America's polity was no longer necessary. Instead, the vital consideration was one the Fathers had fully perceived, popular emotion's threat to America's trusteeship for republicanism. Adams seemed hopeful, convinced that there was "a recuperative energy in the breasts of the American people" which might still save them from evils they had created. Even so, he acknowledged that "our progress of late years has been somewhat downward" because new values threatened "to drown all the land marks of our ancient faith in the one great ocean of expediency." Adams urged that young hearts beat both to patriotism and principle.

Edwin P. Whipple, one of America's early literary critics, wrote in 1844 during what he called "times of turbulence and change." American development had separated its endeavors from its avowed principles. The public passion had been unexpectedly volatile. Such energy, Whipple said, desperately needed redirection. "There is no country in the world which has nobler ideas embodied in more worthless shapes." He went on to repeat what had become *North American Review*'s doctrine. National fulfillment could be anticipated only if passion were placed behind virtue, with freedom safely distant from mere cant. Whipple found in Daniel Webster the embodiment of the ideal Steward.

In 1840, a good Whig year, the *Review* had been guardedly

optimistic about the national struggle toward virtuous freedom. Edward Everett now dismissed the contention that in America "Providence should destine this blessed inheritance of Christian liberty to that miserable failure, which has, in darker ages, over- taken our struggling race in its efforts to be free." He advised America to "place an unshaken reliance in the ultimate triumph of goodness and truth," which was actually faith "in the long course of events." However, by 1848 such confidence disappeared. Instead, men like Lorenzo Sabine were writing that the nation's physical growth was proof that Americans "have made, and are making, no progress in virtue." The fault was in the present generation, "and the consequence of it will be upon our heads and upon those of our children."

Here for the time *North American Review* rested its search. Its intellectual pilgrimage exemplified a more general trend in this period. Events prompted many observers to abandon expec- tations after 1815 of swift results from a self-reliant American stewardship. *North American Review* turned for relief to a mys- terious, ordained process. Human fidelity to immutable princi- ples was key to national fulfillment, but the journal saw little evidence that the age of active faith had begun. Its pages were left to insist that the design of things must eventually invoke a better side of human nature.[36]

While *Knickerbocker Magazine* usually agreed with the great Boston oracle, it resisted *North American Review*'s dependence upon an ordained future. Such belief might diminish America's reverence for absolutes. *Knickerbocker* regularly chastised the more ardent futurists, especially "Young America" and its outlet, *Democratic Review*. Known as "old Knick," the New York mag- azine was the nation's leading commentator upon literary mat- ters by 1846. In becoming so, *Knickerbocker* had advocated that moralists made the best patriots. Lewis Gaylord Clark, *Knick*'s editor, like most other thoughtful Americans, had searched for some years to explain nationality. Clark rejected Clay's materi- alism to acclaim the overarching truths inherent in the provi- dential design for America. Consequently, *Knick* was distressed by the Republic's "corruption and effeminacy." It was a slow business, America's development, as the ghost of Diedrich Knickerbocker had predicted. An editorial fantasy pictured the old Dutchman saying in 1833 that gradualism would work toward good in America's search for nationality. Only slowly could there emerge a genuine America.

In 1848, *Knick* lost patience and talked of the bankrupt search for results in American evolution. The piece, entitled "What Should Be America's Example?" foresaw deepening peril as new and subversive ideas enticed the Stewards. Americans were showing "the effects of evils which have secretly and silently accumulated, while the general attention of all in this young republic has been given to the acquisition of wealth." The antidote was education whose purpose must be to reshape the nation's outlook. There followed a blunt paraphrase of Horace Mann: let America attend "to the formation of that condition of the people on which our welfare, safety, nay, our very existence as a republic depend, and without which we are surely destined, sooner or later, to destruction."

Legislators, clergy, journalists were charged with the emergency steps needed. The masses must be taught, through means beyond sectarianism and demagoguery, that America's future rested not in its name, but in the permanence and purity of its concepts and institutions, all to be grasped and endorsed in the public "intelligence." [37]

Generally in agreement was *Knick*'s neighbor, *New York Review*. It too believed in process while conceding that America's participation might be doomed. It liked to stress the importance of humble living and human frailty. In its first volume in 1837, *New York Review* challenged Protestant churches to seek the full measure of their influence in the nation, especially through the schools and colleges. This need to attain an enlightened, instructed public mind remained a favorite concern of this magazine. A proper system of education would prove "the purifier of the moral atmosphere and the safe conductor of that impetuous energy" which the journal found dangerously evident.

Throughout this era, *New York Review* talked of humility, caution, and education, with occasional reference to patience as destiny worked its way with America. Two statements especially were notable. One of these, in 1840, closed with a frank concern over the error of holding a "flattering opinion of human nature." This could be a fatal absurdity if it became central to the republican philosophy in America, leading to class struggle and the debasement of knowledge. The other article, in 1842, suggested a step toward national self-confidence. This entailed proper affection and respect for England. "We can see no difficulty in preserving a pure and lofty tone of American nationality together with an affectionate reverence for the time-honored country of our forefathers."

True national vigor was yet to come. It would bring a lessening of "nervous irritability" over foreign views. For now, America sought comfort in "the idolatry of our political constitutions." The journal rejected the view that "our safety lay in the mere frame-work of government—the mere presence of a charter." Instead, "a well-constituted national self-respect" would discover nationality in the "sacred Trust" which America shared with England. This was a mutual responsibility to guard constitutional freedom, "the only freedom which has been other than a curse to mankind." From such a broadened awareness would come at last a "sublime sense of duty." [38]

Other journals stressed discipline and duty even more emphatically. *New England Magazine* and *Whig Review* were important examples. Boston's *New England Magazine,* edited by J. T. Buckingham, was possibly the most pessimistic of the major periodicals in this era. Its pages brooded over the likelihood that human nature in America had become diseased by partisanship and sectional strife. It pleaded that private happiness be found in fulfillment of the public good, urging that this was the only way to save a frail American character. Such recognition of the preeminence of public security was possible through education. American stewardship had to hope for enlightened, not natural, circumstances.

Regularly announcing the prospect of "national degradation," *New England Magazine* sang a familiar refrain. Upon the virtue and intelligence of the people depended "whether the future destinies of their country shall be adverse or propitious." Partisanship was allied with man's baser self for the triumph of passion. Certainly the assault on party was a valuable weapon with which to fight the evils of Jacksonism, and *New England Magazine* was no friend of the Democratic party. But the concern over partisanship clearly represented a more profound matter than ironical strategy. *New England Magazine* spoke for a wide apprehension about America's frail stewardship when it predicted that if, after the 1836 canvass, Americans were still party followers, "there will be little hope, henceforth, of a good and rational government."

The rise of the mob was considered especially ominous. The nation "has no guards about it but the moral strength of the people, and when this shall be corrupted the citadel must yield." In these and other articles, *New England Magazine* seemed prepared for a collapse of the American Trust in the face of "anarchy and despotism." If there was hope for national survival it was in teaching men to discern between the self-seekers and those who sought to serve America.[39]

A similar view was taken by *The Whig Review*, founded in 1845. It was a gifted advocate of the attitude which *North American Review* and others had championed. Its willingness to do battle with *Democratic Review* produced some remarkable debate during this search for certainty about America. *Whig Review* was especially successful in blending the nationality of Abraham Lincoln and Ralph Waldo Emerson, stressing the elements of principle, virtue, and selflessness. Edited by George H. Colton, *Whig Review* began by warning that American impatience to develop might mean great physical growth, but it threatened American morals. A frequent contributor, the Reverend Henry W. Bellows, said that America was beset with the illusory goal of perfection. Let this be discarded and "it would allay these feverish anxieties." America had to realize that "individually and collectively" it had "the same passions, weaknesses and vices, as have the men of all ages and nations." This meant that "with us as with them, the demon of popular frenzy crouches ever in the dark cavern of the future."

The *Whig* concentrated on two misconceptions about America's meaning. First, America would never be fulfilled if many individuals remained privately wicked. There must be no distinction between the private aspect and the national aspect. Second, "to think that we are necessary to the preservation of knowledge and freedom among men, were [*sic*] a vanity equally criminal and foolish. The Ruler of Nations will accomplish his plans of benevolent wisdom though we should be stricken from existence." To destroy these fallacies, *Whig Review* said America must reject the notion that change was necessarily beneficial and accept the "sober virtues" taught by "the voice of a buried world." Subsequent issues continued stressing the great American lesson: "that its internal passions need more guards than its external enemies." The *Whig* pointed to the tragic irony of American endeavor. Liberty had triumphed, but at the price of making dishonesty the respected national trait.

This concern filled an 1846 poem by William Wallace, which said:

> The Nation hath gone mad with action now
> Oh many-troubled Giant! . . .

A people so goaded by "hungry Ambition" must seek rest and thought, the poet adding that "the enduring grandeur of a nation" sprang from virtue. If money and greed recede,

> Eternity's calm pyramidal forms
> Shall meet our dreamy view.

So went the *Whig*'s issues, each acknowledging national limitation and the need for a proper set of values. These might arrive with "the sober thoughts of manhood." Uneasily watching "Young America's" exuberance, *Whig Review* advised that "wild rallies and boyish excesses must have an end." A "manlier and maturer" nation required not passion but Stewards with education and culture. These must be America's voice of conscience, disinterested and bold.

By 1847, *Whig Review* seemed to incorporate the rising acceptance of providential process. Henry Bellows led the way in "The Destiny of the Country." Of America's ultimate greatness, he said: "its sure progress we cannot help." Citizens were to seek larger awareness of the role and responsibility "thrust upon us by Destiny." Men could not help but recognize "how little we have done for ourselves and how much Providence has done for us." In spite of national follies and error, a "great Ruler" had devised America "and fitted it for a great display of his power." As the era closed, *Whig Review* offered America's search the vague assurance that God, design, virtue were all at work. Let the citizen accept the outlook made for him. Through this capitulation America might lead much of mankind "to the greatest victory and felicity that humanity can hope to attain."

In contrast, the quest for national meaning led by *Democratic Review* seemed more assured. Like *North American Review* and its partisans, *Democratic Review* was disturbed by the present. As a response to current danger, this journal exploited a venerable element in nationality, America's manifest destiny. Actually, its emphasis was simply part of this periodical's relentless stress upon the times ahead, the ever-impending fulfillment. As the journal put it in 1839, America was the "Nation of Futurity." John L. O'Sullivan and *Democratic Review*'s scouts peered as anxiously toward coming events as any outlook of the time. There was no prediction of immediate triumph.[40]

Democratic Review's pages supplied much encouragement for those seeking American assurance. Editor O'Sullivan and his contributors did valiant service to such topics as America's pilgrimage for God and freedom, the need for penitence and renewal of morals, and even the likelihood that the nation could fail its Trust. While *Democratic Review* was aware that America's career might disclose some fatal internal handicap, it was the stoutest advocate of the power of process, or Providence, or destiny, or God. This journal recommended the mystery of instinctive stewardship, with its hint that American development would summon leaders guided by ordered impulse. A zest for this prescription may have made *Democratic Review* memorable, yet even its spirits were flagging by 1848. Disillusioned with the "Young America" venture, *Democratic Review* was increasingly disposed to talk about the many threats to American fulfillment. The journal was reduced to defending process in the benign function of an inviolable Constitution.

All this was far away, of course, when in 1837 *Democratic Review* launched its career by proclaiming a "critical stage of our national progress" within what it called the "American experiment." Equally conventional was the journal's early concession that it would take many generations to fulfill the American intent. Comfort came with knowing that "we are on the path toward that great result." In the presence of Christianity, America led cautiously toward a "God-implanted" promise of freedom. The way would be slow, for the magazine agreed that much difficulty faced those who had to prove republicanism.

Democratic Review was especially concerned that American youth distrusted the democratic principle. Young people needed faith in human nature. The existing "distrust" was "portentous of incalculable evil." No less alarming was the state of mind among America's great men. *Democratic Review*'s opening pages acknowledged how many "masterspirits" had been "seduced . . . by the intrigues of party and the allurements of ambition." As if this were not enough, the malignant influence of mammon, characterized by the journal as cities and business, was eroding "the moral energies of the national mind." It was logical, then, for the *Review* to conclude that "the ark of democratic truth," symbol of the role "entrusted to us as a chosen people," was not moving "towards the glorious destiny of its future." The journal pledged to rescue "the mind of the nation from the state of torpor and even of demoralization in which so large a proportion of it is sunk."

Issue after issue was used to rally the Stewards. They were reminded of their alliance with Christianity, "incomparably the most interesting as well as the most important aspect" of the American venture. No longer must freedom and democracy fear the "blind rage" of the late eighteenth century. Now they penitently knelt before Christ's throne. A regenerate America would mean a new kinship between the Christian and democratic view of man and the universe. This outlook in *Democratic Review* owed much to Orestes Brownson. As he prepared to leave the magazine, Brownson condemned the extremes of Fourth of July and caucus oratory. Talk of the perfect virtue and intelligence of the people was "all a humbug." American experience found man far from ready to sustain a good society. Religion and wise leaders were still vital. O'Sullivan only mildly chided Brownson in an editorial note which suggested that despite human frailty, Americans would ultimately become faithful Stewards.

Such caution made even Alexander H. Everett comfortable in the *Democratic Review*'s pages. His 1845 lines about "the Young American" would have been equally at home in the Whig organ. Everett called on youth to "follow with unflinching tread where the noble fathers led." Divine guidance would help the young avoid "craft and subtle treachery" and seek honesty, truth, prudence, and dauntlessness.

> Let thy noble motto be
> GOD,—the COUNTRY,—LIBERTY,—
> Planted on religion's rock,
> Thou shalt stand in every shock.

Like all magazines, *Democratic Review* offered conventional remarks on what war might mean to America. It would "be the purification of our own political atmosphere," where now man's lesser qualities were prized. "When the state is in danger, patriotism and ability take precedence of selfishness and medocrity." Furthermore, annexation and conquest were fruits of "the general law" guiding America. In this setting, the *Review* made its famous assertion that there ought to be no doubt "of the manifest destiny of Providence in regard to the occupation of this continent." Historians have exaggerated the significance of *Democratic Review*'s talk about destiny. Providential design was an old and useful idea for a nation accustomed to political and intellectual burden.

With its reiteration of the destiny concept, the *Review* encouraged the search for self-understanding. Americans were called to a duty "not more for themselves than the ages and people that were to follow them." They were warned against the ubiquitous resurgence of selfishness and partisanship, evils sure to retard "the course of the mighty current." In such ways *Democratic Review* surrounded its comments on destiny with the rhetoric of anxiety so commonplace in the era of search. Poems it published in 1846 by William Gilmore Simms were notable instances of the clamor for faith in the American venture. This faith was increasingly the vehicle in which the nation would endure any travail. While Simms sang "We must obey our destiny and blood," he suggested the guides for obedience were inscribed on constitutional parchment. This awkward embrace of process through the sacred federal writings became the ironical way by which *Democratic Review* contributors tried to wrest belief out of uncertainty.

This consideration was increasingly important for a nation whose purpose was being thrust into the immutable course of the universe. The remaining question asked how Stewards were to labor fruitfully amid human shortcomings while awaiting the completion of destiny? The search for national meaning had run upon the shoals of "is" and "ought to be." To this, *Democratic Review* pages offered assurance that soon "all the political experience elaborated during the first half century of our great 'experiment,' is finally to be reduced to scientific principles, and placed in a condition to defy the accidents of time and the ca-

price of men." This explanation of the search was remarkably
like the Websterian glorification of enduring principle. Both
found shelter in the Constitution and its overlord, the mighty
Union. Here were guides for stewardship during the nation's
development as "a living, organic whole" under "an overruling
'Father of the ages.'" The textbook for nationality, the Constitution, was a product of the vast force at work in the universe.

Consequently, *Democratic Review*'s authors were left to cope
with variant readings of the sacred text, as well as differing explanations of the state of the national venture. There was nothing better to do but beg the question. A typical attempt was in
"Poems for the People," published in 1847.

> Let timid men who fear that signs foretell
> The coming downfall of fair freedom's dome,
> Live undismayed . . .

The "threatening signs" were

> But throes of Nature, borne with wise intent,
> Which, heaving for a time, subside to rest
> And earth is purer for the pain endured,

While man's folly and passion provided "more throes"

> . . . when they subside,
> A purer faith and gentler virtue lives
> In graceful beauty, blessing all the land.

Increasingly, wise men would take command, predicted the poet,
and fulfillment would rise from the evil besieging the Stewards:

> Proud of our land, and of its charter proud,
> All pulses beat as one, strong to maintain
> The grandest compact nations e'er beheld.

With offerings such as this, *Democratic Review* abandoned by
1847 any unique contribution to the search for American meaning. Having begun by scolding the young generation for hesitancy and skepticism about the talents of Americans, the journal
in 1848 was snuggled against the warm comfort of immutables.

These would guarantee safety against the depressingly tardy efforts of human nature to transcend passion and avarice.

The most important shelter, America's Constitution, was not "the result of human wisdom," but "an emanation from that Providence, which on more than one occasion, has manifested itself in the promotion of our national welfare, and in preserving human liberty, as exemplified in our institutions." America's danger was man's lamentable effort to violate this guide to greatness. A *Democratic Review* commentator said in 1848 that "he is but a lukewarm American who weighs strictly the words of the document to find some unguarded point through which the rights of one state or states may be assailed to the jeopardy of the whole. That is not the American mode of sustaining a Constitution." [41]

Since it was the most ardently hopeful yet thoughtful voice of the era, *Democratic Review*'s capitulation to divine legalism was influential. It signified that human nature and mystical process had difficulty answering America's quest for assurance. Other periodicals sharing *Democratic Review*'s initial optimism joined in moving to safer ground. Typical were the struggles during the mid 1840's of such advocates as *Boston Post,* a daily paper edited by Charles Gordon Greene; *The Age,* a weekly published in Augusta, Maine, whose editorial department was guided by Richard D. Rice; and *Union,* successor to *Globe* as the Democratic organ, and edited by Thomas Ritchie who had spent forty-one years with *Richmond Enquirer.*

Amid bombast against Whigs and Nativism, *Boston Post* used editorials during 1845 and 1846 to clarify nationality. It first recommended faith in the working out of the future. Doubters were rebuked, with the *Post* especially troubled by the widespread contention that "the Saxon race has already degenerated on this western soil. Luxury has made powerful inroads, they say, upon American energy; faction is at work sowing its poisonous seeds." To all of this, the *Post* replied that it was unfair to compare the present band of Stewards with the Fathers, who were "a peculiar race, raised up by Providence for a peculiar work." While the *Post* hoped the sons would prove "worthy of their ancestors," it also conceded that everyday circumstances were not revealing greatness or large capacity in Americans.

By Thanksgiving 1845, the *Post* had surrendered. America was

part of implacable design. This meant that "men, to be fitting
workmen, must fall into harmony with the great law of progress."
Given the latter, "yet nobler triumphs are in reserve for this
great country." From this should come patience. Celebrating the
Bunker Hill anniversary in 1846, the *Post* conceded that Puritan-
sown seeds had not yet ripened among Americans. Time was the
solace. "America was yet young; her institutions are not yet developed in all their beautiful proportions." In fact, "so far from
beginning to decay as a people, as some assert, we have not yet
by an immeasurable degree, reached our growth." The comforts
of this ideology seemed so apparent to the *Post* that it was indignant at the signs of impatience with process. It insisted that
faith in the ordered nature of things ought to be sustenance
enough for nationality. Angered by talk of national failure, the
Post lamely replied that if one accepted the premise of certain
future fulfillment, then each day should afford evidence of ad-
vancing national greatness.[42]

The Age, in Maine, had a superficially easier time in finding
ideological security for a tumultous America. It accepted the old
Jeffersonian belief that vast size meant nature's relief from any
serious inner tumult. Praising expansion, *The Age* insisted that
once growth stopped, "then will come the day in which republican institutions will be tested in America, as they never yet have
been." If Stewards ever had to live close together, "we could not
vouch for the long continuance of our free institutions." The
nation's anchor was "the vastness of our country." If it gave way,
then came putrification from human evil. It was appropriate
that *The Age* should make materialism the crux of stewardship.
As the Mexican War developed, this journal demanded the capitulation of all opposition to the struggle. Material and military progress were surely now enough to convince all honorable
doubters, so that dissent could rightly be stifled. This ironical
voice for democracy concluded the era of search by condemning
as treasonous anyone who shrank from conceding that American
fulfillment rested in physical growth and martial advance of democracy.[43]

Thomas Ritchie's ancient voice in *Union* called wildly for unquestioning acceptance of national progress. He flayed the Whigs
for their lack of capacity and virtue, elements required to see the
overarching plan for the nation. Once more, freedom and deter-

minism became hopelessly mixed, leaving Ritchie baffled and unhappy. For instance, he denounced passion and war as alien to the Stewards' "Christian policy and their manly character." Yet Mexico would not acknowledge that America was more "conscious of higher motives and a nobler guide" than anyone else. To crush this error in a sister republic, America was called by God forcibly to maintain justice and freedom. When much of America rejected this interpretation, *Union* seemed frantic. It recalled the loathsome opposition during the 1812 war. Was American patriotism to falter again? As the era of search closed, *Union* sadly announced that although the crusade against Mexico was "one of the most brilliant wars that ever adorned the annals of any nation," America was displaying an immoral failure of patriotic faith. It confused and unnerved men like Ritchie to see the Republic divided and uncertain despite destiny's clear message.[44]

For another group of journals the national plight was understood by using traditional Christian interpretation. Although they conceded human frailty, these magazines had their special perplexity. It was the apparent indifference God displayed toward America. Assuming God's immediacy, the Christian patriots had to explain an incomplete and distant nationality. One endeavor was made by a major interdenominational organ in this era, *National Preacher*. The magazine was begun in 1826 with a circulation said to be above 100,000 copies and was in existence until 1844. In articles generally designed as sermons, it advocated America as the land of God's promise to the world. However, national labor for the Almighty would not prosper unless the human heart escaped man's baseness. American fulfillment required man's rejection of self for God, admittedly a distant goal. *National Preacher*'s authors left the burdened Stewards suspended between the Fathers' attainment and youthful opportunity. They said the "National Work" was to combat sin, for human nature in the United States was no less vile than it had been 1,800 years before.

National Preacher united the cause of God and the nation. From this union came helpful answers to the questions about a faltering stewardship. Such explanations featured a Heavenly Father of well-known qualities, whose throne could be approached with supplication and whose capacity for immediate involvement in national affairs was undoubted. God was a more comforting version of process or destiny. It was a formula for personal and national achievement which most men understood. *National Preacher*'s authors tirelessly explained this prescription.

John H. Rice, a professor in the Virginia Union Theological Seminary, wrote "The Power of Truth or Love," an 1828 essay which typified innumerable associations of God, nation, and citizen. National character, Rice announced, must await the evangelization of all citizens. Only then would a world mission for Christ be feasible. Regeneration required a restoration of the primitive simplicities of Christianity which in turn meant firing the inner light fixed in each soul. Here was the true individualism, and only from this inner spirit could come the essentials of American nationality. History, according to Rice, contained many tragic but inevitable failures of nations pretending at Christianity. Form and law were not enough. America was God's choice to disclose what could happen in a nation whose citizens were truly captives of the Most High. It was a difficult assignment, Rice acknowledged, for "unholy ministers of the gospel" were always present keeping the citizens' hearts closed to the magic spirit. In time, however, God would use America to reveal "the entire energy of true religion; and showing . . . the city of God built up, in all its beauty and glory." Such purpose remained evident to Rice despite the "fearful convulsions of half a century." God's Trust was enormous, and his Stewards in America were not yet ready. *"This is not the work of a day."*

Rice made an appealing response to the search for national meaning. When the Stewards were "brought *right under* the full influence of Bible truth," then "all these evils were to be done away with." Thereafter, it would be "peculiarly the duty of American Christians, to enlist and combine their energies for evangelizing the world." The nation had "the fullest opportunity ever enjoyed by any people . . . since the heavenly hosts sang their song of glory." This being so, "heavy indeed will be our reckoning, and terrible the visitation of justice, should we fail—great our glory and felicity, should we feel the extent of our obligations, and bring our conduct up to the measure of duty." The nation's fate rested with a sanctified public sentiment. As Rice put it, "everything depends upon national character." Yet this fulfillment was no closer to realization than was the secular view of America's role.

Another contributor to *National Preacher*, Luther Halsey, a member of the Princeton faculty, urged citizens to pray for those in authority. "We not only find the immoral in office, *but office is apt to make and keep* men immoral and unholy." Office holders were, according to Halsey, especially vulnerable to the most powerful passions, leaving them "secure in sin" and indisposed "to the humility of the cross." The nation's leaders would respond to an exalted morality among the people. This meant substituting God and the Lamb for party. Until this happened, Halsey warned that many in the Vineyard would conceal beneath an outward piety an inner longing "to riot in sin," restrained from such uncleanness only by the law. "I would say then to this nation, Reckon not yourselves secure by the perfection of your constitution and laws. . . . Rely not on the extent, fertility, resources, and intelligence of your country. Trust not to the broad ocean that separates you from the calamities of Europe. Confide not in the piety of your fathers, or the learning and valour of their sons. The Ruler of nations has an arm to reach you." This grasp would bring pestilence, death, riot, corruption, fraud, sectionalism, sedition, and even Europe's contentions. "While man is depraved," Halsey warned America, "there ever will be combustibles enough in the midst of you to . . . leave your country but 'a name.' "

Halsey's America offered peculiar temptations. Especially did frequent elections and a licentious press necessitate a praying band of Stewards. In a divine Vineyard so ironically luxuriant with the charms of sin, Halsey equated supplication to Heaven with true patriotism. To this theme, Lyman Beecher addressed one of the most eloquent essays in *National Preacher*. "The Gospel the Only Security for Eminent and Abiding National Prosperity" contemplated Jackson's inauguration. Beecher's point was simple. It was absurd for any nation to rely upon human nature. Passion and mammon were still at work. "National voluptuousness . . . trod hard upon the footsteps of national opulence, destroying moral principles and patriotism." The more the nation prospered, "the more tremendous our downfall." Beyond this was passion. "Nations, like volcanoes, possess within themselves, the materials of ruin." Beecher was unrelenting. America's malady "is in the heart."

Advocating that the Bible and the Sabbath would keep families together in moral health, Beecher said these might preserve America for its role as "the light of the world." This appeal was significant in its disclosure of the growing uneasiness over American citizens' passion and avarice. A simple act of faith and devotion would bring America into her greatness. To loiter in human weakness meant "the certain destruction of our republican institutions." Unless a transformation took place, Beecher saw good reason why "we tremble with forebodings of evil to our beloved country." Beecher pressed the point. "In our Country's bosom lies the materials of ruin, which wait only the divine permission to burst forth in terrific eruption, scattering far and wide the fragments of our greatness." America's epitaph, according to Beecher, "will stand forth a warning to the world—THUS ENDETH THE NATION THAT DESPISED THE LORD AND GLORIED IN WISDOM, WEALTH AND POWER."

National Preacher had no choice but to emphasize this message as the years passed. Sin mounted and God remained afar. The journal closed its career warning that America's only hope was that man would surrender himself to God.[45]

Other advocates joined *National Preacher* in citing the evidence of American error and degeneracy. Among these were two journals addressed to women. In New York City was the relatively sophisticated *Ladies' Companion,* published between 1831 and 1842 by W. W. Snowden. From Cincinnati in 1841 came *Ladies' Repository and Gatherings of the West,* a journal with Methodist backing whose first editor was the Reverend L. L. Hamline. It remained vigorous until 1876. These two periodicals insisted on Christ's role as key to America's success or failure. The problems were, of course, avarice and passion. *Ladies' Companion* offered an 1842 article on America's fulfillment through principle which made a stale theme sound fresh. Wealth, resources, power, size could not save America from "ultimate and entire extinction." Failing to see this, the United States drifted "farther and farther from the auspicious era when our Country's freedom was achieved." The Republic was obviously "contaminated" by lures of this world, the very things which "trampled into ruin the republics of antiquity." In its material lust and "overweening pride," America was forgetting the lesson the Fathers knew, that "instability is inscribed on everything beneath the sun." Consequently the Trust was about to be dissipated by folly. The conclusion, so typical of the journal, was genuinely despondent. The world might soon behold the "broken fragments of the once beautiful fabric of American freedom."

Ladies' Repository took up the cause. It used Harrison's death to proclaim a nationalist ideology which it tirelessly repeated. Despite its wondrous blessings, America was evil. National boasting was fraudulent, coming from men whose actions menaced hope for a righteous nation. Such vicious patriots "love their Country as Satan loved the Savior when they stood together on the pinnacle of the temple." Indeed, "A Christian demagogue is next to Satan in uncomeliness of character." The journal considered Harrison one of the few public men who resisted vulgar use of God to seek favor with the masses. Only another Harrison could save America by giving the Stewards proper leadership. Otherwise a once devout nation was undone. "Let us not suppose that the piety of our ancestors will save their degenerate children from this deserved doom."

Perhaps the most interesting, if not influential, Christian searching for means of American fulfillment followed Orestes Brownson's establishment of his own journal. *Brownson's Quarterly Review,* published for a brief time after 1844, pictured the national decline as unrivaled in the history of Christendom. In describing the fearful change which time and growth had wrought in the nation, Brownson called the worship of man the great delusion. The moral forces of the universe were abandoned. Turning to the supernatural, Brownson insisted that "our experiment in behalf of popular freedom" must go on. "It will not fail, it will succeed, if we return to God, put our trust in him, and live for the end to which he has appointed us." [46]

America's distinguished journalist for commerce, Freeman Hunt, arrived at an interpretation of the Republic similar to that of his colleagues in religious publishing. His magazine found the merchant to be the prime Steward in the nation's search for honor and success. The first volume in 1839 asserted: "The American merchant, then, should never forget that he holds the character of his country, as well as his own, in a sacred trust." Both could be betrayed by dissimulation and dishonesty. Hunt acknowledged that ambition and obligation were poorly balanced in America, producing wide distrust for the symbolical merchant. According to Hunt's journal, all this could be redeemed through education and Christianity.

By 1840, Hunt was urging a divine community. America's fulfillment required total acceptance of God's will and God's way. God's government and man's government could be reconciled. "Democracy is thus theocracy, and conscience, the vice-regent of God, is placed at the head of our national institutions." New Stewards would be needed, however, since the present generation had faltered. Hunt hoped that America would be given time enough to produce fresh advocates to call for Christian wisdom and restraint as national guides. The latter would return America to the old life of thrift and regularity. By 1848, Hunt's magazine conceded that national progress had become less certain as man's frailty grew more apparent. Evil men now were appealing to the Stewards to take passion as a god. Hunt proposed to face the Republic's future with new caution.[47]

The search for national meaning and fulfillment concluded by producing two groups of advocates. One was implicit in Brownson's somber militancy. The other inspired an exultant insistence upon certain but still distant glory. Caught between a terrifying legacy and its faltering endeavor, America's intellectual preparation meant turning either to God or to the future. Each afforded only limited comfort for the suspense. No matter how ecstatic some of the conventional rhetoric became, it was clear that in 1848 the nation's Trust seemed heavier and the citizen's response remained uncertain.

IV: Responses   Public rejoinder to the dilemma presented by advocates of nationality during this time was usually either jovial or despondent. Extremes, for instance, dominated the annual orations before New York City's New England Society. These splendid secular sermons were noteworthy in their yoking of despair and desire. They suggested perpetual national self-scrutiny as the only way that principles and events might together induce America's successful trusteeship. An address of 1842 by George B. Cheever, a prominent clergyman, acknowledged that although American institutions were noble, the people of the nation were inadequate. "We pray God that this may not prove to be true," said Cheever, who then turned to repudiate the concept of innate human capacity. He insisted America wallowed in luxury and corruption, as it disregarded "our fathers' virtues." Cheever thus was drawn to the theocracy admired by so many desperate Stewards. A favorite sentiment was: "Most fearlessly do I assert that men do *not* know how to govern themselves, except by the guidance of God's spirit." Without active Christianity, "we are lost." Yet this might be destiny's intent. Cheever suggested to the Society that perhaps "God means to demonstrate to the world," through "our passions, our selfishness, our atheism . . . how perfectly inefficacious without the Divine Spirit, are the very best institutions, which the cultivated wisdom and piety of ages could discover or frame, to restrain men's wickedness or to make them free and happy."

A contrasting response accompanied Rufus Choate's message in 1843. The eminent lawyer was convinced that some day America would prove the worth of man and republicanism. It would require that future generations reproduce the virtues of the Fathers. In this fashion the ultimate America would evolve, "as from a germ" toward "a wise, moral, and glorious future." George Perkins Marsh, the New England Society's 1844 orator, offered a third interpretation of American nationality, one considerably more sophisticated than those of his two predecessors. It assumed that nations, like individuals, had stages of infancy, growth, maturity, convulsion, disease, and decay. Marsh could not foretell whether good and evil would continue at open war, or if some day "the reason of state" might attain "a final victory over the rebellious passions of social man." The immediate concern for Marsh was the absence of "an intelligent national pride" and thus the lack "of a well-defined and consistent American character." America had produced only a boastful expectation about the future.[48]

New England Society audiences heard in these addresses the range of sentiment accompanying the search for self-assurance. Some voices were joyous because survival was certain. But those who were uncertain or in despair sounded more tormented, when peace and isolation yielded no flowering of American purpose.

10

Those who expressed assurance about the nation used several familiar themes. Among these was an idealization of the Revo-

lution and the War of 1812. By 1823, process or relentless development was advocated. Around 1825 and 1826 Americans were
ecstatic that the nation had survived for a half-century. Thereafter, a romantic theme was introduced which delighted in the
qualities of both American nature and man. Finally, the dominant contention of the assured response was the promise accompanying faithful preservation. Steadfast virtue became the guarantor of America's march toward completion.

The idealization of the conflicts with Britain usually claimed
an "instantaneous transfiguration" of Americans into free and
able men. The War of 1812 had disclosed that "we are worthy
the palladium transmitted us by our fathers." Now, wondrous to
behold, *"This Republic stands alone in the universe."* In 1817,
one person said the late war's "tempest did indeed shake our political edifice, but without impairing its beauty or its strength,
it was only to make its foundation sink deeper and stand more
firmly." This theme was disappearing by 1828, although a New
York orator then described the 1812 engagement as a triumph of
virtue over corruption. The Revolution "begat our national existence," while the War of 1812 "exalted and embellished our
national character." In Jackson's time, the second war with England entered the sectional controversy. There was also a renais-
sance of cordiality toward the Motherland. Exultation in the
wars of initiation began giving way to less explicit forms of assurance.

Of these, the most engaging presented the nation within a great
progression toward improvement. The Massachusetts legislature
used this in recalling that for 200 years America had held to a
moral and intelligent course of growth. Now stood the nation,
wealthy and powerful, "UNSULLIED BY ANY GROSS DEPAR-
TURE FROM NATIONAL RECTITUDE." In an 1821 poem,
"The Ages," William Cullen Bryant depicted America as a giant
in a "forward race." Into the future would this giant stride with
steady improvement. Bryant was confident of progress, but this
expectation was the most the nation could claim.

> Who shall then declare
> The date of thy deep-founded strength, or tell
> How happy in thy lap the sons of men shall dwell?

Bryant was still relying on abstract progress at the close of the period. In 1847 he used "Oh Mother of a Mighty Race" to describe the United States as a place and people of promise:

> Thine eye with every coming hour
> Shall brighten and thy form shall tower;
> And when thy sisters, elder born,
> Would brand thy name with words of scorn,
> Before thine eye,
> Upon their lips the taunt shall die.

Earlier in the poem, Bryant had said that neither America nor Europe should be caustic about the new nation's efforts, for how could anyone know "what virtues with thy children bide"?

Perhaps because of the vagueness and distance of the concept, it was not widely entertained until late in the nineteenth century. It did help some, however, to talk of the "race of moral improvements" and of the fact that "a whole continent has been set apart, as if it were holy ground, for the cultivation of pure truth." America would undertake to enlarge the boundaries of both the natural and moral worlds. However, in the 1830's the outlines of progress remained vague. The idea used such figures as "a mighty and rushing wind" sweeping America and the rest of the world. Within this universal development, as an 1842 speaker at Princeton observed, America was being used to guide "the cause of civil and religious freedom." Consequently, the outcome was sure, if distant. It was a lonely role for America, there being "no counsel from others" as the wave of human momentum proceeded.[49]

More immediate joy came with the realization that fifty years of American endeavor had elapsed. "The *great experiment* has succeeded," said one person. Mankind now would "behold the spectacle of a land whose crown is wisdom, whose mitre is purity, whose heraldry is talent." Upon America obviously "heaven's highest blessings are descending." But even here the assurance had to be prospective. Though half a century had passed, virtually everyone acknowledged that America's fulfillment was yet to come. The comfort was in asserting: "A gigantic nation has been born." It was suggested that the passing of five decades marked a new era when Americans, still wary of human frailty, could proceed more confidently with building a nation through the Fathers'

ways. Using the best of the past amid the novelty of the present,
America would become wiser and happier than the Founders
could have been in their time.

The Jackson era heard the century's most hopeful sounds about
the impact of nature and man upon America. Virtue, knowledge,
and liberty were nourishment for the national character yet to
appear. In the pure surroundings of America's wondrous setting,
the Stewards could come to speak and act with divine wisdom.
This would be at the behest of the same universal promptings to
move the Fathers. As all men shared elements of this mysterious
character, the popular will was declared ready to carry out the
Trust. Rhode Island's Senator Asher Robbins especially seemed
to enjoy this sense of assurance which he insisted was much more
than "the vain boast of national egotism." Never before, he said,
had a people emerged "whose private virtues were a substitute
for government itself, and a sufficient substitute."

Senator Robbins' view moved to the extreme of an appealing
outlook on national destiny. The transcendent spirit Bronson Alcott stated it simply: "Nature has assumed her rightful influence
and has shaped us in her mould." As time passed, however, it was
more evident that Americans had not completed the second Eden.
Caleb Cushing said in 1839 that, while America's character would
fulfill itself, it must first experience travail. Eventually, events
would produce a nation of one hundred million citizens sharing
one civilization, literature, and character. Cushing conceded that
there could be cautious "national pride," but it must not "degenerate into a blind prejudice against public improvement." By
1848, human capacity was rarely mentioned as an independent
force in the attainment of American destiny. Environment and
institutions were more important in producing a citizen and polity
worthy of the cause.

Since events discouraged the use of man as embodiment of national triumph, the Republic itself became a logical alternative.
Principle and virtue came to reside in the Union, whose security
made an admirable goal as means of national fulfillment. For
many Americans, the Union with its Constitution was "a sacred
inheritance" formed by a "mightier hand," and its sanctity was
the nation's Trust. Here was a responsibility whose discharge was
both plausible and immediate. Unity brought a sense of national-

ity which promised to be borne easier than such other abstractions as character, virtue, and even republicanism. By 1848, those who tried to speak with assurance were more comfortable with talk of preservation than with development. Inspiration had been with America's Founders. Succeeding generations could compensate for their spiritual inferiority by energetic defense of what the Founders had bequeathed.[50]

In groping through these searching years, America drew assurance especially from song, both religious and secular. A favorite theme was the title of one hymn, "Thanksgiving for National Deliverance and Improvement of it." The most eloquent composition was probably Samuel F. Smith's "America," prepared in 1832 after Smith discovered in books of German music that the air for "God Save the King" had broad Saxon ownership. The stanzas following the familiar initial lines nurtured the spirit of assurance:

> Our glorious Land today,
> 'Neath Education's sway,
> 　Soars upward still,
> . . . .
> Thy safeguard, Liberty
> The school shall ever be,
> 　Our Nation's pride!
> No tyrant head shall smite,
> While with encircling might
> All here are taught the Right
> 　With Truth allied.

> Beneath Heaven's gracious will
> The stars of progress still
> 　Our course do sway;
> In unity sublime
> To broader heights we climb,
> Triumphant over Time
> 　God speed our way!

> Grand birthright of our sires,
> Our altars and our fires
> 　Keep we still pure!

> Our starry flag unfurled,
> The hope of all the world
> . . . .
>   God hold secure!

Smith's lines said it all—the Trust, destiny's force, the importance of preservation, and the ultimate dependence upon God.
American assurance was still timid.[51]

11

Despite those who claimed assurance, the predominant response
among the voices searching after nationalism was uncertain. American public discourse during this era kept much of the admonitory
spirit developed in the perilous times after 1798. Americans continued to preach to each other, for the relief in 1815 was too brief
to obscure mammon and passion's threat. No stouter voice was
heard than Hezekiah Niles' *Register.* Disturbed by the sympto-
matic faltering of letters and learning in the nation, Niles advocated new resolve. "In the mingled feelings of humiliation and
hope, we forge the high national destinies we had predicted." He
prayed for the nation's recognition of the importance of learning,
"the only antidote that can be found against the meanness and
selfishness of avarice and ambition." Niles conceded that the
"strongest and most disgraceful trait in our national character . . .
is an inordinate love of gain. . . . It is too true—we see this foul
spirit everywhere . . . carrying patriotism to the market and
principle to the devil." So long as the condition existed, America's
realization was impossible.

Typical of the admonitions inspired by the uncertain American
outlook were the messages heard in the 1820 Fourth of July observance in Charleston. Four such sermons were printed after that
occasion. These accepted an awesome responsibility as the core
of national meaning. America was thus still on probation. All the
world awaited the outcome of the endeavor to bind human passion. As this unfolded, the dutiful stewardship stood guard against
change. These addresses repeated that while God had consecrated
the nation and watched over it "amid the waters of the great
deluge," he now awaited full dedication from all citizen-patriots.

The latter had to show habitual virtue if America was to fulfill its expectations. Such virtue actually meant institutions and beliefs safe from partisan zest. Such a national character could master self and party, meeting the nation's obligation to God and universe.[52]

This same response was put before the American Philosophical Society in 1823 by Charles J. Ingersoll. He talked of American institutions actually shaping a national outlook. Presidential aspirants in 1824 proposed an all-embracing spirit which would place the labors of American Stewards safety beyond partisan or sectional selfishness. A purified presidency meant an emancipated human nature. Occasionally predictions were heard that the day would come when the still unknown and mysterious impulses to be generated by American principle "must regulate the destinies of the world."

The increased scolding heaped on the American public after 1826 had two apparent causes. One was the failure in 1824 to make parties obsolete. The other was that America's fiftieth birthday wrought no lasting progress toward a proper outlook among the Stewards. The heightened sense of uncertainty consequently began emphasizing two themes. First was the importance to national success of preserving principles. Second was the personal surrender of each American in sustaining the national Trust. Together these argued that the uncertainties hovering around America would deepen unless the citizen abandoned the self for the national endeavor.

One of the best exhortations praising absolutes was by Mayor Josiah Quincy to fellow citizens of Boston. He stressed a moral union between times past, present, and future. Only this providentially designed bond through principle kept man from "grovelling in selfishness, wallowing in the mire of sense." These values must guide the nation lest it slip into the "grievous bondage of base, ignoble passions." Such ideals were discoverable in the "purer and better" atmosphere which had surrounded the Fathers. In seeking these, the good American would be alert. "The inventive genius of man is ever striking out new paths for ambition, and creating novelties to amuse and delude us."

This arch-suspicion became a conventional admonition after 1830. America could rely only on the Founders for precept and practice likely to sustain the nation's Trust. "Let us study these great models," said one uneasy commentator, so that American Stewards might "bury beneath the waves of public opinion the passions and prejudices which retard our progress." This strategy expected that when such devices for national attainment were known, successful nationality would have brought a transcendence of self by the citizenry. The challenge of being an American was not only a search for those abiding principles mandatory to the nation's calling. It also meant that each Steward must escape his humanity to embrace the national will and endeavor.

Transcendence of self was a theme cherished by the day's exhorters. A characteristic admonition was one from New Haven in 1826: "National power and virtue are the sum of individual worth." No good American would die having lagged "in the cause of our common country." Each Steward could best display his personal escape by fighting against change. "Innovation," said one speaker, "would surely bring danger; it might bring ruin." These advocates usually had the polity, and especially the Constitution, in mind when they insisted Americanism meant a guardian's labor. This required that education must bring the rising generation to accept American responsibility and the duty it imposed.

This increasingly prominent response appeared cogent by making stewardship a selfless endeavor to "perpetuate the inheritance and deliver it to posterity a treasure as valuable as we received it." The popular New York politician, Silas Wright, preached to this theme in 1839, denouncing individualism as both faithless and unwise. Each American must yield to the nation, never forgetting the "whole country." The equation of selflessness with true Americanism, adopted by Democrats and Whigs, dominated political discourse as sectional hostility added to the uncertainty about America. This was the ideological basis from which compromise became for some the essence of national policy.[53]

With the Founders' precepts, of course, went God. A Jefferson College scholar observed in 1842 that America's essence was Bible-based and that any progress made by the nation was due "to the fact, that God the Lord has been a wall of fire round about her." The Gospel joined the Fathers' wisdom as means for rescuing the nation from moral bankruptcy. The nativist appeal was especially successful in exhortations about preservation. America must be only one nation, "a Christian, Protestant state." Such messages insisted that the Founders desired a Protestant nation in which men admitted to citizenship "should be thoroughly *American- ized.*" The Know-Nothing rhetoric was a natural phase of the searching spirit in this era. American attainment required that national truths "be preserved from contamination" and that "this nation remain distinctively American." Only through such purity might the Republic discharge her "most holy trust."

This response was the specialty of a successful New Haven pe- riodical, *The New Englander.* It inveighed particularly against the "self-admiration" creeping upon the nation. In 1843, *The New Englander* ridiculed those who felt assured that America "will go on in improvement, from glory to glory, until she will become the joy of the whole earth." So many thriving evils re- buked any such confidence. The journal was fascinated by emo- tionalism among the Stewards. "How their understanding is warped by their passion." America's only hope was that citizens accept their Trust in humility. Let it "rather chasten than increase the vain spirit." Awesome responsibility should bring sobriety to the "national breast." The inference clearly encouraged by nu- merous responses such as those of *The New Englander* was that upon the citizen's struggle with evil depended the outcome of America's search for nationality.[54]

12

It was a simple step to a third attitude in public thought. This was a mood of indictment. Its concern went beyond the matter of uncertainty. For numerous observers, the cause of national virtue had retreated after 1815. Consequently, the pursuit for na- tional assurance first necessitated a candid confession of failure or unfulfillment. Typical of this response was a Delaware journalist's despair in 1819 over events since the war's end: "As matters *now go,* in a few years we will, for debauchery, pride, vanity, etc., have pretty fair claims to be compared with Spain, Portugal, and Italy." One particularly emphatic reaction was in issues of the appropri- ately named journal, *American Watchman.* It contended that con- fession was good for the national soul, bringing a salutary chasten- ing and awakening. In *Watchman*'s view avarice and material distraction were the chief villains in seducing America's virtue.

For a quarter-century this sort of self-abasement was common-place. A characteristic charge was one heard in 1841: "It is when men wax fat, and have abundant means and leisure, that they begin to rise up against the ordinances of Heaven and the peace and quietness of earth." On the one hand, grim necessity to strug-gle for physical survival was said to induce social virtue, in that a man's evil had no occasion to vex him and his fellows. Yet Tri-umph in this material struggle emancipated man from one agony only to bring him, paradoxically, the anguish of having time and means for being human. The doctrine of hard work had complex meaning for American thought.

From such varied quarters as citizen correspondence or the sing-ing of popular hymns came the despairing admission that the na-tion and its Stewards were far from the entrusted attainment. This confession entered the letters of such persons as Heny Clay, Harrison Gray Otis, Andrew Jackson, and James Fenimore Cooper. In one way or another all acknowledged "the profligacy of the times," "the unwearied and artfull efforts to corrupt and purchase others," or simply the sad assertion that America had "a want of virtue." The nation's calling notwithstanding, these observers found cupidity and lust distracting the citizens. The public did not lack reminders, such as a hymn familiar in this pe-riod entitled "Humiliation for National Sins":

See, gracious God, before thy throne
   Thy mourning people bend;
'Tis on thy sovereign grace alone
   Our humble hopes depend.

Tremendous judgements from thy hand
   Thy dreadful power display,
Yet mercy spares this guilty land
   And still we live to pray.

What numerous crimes increasing rise,
   Through this apostate land!
What land so favoured of the skies
   Yet thoughtless of thy hand?

How changed, alas! are truths divine,
  For error, guilt and shame!
What impious members, bold in sin,
  Disgrace the Christian name! [55]

In general, there were three theories to explain American short-coming. One of these ascribed evil to contemporary man's loss of the inspiration and comfort of the revered Fathers. Eulogies over the death of Marshall and Harrison usually contrasted the virtue and attainment of Marshall's own generation with the sinful age he lived to see. The second explanation condemned human nature. A Pennsylvania speaker summed it up in 1839: "Our danger is at home." There vice, infidelity, and selfishness brought citizens to abandon the public good. Consequently, as another spokesman observed, the nation had lived "in transgression." This view usually entailed a familiar rhetorical inquiry: "Can we survey the sad realities of our condition without being reminded of our guilt and forewarned of national judgement?"

These two responses normally joined in calling for national penitence. The third approach simply abandoned this era to its sins and escaped through anticipations of virtue in the coming generation. The future was vital to most theories of American nationality. Two quite different journals displayed this response as they began publication in 1846 and 1847. *De Bow's Review* liked to feature talk of a day when mists would lift and human passion would subside. *The American Literary Magazine,* published in Albany by T. Dwight Sprague, was more philosophical about the fullness of time. Its observation in 1848 was the response of many who were exhausted by the search for American meaning: "But, what care we, for nationality now? We can afford to wait, till the preliminary steps have been taken in the grand march of civilization, and moral conquest which is before us." Not before then could Americans expect to discover a nation "harmonious in all its parts, and beautiful in its completeness." [56]

With a mixing of despair and hope, American public thought closed the era of searching for national assurance. It had discovered little more than that its quest led into some tangled issues which had been troubling religious and secular inquiry for generations. As Richard Dana had warned, America could not avoid the old quagmire of human tendency to sin rather than to be virtuous. This ancient problem seemed increasingly to hamper America's search for a presence compatible with its calling. In grasping a continent at the close of the Mexican War, America would soon enter circumstances which would challenge a philosophy that recommended deeds of preservation while awaiting a future brought by process and God. For a short time the challenge in these circumstances would bring an immediacy to the nation's endeavor and invite talk of atonement.

CHAPTER THREE

ATONEMENT
1848–1865

During Polk's time many Americans wanted growth to explain nationality. The compromises of 1820 and 1833, as well as the Mexican War, had suggested that stewardship simply required cultivating a natural development. After 1848, however, this sort of existentialism was besieged by new events which made it difficult for America to talk of both the grandeur of process and the vitality of principles. Numerous politicians suggested that the nation avoid both considerations. Proper Americanism, they argued, was exemplified by the Compromise of 1850. Nevertheless, many younger laborers hungered for evidence that American achievement meant more than perpetuation. Men like William H. Seward, Salmon P. Chase, and Charles Francis Adams claimed that a successful America must have liberty. In doing so, they challenged the doctrine of preservation.

While many Americans took comfort in soothing words from Franklin Pierce, James Buchanan, Winfield Scott, and Millard Fillmore, others listened as Harriet Beecher Stowe used *Uncle Tom's Cabin* to convert stewardship into moral outrage. Her cause was enhanced by developments beginning in 1854. Senator Stephen A. Douglas had difficulty explaining the Kansas-Nebraska Bill, despite its charm for those concerned with growth. Such amoral legislation suggested to some observers that the Vineyard of compromise yielded bitter fruit. The struggle over Kansas' fate and the pronouncements involving Dred Scott increased demands for a critical look at the national being. Thoughtful attention went to the contention that America was being led toward spiritual bankruptcy. A few observers were so eager to associate nationality with militant principle that they claimed John Brown was an exemplary Steward.

Nevertheless, partisan combat in 1852 and 1856 remained largely concerned with guaranteeing the present. Nativism's success was due to its skillful use of the doctrine of preservation. A growing national crisis brought new praise for a stewardship opposed to change, one which raised no questions about human capacity or absolute principles. In reply, advocates like Charles Sumner, George William Curtis, Henry Ward Beecher, and Abraham Lincoln insisted that nationality must embrace explicit righteousness. In calling for a new stewardship such men claimed that the nation had sinned by striving to preserve its form without regard for its essence.

The Civil War was quickly hailed as atonement for truant American endeavor. By 1863 the war was generally accepted as a cleansing act, a purgation of national character. Negro bondage was made to symbolize America's moral dereliction. This important development in ideology dominated Lincoln's great assertion in 1863 at Gettysburg. America was morally obligated to produce a new birth of freedom. Once again war was used to assist nationality. It took violence after 1812 to show national capacity for survival. Momentarily in 1848 war made physical glory America's meaning. With martial victory in 1848, men said the "American Epoch" at last was beginning. Exactly fifty years later, the Republic again used triumph through violence to hail national consummation. This intimate bond between bloodshed and uneasy virtue in America's history and thought is probably the most important revelation of the difficulty in being American. It discloses how frighteningly indistinct is the line between the rational and irrational in the minds of men called to prove righteousness and progress.

Still another moment of bloodshed in this terrifying moral drama was Lincoln's death. It permitted American nationality to emerge from atonement with a symbolic martyr. Lincoln's career became a guarantor of America's new Trust in which moral absolutes were central, and the nation was encouraged to think it had put a clumsy stewardship behind. By confessing sin and claiming national atonement, the American mind believed the Republic would abandon the painful aspects of its past.[1]

DOCTRINE

For a time after 1848, most Americans believed that their duty was to keep things as they were. Stewards rallied to a supreme act of preservation, the Compromise of 1850. It embodied the concept that proper Americanism was an exercise in absolute conservatism. This belief was short-lived. Within a decade the dominant appeals were that stewardship must mean something more than guarding an awesome process. Preoccupation with sheer existence no longer discouraged talk of nationality's fundamental quality. A debate ensued among those claiming that stewardship meant unquestioning acceptance of America as a system and those who demanded a stewardship aggressive in behalf of cherished values and principles. Ultimately, the philosophy of preservation which Clay and Webster had so magnificently represented was overtaken by a doctrine of restoration or renewal. This doctrine, once deemed the unholy premise of fanatics like William Lloyd Garrison, came finally to be the gospel of the American martyr, Abraham Lincoln.

America's Civil War had an even more terrible irony than tradition has recognized. The war came when a generation discovered a sublime opportunity to meet its responsibility for principle in a universal setting. Yet when citizens accepted an active agency for liberty and abandoned the preserver's guise, they embraced passion, violence, and force in an effort to atone for a failure of responsibility. The once dreaded specter of bloodshed became a holy means of discharging the nation's responsibility for freedom's exultation. In this fashion, guarding the museum-piece Republic was laid aside as America's calling. A stewardship of zeal replaced a stewardship of fidelity. So significant a development in American thought required no new idea, but a reordering of elements already in national consciousness. American nationality left 1865 transformed through a brief moment of glorious achievement.

I: Affirmations After 1848 America's Trust came increasingly to require that, before the Republic could symbolize liberty, it must show itself worthy of freedom. This adjustment in doctrine was not easy, requiring confession that the good and the actual had grown far apart and that a negligent

stewardship must make atonement. The generation before 1850
had tried to have human will and national principle coincide.
This undertaking seemed crushed by the Kansas-Nebraska Bill
and the Dred Scott decision. The false sunlight of the compromise
did not shine for long. It gave way to a darkening uneasiness.

One of the last great efforts to sustain a faltering outlook was
made in Boston on the Fourth of July 1851 as citizens were dis-
puting the moral implications of the Fugitive Slave Law. Thomas
Starr King warned that patriotism was natural to the human impulse, so that, when devotion to nation was lacking, virtue and
religion were enfeebled. Patriotism meant devotion "to *the idea*"
represented by the nation, said King. This was impeccable Websterian doctrine. The American nation and its citizens were "consecrated to the office of bearing a just and faultless polity that shall
educate the world." Were not the Biblical prophets at one with
"the seers whose minds have glowed with the American idea"?
Because of the nation's noble system, said King, simply being an
American should make men feel equal, no matter how humble
"the roof and circumstances." All citizens were encompassed by
"a canopy of ideas and sentiments, such as never before arched
over any palace of the world."

For a short time, King's was the most satisfying view of proper
stewardship. Men had to remain devoted to a nation presented by
God, process, and the past. Anything short of this dedication was
"suicide." King moved cautiously among the problems of principle and passion, reverting often to Christian dedication as essential to American patriotism. This would allow selfless loyalty to
soar beyond shallow demagoguery. Only belatedly did King venture into the treacherous waters of definition. While the American
idea was liberty, the nation embodying this idea had to preserve
"the feeling of brotherhood, we need to be knit together in ties
of cordial amity." King warned that slavery threatened to shrivel
the vital "nerve of patriotism."

These affirmations illustrate the insistent paradox in American
doctrine. King bowed before both the polity and the principle,
urging the importance of each. Unless the nation was preserved
in body and spirit, its moral strength would be paralyzed. Here
King took refuge in the warning familiar in the previous era.
Responsibility rested with the present generation, for America's
"patriarchal and heroic periods have passed"; "we cannot rely

for our honors or safety upon the past." The world waited, watching "to see the quality and energy of our patriotism." The crucial implication of this outlook was fidelity to the nation as embodiment of a great idea.[2]

1

After the Kansas-Nebraska episode, King's bland affirmations would not be so easily applauded. Instead, interpretation of the Trust began stressing a supernaturally imposed charge to sustain the cause of liberty. Especially significant was the demand that fulfillment come through the present generation. By 1860 the misgivings once so characteristic of nationality were being supplanted by a new sense of endeavor. Such a transition, however, never removed the Trust from some association with the divine. It remained commonplace to assert, as Henry Ward Beecher could do so well, that the American venture depended upon the Christian gospel and its institutions. For some persons, the Civil War indicated that America had escaped secularism. Holy battle transformed national character, permitting the citizenry, at last properly, to concentrate on personal salvation.

Theocratic talk seemed to thrive in this era. The American frequently heard that he must "regard his country as an abode of the church, and love his country the more without loving the kingdom of Christ the less; the more he is a patriot, the more he is a Christian." An impressive contribution to this doctrine was an 1849 address by Horace Bushnell who announced that God's law and purpose were themselves the essence of the American venture. Both nation and citizens, in submitting to being instruments of a divine plan, could follow right principle to certain triumph. This argument would assume increased importance for a newly aggressive stewardship. If human agency and predestination could exist together, the American Trust might exact from the good Steward an unwavering and even unthinking adherence to principle.

Bushnell advanced what would become a familiar affirmation, saying that "as in the growth of a man or a tree, so also in the primal germ of nations and social bodies, there is a secret Form and Law present in them." Such an element within America had "the force of a creative, constitutive instinct in the body, building up that form by a wisdom hid in itself." The Fathers'

deep faith became therefore a "constructive instinct." Bushnell
declared that America rested not on "man's will or force" but
on "those principles of justice and common beneficence which
we know are sacred to God." Consequently, Americans "do not
understand . . . the real greatness of our institutions, when we
look simply at the forms under which we hold our liberties."
Meaning was in "the magnificent possibilities that underlie these
forms, as their fundamental supports and conditions." Bushnell
was encouraged by the progress of humanity in America, "the
silent growth of centuries" coming from "the seed of Puritan
discipline."

This astonishing address gave the American Trust larger
meaning. Citizens must surrender to the principles inherent in
a nation nestled in the embrace of a mysterious divine process.
In this way human nature would escape the reach of passion
and mammon, thereby permitting the polity to disappear as anything but a wondrous memory and achievement. Bushnell clearly
made this sense of purpose the key to American nationality, "a
feeling not the less universal and decided because its objects are
mostly impersonal." He argued here in behalf of a ripening sentiment about the national purpose which would imbue the rhap-
sodic spirit in the *Battle Hymn of the Republic.* The war easily
meant a coming of God's glory on earth, within America's pursuit of fulfillment. Men should submit eagerly to this whirlwind
of principle surging forward beyond human and social shortcoming. Consequently, Stewards were told to seek "kindly feelings," for harmony was needed for the fulfillment of national
purpose. By 1860 this doctrine of submission readily spoke of
God's plan. The unfolding of grand design seemed to decree that
patriotism and Christianity were presented as "twin brothers."
These brethren, Bibles in hand, carried freedom's Trust.[3]

After 1848 talk of American purpose came to stress liberty's
cause rather than that of republicanism. This was an important
shift permitting an absolute value to supplant a procedural system. An end succeeded a means. While Longfellow's 1849 poem,
"The Building of the Ship," made Union the depository of humanity's "hopes of future years," the "Ship of State" soon held
more than republicanism's cargo. Added was the moral treasure
of freedom itself. The Union changed from a procedure to a
moral imperative. Much as Horace Bushnell reshaped the provi-

dential aspect of America's Trust, so Charles Sumner led in discovering the libertarian features of national purpose. Disavowing
Websterian stewardship in 1851, Sumner asserted: "If I decline
to recognize as my guides the leading men of today, I shall feel
safe while I follow the master principles which the Union was
established to secure, leaning for support upon the great Trium-
virate of American Freedom—Washington, Franklin, and Jefferson." No longer content with a stewardship of conservation,
Sumner announced that America's purpose was "simply morals
applied to public affairs" aided by "those everlasting rules of
right and wrong which are a law alike to individuals and communities." Sumner was, of course, aware that the Trust was still
interpreted by men like James Buchanan as "our blessed Union"
whose presence alone assured "moral power."

Buchanan's was not a partisan view. Democrats and Whigs
agreed in 1850 that American fulfillment depended entirely
upon giving Union "an ever-surrounding care" through "carefully cultivated and acquired habits and states of feeling." The
latter required "a prolonged and voluntary educational process,"
said Rufus Choate, so that "the fine and strong spirit of NA-
TIONALITY may be made to penetrate and animate the
scarcely congruous mass." This spirit, according to Choate,
meant a determination "to leave the Union, when we die,
stronger than when we found it—here—here is the field of our
grandest duties and highest rewards." However, by 1854 republican preservation through Union idolatry was widely challenged.
Important in this development was George Ticknor Curtis' study
of the American Constitution. Union was a vehicle for "republican liberty," but liberty was America's responsibility "to posterity." Gradually national consciousness found Union as a
means to sustain noble principle. More than one voice asserted
in the tumult of this decade: "We have had the temple of liberty desecrated long enough. . . . It becomes our sacred duty,
therefore, to unite as one man, and resolve to bring back this
government to the administration of those principles upon
which it was originally founded."

Events in the 1850's gave no peace to this ambiguity within
the concept of Trust. Did the responsibility for freedom or republicanism demand a peaceful Union at any price? Would pursuit of liberty at the cost of republican discord betray the Trust?

Or would it be a more glorious act of stewardship? These issues still puzzled many Americans as the war began, so that some simply let the need to fight for the nation settle the matter. "It is our Providential calling and destiny to be a *nation*," and the war would show that America "is a perpetual, organic creature, for which, by its very nature and vital law, there can be no secession at will." One observer predicted that from this struggle would appear "a consciousness of nationality, of a Providential calling and destiny, something deeper than geography, or trade, or constitutional agreement, a soul of Americanism." Defending freedom would at last grant the nation "that mysterious sentiment of nationality." [4]

Explaining America by libertarian responsibility had implications for the role of the past and the future in national doctrine. After 1854, the Fathers were made patrons of liberty, a role to be emulated by new Stewards, while the future remained an important and impatient ideological element. Even those who defended a Trust as meaning Union intact felt the past and future watch expectantly as bequeather and inheritor. In the face of these demands the sense of national purpose was all the more divided. Those who saw liberty as America's treasure talked increasingly of restoration. This suggested positive reform action. Others wishing to sustain a sacred republican system urged preservation. This called for circumventing troublesome issues. Between these two views of the Trust, the importance of the past appealed most to the preservationists. For the restoration movement, the past lost some of its charm.

Those who affirmed that America was entrusted with cherishing past attainment were still powerful. Edward Everett said that a reverence for the past was an instinct "deep in our nature." The "Young America" enterprise was exceptional in opposing institution and experience. Not the expedients of the moment but the spirit of seventy-six was the preferred basis for national endeavor. Speakers and essayists often pointed to Mount Vernon where a voice in "trumpet tones" could be heard to say: "Stay the rude hand, already uplifted to disturb the peaceful repose of the mighty dead." It was clear to these spirits that "this mighty Republic has not yet fulfilled its manifest destiny." Let no man then press the awkward question or issue which might "hazard the experiment." Such a doctrine left many in 1861 little more than the affirmation that faithful Stewards could only "wander religiously to the grave of our noble forefathers who have made us one and united, and to seek at their shrine light and knowledge for our fear-beset ways." In such a time men sought balm for their torment, made no easier by the ubiquitous reminders that Washington could be seen afar weeping over his people's anguished state.

The future afforded a broader appeal as national circumstance worsened. Even George Bancroft conceded that the present generation had fallen short. A new age and beyond would have to carry forward the Trust. "I feel myself at most to be but a pioneer, and rest my hopes on those who come after me." It was here, finally, that the variant concepts of the Trust shared ground. Indeed, America had failed to deliver a fulfilled Trust. Major uncertainties about man and nation persisted, and they distressed worshippers of accord as well as those impatient for action. A Phi Beta Kappa lecturer at Trinity College spoke for both sides in 1856 when he said of his country: "But whither? Aye whither!" The "screaming steam-horse" could not disclose what the national ideals were moving toward in a time of awesome change. "The landmarks are all unknown," so no one could predict whether the nation was to complete its passage in "some unruffled Pacific sea" or in "a relentless Maelstrom." And now America could no longer honorably hide in contending that "we are as yet very young." This concept was "Vain, shallow pretext! Foolish sophistry." The nation had become rich and vigorous, so there was no justification for avoiding the matter of "moral worth." [5]

At the close of this period, war and assassination supplied answers to the concern expressed at Trinity College. They were both atonement for and fulfillment of America's responsibility for principle. Bronson Alcott said during the mourning for Lincoln: "The sacrifice is doubtless to knit us in closer and more religious bonds to God and the right, and redound to the preservation of our national honor and glory." A sense of national achievement prevailing at the close of 1865 was more jubilant than Alcott's quiet hope.

It was a triumph arising from Providence's inspiration of a true patriotism. This spirit was said to have brought a matured dedication to the Trust and with it God's promise of long-sought

national triumph. "Thank God, we did not take down the map
of the United States and tear it into pieces; and we never will,"
one person asserted. The American flag was "more than ever the
symbol of irresistible majesty, coupled with endless hope." He
went on to say that in giving so much on the altar of liberty,
America found the answer to its divine call. It would now become "the fountain of civilizing and evangelizing influences for
all the earth."

The sense of atonement brought repetition of this jubilation.
Those who believed that the Trust had been found and discharged joined briefly in the cry: "Righteousness and peace have
kissed each other! Hallelujah!" [6]

2

Discussion of the identity of the Steward was significantly affected by this era's dash toward crisis and action. With freedom's
need becoming the central theme of nationality, the capacity of
the citizen required renewed attention. Affirmations about American Stewards after 1848 showed that America was still being
seen simplistically. There was easy mingling of concepts about
citizen and citizen body. The nation, or the public, remained
ideas virtually apparent to the eye, making the Steward, like the
Trust itself, intensely real. A Boston election "discourse" in 1849
tried to keep personal life as the locus of patriotic pursuits.
"Great misunderstanding has prevailed and much mischief has
been occasioned by erroneous notions of patriotism." These were
said to incite loud appeals and public posturings from many
Americans.

With the 1850 compromise fresh emphasis came to the importance of citizen dedication as the start of a properly committed
body of Stewards. "It behooves then every man," ran one 1850
exhortation, "bearing the American stamp and superscription,
to enlist his best energies in fostering an intelligent, high-toned
public sentiment." The latter implied immediate surrender by
men to their common citizenry. "Our story is a unit . . . in all
we feel of patriotic fervor, we are AMERICANS and AMERI-
CANS only. In all we are or have been, we are bound up in a
common nationality." During the brief calm of 1851, Thomas
Starr King asserted: "It is the striking glory of our land that the
patriotism it asks for is of the highest stamp." He added, "To a

mind of ordinary capacity, the extent of our territory and the various needs of our population, furnish as fine a temptation, certainly, as can well be offered, for the exercise of the sentiment of *universal brotherhood.*"

These appeals to selflessness employed Anglo-Saxon traditions for an encouraging sense of timelessness and endurance. Similarly, some of the insecurity nagging American nationality was eased by the comfort of nativism which often revered the Anglo-Saxon background. For others, the broad mixture of peoples was a source of encouragement. With the blood of all civilized nations within it, American stewardship was, according to a speaker at the Smithsonian Institution in 1855, "the only type of the unity of mankind." But even here the dominant element was the Anglo-American "race." It was the unique capacity of this portion of the populace, asserted the *United States Magazine* in 1856, which made it possible "to Americanize every man, with soul of a man, who deliberately casts in his lot with us." [7]

By 1857, however, talk of stewardship grew more entwined with what Rufus Choate called the critical features of "American nationality." These were "the outward national life, and the inward national sentiment." Like many, Choate pleaded for "the fine sweet spirit of nationality, the nationality of America" that was "a pillar of fire which God has kindled." Such a spirit would take Americans above petty personal and sectional limits to the great accommodation of man and nation preached by Clay and Webster. Choate contended that true nationality meant "you ascend above the smoke and stir of this small local strife; you tread upon the high places of the earth and of history; you think and feel as an American for America; her power, her eminence, her consideration, her honor, are yours." From this must come "the creation of a national life," once the citizen was willing to think about America constantly. As Choate put it, the proper Steward would "contemplate habitually, lovingly, intelligently, this grand abstraction, this vast reality of good." This consummate meditation would produce "a national life, which shall last while sun and moon endure," all buttressed upon "concession, compromise, love, forbearance, help."

Unfortunately for this doctrine of the Steward loyal to a mystical America, large numbers of citizens began asking about the goals of the nation. These Stewards were not content to stand in awe of the fact of an America, whether understood as a Union, a glorious Constitution, or a vast physical empire. They came to represent what one editor in 1859 described as a new "Fanaticism." Such interest in the purpose for which the citizen surrendered to the nation culminated in war. Thus, generally notions about individual Stewards receded. There was little encouragement for such doctrine when the issue was either the national mystique or the claims of principle. The importance of this distinction grew as the war for Union proceeded.[8]

3

Crisis affected the customary affirmations of a physical or a political Vineyard. Those who considered the polity to be a moral entity displayed indignation at claims that God created the political Vineyard merely as a place where other values could seek implementation. Even so, the ambiguous political Vineyard persisted surprisingly well during a time of atonement. Was unity to be cultivated for its own sake or for the pursuit of glorious precepts? Levi Woodbury's plea in 1850 went echoing down the decade in behalf of the polity as an end in itself. "There lurks a serpent in the paths of our political paradise. It is disunion." The American nation was created to "make us conciliatory and kind." In displaying the circular reasoning required by this doctrine, Woodbury said that Americans must resolve "one and all" to behave so as to preserve this polity. As McGuffey's *Fourth Reader* advised in 1854, American patriotism meant "a love of country, mingled with an admiration for our political institutions." Another view, even more candid, called for "a just appreciation of the cognate ties of Union," lest these be destroyed by a "devotion to abstract notions of morality." [9]

The intellectual appeal of a divinely created polity as the American Vineyard was impressive. Men like Wendell Phillips were relatively rare in their disdain for the polity as forced and unripe. Phillips pictured the Union as a vase. Its contents, the principles of the nation, were more important than the vase itself, for they had grown so much that they were about to burst the porcelain. While there was a rising sympathy for this interpretation, moderates like Abraham Lincoln praised the political

Union, waiting until a propitious moment to talk of the national polity as a means. The outlook about the Vineyard as a sublime polity generally was well expressed by one commentator in 1856: "Whether we will or not, we have within us a feeling of unity with all associated with us under the same institutions or laws. All are part of one great whole. It is not mere fancy, a mere prejudice; it is ordered so by our Creator; and when we urge to the cultivation of national feeling, we but carry out His designs."

While many persons shared such affirmation, none did so more grandly than Henry Reed, professor of English at the University of Pennsylvania. He said that all Americans must accept their polity as coming from the "providential government of the world," something evolving out of "Saxondom." It had developed "as a garden grows, and the seed was not sown by man's hands." This doctrine prevailed with much eloquence until the war came. It was widely affirmed that only the "trumpet voice of a god" could adequately proclaim the glory of American unity. The political setting was "to be loved, honored, worshipped at all times." Only the "denationalized" man could think of trifling with "the greatest of the works of social organization yet devised by man." Consequently, the offense of secession was genuinely shameful to most Americans.

Comparatively submerged were those voices affirming that God gave more into America's care than "this ever glorious constitutional Union." Such men, of whom John Brown was the most extreme, had another view of patriotism. To those who appeared confused over Vineyard and labor, Edward Everett would shout, "imbecility!" Putting it more kindly, a Tennessean made the point with admirable clarity: "We may choose which we will, but religion and the Union, or irreligion and disunion, are the dilemma." The latter alternative was as somber as the coffin. Only with the war's coming were most Stewards released to talk of their Vineyard as more than a subject of veneration.

Events after 1848 did little to encourage affirmations about a natural Vineyard. Supreme Court Justice Joseph Bradley was among the last to say that the American Trust would be fulfilled because of its deposit in a vast physical "mutuality of interests." While the organic explanation of natural development was heard in the 1850's, it was mostly in behalf of a political rather than natural Vineyard. Not until the eve of the Civil War did William Gilpin publish his influential study of a material Vineyard. Even here natural assets were most important as aids to political unity. Nature made a blend of politics and hearts inescapable. "It is thus," said Gilpin, "that the holy question of our *Union* lies in the bosom of *nature;* its perpetuity in the hearts of a great democratic people, imbued with an understanding and austere reverence for her eternal promptings and ordinances; it lies not in the trivial temporalities of political taxation, African slavery, local power, or the nostrums of orators, however eminent."

As with the concepts of Trust and Steward, the ideas about Vineyard were profoundly affected by the realities of the 1850's. Reverence for a political setting of almost supernatural capacity for inspiration and safety suffered, as did the once cherished Vineyard of nature. Rarely was it said in this era that nature would inspire Stewards with "stern virtue" and "a holy zeal of regenerating patriotism." The American crisis overwhelmed the Vineyard as a concept.[10]

II: Anxieties   In wresting America away from the majesty of a natural and political union, developments in the nation's career gave the issue of human agency new importance. Good stewardship had to involve more than a worshipful attitude toward the divine Union. National doctrine awkwardly made room for a dynamic pursuit of moral ends. Whether in talk of Americanism as preservation or as advancement, this era listened to the first significant suggestions that dedicated stewardship might surmount those barriers to fulfillment, passion and mammon. Even partisanship, some felt, could be buried beneath devotion to newly important ideals for which the nation had been called into existence. By 1865, American nationality was captivated by the thought that the Civil War was an agonizing proof of this devotion and consequently an explicit act of fulfillment. This was plausible since the evils presumed to detain the nation from its divine call had become explicit and immediate. In facing slavery and sectionalism, Stewards could claim to meet America's obligation to both past and future. Both national design and development became as one, deposited in the deed of Emancipation.

4

This new aggressiveness about the nation's responsibility by 1861 was affecting the ideology of stewardly endeavor. Midway through the horror of civil strife, the American outlook was sharing the exultation voiced by Charles Sumner who spoke of "our national regeneration which is now at hand." But old doubts were not easily forgotten. Sumner was obliged to add: "I am not sure that Providence has given us all the chastisement needed for our case." An easy military victory might not be enough to offset national "sins." The awfulness of the Civil War thus encouraged Sumner to begin talking hopefully of "a redeemed nation." Behind this moment was a decade or more of straining by Americans to see in their labors the potential for fulfilling national purpose. It was with obvious relief, late in the war, that men dismissed the venerable threats to America as temporary aberrations in human nature or as the lure of bad men whom national victory would banish. Even the partisans, the demagogues, the sectionalists were for the moment considered ephemeral evils to be left in the wake of a nation finally roused.

In this transition the old dispute about America's career being an evolutionary development or a system's function gradually quieted. These antithetical explanations tended to be united as American thinking adopted an almost Newtonian view of freedom as permanent and immutable. More credence went to a glorious organic growth within the American experience. National endeavor thus was seen both as preservation and pioneering for morality. One observer tried to explain this in 1852: "It is our pride to have propounded the secret of both permanence and progress, of both order and freedom in the attraction of the people's hearts." The American experience was an extraordinary natural attainment. "The seed was sown with the origin of human society, and the germination has ever since been going on, not to blossom and wither only, but to reach at length an ideal fruitage of future perfectibility." [11]

This merging of principle and process weakened the appeals from professional Unionists after 1850. They fell into their own paradox while often repeating the glib coupling, liberty and Union to be forever one and inseparable. Freedom was becoming an explosive mandate to place alongside the most sacred of contracts. Thomas Starr King showed this confusion in his 1851 address "Patriotism." While Union was a hallowed word, its eulogy must not permit Americans to "overlook or too slightly estimate the conditions of Union." America had been created for an idea's unfolding. King conceded slavery's presence threatened the vital brotherhood among Americans. If this unity fell, with it would go "the ideal beauty of our nation" and "its hovering genius will flee." A year later King tried to scramble out of the pit in a rush of eloquence about the organic character of America's experience. The nation arose from "a feeble germ of order, striving slowly against a chaotic mass of passion." From this came the "mission of our land" which was to show the manner in which liberty must be organized. Finally, the fruition for all mankind would be drawn from the "higher national morality" to characterize America as a result of superhuman development.

King was in growing company as Americans began mixing a sacrosanct polity with treasured principle. With the Kansas-Nebraska realities, this became more difficult, forcing some persons to recall the 1850 prophecy of the radical Ohio congressman, Joshua Giddings. He insisted that Union eloquence was a mask behind which outrages against fundamental principles were committed. The old Union, said Giddings, was deceased. Even so, it was difficult to overcome thoughts of stewardship as total dedication to Union. Delegates to the 1861 Peace Convention were instructed, for instance, to emulate those "immortal patriots who framed the Federal Constitution" and reverently to approach the Union's altar. Like the nation itself, the conference was torn asunder by sentimental loyalty to a once fragile nationality and deep concern over critical issues now associated with the life of the nation.

This confusion encouraged many persons to see the national venture as fostering contentment with existence. One person said, "With us, well-doing is happiness, and duty is another name for prosperity." Another voice prayed in 1856 to Washington for the indispensable "universal spirit of patriotism." Said the supplicant: "We beseech Thee! let thy pure patriotism animate our hearts and direct our lives, so that allured by no temptations and turned aside by no threats, we may follow in the bright path which thou didst make out for us." A New Yorker found satisfaction in saying that proper stewardship meant the advocacy

and support of "the AMERICAN IDEA" which was *"the spiritual worth of every man."* America had made this a "practical
fact." Consequently, America's "great nationality" meant personal virtue, out of whose dynamic quality America would successfully face "a world's work."

Increasingly, however, American thought grew impatient with
such bland assessments of American endeavor. As a Connecticut
newspaper said, following 1860's election, the American purpose
"was to secure the blessings of liberty." The great evil then was
that the Stewards might be lured to labors which would render
the nation "wholly false to its original object." Consequently,
the war once begun was quickly accepted both as a sign of God's
retribution and as the ultimate act of stewardship. This moment
hailed a re-created nation. In atoning for delay in carrying out
their responsibility, Americans had earned a new nation.[12]

By the close of the war, Lincoln's was simply the most magnificent voice in a vast chorus accepting suffering as a divine ordeal
bringing America's Trust at last into men's hearts and minds.
Observers like Francis Lieber, who had become a professor at
Columbia University, foresaw two results of the struggle, the
destruction of slavery—at least in the border states—and "the
distincter nationalization of this country." By 1864 such suggestions comprised an American attitude shifting toward the reality
of its effort. The sins of slavery and rebellion must be overcome,
for even the Fathers in writing the Constitution had not "dreamt"
of these evils. Let faithful Stewards "cut and hew through the
thicket as best we can," leaving political design and mending
until later. This put the doctrine of Constitutional Union, the
inspired polity, distinctly secondary, leaving the "life of the
nation" to pulse in the principles for which war was waged.
National existence, according to such a view, was in the public's
ardent embrace of divine principles making up national meaning. Acording to American doctrine men were penitent Stewards who hoped that the laborer had at last been found worthy
of his hire.

Some of America's most gifted writers expounded this interpretation of war's meaning. In a public letter of 1861, Francis
Parkman spoke of the conflict as national refreshment. America
had let material success distort and diminish its moral outlook,
permitting "a scum of reckless politicians" to direct the nation's

endeavor. Now "like a fresh breeze," said Parkman, "the war has stirred our clogged and humid atmosphere. The time may be at hand when, upheaved from its depths, fermenting and purging itself, the nation will stand at length clarified and pure in a renewed and strengthened life." Two years later, Oliver Wendell Holmes claimed that the war was inevitable since it had to be fought for "national life, for liberty everywhere, for humanity, for the Kingdom of God on earth." The governor of the universe, according to Holmes, had decreed that there be in America an uprising of conscience against the atrocious sin nurtured paradoxically within the Republic. Holmes considered the war as America's abandonment of money-making for the long-delayed "brave deeds and noble thoughts."

By 1864, the atonement idea had fostered a wide exultancy. San Francisco heard one speaker confidently conclude that America could exist only through a willingness to use force against all who would hamper her endeavor. In New York, Carl Schurz drew one of the most vivid portraits of the war as national fulfillment. The conflict was inescapable because only on the principle of democracy could a healthy national organization be built. This made Negro bondage "the natural traitor against the American nationality." A purified Union was an "instinctive" concern of Americans who now acted from "the deepest convictions" and out of "the immovable religious faith of the American mind." Either the evil within the nation must be put to death or the nation itself must die.

Such an outlook quickly condemned the Peace Democrats' philosophy. Its view that national togetherness was so important as to make inner evil worth tolerating was "suicide." A proud new stewardship eager for labor was the concept behind Schurz's rebuke to the hesitant brethren: "Step out of the way of the Nation who marches with firm step and a proud heart after the martial drumbeat of her destiny." The genuine American now knew that the "crisis of this hour" was in truth the compressed struggle of eternity. "It is for the coming centuries that she fights; and already she sees before her what was once only a patriotic dream rise into magnificent, sunlit reality! Liberty!" [13]

Another important development was in the familiar doctrine that personal desires victimized man. After 1861 transcending them seemed likely as Stewards surrendered to the nation's needs.

Americans were urged to "sing the songs of patriotic devotion at your hearthstones," by one 1863 admonition. "Let your country have your earliest and your latest prayers. Frown on every syllable of distrust, of wavering, of disrespect, that pollutes the air you breathe. Require of all your friends to be first the friends of the nation!" This loyalty was nothing less than a "holy spirit of devotion," an "unconditional loyalty that can alone save the land." Stewards should find themselves through "a religion of patriotism." Not only did numerous speeches and pamphlets foster this spirit, but the pledge taken by the Loyal National League, organized at the Cooper Institute in 1863, condemned any questioning of the national pilgrimage. All men should be bound by one concern, "to maintain the power, glory, and integrity of the nation." There were few comments on the ironical swiftness with which many Americans had returned to the doctrine of Webster and Clay, once the act of war had made its contribution as a blow for principle.

5

Although America's ordeal after 1848 briefly made nationality triumph through purification and loyalty, belief persisted that passion and mammon might mar this new stewardship. Even when the war gave human nature a more promising prospect, the Christian reflex was to mention the immemorial dangers from man's own character. In the 1850's such weakness was especially useful to the ardent Unionists who condemned reform simultaneously with passion. James Buchanan said in a public letter of 1850, "God forbid that fanaticism should ever apply a torch to this, the grandest and most glorious temple which has ever been erected to political freedom on the face of the earth." A more positive assertion was that the nation's continuation had about it "a talismanic influence and charm" which would "hush the demagogue to silence." America's problem still was to locate the balance between individual yearning and duty. The former could lead to national shame, if as one speaker said, men let themselves "run wild" and "grow arrogant," confounding "freedom *in* religion with freedom *from* religion."

As crisis worsened, numerous voices called for a revival of Puritan disciplines. It was claimed that sexual impurity was the gravest national threat. Fornication was about to place the

American Samson at the mercy of a Delilah who would bring the nation to a doom "read in the silent streets of Pompeii and among the ruins of the Coliseum." For others it was man's susceptibility to unreason and to flattery, his curious blending of personal insecurity and arrogance, which threatened the success of the American venture. Yet even these human limitations were said to be overcome by the Civil War. Through the conflict, Americans were finding their maturity, their manhood. It was a "smelting-furnace" in which "the metal flows richly while the dross turns to ashes." In being called beyond themselves, the Stewards had left their weakness behind. Said Carl Schurz: "We have a great future." [14]

The other tradition of human frailty also lingered. Many observers continued to insist that inordinate love of gain kept the citizenry from recognizing national peril. Expostulation from New England especially warmed to this theme. Charles Eliot Norton's *Considerations on Some Recent Social Theories,* published in 1853, was a representative insistence that moral excellence was the sole basis for freedom. Yet mammon so appealed to American nature that it "may have the effect of weakening and finally depraving that character." Norton wanted America to recognize that its essence was in the human soul, and the ominous signs within America would not be dispelled without first dealing with the "wild, reckless, and unprincipled spirit" which threatened to capture the citizenry.

The same thing was said by Henry Kiddle who was assistant superintendent of schools in New York City. Writing in 1856 about the relation between mental culture and national character, Kiddle assailed the capitivity of national outlook by the "sordid lust of gain," the "contemptible worship of mammon," and the "degrading passion for money-getting." Education, of course, was the means Kiddle proposed for rescuing a degenerate America. However, he warned that education must offer new values and especially avoid the goal of a national intellect at the "dead level." Often repeated in the 1850's, this doctrine claimed that materialism debased national standards. Everything was judged, said one foe of mammon, "by its present availability."

This presumably left nationality with no respect for public interest. "This Moloch in our midst" was used to explain why the American cause lost ground. Even after Fort Sumter, there were indictments of material lust. For instance, the elder Henry James began an address by rejecting providential assurance of national success as "unscrupulous rubbish." The impact of gross materialism and political corruption had become so apparent that James expected Americans to be jarred from their deluded state. Every man could see "how meagre and mean and creeping a race we permit our rich men to be, if their meanness is only flavored with profusion." This meant America's Trust must first emancipate the human character. What was novel was the rising claim that America's capacities and purposes had been blunted because the charm of material gain had encouraged the rise of a false and pernicious leadership. It was an important shift in the American outlook, charging recent leaders with betraying the nation's Trust.[15]

Pursuit of national atonement was hastened by this explanation of national shortcoming which drew away from general human nature. It produced weaknesses of which America could be readily cleansed. The barriers to national fruition became slavery and false leaders. America admitted to tolerating both, but in the era after 1848 it disavowed them and sought atonement. Slavery especially was called a betrayer of the Trust. Destroying this evil pointed the nation toward long-deferred triumph. The presence of false and foolish leaders readily explained why there had been delay in national fulfillment. Delusion under false spokesmen had brought a near-fatal fall from the Founders' standards. With slavery's rejection, however, Americans believed they might live at peace with the Fathers' memory. Most important, America had a new beginning toward fulfilling universal expectation.

6

In denouncing the leadership of compromise, the nation also attacked its renowned weakness, partisanship. After 1850, the sin of party was more widely assailed. Increasingly the party zealot was pictured as a sectional agitator or a spineless compromiser. This was evident, for instance, when disillusioned men turned upon Daniel Webster. The disgust led to calls for new and noble leaders to return America to the course set by the early pilots. But where was the American, asked one person in 1855, who "has those large and grand national proportions which attract to himself the common eye, and center around him the common hopes of the country"?

Perhaps one of the most eloquent descriptions of how partisanship bankrupted American leadership was heard by students at Miami University, Ohio, in 1856. There an orator ascribed a human quality to nations, giving them a "love of life, which can never be violated with impunity." Since a nation, "being a public person," and having "a distinct personality of its own," existed for moral ends, with moral responsibilities, the character of its leaders was vital. Then followed a typical review of the folly of America's recent statesmen, under whom the nation had departed from Christianity. What resulted was referred to as an orgy of greed, faithlessness to liberty, and public turbulence. This speaker predicted that in God's good time there would appear "a new stock of men, good men and true" who would be concerned only with their duty to the nation. Francis Parkman preferred to call such men "master minds" who could properly guide the patriotism and courage of the multitude. Of interest to men like Parkman was the question: "Why is mediocrity in our high places, and the race of our statesmen so dwindled?"

By 1863, a cautiously optimistic response was heard. Great men would soon re-emerge, giving America the principled, wise, and vigorous leadership which the Founders had provided. According to Parkman, men worthy of the nation's obligation would appear "when a deep and abiding sense of our deep need of them has seized and possessed the national heart, when the fallacies that have deluded us so long shall be thrown from us as debasing and perilous illusions, and the national mind rises to a true conception of republican freedom." In sharing this outlook, Samuel J. Tilden added that the national heart faltered because peace and prosperity had permitted the ideas "of our wise ancestors" to "fall into desuetude." The present generation somehow experienced trials worthy of the Fathers, thereupon arriving at the wisdom of old.

For the realistic outlook, a war for the Republic's nationality and freedom was necessary to transcend the paltry considerations prized by partisans. Thereafter, regenerate America could expect triumphant stewardship from citizen and leader alike. The once gloomy Bronson Alcott caught the new mood when he wrote in the summer of 1865: "The Republic now begins to look sweet and beautiful as if honest patriotic citizens might walk upright without shame or apologies as in years before this rebellion." Stewards whose doctrine of national faith had been the most demanding were joyful in the face of atonement through blood-shed.[16]

As a result, American thought for the first time seriously sought to place its hopes for national fulfillment in the human conscience. Previously, this had been alien ground. Distrust of human capacity had obliged such hopes to look toward the majestic course of events, to indoctrination, to supernatural forces, or to an organic growth. Such misgiving was especially evident in the doctrine advanced by Clay and Webster. Soon, however, these concerns about man's capacity would reappear.

SPOKESMEN

Alcott's description did little justice to the range of sentiment dominating this era in American national thought. Those speaking for nationality, whether eminent or obscure, experienced alternating hope and despair as America sought to sustain the philosophy of Trust. Although only a brief interval separated the deaths of Henry Clay and Daniel Webster from that of Abraham Lincoln, those years transformed America's prevailing outlook. In the early 1850's most men called for pious Stewards who would let nothing distract their energies from preserving the national Union. Ten years later, the clamor was for a stewardship of restoration so that the nation might at last incorporate important values or principles. This development required both a new generation of spokesmen and a modified ideology for the national Trust. Stewardship exchanged a labor of preservation for one of restoration.

III: Advocates   A spokesman whose career and outlook fostered new thinking was George William Curtis. As a man of public affairs and as a commentator upon those affairs, Curtis was a prophet for the stewardship emerging after 1850. He dedicated himself to strengthening public awareness of America's meaning. Curtis had missed the climax to the era of search, for he had traveled in Europe between 1846 and

1850. On his return Curtis broke sharply with Webster's doctrine that nationhood was all-sufficing. Curtis established his
extraordinary influence through lectures, waiting until 1863 to
become associated with the Harper publishers.

An influential lecture Curtis gave at Wesleyan University in
1856 helped to shift ideology in this era. He insisted that zeal,
not awestruck fidelity, was the proper attribute of Americanism.
The fanatics and agitators condemned by the Clay-Webster philosophy thus became champions of principles whose universal
career, they said, was entrusted to American energy. Curtis called
openly for what men like Emerson and Parkman thought about,
new leaders who would minister to the national mind rather
than its body. "While other men pursue what is expedient and
watch with alarm the flickering of the funds," said Curtis with
open scorn for the traditional stewardship, the new national
guardian "is to pursue the truth and watch the eternal law of
justice." The following year, at Union College, Curtis refined
this argument in what became a major statement in the ideology
of American nationality.

The Union College address, called "Patriotism," predicted
that America could triumph over evil as David did over Goliath,
but only by clinging to "the great ideas out of which America
sprang": religious and civil liberty, to which America's Trust
was bound. Stewardship was "a battle, and the victory is to those
who fight with faith and undespairing devotion." Curtis talked
of a long and exhausting national venture. Men still lied,
cheated, and stole, Curtis acknowledged. Two developments
were necessary. The citizen had to see how important his own
action was to national well-being, and he had to recognize that
a nation "is a principle: and patriotism is loyalty to that principle." For too long, said Curtis, "poetic minds" and "popular
enthusiasm" alike had seen nationality as "associated with the
soil and the symbols of the country." This was wrong. Nationality is "the love of liberty." Whosoever opposed man's freedom
was "anti-American."

Here Curtis approached a brink, horrifying many elder advocates. "If we believe that our country embodies any principle,
that it is peopled for another purpose than the early Spaniards
peopled it, and that as moral agents and self-respecting men we
have something to do in America besides turning the air and

water and earth into wealth, we shall need to cling to no principle so strongly as this, that no possible law can bind us to do a moral wrong." In this statement, Curtis proclaimed a Trust which many Americans had come to dread, moral agency. America "cannot be fulfilled," Curtis stressed repeatedly, "without that sovereign moral sense, without a sensitive national conscience." Aware of the familiar hazards which vexed even the Fathers, Curtis denounced mammon in particular. It "tends to make us all cowards."

Finally Curtis offered hope, hope that the same force which had preserved the continent for the American endeavor would introduce a rising moral earnestness to make "the glooms of its morning the glory of its prime." It was a theme Curtis repeated throughout the nation. Meanwhile, the idolaters of Union fought the doctrine of moral agency, even at Fort Sumter. Converts like Abraham Lincoln were forced to proceed prudently. But when war came, Curtis made the ultimate assertion. America was a principle whose nationhood was only secondary. He argued that the vital moral doctrine, liberty, would survive in individual hearts, even should the polity fade. For Curtis, American history had been "the story of a systematic endeavor to debauch the national conscience and destroy the American idea." With this explanation Stewards prepared for a renewed venture. As Curtis said: "We have forgotten, and God is entering into judgment."

The outlook Curtis represented was merciless. "Our very life was liberty, and we denied it. Like Belshazzar, the nation sat feasting . . . its eyes were dazzled." Citizens had not seen that America was entrusted with the spirit as well as the form of free government. By 1864 Curtis spoke encouragingly. America seemed to be arising morally, putting behind it a youth of "doubt, and darkness and despair." He announced that "the golden gates of the future are about to open" and reveal the true nation, and with it a citizenry devoted to principle. However, the past which advocates, including Curtis, berated was the joy of all presidents in this era except one. It was appropriate for Curtis to be chosen to prepare the letter notifying Abraham Lincoln of his 1864 nomination by the National Union Convention. It seemed as if the prophet was anointing the leader who embodied the new stewardship.[17]

7

Not until the end of the period did presidential utterance affirm
the new doctrine of stewardship. Even Lincoln's views on the
capacity of man remained ambiguous. There was, however, nothing equivocal about Lincoln's predecessors in office. Their outlook, best stated by Franklin Pierce, steadfastly reiterated that
fidelity, preservation, and self-surrender were cardinal require-
ments of stewardship. The Trust was essentially to perpetuate
Union. Zachary Taylor spoke of maintaining the government
"in its original purity" and of the need for gestures of conciliation. Sustenance for the desirable "enlarged patriotism" came
simply with knowing that time had been passing and America
had survived. Endurance was everything for Taylor. It would
confound "the predictions of evil prophets" whose foretellings
of national demise "are now remembered only to be derided."

Millard Fillmore, who made the 1850 compromise possible,
exemplified the preservationist type. He advocated national
loneliness, arguing that America's public and private morality
ought to arise from disregarding the affairs of neighbors and
nations. Sensing the Cuban issue's meaning, Fillmore announced
that America resisted involvement out of "a stern sense of international justice" and a "statesmanlike prudence." His goal was
"the permanent safety and interest of the country." According
to Fillmore, upheaval and change were freedom's enemies. Had
not American institutions existed well before the Revolution?
While personal development in a good society was admirable
and wholly American, Fillmore warned against social change,
noting that there were Americans who mistook "change for progress and the invasion of the rights of others for national prowess
and glory." Such zealots agitated against the "organic law" and
advocated "new and untried theories of human rights." These
threatened America's well-being. For Fillmore, the prime affirmation of American stewardship was: "Thus shall conservatism and
progress blend their harmonious action in preserving the form
and spirit of the Constitution."

Franklin Pierce took this doctrine to its extremity. He espoused national fulfillment through preserving the present. This
required stopping speculation, surrendering will, and embracing
faith in God and the Union. The Fathers were hailed not for what
they did, but for their "calm faith" in the nation's innate capac-

ity to carry out its mission. Their great virtue was that they were as practical as they were patriotic. Said Pierce: "They wasted no portion of their energies upon idle and delusive speculations."

Pierce's inaugural message was the ultimate call for a stewardship of preservation: "With the Union my best and dearest earthly hopes are entwined. Without it what are we individually or collectively? What becomes of the noblest field ever opened for the advancement of our race in religion, in government, in the arts, and in all that dignifies and adorns mankind?" After conceding man's vulnerability to passion and evil and his dependence for national fulfillment upon God, Pierce recalled the agony of 1850. "Let the period be remembered as an admonition, and not as an encouragement . . . to make experiments where experiments are fraught with such fearful hazard." Americans must walk with the shades of Mount Vernon and Monticello whose voices could join with Providence in helping the present generation "preserve the blessings they have inherited."

Pierce devoted his later messages to urging that all Stewards believe in national institutions and avoid all internal dissension, intemperate desires, and enthusiasms. In short, fidelity guaranteed progress. Cognizance that America was "the greatest and most noble trust ever committed to the hands of man" required maintaining America's great constitutional doctrines. Even the Kansas upheaval left President Pierce unmoved, for "the storm of frenzy and faction must inevitably dash itself in vain against the unshaken rock of the Constitution." American unity was stronger than "all the wild and chimerical schemes of social change which are generated one after another in the unstable minds of visionary sophists and interested agitators."

By December 1856, Pierce dismissed the nation's "restless spirit" by announcing that America had entered fulfillment, had hardened into maturity, and was now "the great Republic of the world." The Trust had been delivered safely, so that "to us of this generation" there remained the "not less noble task" of maintaining the nation's position. More lively spokesmen than James Buchanan would have had difficulty following the jubilant Pierce. Yet Buchanan talked with a more fatalistic optimism than even Pierce had managed. "We have enjoyed the special protection of Divine Providence ever since our origin as a nation." Heavy danger had often beset the nation. Always "the

impending cloud has been dissipated" and the national danger
"passed away." For Buchanan there was a moral: "May we ever
be under the divine guidance and protection." He rejected John
Brown's adventure as implying any "incurable disease in the
public mind." Love of Union and time's comfort could sustain
the Trust. Ignoring the awkward withdrawal of the Almighty
in December 1860, Buchanan turned to the minds of citizens.
Preservation through conciliation alone would sustain the
Trust.[18]

Abraham Lincoln did not tarry long in such hapless mysticism.
He sought to confess national error and to advocate renewed
stewardship. This required a new philosophy, one which George
William Curtis had advanced. Through atonement, America
might still come to embody dynamic principles and values. The
war was construed as both a sign of God's long-overdue wrath
and of divine cleansing. Lincoln moved cautiously to this position. His First Inaugural Address made prudent obeisance to
national perpetuity before it faced the critical issue, the mood
and motive of the Stewards. In days ahead, these alone would
show whether God was continuing to be with America. The nation itself would recover if Stewards reclaimed "virtue and vigilance."

Beyond these hints at human agency Lincoln did not go, resting content with the message's magnificent close: "Though
passion may have strained, it must not break our bonds of affection. The mystic chords of memory, stretching from every battlefield and patriot grave, will yet swell the chorus of the Union,
when again touched, as surely they will be, by the better angels
of our nature." How long man's evil had disrupted the nation
Lincoln did not say, nor did he choose to describe the forthcoming righteousness. Lincoln was also vague in a speech he
made a few months later. Nationality arose from "the patriotic
instinct of plain people" who knew that America's fulfillment
was the only hope for "the whole family of man." Thus, he
called for a day of national humiliation, saying that "it is peculiarly fit for us to recognize the hand of God in this terrible
visitation, and in sorrowful remembrance of our own faults
and crimes as a nation and as individuals to humble ourselves
before Him and to pray for His mercy."

Not until his second annual message did Lincoln move significantly toward a stewardship of atonement. Nature had granted Americans a wonderful home, a marvelous Vineyard for their labors. It was the people therefore who had caused the national shortcoming. Most guilty was the present generation. Yet the same generation could also bring America to fulfillment, said Lincoln. This required a fresh outlook, for "as our case is new, so must we think anew and act anew. We must disenthrall ourselves, and thus we shall save our country." The present band of citizens could not "escape history," observed the President. "We shall nobly save or meanly lose the last best hope of earth."

The year 1863 was important for ideological as well as for military reasons. Lincoln began discussing national guilt and the implications of expiation. He advised further humiliation and fasting, stressing the importance of beseeching the Almighty for pardon. No nation could thrive unless God was dominant there. This was proven both by Holy Scripture and by all of history. Said Lincoln, the awful war was clearly "a punishment inflicted upon us for our presumptuous sins, to the needful end of our national reformation as a whole people." America's physical progress had been great indeed, but the nation had "forgotten God." It was He, not any "superior wisdom or virtue of our own," that had let the nation prosper. Lincoln rebuked America for having been intoxicated and deceived by material process. Men had ignored "our national perverseness and disobedience."

At the dedication of the Gettysburg Cemetery, Lincoln finally chose to talk of things beyond failure and retribution. In the greatest of American speeches, he quietly accepted a new outlook for nationality. In words so terse as to belie their enormous importance, Lincoln recalled the American Trust as the nurture of two vital principles, freedom and equality. For these the Fathers had established a nation. Men had died in a sublime act of service for this Trust, and with this sacrifice the Trust had been reborn. All men, Lincoln said, were to take renewed responsibility for liberty. Lincoln thus acknowledged that "the nation is beginning a new life." It was a life totally indebted to the soldier, who had made "the home of freedom disenthralled, regenerated, enlarged, and perpetuated." New Stewards must never forget this ghastly chastisement. Said Lincoln: "Human-nature will not change. In any future great national trial, compared with the men of this, we shall have as weak and as strong; as silly and as wise; as bad and good. Let us, therefore, study the incidents of this, as philosophy to learn wisdom from, and none of them as wrongs to be revenged." A nation's atonement, Lincoln knew, simply carried enlarged responsibilities. American fulfillment still depended on this Trust's discharge.[19]

<h1 style="text-align:center">8</h1>

Lincoln became the great figure for American national awareness in the remaining part of the nineteenth century. He had both a contributory and representational role. However, other personalities made important appearances as spokesmen amid a changing concept of nationality. Lingering from the ages of survival and search were Henry Clay and Daniel Webster. Joining Lincoln in the new outlook were such spokesmen as James Russell Lowell and Henry Ward Beecher. Caught uneasily in this ideological tumult were men including George Templeton Strong, William H. Seward, and Ralph Waldo Emerson. In their utterances, these men showed how broad was the range of concern over America's uncertain effort. Equally broad was the concern expressed in the statements of America's leading journals. Both men and magazines found it difficult to assume a posture of atonement. Although few Stewards had ever claimed great assurance, most had taken comfort in a corporate, organic progress. With the latter now weakened, America faced painful questions about what was to be restored that Stewards had not preserved.

Together Clay and Webster continued advocating human surrender to the polity's stately march. Preservation was the ultimate good for which all men ought eagerly to labor without regard to personal or ideological matters. Union's perpetuation was glorified. These two spokesmen appeared content to remind the Stewards of their duty. Duty became more important as Clay and Webster, born in the eighteenth century, saw a new generation's rebelliousness. Both men, so long spokesmen for a rising America, died imploring that citizens lose themselves in the nation. Webster was forced to a totalitarian philosophy. His pleas that national tranquility was the good before which every individual should bow served as scripture for the presidential voice during the 1850's. It was against this concept of nationality that men like George Curtis dared to speak.

Webster had become a desperate man, one who had known

the Fathers and now beheld their legacy imperiled. Preservation of the polity constructed by wholly admirable men seemed to Webster the obvious responsibility for Americans of all time. Both society and the individual fared best in a state of such perpetual reverence. In his Seventh of March speech in 1850, Webster refused to take seriously the talk of Union's dismemberment. But he was alarmed at the presence among the Stewards of the enthusiast, the fanatic, and the sectionalist. Men must take higher ground, adopt an elevated view worthy of the lofty Trust. As for Webster's ideas about the nation itself, he persisted in seeing beyond the Constitution a vague character born of transcendent physical fact.

Webster's advocacy was most succinct and successful in an exchange of public letters with some Bostonians. In praising Webster, they described the contemporary scene as one "when the minds of men have been bewildered by an apparent conflict of duties, and when multitudes have been unable to find solid ground on which to rest with security and peace." In such an hour, Webster had "pointed out to a whole people the path of duty . . . and touched the conscience of a nation." "Duty," "security," "peace," these were words dear to Websterian nationalism, and used with dexterity. Webster's reply to the Boston statement reiterated the importance of Unity. Stewardship must foster a feeling of association, or as Webster put it, "of conciliation and regard . . . those pure fountains of mutual esteem, common patriotism, and fraternal confidence."

At the laying of a cornerstone for the Capitol addition in 1851, Webster admitted that Americans might "betray our sacred trust." For him the critical issue now was whether national well-being could be fully grasped by the Stewards. "The question is, whether we have the true patriotism, the Americanism, necessary to carry us through such a trial." Webster had earlier put the answer to this in another rhetorical inquiry: "What is the individual man, with all the good or evil that may betide him, in comparison with the good or evil which may befall a great country . . . ?" In occasional appearances as secretary of state before his death, Webster elaborated on this corporate nature of mankind. He assailed "misguided men" and pleaded for educating youthful Americans to be properly respectful of the "mighty" achievement of the Founders. His letter to the Austrian chargé d'affaires in December 1850 was designed "to touch the national pride" and to make those improperly dedicated to the nation "feel sheepish and look silly."

Webster was obviously bothered by the gap between himself and "the rising generation." The latter's rebelliousness seemed a dangerous lack of patriotism. Only rarely in his final days did Webster talk of the Trust itself, and when he did it was in terms of a showpiece for republican operation. "Our business is to make proselytes by our example." He assailed without stint "faction and fanaticism." Let "evils" prevailing in parts of the nation be consigned "to the all-wise direction of an overruling Providence." The proper Steward would be concerned only with "those duties which are present, plain, and positive." Thus, "let us stand where our fathers stood."

At his life's end Webster said that social organization could reach perfection but that man's nature was doomed to weakness. If only a divinely created polity would prove unshakable, the implication for America was clear. Well-being depended upon the perpetuation of the Founders' system. Webster's final admonition preached "the Christian religion," "the fear of God," maintenance of "just moral sentiments," reverence for "duty as shall control the heart and life," and above all the preservation of the national polity. With these, America "will have no decline and fall." But if such religion and authority were challenged, catastrophe would "bury all our glory in profound obscurity." Webster's last significant public statement urged "that spirit of union, of nationalism, of Americanism" which came only from following the Fathers' precepts. "I have listened to them as to oracles, teaching me as a young man, the proper performance of my duties." Thus, in eulogizing Webster, Rufus Choate quite properly inferred from the dead voice that the establishment and preservation of the nation was the highest good. Between it and such lesser goods as the curtailment of slavery, the choice for Websterians was easy. The nation had to be maintained if America was to advance "the dearest interests of man, through generations countless." [20]

Shortly before Webster's death, Henry Clay died. The beloved Kentuckian shared the outlook of his old associate from Massachusetts. Clay contended that the burden of America's Trust required surrender of glib notions about individualism. Concern for self must fall before Providence, God, the Fathers, and the American cause. Human existence itself was simply a compromise between life and death, leaving government and society necessarily founded on "the principle of mutual concession, politeness, comity, courtesy. . . ." For Clay, "compromise is peculiarly appropriate among the members of a republic, as of one common family." All who share human nature must live by compromise. Early in 1850 Clay announced that the American character preferred calm and adjudication. "I know something, I think, of the nature of man. I know something of the nature of my own countrymen." In the Stewards, said Clay, there was so strong a yearning to toil for the nation without controversy that, once the current unrest were calmed, the few people who still agitated would be repudiated.

So great was this devotion to national harmony that Clay argued few men really cared about the content of the compromise so long as it brought peace. Prayer for "some healing measure" was everywhere. In his splendid 1850 statements, Clay displayed his astonishing eloquence. "The nation wants repose. It pants for repose, and entreats you to give it peace and tranquility." Clay seemed to accept Webster's totalitarian view. Let men become selfless, yield to compromise, and thus to the fulfillment of God's hope for the nation.

Clay took hope from a good Steward's intuitive awareness that national being was more important than separate being. This brought his chief point: "What is an individual man? An atom . . . a mere speck . . . a drop of water . . . a grain of sand. . . . Shall a being so small, so petty, so fleeting, so evanescent, oppose himself to the onward march of a great nation, to subsist for ages and ages to come—oppose itself to that long line of posterity which . . . will endure during the existence of the world?" Let Americans recognize how little it mattered "if, in the march of this nation to greatness and power, we should be buried beneath the wheels that propel it onward." Again the blunt question: "What are we—what is any man worth who is not ready and willing to sacrifice himself for the benefit of his country when it is necessary?"

Gravely ill by 1851, Clay spent his final moments in the Senate praising a glorious word, "Nationality!" He urged men to unite under its spirit and join in "breaking the miserable trammels of party." A few years later, Stephen A. Douglas would remind the nation: "Clay, to the last, stood forth as the embodiment of Union principles, Union measures, conservative views, which would keep united, as bands of brothers, all the states of this Union, and make the Republic perpetual." Even though he was speaking in 1859 as one who had served the Clay and Webster cause in 1850, Douglas was discovering the limits of America's yearning for repose. Many citizens were insisting that Union had to represent more than unity and that the American Trust implied more than a demonstration of republican perpetuity. Douglas himself was a prime target of those who had become disenchanted when the doctrine of harmony brought destruction of moral monuments like the Missouri agreement.[21]

The strain and confusion about national purpose and citizen responsibility were represented in the outlook of three very different spokesmen in this era. George Templeton Strong, man of affairs in New York City, William H. Seward, aspirant to national political leadership, and Ralph Waldo Emerson, the nation's philosopher laureate variously displayed the difficulty thoughtful Americans encountered with their nationality. Strong saluted the new decade by commenting in 1850 that "words cannot express the destitution and nakedness moral and mental" which seemed to beset the minds of so many Americans. He watched the time's rising excitement with misgiving. Noting that "people will do foolish things when they're in a passion," Strong wished for the moment when men might cherish law above personal values. At the end of the decade Strong announced: "It's a sick nation, and I fear it must be worse before it's better." He confessed in 1861: "'We the People' are disgraced and degraded in the eyes of all Christendom by the events and by the disclosures of the last three months. If these be legitimate fruits of democracy 'after its kind,' Heaven preserve and strengthen all despots."

Strong wanted to believe that the nation's republican design was not itself to blame, but rather that the "national ulcer" of slavery had caused the "national infamy." It was slavery "which blunts the moral sense," observed Strong. He went through the war deeply pessimistic over America's capacity to survive its spiritual crisis. In 1862 Strong said, "We are in the depths just now, permeated by disgust, saturated with gloomy thinking. I find it hard to maintain my lively faith in the triumph of the nation and the law." Even late in the summer of 1864 he was still fearful that the public's behavior meant that the "great experiment of democracy may be destined to fail a century sooner than I expected in disastrous explosion and general chaos." Thus would "our grand republic over which we have bragged so offensively" be cast "as a great milestone into the sea and perish utterly." [22]

Such a prospect was more than William H. Seward could discuss. The New York senator was an unsteady advocate who veered from the Websterian doctrine of preservation to cautious concession that America had a moral purpose. Seward's erratic course represented a wide uncertainty as Americans discovered their search for national meaning had led them into a quandary. In 1848 Seward said: "The first principle of our duty as American citizens is to preserve the integrity of the Union." However, he soon mentioned other duties, which included sustaining democracy, spreading knowledge, expanding physical resources, and ending slavery. In pursuing their responsibility, Americans were impelled by a law above any parchment. Seward began describing the nation as a mystical being unlimited by the constitutional design so treasured by the Websterians. The New York senator was especially fond of reminding Americans that they were the Creator's "stewards" whose "trust" was the enhancement of mankind's happiness. In speech after speech early in the 1850's, Seward told the glorious story of how America had begun nationhood as an "ingenious theory" but that now it towered "in absolute integrity." Once a frail thing, "the republican system is in complete and triumphant development."

However, by 1860 Seward had retreated. He began to stress the emergence of natural impulses which would make one people of all Americans, transcending section and especially "party malice or party ambition." Denying the possibility of secession, Seward insisted that the "wisdom and virtue," the "coolness, calmness, and resolution" of the American people would preserve the nation. But now, while Union was the body of the nation, liberty was its soul. Mature Stewards knew that America had "not yet accomplished what good for mankind" the Creator expected. With this sacred Trust yet to be discharged, the nation might for a time falter and be "cast down." After a cleansing experience Seward predicted that America would "rise again and reappear in all its majestic proportions tomorrow." [23]

Midway between the studied cheerfulness of Seward and the private despond of Strong was Ralph Waldo Emerson's viewpoint. The Concord sage was angry after the 1850 settlement had sacrificed principle, which meant that "nothing seems to me more bitterly futile than this bluster about the Union." For Emerson 1850 had destroyed hope of American fulfillment, leaving the Stewards to "sneak about with the infamy of crime in the streets and cowardice in ourselves." America's presence and purpose had been such as to bestow self-respect on all citizens, but now "conscience and religion" had become "bitter ironies." Worst of all, liberty had been made a "ghastly nothing" by Mr. Webster. The events of 1854 brought Emerson's announcement: "Our politics are bad, past all belief," but there seemed some hope that a healthy recoil would arise from the latest "outrage." Despite the fact that the nation stood "disgraced," every protest was desirable. An awakened stewardship was America's hope, and by 1855 Emerson sensed that a new devotion to freedom was rising. He called for good men to join to save "poor, betrayed, imbruted America, infested by rogues & hypocrites." Let men speak the "plain truth" about the national plight, and "thus we acquit ourselves."

For Emerson, especially, the Civil War had a saving quality. "The shame of living seems taken away," and a sense of purpose could return to America. The war was "immensely better than what we lately called the integrity of the Republic," said Emerson. He demolished the doctrine of preservation by noting simply that "amputation is better than cancer." If the Stewards could keep "a fair share of light and conscience, we shall redeem America for all its sinful years since the century began." Emerson agreed that the Trust had been betrayed by past leaders. Now, the "good heart & mind, out of all private corners, should speak & save." By 1864 Emerson was convinced the "nation shall be a nation." He predicted to Charles Sumner a great age of stewardship. With a regenerate America, "great expansion of thought and moral and practical activity is likely to follow." [24]

Men like Strong, Seward, and Emerson moved hesitantly as America's appreciation of national condition and purpose changed. The old uncertainty about both the capacity of the nation and the individual Steward lingered. Such misgiving was assailed by advocates predicting triumph from a national campaign for right. Especially ardent believers in atonement and regeneration were James Russell Lowell, rising as America's major man of letters, and Henry Ward Beecher, the Republic's most widely followed clergyman. Also, the earnest views of Abraham Lincoln during the 1850's should be recalled.

After 1848, Lowell was urging America to stand for universal principles. Nationality was a pilgrimage of righteousness, and Lowell expected the agony of the fifties to bring an elevated quality to the Republic. He attacked compromise, shuddered over the loathsome demagoguery so often evident, and reminded Stewards that for fifty years America had surrendered to expedience. Lowell considered America's shortcomings to be especially enormous since the nation was willingly defrauded by cheap words. To views like Lowell's war brought an emancipation of opinion and an awakening of principle in America. Men were freed to cleave to morality, as Lowell had pleaded. America's descent into moral indifference was like "the last wretched convulsion before absolute dissolution."

Lowell kept hoping there was purpose in America's disgrace, "that it will somehow be turned to good and that out of this fermenting compost heap of all filthy materials a fine plant of Freedom is to grow. But when?" He took comfort in blaming the nation's past leadership, deemed no better than "a clique of gamblers." They had applied the absurd "glue of compromise," a quack remedy never attaining advertised quality. Such leadership had used the nation's Trust as "a lying phrase to sweeten the foul breath of demagogues." These interpretations no longer sustained Lowell by 1860. "We have been running long enough by dead reckoning . . . it is time to take the height of the sun of righteousness."

For Lowell the 1860 crisis would prove whether American democracy had made "all our public men cowards" or whether some might "learn a little self-confidence from despair." He was sure that to surrender again to the expedient would mean an end "to the experiment of democracy." Lowell yearned for a "great leader" who might, by proclaiming honest principle, "crystallize this chaos into order." Accepting war as a transition for the nation's moral development, Lowell urged the opportune movement. No longer could patriotism evade reality, remaining "a pleasant sentiment" and "a feeble reminiscence" with no "direct bearing on the national well-being." As early as 1861, Lowell bade farewell to "the peddlers of chicane." He said the war "has already won for us a blessing worth everything," the emancipation of public opinion.

In 1864, Lowell announced principle had captured the Republic. Men had escaped being "incapable of lofty sentiment, ready to satisfy everything for commercial advantage." Great moral truths had become America's essence. This fulfillment "will hasten incalculably the progress of equalization over the whole earth." By becoming truly absorbed with "Freedom," America was "a nation alive from sea to sea with the consciousness of a great purpose and a noble destiny." Lowell gladly renounced his earlier doubts about human capacity. Moral victory was due "to the virtue and intelligence of the people" who now sensed "how much dearer greatness is than mere power."

Lowell did much to make the doctrine of regeneration popular. He liked to say that once "America lay asleep, like the princess of the fairy tale, enchanted by prosperity; but at the first fiery kiss of war the spell is broken." As stewardship became an active, meaningful endeavor, "Nationality is no dead abstraction, no unreal sentiment, but a living and operating virtue in the heart and moral nature of man. It enlivens the dullest soul with an ideal out of and beyond itself, lifting every faculty to a higher level of vision and action." This new dynamism freed Americans from selfishness. Life now had "a deeper meaning." "Country" was no longer an abstraction, but had become "a living presence," so that every man could feel himself "a part, sensitive and sympathetic, of this vast organism, a partner in its life or death."

Even so, Lowell was conscious of future obligations, for the real testing of principle and patriotism had only begun. The difference was that now "an abiding faith" in the Stewards was feasible, as they undertook once more "the experiment of democracy," this time "in its fullest extent and not halfway." Lincoln's death was the ultimate wrench in separating the nation from its past. It guaranteed for Lowell the "purifying" of national spirit. Having made atonement, the nation was prepared in Lowell's judgment to advance the cause of principle.[25]

Another apostle of regeneration was Henry Ward Beecher. On

both sides of the Atlantic during the war he denounced America's faithlessness to freedom. "Liberty with us must be raised by religion from the selfishness of an instinct to the sanctity of a moral principle!" As a major advocate for the doctrine of restoration, Beecher preceded Lincoln in proclaiming the guilt of an entire nation. The previous generation, the Websterian age, had seen stewardship devoured by ambition. What the nation needed was a dynamic pursuit of "divine truths," not a passive reverence for order. Insisting "the whole of life must be woven to the heavenly pattern of liberty," Beecher prayed for a new spirit in the land, "that at length we may be an evangelized and Christian people."

Calling for resurrection of liberty "from the graves of our fathers," Beecher gave thanks that God "has begun to recall this nation from a course that would have wrought utter destruction." The new path was the familiar one which Lowell and Curtis had been indicating. It led to the universal principles of justice and liberty and skirted pride, vainglory, and selfishness. Of course Beecher used the supernatural more than did Lowell or Curtis. He said God "has appointed this people and our day for one of those world-battles on which ages turn. Ours is a pivotal period. The strife is between a dead past and a living future." Beecher condemned America's past leadership, which produced "great sins unrepented of." "The whole nation is guilty," especially in sinning against liberty.

Beecher predicted in 1861 that "ere long God will appear and be the leader and captain of our salvation and we shall have given back to us this whole land, healed, restored to its right mind, and sitting at the feet of Jesus." As the war advanced, Beecher found one sin accountable for the national lapse. "Slavery is the abominable poison that has circulated in the body politic and corrupted this whole nation almost past healing." The soldiers went forth in a "sacred mission" which personal weakness had kept Webster and his generation from fulfilling. Here Beecher asserted that slavery was only a symptom of the real problem America faced. The enemy was the human heart. "What is slavery," asked Beecher, "but one way in which lust and avarice and ambition and indolence have sought to enthrone themselves?" Somehow since 1860 God had been rallying enough good men to fight the vipers. Through God would come victory. It would be a triumph for man's freedom, entrusted to America.

Increasingly Beecher talked of God's expectation that America develop human capacity in a free setting. It had thus far been a tragic enterprise. Despite the early republican ideals, "we have steadily marched in the opposite direction." After a trip to England in 1863, Beecher was even more emphatic about a renewed Trust. "This is not our own struggle, it is the world's battle we are fighting. . . . we are struggling for the rights of the common people, but not of this country only." By 1865 he saw some measure of success. The day before Lincoln was murdered, Beecher proclaimed: "This nation has attained its manhood." The four years of war had brought the moral fulfillment which the previous half-century had thwarted. "Our nation has suffered and now is strong." [26]

These contrasting calls for national reconsecration surrounded the development of a long-obscure Illinois politician. The changing quality of nationalist ideology is reflected in Abraham Lincoln's outlook before his presidency. In 1852 Lincoln eulogized Henry Clay as a man sent by Providence to ensure the nation's well-being. With Clay gone, Americans must make renewed effort to please divine Providence. If successful, America could expect that "in future national emergencies, He will not fail to provide us the instruments of safety and security." Two years later, an emergency began that would not cease. After the Kansas-Nebraska legislation, Lincoln and others had to seek a revision of the national faith which could no longer remain simply the Clay spirit of "concession and compromise" or "the national feeling of brotherhood." Lincoln led in taking a step beyond. "Our republican robe is soiled, and trailed in the dust. Let us repurify it. Let us turn and wash it white, in the spirit, if not the blood of the Revolution." By 1855 he said the nation was morally remiss. "On the operation of liberty, as a principle, we are not what we have been." The once ardent pursuit of freedom had been abandoned by the nation "now that we have grown fat, and lost all dread of being slaves ourselves."

Thereafter, Lincoln advocated restoring the values which had animated the Fathers. "Our progress in degeneracy," he wrote in 1855, "appears to me to be pretty rapid." It was a falling away from the truth of human liberty and equality. To forsake this principle would lose the real explanation of national existence and past achievement. By the time his debates with Stephen

A. Douglas had begun, late in the summer of 1858, Lincoln had rejected the Websterian dogma of America as a matter of existence and growth.

Douglas, however, stood fast. "I tell you," he said at Freeport, "increase and multiply, and expand, is the law of this nation's existence." For such a view the only national precept was local determination. Douglas came directly to the point in a speech at Jonesboro. "If we wish to preserve our institutions in their purity, and transmit them unimpaired to our latest posterity, we must preserve with religious good faith that great principle of self-government which guarantees to each and every State, old and new, the right to make just such constitutions as they deserve." A month later at Quincy, Douglas returned to the theme of preservation. Through cherished localism "we can go on as we have done, increasing in wealth, in population, in power, and in all the elements of greatness, until we shall be the admiration and terror of the world." Claiming growth was America's calling, Douglas spoke of it as "this great mission." It dictated "adhering faithfully to that principle of self-government on which our institutions were all established."

The Lincoln-Douglas debates showed how divergent America's concepts of selfhood were becoming. Faced with Douglas' orthodoxy, Lincoln drew for the nation the distinction between cherished localism and the more fundamental *"love of liberty* which God has planted in our bosoms." If this were lost, "you have planted the seeds of despotism around your own doors." Should the evil of the Dred Scott decision be accepted in America, the nation's "genius" would flee. The Stewards would become "the fit subjects of the first cunning tyrant who rises." As the exchange progressed, Lincoln pressed right and wrong as fundamental national concerns. On this continent the common right of humanity must rally against the divine right of kings. For Lincoln, America's purpose was to lead for good against evil in an engagement proceeding "from the beginning of time."

Lincoln's advocacy of moral stewardship was nationally advanced in a widely circulated letter he sent to some Boston citizens in April 1859. Regretting that he could not attend a festival honoring Jefferson's birthday, Lincoln saluted the occasion since "it is now no child's play to save the principles of Jefferson from total overthrow in this nation." These precepts were the defini-

tions and axioms universal for a free society. "Those who deny
freedom to others, deserve it not for themselves; and, under a
just God, can not long retain it." Lincoln hailed Jefferson who,
"in heated times," stood by "abstract truth." Let this same truth
be a rebuke and barrier to "the very harbingers of reappearing
tyranny and oppression." However, the most revealing observation Lincoln made on a new national purpose was a fragment
left among his pre-inaugural papers. In it, he emphatically denied
the Webster-Douglas doctrine that the nation's purpose and
achievement rested in the constitutional Union. The vital element was liberty which must fully claim the human heart. This
treasured precept "clears the *path* for all—gives *hope* to all—and,
by consequence, *enterprize,* and *industry* to all."

As he neared the presidency, Lincoln embellished his advocacy
of principle with graceful professions of faith in man's capacity
to meet the moral requisite. With both shrewd logic and strategy,
the President-elect assured his fellow Stewards that they did have
"composure," "sober convictions of right," and "fraternal feeling," all adequate to restore the nation to its "bright and glorious
future." Principle, combined with patience and restraint, Lincoln informed the New York legislature, would be enough for
the Almighty to bring "this great and intelligent people" to its
fulfillment. But war did come, and Lincoln joined Lowell and
Beecher in proclaiming a nation's sinfulness and the prospect of
atonement through suffering. From civil conflict must stem new
dedication to the truths of the Founders, so long eclipsed by
greed and passion. Then would the sacred Trust be once more
in worthy hands.[27]

9

The transition in nationality evident in Lincoln's outlook was
also apparent among America's significant journals. These magazines became increasingly important advocates of national belief,
worthy companions to spokesmen like Clay, Curtis, and Lincoln.
Perhaps appropriately, the call for a becalmed preservation came
from certain venerable organs which soon vanished. Both the
Democratic and Whig periodicals died shouting Websterian
nationality. Hunt's *Merchant's Magazine* and *Knickerbocker* lived
into the war, each expiring as Copperhead exponents of process
and preservation. Continuing to attack the frailty of human

nature were *Ladies' Repository* and *Country Gentleman*. The latter abandoned commentary on public affairs in 1855, but the Cincinnati women's journal carried on through the war, explaining how man's feebleness affected the national struggle. Advocating old truths restored and a war's atonement were the two Harper journals, along with *Atlantic Monthly* and *North American Review*. These spokesmen, except for *Atlantic*, seemed cautious in urging a nation-wide audience to change its view.

All of these journals used the familiar elements of national doctrine, including stress upon lofty responsibility, citizen stewardship, and the hazards raised by human frailty. All hesitated to predict American fulfillment. The magazines bearing the Whig and Democratic party names were enchanted by the course of events. Like their party masters, the career of these journals showed how the preservation doctrine could not satisfy a new society. Pages of *Democratic Review* testify to the plight of those who suggested accepting things as they were. Briefly in 1849 and 1850, this magazine hinted that human endeavor might affect the uncertain outcome of America's venture. For now no one knew whether the outcome "will be one to make beholding angels weep, or one to give them joy." This reflected the state of moral principle in the United States. As one contributor said, "If we allow bad men to gain the ascendancy, our national existence may become almost a calamity." Another writer urged that America drop its "habit of self-laudation."

By 1850, however, this mild realism gave way to Websterian doctrine. *Democratic Review* readers heard that development of the nation was like a mighty "wheel of progress," or like the Mississippi River. Rebukes were heaped onto those who would "endanger the noble machinery of the Federal compact" merely "to brush away a speck of dust that clings to its band of wisdom-tempered steel." In short, the journal recommended "a firm faith in progress." The route might be "tedious, tortuous, perplexing, and disheartening," but Americans had to take things "as a promise of a better and brighter future."

After this acclaim for the comfort of process, *Democratic Review* quickly lost intellectual quality. It began publishing apologies for slavery, frequent declarations of racist doctrine, and regular praise for English leaders and traditions. Public disputation was called immoral since it would surely hamper America's pursuit of its "noble mission." Experience disclosed that "democratic principle" required peace at any price. Dissonance would bring American degradation and enfeeblement. Harmony promised glorious nationality. For partisans who felt awkward in this Whiggish pose, *Democratic Review* exhumed an 1839 address by the late Democrat, Silas Wright. This beloved party regular proclaimed national being as the ultimate good before which no other issue must stand. The Fathers had willingly tolerated slavery for the larger gain of nationhood. Said the sainted Wright: "Who that loves his country . . . will wantonly trample upon the faith?" To which he added: "If there be those among us, who, misled by a mistaken sympathy, or by a sudden excitement, are forgetting their obligations to the whole country . . . let us use every effort of persuasion and example to awaken them. . . ." With this preservationist scripture the Democrat journal condemned all trifling with the American state of being and becoming.

In 1852, *Democratic Review* entered its final agony through the "Young America" frenzy, a call for evangelical republicanism across the seas. To ignore this mission would be to heed the call of "a dead and indigent generation." The winter and spring issues of 1852 were influenced by George N. Saunders, who later embraced the Confederate cause. The "Great Republic" was told to abandon modest matters like education and literature for a foreign policy of world leadership. America's mistake had been to let men "run round in the circle of perpetual sameness and dullness afforded by domestic questions." America must turn to mankind, to the great needs of the age. Great men and their splendid principles were recalled from the nation's early days, but only so that such virtues could be put in their lofty world setting. Thus did *Democratic Review* seek to renew the old doctrines, but in a context far from embarrassing immediacy. Its proposal to destroy monarchy and bring constitutional freedom to darkest Europe was a safe version of America's Trust. However, the magazine's audience was shrinking. Too many Stewards were now concerned over unfulfilled duty nearer home. *Democratic Review* joined the demise of "Young America," and the death of the party was not far beyond.[28]

Whig Review suffered similarly. Between 1848 and 1852 it blended Websterian reverence for the nation as a monument with international bellicosity. This mixture was spiced with emphasis on human frailty and on the perils of freedom. Like the party it served, *Whig Review* discovered that a preservationist stance would no longer quiet the clamor over national purpose. Some temporary relief came from talk of Anglo-Saxon progress. America and England were said to lead in national vigor. They shared evenly the rich experiences of "centuries of change" guided by divine Providence. The *Whig's* contributors struggled manfully to present national development as far more than momentary excitement.

Consequently, *Whig Review* articles advised Stewards to respect overwhelming development. It was tragic how restlessness and deteriorating statesmanship threatened the cherished national institutions. The *Whig* recalled that the Fathers "had no part in this infatuation of the popular mind." Now man's susceptibility to clamor and wealth was terrifying. American fulfillment clearly decreed that the momentary vigor of the headstrong, the selfish, and especially the extremists must be exhausted. During its final months, *Whig Review* concentrated on the collapsing stewardship. The tragedy of America had come from self-deception. "Reality had been theory, and fiction the sole thing to be revered." One of the last *Whig* authors observed: "The world seems to have made very little way upon the road of happiness for a thousand years past." With this declaration of bankruptcy *Whig Review* disappeared in 1852.[29]

The popular *Knickerbocker* did its part for the philosophy of preservation. A featured article recalled the emergence of "distinctive nationality" in 1754, 1776, and 1787. Generations now rising should hearken to the Fathers' time, knowing then that "America mistook not the lurid glare of the meteor of revolution for the star of freedom." If only the Republic might cherish the wisdom and the deeds of those days. *Knick* employed patriotic poetry especially to preach veneration for institutions. "One mighty heart" was the goal of national endeavor. However, when the war came, *Knickerbocker* altered its course. It pronounced the struggle necessary to purify the national heart. Venerable foes, mammon and passion, were said to have captured America with "luxurious weakness, effeminacy, and corruption," so that only by "hardship and trial and desperate extremity" could redemption occur.

Knick predicted that an extraordinary good might come from national distress. "A new energy will prevail. The nation, purged of treason, its insulted majesty vindicated, will resume its grand march, chastened into a divine harmony of action." This was probably the last editorial by the remarkable man of letters, Lewis Gaylord Clark. His successor, Charles G. Leland, likened the war to man's greatest challenge. It was petty materialism that blinded the citizens, denying them "a stupendous, all-demanding faith" in the great purpose of the war for national cleansing and fulfillment. *Knick* continued to call for a confession of national sins, for destruction of "all old party prejudices," and for ending the mad dollar-hunting which led to "forgetting the Beautiful in mere Mammoned ostentation." America had fallen so low, argued Leland, that knaves had become deities and public expression sailed in sewers. No wonder there had come "a thunderstorm to clear the air."

By the end of 1861, *Knick* had found its theme. The nation had been humiliated by crassness and the power of demagogues. Citizens and leaders had failed to see that American circumstance had changed. Now let the Stewards push aside "the gangs and cliques of wretched old politicians, who . . . still utter untimely cowardice. . . . Away with them . . . we are entering upon new times . . . for which the old demagogues are utterly unfitted." This positive version of "Young America" was short-lived. In 1862, the *Knickerbocker* editorship changed again. Thereafter it opposed Lincoln and urged the nation's "conservatism" to restore the old principles. *Knick* revived the old Websterian pose, urging Stewards to shun "the impulses of passion" and to seek renewal through peace. War brought only "ruin, anarchy, and confusion."

The doctrines once advanced by Henry Clay were used in peace propaganda. A nation, said Kinahan Cornwallis, *Knick*'s editor, could not simply identify an evil and then destroy it. Life was more complex than that, especially in America. Despite slavery's sin, there were more important factors. "We are bound to act in accordance with the most reasonable prospect of the highest good to the greatest number." *Knick* said that the nation's values and laws were admirable. It was human collapse which had caused America to falter. Let honesty and faithfulness replace corruption and the Trust would again be safe. "The

American people must now awaken, arise, or be for ever fallen."
In its final days under John Holmes Agnew as *The American
Monthly*, the shadow of old *Knick* called the Lincoln philosophy of "national regeneration" through war a deception to subvert the true America. Until "the masses" were roused, "the
spirits of the fathers of the country hover around us; their
prayers are for us." Atonement thus meant undoing all that passion and mammon had achieved through Lincoln's evil agency.[30]

A fate similar to *Knickerbocker*'s came during the Civil War
to *Merchant's Magazine*. Freeman Hunt died in 1858, maintaining to the last an editorial policy dedicated to cautious
growth and high morality. Praise for transportation and brotherhood had filled the journal. Writing in 1852 on the "Moral
View of Railroads," Hunt emphasized that the good Steward
kept uppermost the broad national process. "So when men
build their steamships and their Railroads which are to unite
nations, and bind the ends of continents together, they may look
to their dividend as sharply as they please, but let them give
some thought to those higher purposes of civilization also, which
their enterprises subserve." Special mention was made of "the
good of the race." This meant that Americans must be mindful
that "the great process of human progress, which they are perhaps the unconscious instruments and agents of, is a greater
and better thing than the largest fortune of gold and silver ever
got together." Article after article in *Merchant's Magazine*
warned during the 1850's against man's susceptibility to greed.
At the same time the national drama was pictured as a great
plan which would, as one person said, finally give "the mental
manhood of the twentieth century" to America.

Hunt's journal seemed as eager to exchange the present for
the future as it was to lament the deterioration of the Stewards
for whom the future was a charge. Mammon once more was the
culprit, and the journal sadly admitted that "the leaven of decay
already begins to work." It was "making false the stout heart
of oak that nerved our patriot sires." The golden calf had replaced the Fathers' truths, which meant that despite its physical achievement, American greatness "will come to naught." By
1864, Hunt's successor, William B. Dunn, was announcing that
the wondrous national institutions created by Washington and
Franklin had been "well-nigh destroyed." The elements of na-

tional greatness, designed to be cherished in purity, had fallen before "intriguing, unscrupulous and selfish men." Small wonder, then, that true patriots were filled with "the fear of approaching national dissolution." [31]

Knickerbocker and *Merchant's Magazine* defended to the end the doctrine of preservation. For them strife was a malicious disrupter of the mysterious but intended working of institutions and affairs. It hampered man's surrender of himself, thus denying him opportunity to sustain national development in the only possible spirit and form. For this outlook, there was little comfort or promise of atonement in a war for special and immediate ends. It meant not a purified nationality, but a desecrated Trust. Much of the Copperhead philosophy was therefore a refinement of the old Websterian formula for national fulfillment.

Using many of the same assumptions, two other magazines came to quite different conclusions. For *Country Gentleman* and *Ladies' Repository* the national challenge was still its traditional foe, faltering humanity. *Ladies' Repository* remained consistent in this, thanks to its clergy-controlled editorial office. The editors assaulted the dynasties of unbelief and mammon. One contributor during the furor of 1855 described his thoughts on visiting General Jackson's tomb. "I could not but sigh that he did not give his heart to God years before." Tardiness of great Americans in acknowledging God had serious implication. "Jefferson, Jackson, Clay, and Webster, all professed to love and submit to Christ late in life. I would it had been different. If they had made their lives sublime like that of the peerless Washington, the nation would have been better."

Not only was leadership in America remiss, but *Ladies' Repository* supplied evidence of the citizen's fallen state. Somehow inspiration must gather momentum to reclaim Americans from "narrowness of soul" which was companion to "an avaricious selfishness." The American mind was becoming dwarfed by a pattern of life which stopped with materialism. Let the spirit soar, so that men could be roused "to be *doing* something for one's country which will go to make its future more glorious." Serious stewardship intended there "must be a daily *doing* as well as a daily *babbling* of patriotic devotion." The journal summarized the proper outlook: "Here is my country—what can I do for its dear sake?" It also supplied the answer, a renewal of stewardship that "will destroy the dynasty of mammon, confiscate the possessions of his mercenary courtiers, and establish the reign of the excellent—an aristocracy—the majestic rule of the good."

Ladies' Repository found this renewal in the war's impact, making it a national blessing. Not only would battle vindicate human rights, it would defeat demagoguery, correct national extravagance, bring greater respect for government, enlarge the American view of justice, and finally instigate a moral transformation. America's betrayal had been at the hands of men who infested government, seeking "to turn corruption to their own personal advantage." Indeed, "a godless crew" had now been overthrown, left to skulk behind the peace movement. These evildoers had once captured the nation because Americans had been drawn from spiritual things by prosperity. Now came the war, driving mammon and passion both from the national temple, "awakening us to a nobler, sterner manhood—giving us nobler passions, infusing into our natures grander energies, lifting us from the mire and rot of prosperity, deepening and intensifying our love of principle, of duty, of manliness, and of true glory."

In short, the view taken by *Ladies' Repository* was that the person most emancipated by the war was the American Steward. It was fitting, for America now dwelt "in a time when God's purposes are ripening fast." Needed was a mature national character. "Verily are we not on the eve of wonderful events?" asked the Reverend H. H. Howard, an editor. "Do we not already hear the instruments tuning on every hand for the eternal jubilee? Let us help." This apocalyptic view of the Civil War sought to reunite America and God, a partnership vital to universal fulfillment. With an awakened and wiser public conscience, the American Steward would pursue the sacred work before him, freed of the promptings of party, wild majoritarianism, and unholy compromises. From the war's tribulation had come a nation's "moral transformation." *Ladies' Repository* advised its readers to accept "the designs of the Almighty" and exult in the strife.[32]

Country Gentleman, published in Albany, generally shunned comment on public issues during the war. In the 1850's, how-

ever, it had campaigned for national reformation on a physio-
cratic basis. The need for America's regeneration was evident,
and "country life" was this journal's means. Conceding that
Stewards had sound instincts, *Country Gentleman* argued that
much of America was afflicted with a "vitiated appetite" to which
demagogues pandered. The instincts, apparently, needed environment and instruction if they were to emerge and function.
"The masses are pleased with barbarisms, because they have
never been taught to love anything higher and better," this magazine contended in 1853. Human nature never changed, and now
"the same amount of severe discipline is necessary to sound
culture that was requisite in earlier times." Let men see that virtue was embodied in hard work and perseverance. From such
would a heroic America reappear, despite wide evidence of current degeneracy and of treachery to republicanism.

As times worsened, *Country Gentleman* steadily maintained
that America was the victim of mammon. Because of the hurry
and bustle, the selfishness and grasping so common in the day,
men were distracted from meditations upon the importance of
principle. Freedom, virtue, and education must be restored to
an "uncorrupted" state. It was the "duty" of each citizen to
achieve this restoration, whereupon the long-awaited mature
national character would appear. The journal observed that,
ironically, America already knew what man's character should be,
for the Founders had exemplified it.

However, a change in personal inclination not only seemed
unlikely, but it appeared insufficient to the need. Something
more dramatic was necessary if American thought would take
seriously the prospect of national rejuvenation. Man had been
errant too long for any wide belief during the furious fifties in
the quaint idea that from individual adjustment would spring a
transformed America. Therefore, by the eve of civil war, *Country Gentleman* had retired from further admonishment on nationality. It left to others the proclamation that in war's fury,
the true national character would be reconstructed in time to
save the republican Trust. It was a remedy both immediate and
massive. *Country Gentleman*, like its title, had proven out of
date.[33]

Filling the gap were several magazines who joined spokesmen
such as Curtis, Lowell, Beecher, and Lincoln to advocate that

war would atone for the sins brought by mammon, passion, and party. In battle Americans should find their true selves, making warfare the major venture of American stewardship. Most prominent of these magazines were the Harper firm's weekly and monthly periodicals, and *Atlantic Monthly*. These used differing philosophical routes into the satisfactions of atonement. On the other hand, venerable *North American Review* was properly cautious, given its national circulation. It seemed even indifferent to the rising crisis until late in the 1850's. Thereafter it capitulated, making James Russell Lowell its chief spokesman on the opportunity for nationality. This was defined as public rediscovery of righteousness.

Harper's Monthly, launched in 1850, showed the compromising temper of editor Henry J. Raymond. But its strongly fatalistic outlook readily found a place for the war's beneficial work. *Harper's Weekly*, founded in 1857, concentrated on man's tardy development, his failings, and especially the folly of his leaders. The war would restore the nation to the embrace of citizens made newly worthy of it. Also begun in 1857, *Atlantic Monthly* was immediately an advocate of regenerate nationality. It was eager to assail the old preservationist dogma. All four of these journals made fresh grasp of old truths their denominator in common.

North American Review generally conceded during the 1850's that America was corrupted. But it preferred to leave most causes and implications of this for others to discuss. This journal was still clearly uneasy with majoritarianism, which one leading contributor said had made cowards of men like Henry Clay. As a result license and greed triumphed. In facing a deteriorating nation, *North American Review* authors continued to insist on religion, selflessness, justice, industry, and reverence for the Fathers. With these America would "grow up into its own full proportions." As late as 1859, a *North American Review* voice said: "this much is certain—to preserve our institutions, we must preserve and foster an habitual respect for them." The precepts precious to the Founders must have a contemporary meaning. "When these no longer hold sway, the form may indeed survive, but the animating soul of the republic will have departed." Uncharacteristic sharpness was heard from the literary critic, Henry T. Tuckerman in October 1859. Praising James

Fenimore Cooper's frankness on American shortcomings, Tuckerman added that now "every candid mind acknowledges the
evils, every brave heart laments them; but very few of our citizens have dared to risk their popularity by openly contending
against the state of things which custom and interest have so
firmly established." Tuckerman might well have had his sponsor,
the ponderous *North American Review*, in mind.

Not until early 1862 did this journal announce national failure. It came from "blind trust in leaders, sometimes atro-
ciously corrupt, sometimes upright in purpose, but warped by
sectional or party prejudice." The nation had discovered that
when the Fathers had died, none like them remained. Consequently, the war must induce America to shift "our allegiance
from men to law." Thereafter, *North American Review* talked
of the importance of immutable truths. They had become tiresome to most Stewards and had to be "made to appear new, with
paint and varnish, or sound old oak must give way for slight
new pine."

By 1864, the journal's contributors conceded that war had
given America a new receptiveness to vital moral sentiments.
Standing for freedom, the nation could now anticipate "a nobler code of political morals, for truer conceptions of the nature
of the Constitution, and for heartier and more faithful devotion
to the principles from which our institutions derive their worth,
their power, and their endurance." Especially among America's
youth, drugged by prewar pettiness and selfishness, would there
be a new manliness. But *North American Review* quickly reminded America that only renewed opportunity, not fulfillment,
was at hand. Charles Eliot Norton wrote: "The progress that we
have made as a nation is very little compared to that which lies
before us; but in the future, as in the past, progress will be difficult, slow, imperfect." Despite the war's awful price, the present
generation held America's ultimate success still in trust.[34]

In 1855 *Harper's Magazine* began discussing national philosophy, relying on a polished Websterian doctrine. Even in January 1861 the editors persisted in a warm affirmation of a happy
outcome for the mystical process which was using America. A
spokesman, probably Alfred Hudson Guernsey, announced:
"The great instincts and habitudes of our people will have their
way, and it is the true wisdom, and we believe the true humanity

also, to leave each section free to develop its activities and institutions upon its own ground, and leave the will of Providence and the mighty forces of civilization to work out the great future of the country and the race." This view needed only one precept, the nation "is a great Providential fact." It could never be susceptible to public opinion. With this Clay and Webster would hardly have demurred.

For six years, *Harper's Magazine* had acclaimed Providence and the "organic" essence of the nation. There were instincts and sentiments guided by this process, making the fundamental fact about America its momentum toward destiny. This was true even though "men are often unconscious agents of Providence, and, like Abraham, they know not whither they go." *Harper's* thus interpreted the glaring inconsistencies between the nation's ideals and its practices. In due time America would attain "the highest grade of development." Because the journal was distressed with America's faltering, it heavily emphasized the future: national error was insignificant in the face of inevitable momentum.

By 1862, this fatalism helped *Harper's Magazine* to announce that the war carried a regeneration of national life. With victory, America would clarify national ideas and purpose, thus making nationality "a life, not a mere opinion." Men would at last believe "we are not *made,* but *born* a nation . . . and a nation we will be." Thereby greed and passion would be quelled. The act of atonement foresaw national completion through man's acceptance of America's enormous meaning. The Stewards now "believe that national life grows. . . . They believe that nations, like families, are under Divine rule." As the journal observed in March 1865, war had invigorated the national character by creating a submissive band of Stewards. Nationality had become part of religion, so that men were "singing and praying and preaching patriotism as of the essence of true faith." Again, Webster and Clay would have rejoiced.[35]

When the Harper firm began a weekly in 1857, its concern was over personal and political corruption. This magazine concentrated on the individual's capacity to wreck the nation's progress, so lauded by the *Monthly.* Corruption threatening the nation's very life was far more dangerous than slavery. After confessing that good men abstained from national affairs, and presidents seemed willing only to defend oligarchy, *Harper's Weekly* was delighted with Abraham Lincoln. The journal embraced the President's contention that the Civil War was a people's struggle to re-establish America on its original principles. Even so, the weekly reported that war's freshened patriotism "had not entirely purged the nation of the deepest selfishness and the most threatening corruption." In fact, the war had made such evil all the more conspicuous. Material lust kept America from "a high moral tone." Once Lincoln was re-elected, however, *Harper's Weekly* discovered a Trust fulfilled and a nation vindicated. It acclaimed the completion of the great experiment and the virtual discharge of national obligation. *Harper's Weekly* emerged from the war exultant. For it, atonement seemed like attainment.[36]

Atlantic Monthly was unique. From the first it proclaimed a new nationality. Speaking bluntly in 1857 to the still popular preservationist attitude, *Atlantic* insisted that the indispensable old values had been perverted by the monstrous evil of slavery. In proper time the ideal of freedom would win the national mind. Ideas were meant to dominate, for both the kingdoms of heaven and earth must be in the souls of men. The coming generation might thus produce the true republic, inspired to righteousness, an explicit triumph of truth. "Angels wrestle with the men of this generation, as with the patriarchs of old, and it is our own fault if a blessing be not extorted ere they take their flight." However, until the war arrived to serve as a symbol, *Atlantic* had difficulty being more than a sophisticated successor to *Country Gentleman*. It talked of "the aggregate fidelity to personal rectitude" and of need for "a thorough awakening of the individual conscience." Household reform must save America. "Our sense of private honor and integrity must be quickened."

Generally, *Atlantic* seemed more hopeful about human capacity than were most advocates. It sought to keep national purpose ensconced in the Stewards' conscience. Religion, justice, sobriety, and magnanimity were simple universal truths. It was "the peculiar feat for which the American is born—to bring together seeing and doing, principle and practice, eternity and today." The nation must take the "eternal truths" and place them "with the newest work, the toil and interests of this year and day." Yet, as Charles Francis Adams, Jr., observed in 1861, King Cotton had forced half a nation away from such basic values.

For *Atlantic*'s authors, the war was a glorious experience. It was a struggle "for humanity, and for all time." Suddenly America had proved that "we are a nation equal to the task of self-discipline and self-control,—a new thing on this planet." Onward, then, "to the accomplishment of the grandest mission ever yet entrusted to any people." If more atonement for national sins was required, let it come, for there was nothing more vital than "the work of national purification." Ironically, it was in this exultant mood that *Atlantic* first permitted itself to display misgiving. "Only from ourselves have we anything to fear." This magazine realized that atonement and purification restored nothing more than a chance for noble endeavor to each American. The path ahead was once more uncertain.[37]

IV: Responses   Skepticism over human inclination mounted as 1861 approached. Those responding to the major spokesmen found it difficult to accept the satisfactions of process. Evidence of man's weakness seemed each year more damning and the plight of the Trust became more desperate. Voices of assurance were clearly more subdued after 1848. For instance, blandishments from the "Young America" movement, designed to introduce less awkward topics, were little heeded. Americans hesitated over a Trust of international proportions when evidence suggested that their country was itself morally and politically ill-formed. Not until 1898 would the nation accept world involvement as a solution to vexations at home.

10

During the 1850's there were, of course, recountings of America's simpler meaning. Increasingly rare, however, was the voice of complete assurance. This response entailed an elaborate review of the Fathers' deeds and claims of how the present generation would move finally to disenthral the world. The major delight came from vaguely affirming the progress made by America. This usually was limited to such rhetorical flourishes as "Our Country! Our Whole Country!! There she stands—Queen of the Nations! Her name entwined high on the Temple of Fame." Her sons were

"as one man" happy to battle for the nation, since "purity of
purpose is our breast-plate—and the favor of Heaven is our
shield."

Perhaps the best expression of an ecstatic national consciousness, so infrequent in this era, came from young William Dean
Howells, who had gone abroad in the American foreign service.
The future novelist quickly announced to his sister that "no one
knows how much better than the whole world America is until
he tries some other part of the world. Our people are manlier and
purer than any in Europe," owing to "strife and combat" prevailing among individuals in America.

Howells derived his assurance from an important vantage point
in the mid-nineteenth century. Comforting thoughts about American purpose and attainment usually came from either of two
positions. One was the understanding that national responsibility
came from a sympathetic God or Providence. The other, which
young Howells took, favorably compared the United States with
history in general, and with Europe in particular. If the analysis
stopped here, it afforded some comfort about America's venture.
However, most thoughtful minds felt it necessary to go beyond
Howells' simplistic advice: "prize America all you can. Try not
to think of the Americans' faults—they are a people so much
purer and nobler and truer than any other, that I think they will
be pardoned the wrong they do."

Certain hymns of the years after 1848 best reflected the discovery
of divine assurance. Rejoicing was mostly over "our fathers."
They had left an assignment to maintain "the altar and the
school, the sacred pillars of our trust." Stewardship by preservation depended on an "almighty hand" whose touch must enter
"every peaceful private home." The Civil War affected this earnestness, as a popular collection of secular hymns, *Lyrics for Freedom,* showed. Some spoke of the "glorious fruit" certain to come
from "Freedom's travail." The nation would emerge from war
with renewed purpose "upon the path that godlike heroes tread."
However, most verses were inclined to see the bloodshed as a
catharsis. This turned wistful gazes ahead "when Time's chariot
had rolled a thousand years."

There were some instances of an inane assurance, as in "Columbia Needs No Heraldry."

Columbia needs no heraldry,
   Nor strange, time-honored crest,
To stamp her name and title clear,
   The queen of all the west.
From sea to sea her cities spread
   While fields of golden grain,
And thriving villages, give note
   Of Freedom's prosperous reign.
And though rebel foes assault
   Her legions could withstand
A world in arms, when battling for
   Their honoured native land!

More cautious lines came from the venerable poet, William Cullen Bryant. He sought to rally the remnants of American assurance in the New York *Ledger* during 1861:

Oh Country, marvel of the earth!
   Oh realm to sudden greatness grown!
The age that gloried in thy birth,
   Shall it behold thee overthrown?
Shall traitors lay that greatness low?
   No, land of Hope and Blessing. No!

Bryant simply suggested that "the arm that gave the victory in our fathers' day" would not desert the nation. Let the Stewards go forth and

Strike, for that broad and goodly land,
   Blow after blow, till men shall see
That Might and Right move hand in hand,
   And glorious must their triumph be! [38]

Such hollow delight relied on simple versions of national doctrine. Organic process was taken by many to mean reassuring growth. "It is the true secret of our political institutions; for they have grown; they have been growing since the planting of the colonies." Others found comfort by advocating an instinctive stewardship. Both views recalled Anglo-Saxon endeavor through fourteen centuries. America would succeed, despite its folly and vice, for "we are but a branch of that great Anglo-Saxon tree."

Those who quibbled about nationality were as "children playing at cursing and swearing." Trifling with national meaning, said one Kentuckian, was to "rattle the dice upon our fathers' gravestones." Other uncomplicated rejoicing utilized the doctrine of assimilation. It opposed nativism by depicting America as liberty's asylum. A New York advocate called: "Come, ye men of every clime and every nation; come in your misery or in your affluence." From this hearty mixture the nation would take strength and renewed dedication to preserve itself from demagogues and pretenders.

The favorite doctrine as a source for assurance was claim of the inseparable nature of Union and liberty. Any other arrangement was forbidden by the "moral sense of the nation." From this bond, American endeavor was certain eventually to escape the petty strife of the hour. "Perfect year by year the noble edifice of American freedom, until it shall rise a magnificent cathedral." The publisher, James D. B. DeBow, was important in this litany of assurance. During the mid-1850's, while in Washington directing the Census Office, DeBow often wrote on national progress. Inferring success from physical growth, DeBow believed in "an undeveloped genius" within America. His system of material inevitability made spiritual riches certain. From the American citizen's "practical and working faith" would soon come spontaneous rebuke to corruption and demagoguery.

Like many others, the Kansas-Nebraska struggle left DeBow uneasy with the blessings of expansion and mobility. He began saying that a steady, century-long effort was needed for appropriate use of what America possessed. Even if "the civilizing and godlike influence of machinery" were relied on, a fulfilled America must expect to find that "want, and disease, and misery, should be the next door neighbor of wealth and unbounded prosperity." This was the manner of a wise but unscrutable Providence which "strikes down without reason or explanation, and teaches the utter nothingness of man by her frequent indifference to his fate." DeBow left his astonishing paradox at this point, praise of American effort within an inexplicable universe.

More consistent or conventional comfort was claimed by the new poet, Walt Whitman. His 1855 preface to the first issue of *Leaves of Grass* posited a universe of good centered on America, a nation which itself was "essentially the greatest poem." History offered nothing so inspiring as the American venture, where the fundamental energy was "always most in the common people." A big nation exacted "a corresponding largeness and generosity" from "the spirit of the citizen." For Whitman, America was an inspiring Vineyard where Stewards would willingly labor to produce a noble humanity. This was the Trust, an America which, as "the race of races," must confirm symbolically and in fact the "full-sized man unconquerable and simple." Like others, Whitman had to be content with anticipation, for he too saw the vulnerability of uncertain Stewards. Whitman expressed the spirit of most who insisted on a joyful stance in the 1850's. For him, America was not a past or present so much as a theme that "is creative and has vista." Yet almost in the same breath, Whitman hinted at an unspoken concern by thrusting the American into the Anglo-Saxon racial progression.[39]

11

A response more characteristic of this era made Whitman's covert uncertainty explicit. Whether the departing point was the preservation or the restoration philosophy, men agreed that every year brought new evidence of human frailty. This insight challenged the doctrine of an organic development by talking of a dedicated stewardship. Fidelity to America should be "as unchanging as the great luminary of day." Yet the citizens "are becoming more unworthy of the glorious inheritance," while God demanded from America a "new type of national character." The feeble steps men took in their pursuit of responsibility attracted a widening fascination.

Philip Schaff's popular 1855 interpretation *America* saw the nation's "deformities" as something stewardship would develop enough "soundness and vitality" to overcome. The "morbid matter" Schaff had in mind was a blend of slavery, materialism, radicalism, and sectarianism. As a distinguished immigrant theologian, Schaff was comfortable in stressing a future state of national bliss, with America momentarily "unripe" or "the land of promise." But he added this would come to pass "if we are true to our calling, if we fear God and love righteousness." Although a capacity for hard work, a rational view of liberty and law, and a sound racial mixing all suggested eventual triumph for America's mission, Schaff still feared the "bottomless materialism and worldliness" through which American pilgrims must pass. America's battle with mammon and passion, Schaff predicted, would "bring forth fruit for the weal or woe of generations to come." [40]

Schaff had been in America a decade when he wrote his perceptive account of the national dilemma. His triumph over uncertainty was considerable when compared to the moral didacticism used by an educator with a name long honored in America. An 1856 essay by Miss Elizabeth P. Peabody was one of the most extraordinary responses of this. era. A sister-in-law of Horace Mann, Miss Peabody announced that America needed an awareness of history to retain proper appreciation of human frailty. Material power was useless if American society became diseased by human passion, which the author called "these fatal tendencies." History's main lesson was the unchanging character of mortal man. If America hurriedly learned this, there might yet be time to escape national failure. "We have seen that we are in no less peril here in our day in this new world, than was Adam and the old world."

This made clear to Miss Peabody that men must depend on God. Yet seemingly "in vain does the spirit of God intimate this destiny to us." Unless men responded to this divine call "addressed now to a nation, not to a single man," there would be a swift ebbing of mercy. In Miss Peabody's judgment, Americans must embrace eternal verities. The journal in which she published also stressed the vital link between Protestantism and higher learning if the nation was to develop what another contributor called "a grand Christian manhood."

Pleas for national capitulation to divine mercy remained omnipresent. Among these was the popular 1857 volume, *The American Citizen: His Rights and Duties,* by the Episcopal bishop of Vermont, John Henry Hopkins. It argued that national character in America was religious, so that successful stewardship meant ceaseless religious endeavor. Talking about the Constitution as a Christian document and citizenry having no significance other than Christian association, Hopkins ascribed the awful peril of the hour to "the increasing spirit of religious infidelity." Indeed, "the whole tendency of the times seems downward, to anarchy and confusion." Another response said that if America was a divine nation as many believed, then Stewards "are under obligations to obey the law, whatever as an individual you may think of it. Your consent is not asked, it is required. Your reason cannot set it aside." Or so an Ohio crowd was informed in 1858.

An opposing view was expressed by Carl Schurz in a Faneuil Hall address in 1859, "True Americanism." He admitted that America's great opportunity might be "recklessly thrown away by imbecile generations." Here, indeed, was the plight of American self-awareness, to seek certainty despite doubts created by an age of evil. Schurz's solution was to recommend faith in the ultimate efficacy of liberty and equality, not only for America but through America to the world. Sustaining this faith was the Steward's first obligation, with destruction of expedience the initial harvest of his effort. Acknowledging that the "billows of passion will lash the sides of the ship," Schurz insisted that a renewal of the Fathers' faith would mean "the resurrection of human freedom." For Schurz, this was "true Americanism."[41]

The storm exceeded anything Shurz was likely to have foreseen. In response to the gales of civil strife, an attempt to bolster Americanism was made through publications of encouragement or instruction. Most evident were espousals by Union Society members whose consistent theme was, as Lewis Tappan put it, "We are a nation laden with trespasses and sins." The Almighty "has come out in judgment against us." Attention then turned to the reasons for such iniquity and the prospect of national salvation. The former was usually portrayed in Union tracts as the familiar enticements of mammon; the latter was based on a fresh discovery of ancient truths. Now there was need "to concentrate and to manifest, to make evident and to make intense, the matured purpose of the nation." No longer "craven and contented," America must teach the true efficacy of freedom. A successful war would begin this instruction, after cleansing the nation of faithlessness.

Such Union Society propaganda had one purpose, to start a second pilgrimage in pursuit of the "sacred trust." Andrew Johnson considered this to mean a restoration of the nation of the Fathers. Johnson told an Indianapolis audience in 1863 that this national momentum would not stop, even for blacks. Should they "get in the way let them be crushed." America must allow nothing to interfere with the restitution of "this great fabric of human liberty." Even so, the war's distress brought larger reference to

America's religious role. One 1863 booklet, *Christian Patriotism,*
called for an American outlook "invigorated and exalted by that
class of motives which can be drawn only from our religion." It
needed to be "redeemed from all association with that cheap and
vulgar quality which is so much eulogized in vapid declamation."
This required "loftier conceptions of our nationality, as related
to the Providence of God in the progress of His eternal kingdom." Surrender to this "sacred cause" of nationality must be
complete, as one Rhode Island response said. To hold back from
this cause "is suicide." [42]

These admonitory responses became most fervent in the commentary upon Lincoln's death. The personal sacrifice of Lincoln
was made to appear as a dramatic rescue of individual Americans.
Lincoln stood beside Washington, one the Father of the Country,
the other the Savior of his countrymen. Mourning for Lincoln
centered upon his precious example. He had vindicated republicanism. "Men will receive a new impulse of patriotism" for his
sake. Now they will guard with zeal the whole country which he
loved so well. It was customary to contend that God had taken
Lincoln so that America could have a martyr "to inspire us from
his heavenly seat." A sobered nation must turn to "stern and
solemn duties." The eulogies, however, said that America began
anew as a "confirmed" nation with a cause now "eternally secure."
The war and the symbolic death of the leader brought at last an
end to childish excesses, leading Stewards "from the careless and
boastful youth to the more firm and thoughtful manhood of our
career."

A somewhat different response was the burial oration at Springfield, by Richard S. Storrs, Jr. It was a statement reminiscent of
Lincoln's old mentor, Henry Clay. Storrs dismissed the individual
as decreasing in consequence for civilization. The nation had
become a "mightier presence" and had done so according to providential plan, the outcome of which lay beyond comprehension.
More important, the Stewards knew "instinctively" what remained
for national fulfillment. Storrs' interpretation of the Trust was
hardly startling, calling for America's demonstration to the world
of true Christian democracy. This would mark the moment when
"the spirit of the nation shall be finally formed and declared."
Apparently it would also signal the transition of a model republic

into active agency. Storrs suggested an enlarged sense of nationality would soon be needed. With the approaching completion of itself, America "must pour abroad through constant channels, an infinite influence." For men like Storrs, atonement brought a comfortable view of the future and a glimpse of stewardship in distant climes.[43]

12

Not all responses, of course, could be so confident. The decade of the 1850's had heard too much lamentation for everyone to put despair aside easily. It was Henry Adams who wrote after the Harpers Ferry incident: "adieu my country. . . . We shall have made a brilliant failure with our glorious Republic and the prophet can't say what'll turn up." Francis Lieber thought "a daily whipping" might help the nation. He wished it were not wicked to "pray to God for a chastising calamity to befall our whole nation." Only this might bring "regeneration." Men like Lieber brooded in their time, as had previous generations, about America's defiance of right and morality, its drinking and dancing, and its "money-making and murdering." As the only means of restoration a merciful God might smite America. Lieber was so depressed late in December 1860 that he wished he were a physical scientist, shut away from human corruption and investigating "that portion of nature which knows no question of right or wrong. . . ."

Such despair was not limited to the intellectuals. Senator Lyman Trumbull received a letter during the frantic Christmas season in 1860 from an Illinois constituent who considered Buchanan's call for national repentance belated. Blaming Buchanan and previous leadership for the national agony, the writer described America as "bleeding and prostrate in the dust begging for existence." A response from New York ascribed the nation's destruction to "our craving for wealth." There was little hope in such an outlook. The best to be said was that "out of our sore afflictions" America would come to "build up a purer nationality." If this ever occurred, "we shall vindicate our true national glory."

By autumn of 1861, such despair over national sin was commonplace. A Thanksgiving Day sermon in New Jersey was a characteristic response. Nations which had grown prideful, fraud-

ulent, and treacherous must suffer. America had no choice but to
accept "dire public calamity." The hope was that this affliction
would somehow "awaken reflection, and lead to private and
public reform." Meantime, men must wait to see if God sent this
great trial in a spirit of mercy. Then an attempt at amends could
be made. This usually meant restoration of forgotten principles.
As another New Jersey spokesman said in 1863, "The only hope
for this nation . . . in the furnace of fire through which it is
passing, is our return to wisdom's way." The sense of despair
made national self-abasement a popular theme. A hymn of 1863
had as a typical stanza:

> Lest we pray in thoughtless guilt
> Shape the future as Thou wilt!
> Purge our realm from hoary crime
> With thy battles, dread, sublime
> In thy well-appointed time!
>   Help us, Lord, our only trust
>   We are helpless, we are dust!

A hymnal published in 1864 specialized in supplications for
the sinful nation. Such lines had America usually prostrate and
"with tears the nation's sins lament." In such a posture, amid
terrible battle, Stewards awaited the dread decree. Nothing remained but to pray for deliverance:

> Let that love vail our transgression
> Let that blood our guilt efface
> Save Thy people from oppression
> . . . .
> Lord, with deep contrition turning,
> Humbly at thy feet we bend;
> Hear us, fasting, praying, mourning,
> Hear us, spare us, and defend.[44]

The era of atonement established a bond between this earnest
Baptist hymn and the supplications of Abraham Lincoln and
James Russell Lowell. An all-powerful God and sinful man had
been polarities in New World thought long before the Republic
undertook a mission for the Almighty. The Fathers had once

trembled for America's real and anticipated shortcoming. Such apprehension captivated the America of Lincoln's time. Yet when the ordeal by blood was somehow endured, the nation characteristically announced God's restored favor. Perhaps because of the awful price of their atonement, most Americans began renewed stewardship with stout expectation.

CHAPTER FOUR   RENEWAL
1865–1876

Despite the anticipations kindled at Appomattox Court House and Ford's Theater, the dozen years after Lincoln's death proved anything but comfortable for national consciousness. Events in the era suggested that man had not rightly used the recent atonement. New trials vexed the nation. Fresh revelations came of man's surrender to mammon and passion. By 1876, the nation's centennial, America's spirit was a new compound of indignation, despair, and stubborn anticipation. It seemed far removed from the exultancy of 1865 which gloried in "The Founder and the Restorer." One celebrant had then claimed that, while Washington "first gave life and form to our National existence," Lincoln had "saved it from destruction in the crisis of its fate." Thanks to these two men, America now stood "in the majesty of our triumphant republicanism." There was heady talk of "the conscious power of our renovated nationality." The atonement just completed, many observed, would prove "a great gulf between what happened before it in our century and what has happened since."

Such enthusiasm quickly subsided, for the memory of past achievement was fragile. It was not so much that men still recalled the feeble stewardship in Jackson, Webster, and Buchanan's times. In 1865, the nation had thought that the brave Fathers of 1776 had been succeeded by a new group of heroes. These same gallant men soon became shabby Stewards in the era of Crédit Mobilier. The days of Jim Fisk and Jay Gould were an unnerving aftermath for those who predicted a national rebirth through the restoration of ancient virtue. Men asked if a century of national life, including the sacrifice of two sets of soldier heroes and a martyr President, might still go for naught.

The celebrations beginning in 1876 only fostered this uneasiness by underscoring the contrast between the nation's incredible material development and its faltering spiritual growth. Little occurred after 1865 to narrow this gap. First, the issue of reconstituting the nation forced the executive and legislative branches of the federal government into open warfare. They did so amid an economic rush that brought difficulty and vast temptation to both the local and continental spheres. Agrarian, monetary, industrial, and civil troubles assailed the citizens in an unprecedented way.

The world watched as the Republic's chief Steward, President Andrew Johnson, was accused and tried for what were allegedly high crimes and misdemeanors. His successor, the heroic U. S. Grant, was soon struggling to explain why his colleagues were spectacular victims of mammon. The anticipated fraternal peace, espoused by President Grant, seemed more remote with each year, in spite of constitutional amendments, Supreme Court mandates, and Ku Klux Klan legislation. It seemed that in both public and private, American stewardship was devising an unworthiness which even civil service reform legislation could not diminish. Consequently, George William Curtis' despairing resignation in 1875 as the first head of the Civil Service Commission symbolized how thwarting the renewal of national fulfillment had become.

Curtis was simply one of many Americans disappointed in their expectations of swift triumph for American endeavor. Instead of completing the American mission, men struggled to retain hope of eventually doing so. In 1871, for instance, New Yorkers sought to overcome the political misrule of Tammany Hall and Boss Tweed, while Illinois grangers tried to end railroad tyranny. Then, in 1872, the Republic's virtual captivity by the owners of the Union Pacific Railroad was disclosed. Faced by this debacle for the national Trust, some members of Lincoln's party attempted to organize a new crusade. This Liberal Republican movement ended in further chagrin, embodied in the quixotic Horace Greeley. Barely was the election of 1872 over when America discovered that moral ignominy was to be joined by economic collapse. This discovery suggested to many citizens, whose lives had largely political and economic dimensions, that the American experiment was entering its gravest peril.

The year of the centennial, 1876, brought no basis for renewing national hope. In that year the Steward in whom so many saw so much, James G. Blaine, emerged as mammon's prize captive. Also, the presidential canvass produced party antics which further confirmed George Washington's fears. Consequently, the centennial celebration had to be largely an effort to find something beyond sheer physical testimony to prove the nation was progressing in step with its responsibility. Wisdom suggested that everything be ignored except the past. Official admonition led citizens to study the establishment of their localities. No more pathetic declaration of despair appears in American history than this design of centennial activities in 1876. It meant marveling at material growth while overlooking the moral tribulation of the nation. For many observers, therefore, the era of renewal was noteworthy primarily in supplanting Lincoln's supreme sacrifice with a procession of scoundrels and scandals. It was so disappointing a climax to a century of nationhood that America was tempted to forget itself. Solace came either in celebrations of days and scenes long gone or in stout calls for a new morality for a second century. In these directions national thought hurried away from the unseemly present. Despite a hundred years of life, Americans still put themselves either in the past or the future.[1]

DOCTRINE

After 1865 thoughts about American meaning and endeavor were forced often to re-examine fundamentals. Although the war was said to confirm the political and institutional setting for the Trust, man's nature and achievement required further calculation. The hope was that the citizen would succeed in bearing his moral and rational responsibility once republicanism had been proved at places like Gettysburg. After Lincoln's murder the nation watched for signs that triumphant republicanism would be joined by a new human nature freed from weakness. It was hoped that in emancipating the

slaves America would chain the mortal frailties which until then
had thwarted stewardship. However, this season of renewal did
nothing to soften the dissonance between affirmation and anxiety
which so long had disrupted American doctrine.[2]

I: Affirmations   Americans entered the
era after Lincoln's death still believing that the nation carried
an enormous responsibility. On its discharge rested the completion of the national character, a goal many observers considered
closer because of the Civil War. While men might dispute this
immediacy, there was general preoccupation with moral fundamentals. More than ever, the sacred Trust meant the endurance
of ancient virtues. This was a fitting aftermath to Lincoln's philosophy of restoration.

1

The idea that national purpose was meeting God's expectation
continued especially vivid after 1865. Both the war and Lincoln
were widely accepted as divine instrumentalities for eliciting the
ultimate nation. The Declaration of Independence became a
codification of divine principles and goals for America. It was
joined by the Emancipation Proclamation, then hailed as the
implementation of eternal verities by a triumphant stewardship.
Momentarily in the postwar season, the familiar gloom over the
nation's stubborn resistance to providential mandate brightened.
Man and God seemed companions amidst the beauty of a
cleansed America. An inspired humanity was said to have assumed the Steward's role.

Lincoln's sacrifice encouraged the contention that America was
thereby freed from the malevolent experiences brought by errant
leadership. As Henry Adams said in May 1865, the great change
occurring in the nation was the arrival of a fresh outlook. "New
men have come." The insistence that America's recent ordeal
had called forth "a new and nobler humanity" dominated the
ideology of nationality for a time after Appomattox. Members
of the Grand Army of the Republic, gathered in the summer of
1868, heard this view acclaimed. But even with a new stewardship, the veterans were urged to join in "an anxious regard for
that future which is all in our hands." The world watched closely
to see if the American venture would again exhibit "gradual

degeneracy." To avert this, the new men got old advice: embrace natural surroundings to retain Anglo-Saxon vigor; and make final escape from a "love of ease and luxury." A new generation still had to live in hope. With proper faith and deed, Americans might at last reach "the accomplishment of our high-written destiny." [3]

This meant that while unsullied hands were welcomed to the toil, the new laborers would have to accept the old chores from a divine taskmaster. American doctrine could affirm a change in manpower, but God never varied. The divine scheme as articulated by Protestantism remained dominant in America's self-perception after the Civil War. Protestant views and Americanism continued to be interchangeable. Patriotic occasions after the war regularly claimed that God had awakened true nationality in American hearts. Having created America, God finally granted it a mighty spirit. Only thus would come what one individual called "a deeper perception of the foundations of our nationality." Out of "this self consciousness" would arise those "supreme convictions of the soul" which the nation would need in a "divine administration."

For several years these claims of a national spirit from heaven served as the most satisfying recognition of God's ultimate gift to America. Postwar doctrine was especially eager to portray America's new heart as God's itself. The advantages were obvious. Having shown His most "distinct token of a benignant purpose" for America through the North's victory, God now granted "a spirit of nationality." One person called this the final bequest needed "to fulfill the great mission that is before us." In the era of search the nation had relied on human rather than divine inspiration. A renewed America appeared eager not to err again by unleashing the old Adam.

However, events soon took an alarming turn. Eighteen seventy marked an important point in the tribulations of nationality. For five years after the atoning Civil War, Americans talked of immediate realization of national goals. God's manifest inspiration and intervention were to bring swift completion of American purpose. Yet citizens soon realized that their neighbors loitered unmoved by the divine invigoration. This forced nationality gradually back to the stance of distant anticipation. With 1870 the sense of expectancy grew noticeably subdued.

There would be a final, winning gesture from God, but at a later time. This revived patience was also encouraged by the official recollection, in 1870, that 250 years had passed since the Pilgrims first came with God to America. Perhaps the work of God was slower than America had perceived. But ultimately, it was said, his "heavenly and angelic food" would replace "the materialism with which many were now trying to feed the people." [4]

Similarly, the acknowledgment that America carried the fate of liberty made a forced retreat in this era from claims of victory to an uneasy expectancy. A nation had been reinspired, under God, but the new endeavor stumbled. The cause was noble, but the champions weakened. At the war's finish, liberty's fresh hopes had been typically expressed at Tammany Hall in 1866. Among its seventeen stanzas, the occasion's ode affirmed such sentiments as:

> While the foes of Freedom tremble
>   From old Spain to classic Greece,
> And the hostile hosts assemble,
>   Blood the only road to peace,
> Brighter beams *our Constellation*
>   In the upper sea of blue
> Emblem of the *reborn* Nation,
>   Guardian of the brave and true.
>
> . . . .
>
> Fairest flower among the Nations
>   Thou shalt rise in majesty,
> Bearing Freedom's declarations
>   To the great futurity.

The recent war was only a phase of America's battle for liberty. Yet to come was "that great day." Until then, the nation was advised to make wise use of its great blessings, for only thus "shall we begin to find a realization of the great destiny which lies before us."

In looking for sustaining ideals, the nation thought more about the future as the setting for American achievement. The sacrifices of the Civil War, which had briefly represented final fulfillment, soon became only more inspiration for appraising American meaning. Widening political and economic squalor provoked awkward questions, leaving men to wonder whether the first century of national endeavor had been a delusion, a pathetic pursuit of an impossible ideal, or a shouldering of responsibility beyond even America's capacity. Even if a reassuring answer somehow were found, the incessant asking suggested the alarming national health in 1876. There was little left but the affirmation that, despite the Civil War's noble attainment, being an American meant looking to a succeeding generation. The latter might hope to attain for America the fulfillment long anticipated and advocated. Private morality remained the locus of national progress, in spite of trumpetings over destiny and evolution. Human sinfulness so widely displayed in this era made the Trust disagreeable and disconcerting.

As a consequence, some men faced the future by fresh retreats to the past. James A. Garfield joined this march while speaking in 1868 at a decoration of Union soldier graves. He insisted that no heroic sacrifice was ever lost, since "the characters of men are moulded and inspired by what their fathers have done." This brought the comforting assurance that "treasured up in American souls, are all the unconscious influences of the great deeds of the Anglo-Saxon race, from Agincourt to Bunker Hill." Garfield's effort to blend principle and process was often duplicated. The 1870 plea that Philadelphia's Independence Square be made a national shrine was justified because American youth needed a place of patriotic inspiration where they "could visit this fountain of freedom to be refreshed." Such a site would prove "the moral light-house of our beloved country."

By 1876, circumstances required blunt affirmations that America would complete her destiny only "as long as piety, religion, and morality shall prevail in the land, and no longer." Recollection thus gloried in the labors of "plain folk, with homely traits" whose stewardship did justice to the Republic's intent. This revived a modified doctrine of preservation. The polity was secure as a framework, but the task remaining for America was "to see that no moral decay—the sure precursor of physical decay shall sap the structure. . . . Our aim should be to leave to our children an example as noble as the one that was left to us." The centennial itself largely celebrated ancient verities. Usually voices of 1876, forgetting any recent claims to national purification, pleaded that "the spirit which actuated our fathers and brothers

will animate us, and we shall then repair and restore what we
have suffered to fall into waste and decay." The nation could
enter its second century with hope of success only if it were devoted to the habits of the past.[5]

Centennial concentration on the past usually tried to pledge
faith in the nation's ultimate completion. While the era began
with claims of renewal and attainment, it closed with acknowledgment that national completion still lay far ahead. Both self-
government and equalitarianism remained uncertain blessings
in view of man's faltering nature. The venerable poet, William
Cullen Bryant, concluded his long lifetime in the Vineyard by
acclaiming the future, the habitat of "a nobler age." Then would
good at last prevail, and:

> The hand of ruffian Violence, that now
> Is insolently raised to smite, shall fall
> Unnerved before the calm rebuke of Law,
> And Fraud, his sly confederate, shrink, in shame,
> Back to his covert, and forego his prey.

Bryant's "Centennial Hymn" showed the pathos in much of
American affirmation about its Trust. Even the aged had to peer
impatiently ahead, for experience served mostly as a warning. In
Bryant's call went much of the tragic irony of American nationality:

> Oh, chequered train of years, farewell!
>   With all thy strifes and hopes and fears!
> Yet with us let thy memories dwell,
>   To warn and teach the coming years.
>
> And thou, the new-beginning age,
>   Warned by the past, and not in vain,
> Write on a fairer, whiter page,
>   The record of thy happier reign.

New pleas for preservation argued that "if we live long
enough, a day will come to reward our faith." The latter, according to further affirmation, required truthful history. "In expos-
ing the errors of others, we fortify our faith in our own principles. We want no sham or pious frauds in our annals; the lessons
of the past are most wholesome when unadulterated." This was

folly for those who wanted to forget former evil, and "let the dead past bury the dead." As one person put it in 1876: "The star of our country's destiny is hope, not memory. It is a morning, not an evening star."

This outlook brought some early affirmations of what would finally be the only tolerable version of the Trust, a world-wide mission. The European opposition to the North had revived the belief in Old World evil. Thereafter it enabled some persons to ignore domestic travail in the glare of Europe's troubles. One contention was that the Civil War's results "must amaze the people of the earth, and strike a chord of sympathy that will course like the electric fluid, and arouse them to action." Let America stand, "full of glory." An 1876 series in *Lippincott's Magazine* said that America's first century must be seen in a global drama. America had actually been in an Atlantic community, with its culture drawn from this international setting. While rare, there were significant efforts to have the centennial celebrate a universal story in which America's contribution would be more distant and impersonal.[6]

2

As affirmations about the future and the globe indicated, talk of America's responsibility grew more vague. In part, this was because the issue of national design disappeared at Appomattox, leaving national doctrine to concentrate on questions about man and society. After 1865, national consciousness began facing an issue central in the doctrine of the late nineteenth and twentieth centuries. Was the nation moved by and dedicated to the interests of total society, or was the individual citizen the beginning and end of national concern? It grew tempting to see national fulfillment in a vast organism, American society. However, the deeply rooted beliefs in individual meaning remained to complicate the discussion, as they had for Webster and Clay.

For a time after 1865, individual capacity to effect good or evil in a personal ministry for American fulfillment seemed newly significant. It was briefly so, however, given America's speeding institutional development. In every aspect of life, stewardship appeared increasingly to be a mutual venture. Business, agriculture, and labor were absorbing the person into a corporate undertaking. It was much like Union's earlier significance for the free individual. By 1876, American thought took increasing solace in placing the citizen in a great drama stretching far into a romantic past and moving toward a glorious future. The comfort of Anglo-Saxon mysticism made more acceptable the integrative implications of Herbert Spencer's dogma. The Steward approached the time when his role would be pleasantly indistinct.

Some eagerness remained in this era, especially in American literary circles, to concentrate on the individual. Since battle had restored and assured the moral precepts threatened before the war, only the proving of man faced America's calling. So argued commentators like Charles Eliot, Emily G. Balch, William James, Edward Atkinson, Edward Everett Hale, Thomas Wentworth Higginson, and John Graham Brooks. They sought to restore the old idealization of man. Much of this talk about man's dynamic capacities seemed devised to impress the youth who were again the target of a campaign to instill correct ideas. Exhortation in *Youth's Companion* used such tales as one about an American lad who so charmed the Czar of Russia with "simplicity and artlessness" as to persuade him of America's greatness. Addresses to youthful gatherings typically insisted man made himself.[7]

Nevertheless, it grew easier to argue that stewardship was a matter for society. This concept was more believable after 1865 than insistences that America's Trust still rested with the individual. New exuberance was evident in affirmations that the national undertaking "moves upon grand centres, and not upon the separate axis of each individual." America drew its real meaning and inspiration from the group. Nathaniel P. Banks observed: "All are wiser than a part. . . . The ark of safety is the heart of the people—the instructed heart of the people." The spelling book and the love of God brought this ark its essentials. Society portrayed as the embodiment of national purpose drew an eloquence appropriately reminiscent of Webster: "The country claims all our strength. We owe to no earthly mistress a holier love."

More doubt about the separate Steward existed after 1865 than had been heard since 1798. A typical statement said that America's undertaking now required "not only the political oneness and nationality, but the fraternity of the American people." In short, a union of minds was the basis for stewardship, as the nation began "the era of manhood," having paid retribution for "national guilt and crime." The talk of individualism tended to become affirmation that a young man could learn universal principles. "Harmony," "collaboration," "accord" were popular terms after 1865. The nation was seen as "a vast Syncretism," having at last established "One Life."

For this doctrine, advanced by men like Francis Lieber, the remaining need for American fulfillment was that the individual citizen feel "an organic unity with one another, as well as being conscious of a common destiny." Success required "but one nationality," for in "the organic unity lies the chief difference between the words Nation and People." Charles Sumner chose to call this the "national faith" which now served as the "pivot of the national hereafter." Henry Ward Beecher by 1876 was preaching the gospel of the "common senses" rising from a unity of people. The spirit displayed when men said "Our Fatherland" after "Our Father" was for Beecher the assurance of a fruitful America. The latter was thus advised by a centennial poet:

> Let us clasp hands, to work as one
>   for all the Nation's good
> And stand together as one Man
>   as once our fathers stood.
> . . . .
> We live in freedom; let us clasp each
>   other by the hand
> In love and unity abide, a firm,
>   unbroken band.[8]

3

Closely tied to the emerging doctrine of human interdependence was this era's thinking about the place in which America centered its endeavor. With the Union triumphant, the old natural and political Vineyards were newly important. Both were rediscovered as sources for the morality which national renewal required. More than ever Stewards needed inspiring surroundings appropriate for duty. Nature was restored to an active force for some observers. It did not seem important whether the setting was unmolested or machine-enhanced. America's physical glory brought human enhancement. James Garfield told his diary that an appreciable change was being wrought in the American people, physically and spiritually, by "the vital and atmospheric influences of this continent." More generally heard were such assertions as Bronson Alcott's that America's interior gave national endeavor what the East had lacked, a broader and more liberal spirit, something "our century dictates."

On the whole, however, Stewards took unprecedented satisfaction from rejoicing over the political system recently made glorious by a shedding of blood. It made possible the rediscovery that proper stewardship derived an instinctive patriotism and political capacity from a surrounding institutional legacy. The American polity as a Vineyard challenged nature as a source of inspiration. It was a bequest from a second group of Founders, led by Lincoln. In a proven Constitution there was substance which the appeals of Clay and Webster lacked, leaving men to claim: "A new era of the republic now opens before us." The idea would further the notion of a corporate society. Political cohesion was now "the instinct of the people." Even after a decade of fiscal panic and presidential misrule, such affirmation persisted. The reason "that the nation is not ruined, that liberty is not destroyed" was ascribed to the sustaining institutions "given us by the wisdom and virtue of an heroic age."

The Civil War and Lincoln's sacrifice obviously enhanced the once controversial and artificial polity, so that powerful stimulants which man once drew from physical environs were replaced by institutional sustenance. These "subtle forces" were traced from the Constitution and ripened Union back through the first Fathers to the English origins. American Stewards should take heart from "the dignity of our pupilage." In the age of renewal, Americans discovered deeply planted customs. These brought the nation both instincts and practices "to carry her through the tremendous process God had ordained." The "first conception of an American nationality," said one voice, had come in the battle against kings. Now, thanks to the legacy of enduring political inspiration, America had a "sentiment of nationalism . . . which became compacted and unified with the very fiber of the American people."

Not everyone, of course, was certain that the season of renewal warranted America's relying on the encouragement and guidance inherent in the polity. There was discussion of amending the Constitution to remove from these scriptures any lingering hints of a discredited divided sovereignty. One newspaper conceded that such an amendment might prove necessary if the entire populace was to accept "the inherent nationality of the country." Such insistence that the printing of a political affirmation would make America "truly and thoroughly national" indicated how far beyond the days of John Taylor and Thomas Jefferson America's concept of a political Vineyard had moved. As one speaker at the Centennial Parade in Philadelphia observed, the American people appeared at last to show a "patriotic instinct," derived from the scenes and facts of political trial and triumph. This sort of affirmation was the response to the fresh anxieties which crowded upon a renewed nationality.[9]

II: Anxieties   With Lee's surrender, men no longer had to contemplate whether republicanism and Union were possible. Instead, the travail besetting the renewed pilgrimage arose more from the effort to meet the demands of institution and law. Since the latter had been confirmed by noble sacrifice, Stewards anxiously faced expectations as awesome as any before the Civil War. Here was the agony of America's renewal. The actual task of being an American with the hazards traditionally accompanying it became even more important for national doctrine. Carl Schurz spoke of it as the burden of "coming of age."

While the era had its clichés about freedom, destiny, and glory, thoughtful citizens recognized that civil war had not settled the uncertainty over man's capacity to succeed as an American. It was significant that one of Reginald Heber's hymns from the early days of the Republic was republished in 1871. The lines were apropos in their plea for divine protection against "guilty pride, and lust of power . . . blinded zeal, by faction led . . . giddy change by fancy bred . . . poisoned error's serpent head." More testing would be necessary before American character was proven worthy, or so the New York City Young Men's Christian Association heard in 1876. "We stand today, nationally, very much like a school of boys passing up into a higher grade of education. Hitherto we have been but in the primary department." The anxiety this condition provoked was enlarged by

the insistence that renewed pursuit of the Trust made it mandatory that "there shall be no confusion in our national morality,
between right and wrong, between patriotism and treason, between the effort to preserve our national life and the attempt
to destroy it." Despite Lincoln's toil, American thought still
sought to understand both the nature of American endeavor and
the character of man himself.

4

Americans approached this challenge with talk once more about
adequate preparation. This meant indoctrination and education,
despite the encouragement rising from the concept of an organic
career. It was still important that citizens fully perceive what the
national drama implied. This was true whether one was concerned over behavior decreed by undying principle or required
by awesome social evolution. This was not a period which praised
rampaging individualism. The concern was to create a dutiful
citizenry submissive to whatever the national purpose entailed.
Americans had yet to face an increasingly troublesome aspect
of nationality. Theories about American character and purpose
still provided no satisfactory place for human corruption. A
stewardship prone to evil had always embarrassed America's
Trust for God, liberty, and the future. The chief rejoinder had
to be that somehow Stewards would discover the inner resources
needed to comply with America's meaning. After the Civil War,
this aspect of interpreting America's endeavor became the para-
mount consideration in national doctrine.

Two college addresses in 1868 faced the troubled implications
of a stewardship newly conveyed by American purpose. At Princeton the concern was over persisting fatalism. Americans, said
Thomas N. McCarter, "have become so accustomed to admire
and laud the mere form of our government, that we have come
to look upon it as a self-acting agency, which cannot move in a
wrong direction, and which, left to itself, will of its own inherent
goodness accomplish the greatest good of the greatest number."
McCarter warned against seeing America as "a perfect machine"
headed for national fulfillment no matter how badly driven.
Toil by Stewards was still important. Speaking bluntly about the
shabbiness of stewardship, McCarter pointed to "the insidious
progress of corruption." Not during the war but now was

America's gravest moment. Human delusion and weakness had "brought us to the verge of destruction." Despite the war's result, America now faced "the greatest peril for the future."

McCarter's remedy was as old as the Republic. Stewardship and education must be close companions. This was the doctrine also advanced in 1868 at Yale where Joseph P. Thompson spoke on how to build a nation. He said America's "entirely changed condition of affairs" required that education perceive anew the need for principles in politics and society. Like McCarter, Thompson rejected thought of America as a benign process. Only a wise adjustment of "old truths to new conditions and of squaring new facts to old foundations" would make it possible to "avert the fall of the Nation." America's purpose was still "to build a model nation for mankind." It must use the family, Anglo-American stock for social purity, individual obedience "to the national spirit and life," hard work, glorification of women, encouragement of culture, and a thorough education of the people. Once more indoctrination was the nation's weapon against man's weakness. Thompson insisted that by instruction the public be imbued with "sound views, and pure and noble aims." This in turn brought "allegience to God" which must pervade "all political forms, institutions, laws," as well as "the souls of men." For those with Thompson's outlook, America more than ever needed a theocratic perspective in order to gain eternal life.[10]

There was a continuing clamor for religious quality in American labor. The nation's "integrity and rectitude," it was still said, would be established only when men let "Christianity prevail among us in its original purity." Such admonitions usually added that this dedication would ensure reverence for the constitutional system. It was also the most acceptable form of the familiar argument of citizen surrender to eternal truths. "For well we know that whensoever this nation shall depart from these great lights, and wander darkening in the gloom and sorcery of despotism and oppression," God would "strike down the whole political fabric under which we live." Before the Civil War, men had talked of America's fulfillment through labor dedicated to virtue and truth. Generally, these precepts had been secular, and the Websterians had even made them constitutional in character. Such absolutes theoretically had been sanctified by the

Civil War, as were citizen lives. Yet human transgression thrived after 1865.

Consequently, increased attention went to those who put the national experience into a natural development which made fragile principles safely subordinate. While biological certainties grew more appealing, they required a high ideological price. If, as Emerson observed in 1870, America "moved as the sea does," individual stewardship stood in awed respect. Nevertheless, to interpret American momentum as an ocean or an eternal race tended to free stewardship from personal responsibility. This brought a rising insistence, aided by men such as Horace Bushnell and Francis Lieber, that national well-being could thrive apart from human misstep. The majesty of events, the revelations of an organic social development, all hinted that, after all, America's pilgrimage need not be troubled by individual aberrations.

Like everything else in such a doctrine, human error was natural. Such doctrine removed the sharp point of America's Trust from the backs of individual citizens, leaving them to offer passive homage to the universal truths which their nation guarded. Responsibility thus discharged, the citizens could follow private inclination believing that America moved toward fulfillment through an implacable course of events some called progress. At last men might be Americans and yet be comfortable. Fatalism thus became invaluable for American thought. It gave many anxious spectators a way to believe in national purpose despite reality.

5

No matter what the philosophic comforts were, interest in the familiar vicissitudes increased during this era. The power of mammon and passion seemed untouched by the symbolic expiation of emancipation. Much of America was not yet able to equate the pursuit of gain or power with moral and physical inevitability. Meantime, money was running amuck in railroad tyranny, monetary policy, and corporation growth. The political and economic distresses after 1865 suggested that the anchor dropped by Lincoln had been loosened by a thoughtless new generation. Many saw the American ship newly threatened by the shoals of human nature, which had wrecked republics of the past.

The resultant burst of sentiment, especially during 1876, showed how the nation was torn between its material achievement and the dangers entailed in it. National virtue stood uneasy in the midst of money policy, railroad tactics, banking practice, and monopolies. The faithful patriot was asked to ponder these and also the presence of cities and disgruntled multitudes. Here were new challenges to national endeavor. Sensualism, barbarism, and selfishness were ancient charges a weakening stewardship heard again. One antidote, education based on strongly Protestant truisms, continued to be an equally venerable paradox. While training in citizenship was urged, tributes to instinct grew commonplace. Apparently, good impulses could be aroused only by accepting established truth. Rationalism seemed more anachronistic than ever. Mobs and materialism prompted many thoughtful persons, including Walt Whitman, to espouse a spiritual essence for nationality, one reaching beyond the repulsive mundane.[11]

A former schoolman turned politician, James A. Garfield, regretted that many of his new associates failed to see the ideological crisis. Garfield urged an older stewardship. "I appeal to those who care more for the future safety and glory of this nation than for any mere temporary advantage." This was the issue invoked by experience. Would public effort worthy of the nation succeed when human nature tugged man aside by selfish strings? Garfield's friend, Robert Ingersoll, was dubious. America was the "same old story," he said in 1868. After a glorious national beginning, wealth had captured public esteem. "Authority gets shabby. Rebellion rises. Debt is created. A tax gatherer at every door. Law becomes odious."

In another direction went Henry Adams, who scoffed at expectations of a renovated public integrity. He called the purification of human nature "one of those flattering fictions which have in all ages deluded philanthropists." His brother, Charles Francis, brooded over an America now "prolific of knaves as well as of heroes—of evil as well as of good." For a nation adrift from its "moorings," it was clear to Charles Francis Adams that "our future is not to be our past." In conceding that "we have overcome one enemy only to encounter another," this Adams apparently had no remedy except creating selfless Stewards. Like so many who watched a renewed America become a scene of moral and economic contrasts, Charles Francis Adams could find no new inducement for proper stewardship except a "nationality" of feeling which education might bring. Without it, America would fall beneath what a *Country Gentleman* contributor called the "struggle between Equality and Aristocracy in Free America."

Thoughtful Americans were well aware of the new hazards, those "fearful moral storms that sweep over our land with a deadly force." These seemed to overwhelm "our noblest and fairest," making familiar a lament of 1871 that mammon held America captive. The Republic's fulfillment must again be deferred until, as one observer noted, men learned that "wealth basely acquired and ignobly enjoyed" was "a reproach and not a glory." During the centennial, newspapers especially insisted on programs of indoctrination through education. A characteristic observation suggested that in the national peril, schools should discard concern for languages, literature, and the sciences to concentrate entirely on one goal, to "strengthen the government by qualifying American youth for the duties of citizenship." Another said, "We need the rod to correct quite a number of serious faults."

Centennial ceremonies were often confessions of national surrender to fleshy appeals. Human weakness explained for most commentators why America had not completed its assignment during its first century. A moral revival was demanded. Schools and churches were exhorted. Also important was the reappearance of an explanation of American distress which Lincoln's era had used. The corrupt man of politics or affairs was newly indicted. Here were "the devil's own princes." Such "unnumbered enemies" were once more for American nationality the cause of delaying "political right and liberty." [12]

6

Evil leaders introduced an old curse, the party. Faction now became the agent of greed and monopoly, threatening the last vestiges of a selflessness which centennial speakers recalled had flourished a hundred years before. Politicians became "parasites" and President Johnson's case was called one of those painful moments when man's deformity "is exhibited in a high place before all the people."

Partisanship easily resumed its convenient place as the reason, for many Americans, why effort to sustain the Republic through reason and selflessness had failed. As one aged Steward said in 1872, "I suffer in thought and mourn the depravity of the people," and do "not regret that I am near threescore years and ten. The future has but little promise, and I have little hope." This matter of political debauchery seemed especially to fascinate centennial sentiment. Men apologized for being trite as they acknowledged in countless statements that during America's hundreth year "we are living in an age of low standards and cheap fame." It was argued that since Jackson's generation "there has been in our political system a poison, now torpid, now active, but ever increasing in virulence until at the present time it has permeated to the utmost extremity of the body politic."

Escaping this curse needed no new device. American Stewards once again were urged to produce enlightened, selfless leaders, especially by overcoming "the material tendencies of the day." From this the next generation would have leaders who would cleanse the poison from the body politic. There were few efforts after 1870 to deny the realities of political evil, or to praise political endeavor. Even the parties acknowledged America's distress, fixing the blame, of course, upon the opposition. With massive irony, the centennial year closed in a presidential election which confirmed for most Americans how serious was the moral blindness afflicting the nation. Consequently the era of renewal was left with little but prophecies of national collapse. The Republic ended its first century unfulfilled, with "the fountain of all political power . . . disturbed to its depths." Hopes born in 1865 changed to fears that Stewards were about to destroy themselves. Beginning with high expectancy and closing in anxiety and anger, the centennial year itself was an appropriate climax to the era of renewal. The doctrine of nationality fast approached exhaustion.[13]

SPOKESMEN

The irony and chagrin which events after 1865 forced upon American introspection variously stirred the personalities speaking for this era. Men who considered the Civil War to be republicanism's affirmation had turned expectantly to watch the final act in the drama of American achievement. This would feature the Steward's surrender of self-interest to the well-being of principle. Like advocates before them, spokesmen in this era took their ideas from doctrine venerable to Western culture. Emerson was not the first who pointed to the true self through identity with universal need and values. Each generation of American advocates seemed obliged to sense anew this aspiration. Each also had to rediscover how easily selfishness would assert itself. The American outlook in the era led by U. S. Grant was no exception.

There was a pathetic quality to the expression of nationality after 1865. Circumstances encouraged for a brief, wonderful moment the hope that America was about to realize humanity's dream. America's Trust carried more immediacy and thus more heartbreak after 1865 than at any other point. The time of renewal seemed at last a moment when America might show man freed from the ancient enemy, his uninspired self. It took only a decade to blight this hope and return American nationality to the plight facing the generations of John Adams and Abraham Lincoln.

III: Advocates   Speaking for the anticipations of men emerging in a time of national renewal was young Henry James. American literature would be profoundly affected by James' disappointment with his nation's stewardship. However, at age twenty-five in 1867, James described himself as a man "of the future." Others like him would carry out America's extraordinary contribution to the world. James believed this because the fresh Stewards had a unique possession, "our moral consciousness, our unprecedented spiritual lightness and vigour." With this they would at last meet the challenge of civilization, producing on a moral foundation "a vast intellectual fusion and synthesis" of the world's tendencies. James did not expect this fruition to be completed in his lifetime, but he anticipated soon "to see something original and beautiful disengage itself from our ceaseless fermentation and turmoil."

Momentarily enchanted, young James handsomely expressed

American nationality as it awaited the ultimate man and society to arise from the Republic's renewed opportunity. James was more explicit than most advocates when he concluded: "I am willing to leave it a matter of instinct. God speed the day!" By 1869, however, hope of fulfillment was fading. A despondent James watched material greed and spiritual shortsightedness reassert control over what he still considered America's innate capacity for "character." In a celebrated statement of 1871, young Henry may have said it all when he observed: "It's a complex fate, being an American. . . ." By then James was attacking the nation's dependence on old traditions and norms. Increasingly he believed that American fulfillment required rejection of the past.

James' view thus came to surpass the general American outlook. He followed the implications of America's Trust more fearlessly than most persons could as he pushed toward a new self and society. Consequently, James' expectations steadily dwindled and he spent more time in Europe. One would think, he wrote sadly in 1874, "that in our great unendowed, unfurnished, unentertained and unentertaining continent, where we all sit sniffing, as it were, the very earth of our foundations," Americans "ought" to be able "to turn out something handsome from the very heart of simple human nature." [14]

7

More typical of America's mixed apprehension and hope were the views of Andrew Johnson and U. S. Grant, the two presidents of a renewed nation. Their assertions displayed the ambivalence which once more came upon America. The nation faced expectations after 1865 which were unequivocal. Man must transcend both self and past error for national fulfillment. In this venture, supernatural aid was indispensable. For most Americans, President Andrew Johnson did the proper thing in 1865 when he called upon "the whole people" to join in "confession of our national sins" before God who had concluded the recent war so gloriously. He suggested that men implore God's guidance toward the final goal, "national virtue and holiness." Probably influenced by George Bancroft, Johnson's first general message predicted that America would continue to be led by an "Invisible

Hand." Such aid was crucial if a "purified" America would arise from the battlefield to meet "the pledge of our fathers" by demonstrating the ultimate success of republicanism.

Andrew Johnson's hope was doomed. He soon abandoned talk of an emancipated human spirit for eulogies of law and constitutional decrees. Surrounded by tumult, Johnson spoke of limiting the ballot, of "faithful obedience" to the nation's fundamental rules, and of maintaining that which emerged from the war. Forced by circumstances to embrace the old Websterian dogma of preservation, Johnson sorrowed over the great public wrong existing in America. He looked to some remote moment "in the end" when patriotism and integrity might rescue the nation.

Johnson considered America to be far from what "our fathers" had wished. If this persisted, especially in the face of the war's pledge, it "would be a rude rending of that good faith which holds the moral world together." Consequently, "our country would cease to have any claim upon the confidence of men; it would make the war not only a failure, but a fraud." By December 1867, the President asserted that despite its renewal, the nation faced a crisis which would challenge "all the wisdom and virtue of the great men who formed our institutions originally." Constancy, obedience, morality, were familiar admonitions used anew as Johnson warned: "the public conscience swings from its moorings and yields to every impulse of passion and interest."

Upon leaving office, Andrew Johnson freely predicted new civil wars arising from law's collapse. He also foresaw tyranny accompanying the bond-holders and tax-gatherers as they raised upon the ruins of the Trust "a moneyed aristocracy." His optimism long vanished, Johnson was left with only the ancient rhetoric. "It is our sacred duty to transmit unimpaired to our posterity the blessings of liberty by the founders of the Republic, and by our example teach those who are to follow us carefully to avoid the dangers which threaten a free and independent people." [15]

U. S. Grant used his inaugural speech to place the burden on the rising generation. These future "rulers" of America, Grant said, had a special interest in maintaining the national honor. "A moment's reflection as to what will be our commanding influence among the nations of the earth in their day, if they are only true to themselves, should inspire them with national pride." Soon Grant undertook his own stewardship by seeking to annex the Dominican Republic as "a measure of national protection." The result was to be "a rapid stride toward that greatness which the intelligence, industry, and enterprise of the citizens of the United States entitle this country to assume among nations." This and other missteps may have encouraged Grant to confine his later remarks to gratifications over Europe's purported surrender to United States' ideals and example. Comforting thoughts of America guiding the world prevailed in Grant's second inaugural message. He avoided elaboration, however, asserting simply that "our own great Republic is destined to be the guiding star to all others." Ultimately, "the Great Maker" would ready the world for America's political outlook. Meantime, let the nation keep growing and doing, while education assisted the masses in appreciating the need to preserve institutions.

By 1875, Grant's uneasiness was more apparent. He called for a constitutional amendment requiring states to maintain free public schools for all children. Only through the ensuing understanding could America elude demagoguery and tyranny. Education meant conservation, of course, and Grant stressed that "the preservation of our institutions" was crucial. "They have secured the greatest good to the greatest proportion of the population of any form of government yet devised." However, republicanism could not be sustained by instinct. Like Jefferson and Adams of long before, Grant urged a trained stewardship, suggesting even that literacy be required for the franchise. This penchant for indoctrination carried into the centennial spirit. Grant enthusiastically endorsed Congress' establishment of the hamlet as the centennial idol. The early career of each locality was a topic for celebration which need not fret over America's later meandering. Grant stubbornly insisted America had now achieved that for which in a feeble time the Fathers had besought "Divine Providence." With divine aid America "has been enabled to fulfill the purpose of its founders."

Not until his last message to Congress did Grant acknowledge his errors. He then blamed Congress for joining in them. As if explaining the nation's own plight, Grant said his desire to act righteously had been thwarted by blunders in judgment. With this poignant revelation about a stewardship well designed but enfeebled by human frailty, Grant fled to less painful comments on foreign affairs.[16]

8

These presidential reflections blended three attitudes dominating America's self-awareness after 1865. As with Johnson and Grant, the national outlook entailed a simplicity of American meaning, an expectancy of immediate achievement, and a tremulous doubt that men would soon live to see national fulfillment. As the White House mingled despair and hope so did most advocates find comfort or explanation in one or more of these three vantages. Speaking for the simple outlook, one which relied either upon God's guidance or upon past virtue, were two famous New Yorkers. Henry Ward Beecher and Samuel J. Tilden advocated stewardship through inspiration. Beecher sounded passive after the war, compared to his exhortings for human endeavor during the conflict. In proposing Christ's steps, he argued against mundane guides and needs. Too long had America tolerated affairs "in which men have sacrificed principle for the sake of quieting the community." God sent war's horrors because the nation had refused "to come up to the grounds of moral truth and moral principle." Beecher now summoned all America, "laden with sin and burdened with iniquity, to rise and come to judgment." Though the nation had suffered "through five bloody years," once again great moral issues were "at our doors." Man's attitude was built on "lies." Only God had truth.

Watching the American debauch after 1865, Beecher tried salvaging the next generation of Stewards. To the youth of America he said, "take your ideal of what is right not from the great of this world. Go not to presidents, or secretaries, or generals, or merchants, or ministers, nor to any man, for your ideals." All of these were too entranced by the nation's reigning values "to be models." Beecher's prayer in 1869 would have been appropriate for John Adams' time. In America's behalf, he begged God "to save us from our wanton passions, from impertinent egotism, from pride, arrogance, cruelty, and sensual lusts, that as a nation we may show forth his praises in all the earth." The three greatest national dangers, in Beecher's judgment, were materialism, centralism, and Romanism. One and all they threatened to retard or destroy the Republic's desperately needed spiritual maturity.

By the close of the era, with political violence threatening, Beecher was obviously torn between capitulating to human evil and anticipating salvation. He admitted "the peculiar exigencies of today" posed a strain greater than America might sustain. Among the dangers at hand, that "springing from riches is great [but] not the greatest." More ominous was that American citizens no longer were guided by conscience. Beecher predicted: "our greatness will be the measure of the pangs that we shall suffer in coming disorganizations and revolutions." Yet, despite these maledictions, Beecher usually managed to conclude that some day the nation would complete its wilderness travail. Strongly hinting that the Republican party might find a shortcut to the goal of national safety, Beecher lamely told the sinful land, "A glorious future lies before us." Though its arrival might be preceded by "pain and tears," Beecher insisted "that *it will come,* I have no doubt whatsoever."

Samuel J. Tilden, whose presidential aspirations were in jeopardy at the time Beecher spoke of pain and tears, had employed another simplistic version of national endeavor. Where Beecher advised surrender and God's paths, Tilden liked to stress fidelity to America's "peculiar" ways. Admitting in 1868 that men rightly feared "for the future of our country," Tilden recommended his personal method of solace—to revere again those institutions which Americans as children had learned to cherish. In those days Tilden recalled his own expectation that "the great traditions" of America would flourish, securing "prosperity and happiness to our people evermore." Now, "my mind still clings to that illusion, if an illusion it be—I would fondly believe that it is no illusion." It was only from "the simple habits, moderate tastes, and honest purposes of the rural community [that] we must largely hope for whatever of future is reserved to our country." Tilden admitted again that he might be deluded, but he could only cleave to "the teachings of the great fathers of the American Republic." Remembering his personal talks with Revolutionary heroes, Tilden announced that he always must believe in "a great destiny for humanity before my country."

Tilden's concept of the sacred Trust was of something "broader

than any class, broader than any interest—a destiny extending
to all men, and particularly to the portion of the community who
in other countries have been the hewers of wood and the drawers
of water." But this was future business. Now the dutiful Steward
must have faith in the national purpose "as a man clings to the
only fresh and unbroken hope that there is in life." Comfort and
inspiration came from knowing that, as the Fathers watched
"from the ethereal heights," they were concerned with America's
plight. "Washington himself—his tall and peerless form leans over
from the midst of those patriots and statesmen . . . to see today
what we are about to do." For Tilden the critical moment in the
American pilgrimage had arrived. "Shall we prove ourselves
worthy of our ancestry?" If so, then the nation would attain fulfillment by bringing salvation "for the oppressed and downtrod-
den in every clime and in every age."

In the early 1870's Tilden managed to discover that the Democratic party was guardian of America's venerable traditions.
During the "midnight darkness which has brooded over the
Republic," Tilden saw light. The nation had left civil war to
rush "blindly toward the opposite peril," public and private corruption. But in drawing back to the Democratic movement,
America would escape final destruction. When the Democrats
asked him for leadership in 1876, Tilden used his favorite themes.
He advised his fellow Stewards to believe "that we now see the
dawn of a better day for our country, that . . . the Republic is
surely to be renovated." Through embracing the past, the nation
"is to live in all the future." By using Jefferson's blueprints as
guide to another national reconstruction, Tilden predicted that
once again the nation would prove "a hope to all mankind." [17]

This naïve expectancy through ancient verity bolstered the
belief in immediate achievement. This concept was typically advocated by two men who combined letters and life in a splendid
manner. George William Curtis and Carl Schurz resumed after
the war their earlier roles. After the cleansing by battle these experienced champions of principle were obliged to expect American fulfillment quickly through citizen rejuvenation. One of Curtis' most successful lectures was "The Good Fight," given in
1865–66. Through punishment America had discovered "an overpowering instinct" which made it truly a nation. This "living
consciousness" would thrive so long as the citizens retained moral

insight. "Our America shall be the Sinai of the nations, and from the terrible thunder and lightnings of its great struggle shall proceed the divine law of liberty that shall subdue and harmonize the world."

The iniquities following 1866 required astonishing reasoning for Curtis to retain his expectations. He insisted the Civil War proved that "national greatness is a moral, not a financial fact." The new era was one in which America must ready itself to show the power of morals in politics. The rising corruption and fraud were intended to quicken the Steward's perception of mammon's dangers. "Materially and morally," insisted Curtis in 1872, "the country was never more hopeful, never fuller of promise, than now." He saw national sorrow over Charles Sumner's death in 1874 as disclosing "how true, how sound, how generous is still the heart of the American people." This was refreshing insight "when politics seem peculiarly mean and selfish and corrupt, when there is a general vague apprehension that the very moral foundations of the national character are loosened." Sumner had shown that morality remained "the sole salvation of America."

In April 1875, Curtis spoke to persons, including President Grant, gathered to celebrate the centennial of the Concord battle. He kept trying to prove that America could meet the new century's demands, despite problems unforeseen by the Founders. Now immorality had a new ally, the "fashion of scepticism of American principles" which led to a "despondency" and a conviction that the once proud Republic "sits today among shattered hopes." This national pessimism was a mortal enemy. Against it Curtis could offer only faith in American principles. He stolidly proclaimed during 1876 that American fulfillment was dependent solely on "the moral character of the people." Consequently, such afflictions as civil war and recession were welcome in forcing the nation to emerge "greater, better, truer, nobler."

Until the close of the era Curtis insisted that American fulfillment was near. Both "the spirit and principles of our fathers" would enable the present generation to deliver "our noble heritage" to the new century "enlarged, beautiful, ennobled." Not even the unnerving election dispute at the close of 1876 shook Curtis' insistence on the power of venerable national truths. Edward Everett Hale contended that Curtis' speech on puritan principles during December 1876 moved the nation to accept electoral conciliation. There could be only one America, Curtis proclaimed, for the land was dominated by a spirit which began with the Puritans and had "ripened into Abraham Lincoln of the Illinois prairie." To sustain this spirit, there was "the free State, the free Church, the free School—these are the triple armor of American nationality." He called on the strength and wisdom of three centuries to curb the furious spirit abroad in America. The wondrous truths from the past would encircle "our native land, against the mad blows of violence or the fatal dry rot of fraud." [18]

Somewhat more realistic was Carl Schurz, who had become a senator from Missouri. While he eloquently predicted America's fulfillment through moral awakening, Schurz joined in the liberal strategies to have principles seize the regular Republican organization. The latter for Schurz and others represented what was detaining the nation. Party indifference explained American tardiness in building a nation upon virtue and law. Across America Schurz described national completion through "the infusion of a new moral spirit into our political life." Looking back from 1874, Schurz could recall one moment when America came close to such fruition through the promptings of Daniel Webster, "a huge Atlas, who carried the Constitution on his shoulders. He could have carried there the whole moral grandeur of the Nation, had he never compromised his own."

Despite these memories, Schurz peered more openly than did Curtis at the ugliness of human weakness. In 1874, Schurz said the American eagle was too ashamed of his nation to soar on the Fourth of July. However, Schurz's outrage brought no remedy save recourse to ancient truth. National rescue lay in man's heart. Schurz rejected immutable process as controlling America's drama. Only the decision made in each soul would spare the nation. Schurz agreed with Curtis that from a divine past came the wisdom to carry America forward. To ignore the verities from that past jeopardized America's future. Renewing these truths in the Republic's later days would ensure the ultimate America.

Although Schurz would casually mention "the National will" and America's "exalted mission on earth," his preference was to speak for a decisive individual stewardship. Mammon and passion most threatened the nation by creating organized political and economic forces which overwhelmed the citizen. Schurz especially regretted shouts for Manifest Destiny. Such cries were "pathological phenomena" and "sinister," all "deadly contamination" to destroy the Republic. He argued that America had "come of age." It was now time amid trials and dangers "to consider calmly . . . in what way the American Republic can achieve the most useful, and therefore the most glorious position in the history of the human race." Self-evaluation was the technique required of effective Stewards, Schurz argued. Men must discover the precarious relationship between the theory and the practice of republicanism. Candor would combat "inveterate habit, prejudice, and the corrupt influences developed to such alarming power" in America.

After the Liberal Republican failure in 1872, Schurz found himself in the quandary generally gripping America's nationality. He still had difficulty anticipating good from the nation itself, since it was an instrument, not a power or force. The individual Steward remained for Schurz the essential reaper in the fields of American achievement. But seeing the plight of private morals, Schurz acknowledged in 1874 that there was sound reason for wide despair. He had nothing new to offer except a revival of tested precepts in man's heart. These would "regenerate and put upon a firmer footing than ever the free institutions of this Republic." Unless this happened, Schurz predicted national failure; America would be not a glorious model "but only another warning example." This made the centennial especially welcome to Schurz. It might rekindle the "dutiful spirit" needed to slow the deep disgrace America was entering "in the estimation of mankind."

As chairman of the Reform Conference which gathered in New York City in May 1876, Schurz obviously influenced the "Address to the People" which the conclave issued. It was a blunt document, aimed at what it called the moral squalor across America. Surely, it said, "every patriotic citizen feels the burning shame of the spectacle presented in this centennial year." On the one side, "momentoes and monuments of the virtues of the past," and on the other "the shocking evidence of the demoralization and corruption of the present." The only hope for America was private morality. In a later speech at Cincinnati, Schurz confessed that favorable physical circumstances alone had spared the Republic. A regenerate citizenry might yet rescue the nation. Thus, to the close of an agonizing era, Schurz preached the magic of spiritual renewal.[19]

Another approach was taken by men like Walt Whitman and
James Russell Lowell. For them America's renewal in 1865
granted a new chance to cover the long distance facing national
responsibility. The future had always been important in American opinion, but Whitman and Lowell gave it an enlarged significance. The difference between these two writers and Curtis
and Schurz largely was one of tactics. These four advocates, along
with Tilden, Beecher, and nearly everyone else, agreed on the
importance of moral reformation. They shared in the last campaign for the individual. The source, pace, and fruition of individual renewal brought differing interpretations, but there was
agreement on the need for awakened Stewards to complete the
triumph begun by Lincoln. Whitman and Lowell provided a more
thoughtful exposition of this doctrine.

Whitman's famous essay "Democratic Vistas," written in the
troubled year 1868, was built upon familiar beliefs. The obvious
discrepancy between American opportunity and shortcoming
vexed the poet. Gone was his more sanguine outlook of 1855.
"Democratic Vistas" acknowledged that America would be either
a great triumph or "tremendous failure." After dismissing material achievement, Whitman proposed to talk of a superior "nationality." America must be a spirit or idea, surpassing written law,
self-interest, and material objects. The latter now dominated,
leaving Americans "canker'd, crude, superstitious, and rotten,"
with "hollowness at heart." Men did not believe in men, and
until they did, America was in peril. The absence of a national
soul obviously tormented Whitman, who consequently dis-
counted America's previous growth. "Far, far, indeed, stretch in
distance, our Vistas! How much still to be disentangled, freed!"

Freedom, for Whitman, meant an emancipation from the human frailty, blindness, and superstition implicit in past belief.
Morality would come when men confronted the human self.
Whitman was vague about the likely qualities of the American
Steward, but he was quite explicit on the travail which must
accompany self-scrutiny. American nationality rested with the
inner struggle in every American soul, made the more difficult
because of the evil abroad in the land. "We sail a dangerous sea
of seething currents . . . all so dark, untried—and whither shall
we turn? It seems as if the Almighty had spread before this nation
charts of imperial destinies, dazzling as the sun, yet with many an

intestine difficulty, and human aggregate of cankerous imperfection." This summary by Whitman of the tormented American nationality is incomparable for beauty and accuracy. But not everyone could accept Whitman's belief that America would require "ages, centuries" to outdistance the omnipresent foes, greed, deceit, passion, and lethargy.

The matter of time troubled Whitman in the prefaces to the 1872 and 1876 editions of his poetry. Particularly in 1876 did he stress that the nation faced a mighty age of change, with "violent contrasts, fluctuations of light and shade, of hope and fear." America was seething material out of which might arise "the grand nationality of the future." Surrounded by material triumph and human decay, such Americans as Whitman had to establish the Trust in spiritual dimensions and in remote settings. For this viewpoint, the Republic's fulfillment seemed more distant than men had perceived even a hundred years earlier. Whitman emphasized this. The first century "has been but preparation, adolescence," a "formative career" in which "the morbid facts" of politics and people were "but passing incidents." Now let the ship of state start "upon deep water," to enter upon its "real history." America was still, Whitman said, "a prophecy." [20]

James Russell Lowell began the era with more confidence than Whitman displayed. He concluded it with a deeper, quieter concern. In 1866 Lowell was talking of a nation which had displayed such "hardshelled virtue" in the war as to justify at last "more confidence than apprehension" over the country's remaining difficulties. While a nation's judgment developed and moved slowly, Lowell thought he detected a popular faculty appearing that was prudent and principled. From this would come the dedication to fundamental values so necessary to nationality. "We have only to be unswervingly faithful to what is the true America of our hope and belief, and whatever is American will rise from one end of the country to the other instinctively to our side." Stewardship and national cooperation thus rested as far as Lowell could perceive with "being loyal and faithful to Truth. . . ." Such dedication Lowell at times elevated to *"instinct."*

What Lowell opposed was any determination to believe that America's future was assured. He warned in 1867 that it was nonsense for Americans simply to claim "from the flight of our eagles that tomorrow shall be ours." Great though the nation might be materially, it was still only "a phenomenon" until "the germ of nationality" could bring each Steward to appreciate great ideas and great men. Lowell even accepted Europe's criticisms as means by which American thought might rise beyond provincialism as well as "our absorption in the practical, as we politely call it, meaning the material."

By 1873 Lowell was reduced to advising that national misbehavior not force generalizations about American character. "I hope that my feeling that the country is growing worse is nothing more than men of my age have always felt when they looked back to the *tempus actum*." The centennial atmosphere prompted Lowell to join most of his countrymen in nostalgia. He recalled the day when John Adams died. "I wish I could feel, as I did then, that we were a chosen people, with a still valid claim to divine interpositions." In 1876 Lowell said that Satan seemed to have become guide for national endeavor. This left him to observe that "our experiment of innoculation with freedom is to run its course through all Christendom, with what result the wisest cannot predict." Lowell saw in the future "a constant fight against weeds, against the wild growths of nature that are pushing while we sleep, and some of us have been foolish enough to think that in a Democracy our weeding would be done for us." [21]

9

Concerns expressed by these spokesmen also touched the era's periodicals. Some made of expectation a joy, while others accepted uncertainty as stimulant for deeper faith. There were also those whose misgiving deepened. If there was thoughtful assurance about national fulfillment, the magazines published by Harper and a new journal in San Francisco, *Overland Monthly*, reflected it. *Harper's Monthly* entered the postwar era with grand spirits. By 1867 it retreated to a cautious pose. *Harper's Weekly* even advocated the Republican party as overseer for fruitful stewardship. Both magazines for a time shared the spirit of an 1866 poem in the *Monthly*:

> I am a live American,
> Life's meaning on my breast.
> . . . I grapple savage Nature's mane,
> And make her to me bow . . .
> Push along, push along, keep moving!

Harper's Monthly featured an article in 1867 which found that the experience of the 1860's had "made of us a new and better people." Patriotism was producing a more powerful idealism in the nation. It would combat the materialism which had blinded men from seeing that "the God of our fathers has called us to organize liberty in this nineteenth century." Indeed, "this is the American's mission and ought to be his inspiration." At last the nation had an instinct, an intuition, for "primal ideas are lighting us on to our daily work." There was a "national will," an awareness now of a divine purpose. The author, Samuel Osgood, said an overpowering national spirit had captured America, giving the sense of mission a "religious dignity." Osgood insisted, "It possesses us more than we possess it."

While Osgood talked of a "far-sighted sagacity" guiding the Republic, other contributors to *Harper's Monthly* began conceding that national mishandling "would shame a bungler or a knave." Moral rearmament was needed to complete the renewal begun in the Civil War. Then "official virtue will cease to be a by-word, and private faithlessness lose the excuse it takes from public laxity." America could thereafter for the first time show "a model republicanism, as a commonwealth ruled by common-sense and common virtue." Another poem, appearing in 1871, showed the journal's drift in sentiment:

> When this old flag was new
> The manners and the men
> That are so pretty now
> Methinks were better then.

Among the reasons for the Founders' superiority was their willingness to work, and also:

> They read the Bible then
> And all believed it true;
> For they were simple folk
> When this old flag was new.

In 1875 *Harper's Monthly* began a series of "Centennial Papers" which expressed alarm at the "demoralizing influences" working in America since 1865. The once jubilant magazine found "the want of uprightness" so desperate at the close of America's first century as to leave only one question: "Is there such a poison in the political system that there is no cure for it?" It seemed that America could become merely "a degenerate form of polity within the next hundred years." The nation's Trust stood waiting much as it had in Jefferson's day. "All our future, then, hangs on the strength of the moral and religious causes at work or that can be used for the elevation of the American character."

Harper's Weekly was less cautious. Its attitude after 1865 was one of the few benign views of America's successful renewal. A long Fourth of July editorial in 1865 contained the journal's philosophy. The nation had begun as an experiment. The trial had been frightful, yet "the people breasted the combined and prolonged fury of anarchy and despotism, and triumphed. Today they stand erect and victorious under the perfect rainbow of the departing storm, and that bow is the promise of peace to mankind." *Harper's Weekly* liked to repeat: "The experiment is complete." Now men should realize that "every question within the nation will be wisely settled by the same popular good sense and patient patriotism which has saved the nation."

As time brought new public folly and evil, the *Weekly* kept claiming confidence in "the moral force of the nation." Once dubious, such power "is indisputable now," so that every American could trust "the public sagacity and heroism as he never did before." Yuletide in 1868 found the journal conceding that "passion seethes" but still insisting no threat existed to America which its "sagacity and resolution will not remove." By 1870, *Harper's Weekly* was less certain that America had found the path between politics and morality. "Intelligence and honesty, these are the charmed lance and shield. Without them there may be a vast nation, but only with these can there be a free and progressive people." As the centennial approached, the *Weekly* admitted this lance and shield gathered dust. Citizens were not adequately responding to the wonderful, renewed polity. While national principles were clear, the Stewards apparently needed more time for moral and social growth.

Harper's Weekly managed to find joyful meaning in the centennial. While a century earlier men fought for their independence, the Founders' sons "are today contending for the mastery with corruption and decay, in order that the security of those rights may be confirmed and strengthened." In this way, even the ebullient *Harper's Weekly* acknowledged America's incompleteness. It left the journal scarcely differing with the general American outlook. The national design was complete; now the individual must prove his capacities to carry forward America's institutions.[22]

Overland Monthly, a California journal originating early in this era, enjoyed using material which considered the peopling of the Far West as fulfillment of America's destiny. The nation's physical attainment could bring further national accomplishment not now foreseeable. Toward this end, *Overland* proudly offered Mrs. Sarah B. Cooper's 1871 essay, "Motherhood," which said that America's disease of "selfish wickedness" was dangerously advanced. It even dissuaded American women from bearing children. Of all the day's "moral maladies," this was the gravest. Mrs. Cooper contended that "a genuine Pentacostal season of sweet and loving maternity" would launch America's moral victory. The nation's "public conscience" had become "very rusty and slipshod" and "so attenuated as to be hardly recognizable."

According to Mrs. Cooper, detestable attitudes of selfishness and sloth were now bequeathed to the temperament of America's youth. This explained why the nation had fallen "upon degenerate times." What was once a "race of noble men and women" had become "enfeebled." Mrs. Cooper predicted that if parents adopted new zest and vigor, the next American generation would reflect it—"let virtue bequeath virtue." If a plodding, unaspiring mood dominated the generative process, America would revert "back to barbarism" or would be "blotted from the eath." The article's conclusion was provocative. "Is America, the presumptive mistress of civilization, keeping abreast of her own projected work?" If so, then let husbands "fall newly in love . . . every morning" with their wives.[23] Mrs. Cooper's doctrine of national fulfillment through eugenics was probably the most ardent approach to this era's chief concern about nationality, the disappointing personal life of the citizen.

Why did citizens so readily submit to selfishness, corruption, and laziness when a splendid Trust had been restored in 1865? This question formed the major intellectual concern of this era. Spokesmen for nationality consequently were involved in the last meaningful defense of primitive individuality in American existence. The issue's powerful appeal can be seen in the extent to which it still claimed the attention of three major journals. The trio of magazines was *Atlantic, North American Review,* and *Galaxy,* a newcomer. *Galaxy* thrived briefly in New York City, where it boasted of Samuel Clemens on its staff.

By 1868, *Galaxy* was conceding the new inroads materialism made upon the Republic. America was gripped by coarseness and sordid selfishness. "Among the fathers and mothers of this generation such hard, self-seeking behavior was unknown." However, the journal refused to share the gloom it said was spreading over American prospects. Surely with men of 1861 still about, America could be saved. *Galaxy* became pessimistic in 1875, observing that cynicism was now abroad, afflicting even the nation's last hope, its youth. Although *Galaxy* conceded that American "public life is shockingly corrupt," it disagreed that this was a result of the republican system. It was human nature, captivated by money, which had failed.

Meantime, many *Galaxy* authors joined the discussion. For instance, Walt Whitman and Eugene Benson debated America's chances of ever escaping the ravages of mammon. This exchange concluded, as did so much of America's view at the time, that any hope rested with a return to first principles, those of the Fathers. Here, too, *Galaxy* seemed content. Its centennial commentary announced that eventually America's Stewards would embrace the moral guides needed by a great nation. As one voice insisted: "All we want is time for our national stream to settle. It will settle in time, and our national character will become apparent." [24]

Rejoicing in the nation's renewal, *Atlantic* had asked Charles Sumner to sound the jubilance of victory. He promised that "the name of the Republic will be exalted until every neighbor, yielding to irresistible attraction, will seek a new life in becoming part of the great whole, and the national example will be more puissant than army or navy for the conquest of the world." *Atlantic* authors spoke often about "the renewal of our national life" and "the second birth of the Republic." In 1870 Thomas Wentworth Higginson urged an "attitude of hope," arising from "the consciousness of a new impulse given to all human progress." With this faith, the Stewards were "entitled to an imperturbable patience and hopefulness" as they watched the nation's character emerge slowly, with "vacillations and vibrations of movement." Higginson was one of the first to suggest relief for the old individualism. "We need to become national, not by conscious effort, implying attitudinizing and constraint, but by simply accepting our own life." Eventually "the higher Americanism" would emerge, although "centuries" might be required.

Other contributors to *Atlantic* were less assured. Greed and ignorance were for them so powerful that America needed new policies. These, combined with education and the reassuring knowledge of Anglo-Saxon vigor, might permit America to survive a time of spoliation. Two important 1875 essays joined this debate. One was anonymous and the other was by Horace E. Scudder, biographer and later editor of the *Atlantic*. Scudder called America "a nation slowly struggling against untoward outward circumstance and inward dissension, collecting by degrees its constituent members, forming and reforming, plunging with rude strength sometimes down dangerous ways, but nevertheless growing into integral unity." Scudder condemned the "uneasy national consciousness," which should be replaced by an "instinctive sense of nationality." This was needed "when gloom overcasts the political landscape." Such times called for "a sturdy belief in the nation as a divine fact." Scudder's most substantial comment said America was "making ready for a new start in history."

The anonymous article by a Philadelphian rebuked the mystical futurism which persons like Scudder accepted. The writer preferred to ask: "What has happened to us? Are we rotten before we are ripe?" But after he insisted that America was a "deplorable spectacle of a country without solidarity, without a soul . . . a base mart," the writer could suggest only a return to the Fathers' path guided by the Founders' "fundamental ideas and principles." Such a route led to the "moral greatness" America must have for its ultimate completion. It was clear that the greatness of the Civil War had vanished. "Where are those Americans? Where, alas!" Meanwhile good men hid in shame before "the disgraceful spectacle" of centennial America. *Atlantic*'s anonymous writer insisted that such shy souls "are only less guilty in degree than the men whose villainies are making our name a hissing at home and abroad." With principle at bay before greed and ignorance, America's character had been captured by "low rascality." This grim candor and Scudder's surrender to process put before *Atlantic*'s audience in 1875 the two important ideological alternatives facing most thoughtful Americans.[25]

North American Review authors began this era by acclaiming the Civil War as a watershed. "The Civil War which has changed the current of our ideas, and crowded into a few years the emotions of a lifetime, has in a measure given to the preceding period of our history the character of a remote state of political existence." National feeling now commanded American minds as the nation completed its growth guided by "supreme forces" of which men were unconscious. These forces were part of a principled universe ultimately mastering men's thoughts. According to these spokesmen for naturalism, any American blunder was not from innate defect but from "excrescences which time would rid." The American purpose was still to prove moral law triumphant in human affairs.

Misgiving began creeping into *North American Review* pages by 1868, as E. L. Godkin and others acknowledged trouble. Americans had failed. They preferred their wits to tradition and law. Godkin rebuked naturalism, pleading that America stop relying upon the popular concept of "inevitable progress," and instead make "special efforts toward reform." Cosmic design was a stumbling block, Godkin argued, while Henry Adams wrote of riotous passion and corruption in the land. Adams appealed to "fundamental principles" in a thoughtful definition of stewardship. "To build by slow degrees this deep foundation of moral conviction . . . a work not inferior in quality to that of the Republic's founders, is an aim high enough to satisfy the ambition of one generation. Such a movement must necessarily be slow."

By 1874, voices in *North American Review* found conditions in America "anything but the golden age expected." The free individual, even with deep Anglo-Saxon roots, had not responded as anticipated to the transformation of American life. "Private interest empowered, escaped control, and running at last into sheer corrupting disease"—this was the plight of stewardship. One shrewd observer said Americans had "enthusiastic faith" in the form of their beloved polity, but when implementing it they showed only "prodigal distrust, incrimination, contempt. . . ."

During the centennial, however, contributors to the journal withdrew from this grim philosophy to share in the hour's conventional comfort. America's fulfillment was said to require recognition by thoughtful citizens of the forces and principles at work both among and within them. Such citizenry would in time strike blows at "impudent wrong." Authors, including William Graham Sumner, Daniel C. Gilman, and Simon Newcombe, preached the era's ambiguous philosophy. Both the presence of immutable laws guiding national development and the need for an intelligent stewardship to discover and use these laws were stressed. Sumner's article was especially instructive. The Republic must use its power to meet the grave tasks ahead. While the Civil War had brought good out of simple instincts, the issues facing America in 1876 were such as to call for high intellect and training. These must be linked with a renewal of the moral fervor of the war years as man moved through awesome new economic and social challenges to justice and right.

Sumner and his colleagues showed how nationality was being forced to make prospect out of retrospect. American fulfillment asked that men learn the rules, the absolutes inherent in their system which determined a majestic process of development. Consciousness of these laws implied a triumph of individualism as men obeyed or used, the verbs being interchangeable, these rules. Stewardship had come to mean awareness of life's facts. This confusion over national fulfillment was especially evident in *North American Review*'s October 1876 issue. A discussion of Benjamin Bristow's futile assault against evil concluded that corruption so commanded America as to muzzle the nation's leaders. "And these silent men are today the worst enemies of the Republic." Somehow the people must "rise in might to save America."

However, a few pages later, Henry Adams and Henry Cabot Lodge announced that the last ten years had allowed most Americans to recognize their weakness. The old "boastfulness and arrogance" were vanishing as the nation prepared to watch the monumental progression toward American completion. Human weakness and corruption had their place. But above such mo-

mentary pettiness there was "the real majesty and force of the
national movement." Adams and Lodge implied that the mature
American beheld at the nation's heart "a silent pulsation that
commands his respect, a steady movement that resembles in its
mode of operation the mechanical action of Nature herself." [26]

The era's mingling of will and process was less convincing to
other journals. These were consistently pessimistic about America's renewal, drawing upon the Christian position. Important in
this outlook were the veteran *Ladies' Repository* and *Hearth
and Home*. A new journal, *Scribner's Monthly,* advocated the
old moralism. It opened its career in 1870 by announcing that
in "the old bigotries of Puritanism" were the roots of "that
which is purest and best in American life." Admonitions from
Scribner's were expressed in an editorial column entitled "Topics of the Times." Its theme was America's retrogression since
1865, and it condemned even the nation's best quality, its good
nature, for enduring the rascal and the rogue. "It begets a toleration of every kind of moral evil that bring at last insensibility
to it." The journal assailed any axiomatic belief in the superiority and certain progress of America. Such nonsense titillated
the "traditional vanity of the American people." The "national
edifice" had to stand or fall upon the virtue and intelligence of
each citizen. This meant that the ignorance and anarchy now
rising could prove fatal. Clay and Webster were called victims
of the lust for place, a passion which had become dominant. If
unchecked it meant "our republicanism will be as contemptible
among the nations as it is unworthy in itself."

Scribner's approached the centennial in desperation. Believing
that America's completion required the awakening of dormant
morality, the magazine pleaded for the nation to become righteous in 1876. It meant that "the rotten houses should go down,
and that we shall, practically, start during our Centennial, on a
new and prosperous national life." The closest *Scribner's* came
to the doctrine of process was in a long editorial in July 1876.
It said that America lingered in childhood, despite a pace of
growth which made men feel old. National survival was due
only to those "stern virtues of the fathers of the Republic." Now,
after a "momentary eclipse," these principles were enlarging
their hold. "The call for reform and purification, that rises

everywhere today, is but an echo to the cry that reaches us across the century, from men who sealed their incorruptible patriotism with their blood." The new stewardship was "to make the next century as notable for its political integrity, and its moral beauty, as the last has been for its progress in material good." [27]

A similar concern dominated *Hearth and Home,* which was begun in New York in 1869. It looked openly to the next generation, a view especially appealing to Edward Eggleston who joined the journal in 1871. The magazine ably summarized the frustration of nationality: "As a people we are becoming fearfully demoralized by this tempest of endeavor." Rescue could accompany an awakening of "the good sense of the country." Debauchery would diminish when America discovered that "all success is not a success of gold."

Until it ceased editorial comment during 1874, *Hearth and Home* had eloquently expressed distaste for the present and uneasiness about the future. However, American circumstances were so scandalous that the journal veered helplessly from deep gloom to hope derived from a new generation. The Fourth of July in 1873 brought from the journal a reminder that, although national morality was feeble, the republican system had been proven. The next month, however, featured tormented speculation as to whether "the deadlier disease of luxury and dishonest money-getting, which killed the old republics," had not fastened itself upon America.

Hearth and Home opposed an ostentatious centennial display. What irony it would be, considering the "debauching of the public conscience" by mammon after 1865. Rather, the nation should study "the type of manhood we have evolved." On the nation's birthday "we shall do well to search ourselves and see how much of our boasted progress is superficial and coarse." The answer was painfully clear, so the weary journal passed the Trust to the next generation. The latter must face "largely social and moral" issues, for the Founders' opinions might well be outmoded. Apathetic youth should recognize that each generation must meet its own issues afresh.

As for the shameful present generation, the magazine said: "the sooner we return to the good old paths of our fathers the better it will be for ourselves and our children." Contemporary

America was so debased that it could survive only with the sword of law. With this *Hearth and Home* ended its editorial career. There was nothing further it could safely say.[28]

After long exhorting America, *Ladies' Repository* gave up the battle in 1876. To the end, however, it advocated a Christian nation against passion and mammon. For a short time it joined the exultation at the close of the war. It called the experiment of America a success. With liberty and Protestantism, the nation had a sublime prospect. The prospect had diminished by 1867, leaving the future a more dismal caste. Now even American women were victims of economic desire. If the female accepted "the yoke of modern materialism," America's last hope for moral insight was gone. Except for one Websterian article in 1868, *Ladies' Repository* used contributors who saw only America's danger. Its analysis: "the public conscience is drugged with immoral maxims." The evils were so deadly that America "shall die of them unless we return our steps to the plain paths of the Constitution." Once more the act of preservation was made to promise individual regeneration. This was the closest the journal came to a means of national deliverance.

Centennial articles in *Ladies' Repository* concentrated on a national corruption whose origin was evident. "Let the whole blame of our public disgrace be put where it belongs—upon the natural depravity of the human heart." Total spiritual "regenertion" was the nation's only hope. This transformation would need the help of Christ, who alone could "extinguish the passions that have caused us our national shame. . . . It was the Christ-power in the hearts of the founders of the Republic, more than anything else, that gave grandeur and permanency to their labors."

Along with other spokesmen for nationality, *Ladies' Repository* did what it could to comfort contemporary America. National shortcoming would persist until God produced a new people. After the old American was discarded, the journal predicted God's nation would emerge. Citizen endeavor was not rejected completely. If "the people will be aroused," and join in God's great purpose, America could expect to see its Trust discharged. *Ladies' Repository* said that by 1976 there could be "mankind perfected." The journal showed how desperate and confused the advocacy of nationality had become. Its final pages

talked alternately of mortal hopelessness and eventual supernatural intervention. The only clear thought was that national
renewal had made a false beginning.[29]

IV: Responses   After 1865 voices across
the land joined in more ardent praise or more earnest despair
than had been heard before. The time of national renewal was
the most difficult moment in the nineteenth century for America's
assumptions about individualism. Completion of America's Trust
momentarily rested on man's shoulder. The brief delight at this
in 1865 quickly became a fatuous assurance which subsided by
centennial time. Grim disclosures from the lapsed decade had
brought endless sermonizing on volatile humanity's total dependence upon principle and a repudiation of America's advance as a
complex, material culture. Confidence in a model republican
organization had been dispelled. American thought generally
conceded that the nation's renewed Trust had not yet elicited
the understanding nor the endeavor it deserved.

10

Happiness prevailed on the Fourth of July in 1865. Words
spoken at Burlington, New Jersey, were duplicated across the
country. "We have gained immensely in national character, and
in the grandest result of character—power for good." By embracing liberty, "we have renovated the national life. We have un-
burdened the national conscience." America could give thanks.
The nation could act with confidence, for its system had "power
to benefit mankind." In Chicago, the war's great result was
ascribed to the "instinct," the "impulse" of the "masses of the
people." In New York, the nation was acclaimed as "a great vital
and intelligent organism, whose heart and arteries pulsate with
healthful, loyal blood." This made certain that the "powers of
evil cannot prevail against it." In Connecticut, the nation's
"eager and confused" career was now finished, and "a more ex-
pansive national life" with "a calmer, steadier progress" had
begun. All of this revealed "a higher moral sphere." Others talked
of ordeals completed by fire and baptisms of blood.
    Such general gratification captured an early editorial in the
Nation which claimed that the very being of the nation "had
been cemented by the blood of thousands of sons." The American

polity was now permanent and proven. For men like Governor
Conrad Baker of Indiana this meant that the war had proven
freedom, and "a regenerated Republic shouted Amen." A Methodist hymn of 1866 caught the assurance from renewal which
many articles and speakers were showing:

> No murm'rings through the land resound
> But sweet content spread all around.
> Happy the people thus at rest,
> With laws, and peace, and commerce blessed.
> Then happy we—no good denied
> Who claim the Lord *our* God beside!

The bliss lingered merely a moment. By 1874 a typical song
conceded that the Civil War had created only the prospect "of
better day and clime" for America. "A nation from itself
redeemed," was still possible, but not if

> . . . greed and lust
> Eat out our faith, eat out our trust,
> The fibres of our manhood loose.

Even the most optimistic could not overlook this concern. While
the war might have demonstrated the endurance of America and
thus of republican design, the nation's pilgrimage moved on.
Americans themselves must further serve the Trust in a manner
to prove themselves worthy of their calling. While Lincoln and
his army had suggested the value of both nation and citizen,
events by 1876 had forced a more cautious tone upon any remaining celebrants. The poet, Bayard Taylor, was reduced to telling
a friend in 1875: "Our Country is still worth something, in spite
of all you may hear against it."

The limited centennial jubilation appeared mostly in newspaper editorials and in song. These expressions struggled with
the problem now crucial to national ideology. They tried to acclaim America's triumph as complete while admonishing the
citizen to seek still distant goals. A typical effort began:

> Columbia, thou wast in thy youth
> A hundred years ago.
> It scarcely sounds like honest truth,

> So fastly thou dost grow.
> Such noble triumphs have been thine,
> Within a hundred years,
> That nations come from every clime,
> To crown thee with their cheers.

But then the inevitable mandate:

> And we pray God, in the future,
> Thy motto e'er may be,
> Onward and upward ever, till
> All people shall be free.
> And in one glorious union
> The nations shall unite,
> Enjoying sweet communion,
> And glory in the right.

Philadelphia, center of the formal rejoicing, had a newspaper whose struggles for assurance typified this phase of America's response. *North American* began the centennial year strongly implying that material achievement was evidence enough of both citizen and society's blessedness. "All that wealth can command, industry produce and ingenuity accomplish" attested to "a people self-created, self-taught, independent and sovereign in their own rights." On Washington's Birthday, *North American* proudly claimed that the nation had so exceeded the Father's dreams as to be "freed from the great danger of its beginning and youth." Moreover, the original principles producing the Republic were "confirmed in their sufficiency."

By Easter time, however, such talk was weakening. Conceding that grave evil still existed in America, *North American* used the great Exhibition's opening to emphasize the future. The commemoration must serve as an educational experience, demonstrating "what the country may anticipate from what it has accomplished—what the world may hope from this progress in the past." From all celebrants must come "a more glowing patriotism, a more ardent national spirit, a stouter resolution that . . . industry, intelligence and virtue are crowned here in public and private life."

Further tempering of joy occurred on the Fourth of July when *North American* adopted a conventional outlook. It regretted

that America must suspect itself. New courage was needed in the
struggle toward fulfillment, said the paper as it urged faithful
Stewards to rescue the Trust. "We do not know of any work
nobler for the citizen to do than save the nation. . . . Nations
must be taken care of." This would be America's achievement
"if once the mass of the people can be trained up to the proper
standard." No longer acclaiming virtual fulfillment, *North American* concluded 1876 hesitantly. Noting the exhibition's finish, it
spoke of hope that "as the meeting of a few in this city an hundred years ago inaugurated all we have seen and have now, so
the meeting . . . now closed may prove the precursor of a still
greater progress and the herald of absolute complete national
and individual happiness."

Not all the voices of assurance were so reasonable. One was
the Albany *Journal,* a Republican newspaper whose editorial
practice illustrated why many Americans feared partisanship.
"Let the Eagle scream, and the Flag float," it said. These
deserved "the jubilant and unqualified homage of every thorough
American." According to the *Journal,* America's joy should be
unconfined. The nation had increased in power while keeping
sight of morality. All of this meant that America must not again
turn to the Democratic party. In Indianapolis, another newspaper
editor was certain that not until 1876 had the nation's principles
been so well understood. Scandals and scoundrels had no effect.
All true citizens could swell "with patriotic pride at what we
as a nation have done." There was pleasure even in mammon.
"Industry rules the world. This is the grandest teaching of the
past and the brightest promise of the future, and it is the lesson
of the Centennial."

However, even this Indiana ecstasy paused occasionally to
acknowledge the unfortunate occurrences before 1876. These
really did not matter, said the Hoosier editor, for the American
polity was "incomparably superior to any other now in existence,
or yet devised among men." Given this wondrous system, faults
of practice were inconsequential. The equation of political design with American fulfillment received little support. Instead,
most optimistic responses preferred America as an unfolding
phenomenon whose triumphant completion was still to come.
Such was the view of William M. Evarts, soon to become secretary of state, who spoke in 1876 to the multitude gathered for

the Fourth of July services in Philadelphia. Be of modest cheer, Evarts seemed to say. He insisted America's fundamental spirit was not dead and that the original principles would yet be revived. "We have not proved unworthy of a great ancestry; we have had the virtue to uphold what they so wisely, so firmly established." But Evarts conceded that the manner in which the inspired legacy was being passed on to the next century had become alarming.

Other optimists took up talk of expansion. The final act of stewardship was beyond the continent. Here were "Heaven's decrees" for America to carry out. Americans were "graduates of the universe," said an Ohio speaker, who predicted that with every assignment the Republic would also receive from Providence the proper leader. This assured America as "a people of great destinies." Another joyful noise added: "I think we are bound to attain the maximum of our power. No human hand has led us hither, and no human hand can curb that destiny or arrest its progress." Thus would America "rise grandly up to the utmost of our hope" with a "resistless sweep," leaving the planets to mark footsteps, and the universe as "our throne." Generally these responses, determined to be hopeful about America, emphasized relentless process or towering principle. Postwar events had left them small ground for talk of human adequacy or individual contribution.[30]

11

With man's weakness troubling even the joyful view, much of the broad reaction to national purpose became a redoubled exhortation of the Stewards. Here the uncertain spirit of the age found comfort. One of the most pointed of such responses appeared in an early issue of *Nation,* a journal eager for citizen rehabilitation. The article called "The Paradise of Mediocrities," by Charles Eliot Norton, openly expressed the misgiving often disguised before the war. Low morals and weak intelligence were clearly the enemy staying the nation from answering its divine call. "It is hard to say it," Norton announced, "but there are very few first-rate things in America, and scarcely any first-rate work done here."

In stressing what he called the irony in the American situation, Norton faced the era's fundamental issue. The irony ap-

peared, he said, when America's reality was placed against that
superiority "to which we look forward and in which we believe
as the genuine and inevitable result of the unimpeded development of democratic society and institutions." America's devastating pace was the culprit. "We have had too much work to do in
a given time to do it well." Norton restored an old challenge.
Henceforth, the good Steward would advance the nation through
personal adherence to high standard. Later, in the upheaval of
nationality during 1898, Norton would be one of the few to suggest that America should learn to live with the fact that citizens
were imperfect.

Appeals to individualism brought new didacticism after 1865.
An address at Amherst College tried to put a fresh face on the
opportunity for improved individual and social effort. "Many
new questions are before us," therefore men of learning must
"take up politics to purify them." By centennial time, much of
American thought turned upon the challenge issued in *Nation*
and at Amherst. Given the record of dismal stewardship, men
again turned to past precepts for future sustenance.

A Michigan statement was typical. It first asserted that "our
national temple" now had its "finishing arch." Men could not
contend that "here is a partially completed structure." It was at
last "a fitting abode of freedom." Yet those who would enter this
temple were dallying with mammon and passion. This left the
Michigan expression to close helplessly with admonitions for an
"unfaltering faith in the final success" of the nation. This "perpetual inspiration" needed for being an American would somehow "secure from us a corresponding return of obligation."

Many centennial exhortations called for return to "that better
era of the Republic in which when men consecrated themselves
to the public service, they utterly abnegated all selfish purposes."
America must revive that spirit of honor and self-denial which
had once flourished. Boston's *Post* was among those urging that
the centennial observance stress America's "reformation and
purification." In re-establishing a "sense of personal responsibility," revelations of failing stewardship would more impress
the people than "illuminations and music." America's success
rested with the creation of a purer citizen. Unless this was
achieved, said the Boston paper, "we are gone as a free people,

and it will have to be written in history that we did not care enough for our liberties."

A numerous company in 1876 joined these calls for national salvation through candor. America could be undone by "indulging in noisy hurrahs." Loose talk of a nation truly renewed was condemned as "a ridiculous travesty." The principles of 1776 were far from vindicated. It was an oft-repeated assertion in a time straining for celebration that the life established by the Founders was "decaying and dying." The individual Steward could be true to his charge only by resuming the labors inspired by the Fathers' memory.

Typical was the centennial address made to the National Education Association by its president, William F. Phelps of Wisconsin's State Normal School at Whitewater. Phelps dismissed any thought that American national responsibility had been fulfilled. Still undeveloped was individual attainment. This brought the traditional charge that only by educational indoctrination might Americans "enter upon a career of prosperity and true greatness, of which the past is but a faint foreshadowing." Faithful to the spirit of Horace Mann, Phelps urged that education teach individual surrender. America's success awaited the time when each citizen "honestly and faithfully seeks the greatest good of the greatest number."

There was ample worry over the difficulties awaiting even the most stoutly inspired Steward. In New York City, Richard Storrs, who had preached at Lincoln's interment at Springfield, admonished a faltering nation toward a life of self-denial. National completion required a dedicated existence now threatened by "a swiftly increasing luxury of life," which diminished the "old humility, hardihood, patience," all requisite if men endured the burden of being American. Storrs' message was echoed in Boston by another voice familiar to the nation, Robert C. Winthrop. He said that the delinquency sweeping across America like an Arctic wave would be thwarted only if citizens could "catch larger and more exalted views of our destinies and responsibilities."

Storrs and Winthrop were two of the men who were preaching fulfillment through restoring the life of simple virtue. This response challenged those who began to see America as process, pushing before and beneath it the puny citizen. The message of

Clay and Webster was frequently set aside as centennial speakers praised the primitive life, simple in form and outlook. One exhorter ably summed it up: "The founders of our nation were not of that heroic character we find so glowingly described in romance and song, but were distinguished rather by their sober every-day common-sense." He added: "Bravery, honesty, and a steadfastness of purpose, which faltered not in adversity, and which was not corrupted by success," were the qualities which alone would sustain America. Admonitions like these were among the last efforts to portray America as a combination of single-handed endeavors.[31]

12

There were others whose view of America's plight denied them such solace. Hartford centennial celebrants were told: "We are caught in the contemplation of evils that exist and that occupy us with a sense of what has not been done and of unpleasing aspects." Most distressing was the timeless reminder: "If we forsake our calling, God will take away the crown he has given us. The kingdom of God will be taken from us and given to another nation which shall bring forth the fruits thereof." Tribulation after 1865 had quickly revived doubt over the American's capacity to support the nation's calling. Circumstances were so changed that many persons argued man could no longer hope to meet the expectation laid by God and the universe upon the United States. Consequently, responses of the period included more despair than American thought had espoused since the days of John Adams.

Disappointment came quickly after what many believed had been an ordeal of purification, of vast sacrifice, and even of martyrdom for a sacred Trust. As early as 1867, that ardent nationalist, Francis Lieber, had to confess: "Times have become so nauseous—and so soon after our heroic period." Lieber recoiled from both the executive-legislative tumult and the broader private squalor. Together these seemed to have *vulgarized the United States in a short time.*" Lieber's chagrin was expressed another way by two Baptist songs, published in 1871. One asked:

> Why, O God, thy people spurn?
> Why permit thy wrath to burn?
> God of mercy, turn once more;
> All our broken hearts restore.

Thou hast made our land to quake,
Heal the sorrows thou dost make;
Bitter is the cup we drink;
Suffer not our souls to sink.

. . . .

Give us now relief from pain;
Human aid is all in vain.
We, through God, shall yet prevail,
He will help when foes assail.

The other hymn, entitled "Oh, Spare Our Guilty Country, Spare!" was less confident:

On thee, O Lord our God, we call.
Before thy throne devoutly fall;
O whither should the helpless fly?
To whom but thee direct their cry?

Lord, we repent, we weep, we mourn,
To our forsaken God we turn;
Oh spare our guilty land,
Spare the church thine hand hath planted here.

By the 1870's, such despair was an important part of nationality. Vanishing integrity in personal life was especially devastating, for individual purity was now said to have been more important to the Fathers' success than their principles. Personal dedication to honesty was widely described as the key to American attainment. Emphasis declined on noble principles like freedom and equality. These were presumed as evident. But it was also exasperatingly clear that Stewards seemed drawn increasingly to those things which "satisfy a low and personal ambition." This made the individual responsible for the nation's disgrace. "We make that which we allow." The response of concern usually agreed that there was no longer in America "that quality of manhood which must underlie the nation." George Templeton Strong's anguish was typical of this dispirited mood: "Whom can we trust, and who can feel sure of even his own honesty?" Strong said that "the Devil must certainly be unchained in these days." Robert Ingersoll was so disillusioned by 1875 that he asserted "the sooner this nation dies and rots the better."

Ingersoll's reaction was extreme. Even the most despondent voices rarely conceded America's failure. Admissions of national guilt usually accepted some scheme for renewing the nation's pilgrimage. Later, the ideology of determinism or process came to the rescue, signalling the capitulation of a stewardship with immediate responsibility. However, during the gloom of the centennial season, despair brought some persons to urge "the severe and practical creed of the fathers." Without it, "the plague must come." With "a double portion of the spirit of those whose mantles we wear," it was still possible that "lust will not usurp the throne of virtue, nor liberty lapse into anarchy." All this was aptly displayed in a centennial poem where a pitiful freedom shrieked: "Oh, shame in woe . . . from my country's sons I shrink, who . . . waste, corrupt, despoil, and steal." Freedom called desperately upon the spirit of '76 for a restored purity, so that "my republic" might yet "be the world."

At the close of the age which began with delight over the Republic's renewal, the spirit of nationality sagged. When Americans had to complete their responsibility by guaranteeing republicanism through a renewed citizen morality, nationality's troubles deepened. Telling Stewards to embrace "the precepts taught by their forefathers" was an admonition many realized was born of intellectual desperation. "Our outlook is far from bright," said one person in 1876. "This very year, when national pride should justly be at its height, when of all times we should most exult in the name of America, we have been compelled to face revelations so humiliating as to bring for the time, almost a willingness to disown our country; almost a shame at being obliged to admit we were Americans."

By 1876 individualism was indicted. If America's role was to be successful, either human nature would have to change or the ideology itself would have to accept new alternatives. Somehow American thought had to escape the spiritual dilemma posed by an intolerable present.[32]

CHAPTER FIVE

ESCAPE
1876–1898

America's self-expectancy profoundly affected what one historian calls the psychic crisis prevailing between 1876 and 1898. The national consciousness grew more troubled by irony and frustration. Then, in 1898, events suddenly permitted many weary Americans to escape the nationality so burdensome for a hundred years. The traditional Trust was exchanged for a new duty.[1]

Citizens found material attainment more difficult after 1876. Diminishing natural blessing and more complicated business-industrial existence encouraged acts of passion which threatened liberty and republicanism. America's irrationality, always a problem, appeared to be increasing in both rural and urban areas. In addition, the evils of political practice not only thrived but claimed the life of another President. Considering what Americans expected of themselves and their nation, occurrences after 1876 were clearly distressing.

The centennials celebrated between 1876 and 1889 were distracted by violent acts. At this time there were appalling economic reverses. As Americans tried to concentrate on commemorating the Fathers' noble struggles, attention strayed to the railroad strikes and their aftermath. During official recollection of how the Founders made a constitutional basis for freedom and law, citizens were diverted by bloodshed in Chicago's Haymarket Square and the execution of men presumed dedicated to overthrowing the Republic. While Americans remembered the divinely led voyage of Christopher Columbus to a new Eden, the garden seemed befouled by avarice and hunger at such places as Homestead, Pennsylvania, Pullman, Illinois, and Massillon, Ohio.

Farmers and workers were outraged, businessmen and professionals, disillusioned. While the public deplored persisting partisanship, quarreling began over who was most poorly serving America's responsibility. For many citizens, the spoils struggle measured the weakening of America's labors for republicanism. Calls for reform and regeneration became frantic. Whether money champions, social manipulators, immigration restrictionists, or the followers of Edward Bellamy, many advocates suggested changes in the national design. Others redoubled their efforts to plant loyalty in the mind of American youth and to keep the adult properly inspired through such symbols as the flag and the veteran.

These circumstances encouraged change in the ideology of nationality. The 1895 controversy over Venezuela's boundary widened speculation that America's calling had become one of universal involvement. Men talked seriously of the timeless process and instinct found in Anglo-Saxon destiny. Using these possibilities in 1898 American thought created a new identity and claimed a different duty. By entering an immemorially dynamic racial crusade across the globe, America was diverted from its traditional ideology. This metamorphosis in American self-awareness, for it was nothing less, was best evident when spokesmen began insisting that George Washington would advise his countrymen far differently at the close of the nineteenth century than he had in 1795. The Father, it was said, would readily see in 1898 that his nation had become a global leader for universal, primordial righteousness. Imperialism was not greed, asserted the new trustees. It was a costly, even painful responsibility which a nation with America's background, composition, and attainment could not shirk.

Such escape from tradition was more than some citizens could accept. For them the followers of President McKinley were claiming America had carried out its first responsibilities simply because it perceived some new duty. However, these dissidents could help the painful present only by invoking the original national truths. Their concern was that domestic and international travail threatened the Jeffersonian hope for America. Preserving the old Republic remained for some observers the only way to seek America's fulfillment.

DOCTRINE

In changing their sense of purpose, Americans used most of the rhetoric familiar since the days of John Adams. Advocacy continued for a sense of duty, for a cultivation of stewardship, and for an awareness of a special Vineyard. The difference was in the interpretation of the new ministry. At the close of this era, America eluded the incriminating aspects of the old Trust by adopting a new view of man's role. Human nature had never ceased troubling American nationality, bringing this ideology finally to adopt impersonal and distant duty as the locus of the nation's new attainment. The astonishing events of 1898 seemed to make prophetic the funeral sermon Richard Storrs had uttered over Lincoln's martyred form. In 1865 Storrs thought he spoke for a penitent nation about to prove the capacity of Christian men to be worthy of a democratic society. Once this was shown, Storrs predicted the nation's responsibilities would shift to a world setting. In words that forecast the outlook adopted in 1898, Storrs asserted that when America's energies "shall cease to be consecrated, as they hitherto have been, on the preparation of the country itself for its habitation, and the swift and mighty mastery of its riches, and on the fashioning and up-building of its own institutions—when the educational influences that mould it shall have come to their fruition, and the spirit of the Nation shall be finally formed and declared—it must pour abroad, through constant channels, an infinite influence."

A great pouring forth in 1898 was literal enough for most observers suddenly to claim fulfillment of the long-abused Trust. The prologue to a revised doctrine was uttered by President William McKinley. Speaking at the great Peace Jubilee in Chicago late in 1898, McKinley showed the change in American nationality. "Duty determines destiny," he said, quickly adding a display of confidence appropriate for emancipated stewardship: "Destiny which results from duty performed may bring anxiety and perils, but never failure and dishonor." Since failure and dishonor had always been real eventualities for American thought, McKinley prudently said that God had initially assigned America a Trust "whose full meaning was not apprehended even by the wisest statesmen of their time." Now, said the President,

Americans had learned that "Patriotism must be faithful as well as fervent."

Faithfulness was important since the nation's true meaning had been found in a vast universal progression. Development, and therefore progress, was always a part of America, said McKinley, even though the citizen's vision was "often defective." Accordingly, men must accept national growth as necessary to "prevent degeneration." McKinley kept stressing the comfort of a doctrine of process over preservation. "There must be new life and purpose, or there will be weakness and decay. . . . There must be a constant movement toward a higher and nobler civilization." To others, like editor Henry Watterson, the new duty's meaning called for more realistic terms: "From a nation of shopkeepers we become a nation of warriors. We escape the menace and peril of socialism and agrarianism, as England has escaped them, by a policy of colonization and conquest. From a provincial huddle . . . we rise to the dignity and powers of an imperial republic incomparably greater than Rome." Watterson conceded that "we exchange domestic dangers for foreign dangers" and that there was a threat from Caesarism, but all this was preferable to "anarchism." In contrast to McKinley's loftiness, Watterson said that "anything is better than the pace we were going before these present forces were started into life."

Beyond McKinley and Watterson was the cool glance of Henry James. As 1898 waned he wrote of the strange "consciousness" now entailed in being an American with the new expectation "that we *shall* swell and swell, and acquire and *re*quire, to the top of our opportunity." James admitted that "we have not been good enough for our opportunity." Although he could not join McKinley and Watterson in ignoring the question of America's merit, James acknowledged that with its fresh impetus America might improve. However, this dropped him into what James Russell Lowell had long before warned was the deepest pit facing the doctrine of nationality, enrapture by the sheer phenomenon that was America. James himself conceded: "I fear I am too lost in the mere spectacle for any decent morality." His comment was an apt summation of the plight of America's self-perception after a century of troubled nationality.[2]

During this last phase of America's struggle with its Trust, most thoughtful citizens were trying to make the doctrine of na-

tionality, by then so familiar and yet so disquieting, retain meaning and appropriateness. With so much of both heaven and
earth in the American consciousness, endurance of its traditions
is hardly astonishing. After 1876, men still clutched the idea of
a divine bequest or assignment. In doing so, they merged the
proving of liberty and republicanism, while enlarging the disputes between past and future and between domestic and international claims for attention. Concern over the Steward led increasingly to dramatizing the sweep of teutonic strength. Pleas
for exhuming private virtue became shopworn. Most appealing
was talk of a new Vineyard, the great globe itself. The old settings of garden and polity had been trampled into comparative
uselessness.

The profound adjustment in American doctrine occurred in
reflections upon the anxieties of existence. In this era the inroads of mammon, passion, and partisanship seemed about to
overwhelm the Republic. This eventuality, so long predicted,
appeared dramatically averted when success in the task of liber-
ating Cuba offered to lift the nation beyond the old vicissitudes.
As many observers put it, the experience of the war brought the
long-awaited revelation to America, opening its appreciation of
what its real Trust should be. After the Spanish-American War,
nationality rested easier, comforted in believing that American
undertaking had escaped the caprices of human nature.

I: Affirmations God's presence still
shone through the twilight of the Trust ideology, illumining
especially those who urged deeper faith in Heaven's eventual
rescue of America. Since Christianity remained "the essential
framework and being of the republic," new Stewards capable of
the divine calling would surely emerge. In 1888, the venerable
Philip Schaff summed up the broadly held belief that God was
far from done with America. Heaven's "great surprises" might
even include using America to combine the best of Christendom
in a new "concord of Christ." [3]

1

America waited for God until 1898 when the suspense ended.
The old national assignment was replaced by new tasks from
above which required less thought about God's stern gaze or
about man's weak nature. Instead, Stewards of 1898 eagerly

heard what students at Union Theological Seminary were told about God's placing America, "like Israel of old," in "the center of the nations." The Trust became more welcome. America was missionary and teacher. Men rejoiced to hear the long-awaited tidings that they had "fulfilled the manifest destiny of the Christain Republic." It was easier to talk of America's election, with little need for further mention of proving national worth. As the Episcopal mission board declared, it was "the providence of God" which had sent abroad "American civilization and American ideals and institutions, with American power to uphold and extend them."

The power of God was sorely needed to sanctify the Republic's abrupt departure from the ways admonished by George Washington. McKinley's affirmations recognized this. As the Heavenly Father once assigned America to purifying remoteness, so He surely called her now to lead in man's final redemption. Senator Orville Platt of Connecticut was especially skillful in such exhortation: "We of this country have always asserted our firm belief in an overruling Providence. We have professed to recognize the hand of God in history. Does not Providence, does not the finger of God unmistakedly point to the civilization and uplifting of the Orient, to the development of its people, to the spread of liberty, education, social order, and Christianity there through the agency of American influence?"

Like the bulk of American expression, Platt exulted in explaining American energy as part of the transcendent Anglo-Saxon global mission. America's revised purpose was obvious, he insisted. "The National Policy of isolation is no longer for our best interest. To pursue it . . . is selfishness." A new work was decreed for America. "We are first in the family of nations," so that stewardship must now hasten to far places. Platt called each American ship in Manila harbor "a new *Mayflower* . . . the harbinger and agent of a new civilization." To President McKinley, Platt wrote reassuringly that 90 per cent of Connecticut's citizens believed in the changed America. They could see that "God has placed upon this Government the solemn duty" of spreading the joys of liberty "no matter how many difficulties the problem may present. They feel that it is our duty to attempt its solution."

The century of debate over nationality found Americans more

comfortably allied with God at its close than in 1798. A similar reconciliation with its responsibility for liberty and republicanism proved to be more difficult. Man's misuse of the republican elements remained so evident in America after 1876 that observers had difficulty interpreting so distressing a scene. While he might well have had special feeling in the matter, Samuel J. Tilden advised a friend in 1880 that America's corruption placed the welfare of republicanism in grave jeopardy. The commonplaces about liberty's dependence on America became infrequent as the outlook steadily darkened with reports of larger violence, economic aggression, and political corruption. One who continued to insist that America had been chosen to demonstrate "the compatibility of Liberty with Order" was Putnam P. Bishop. However, even he agreed with those "many leaders of opinion" who said that America's responsibility for liberty had not yet been fulfilled. "It is safest for us to assume the justice of that view," Bishop conceded, adding the hope that each citizen might eventually feel "divinely called" to carry forward this Trust.[4]

This concession had to rely on another familiar part of American doctrine. Continued abuse of republicanism made it indispensable to talk of the past or the future. The advantage went quickly to the future when it displayed an enticing new duty. While the past offered a grand legacy, it clamored for execution. The interminable festivities between 1876 and 1889 had been ever-mindful of the nation's debt to the Founders. The appeal touched everyone. Edward Bellamy insisted that his nationalist program would usher in the true nation, for it "follows lines laid down by the founders of the Republic and proves itself the legitimate heir to the traditions and spirit of 1776." Bellamy contended that if America were "guided by those traditions, sustained by that spirit," it "cannot fail."

In contrast was the 1889 declaration of *Collier's Once a Week* magazine that America's pleasure in anniversaries demonstrated the nation's faithfulness to the mandate left by the past. This journal insisted that simply by celebrating "the amazing progress made in a hundred years," America showed "the realization of the ideal commonwealth which De Tocqueville eulogized." However, events at New York City's centennial ball in 1889 punctured the editorial euphoria. Throngs of the uninvited, described as disreputable persons, crashed the party and drank all

the free champagne. *Collier's* said that while policemen and
messenger boys reeled about, judges and governors thirsted. Un-
daunted, however, the magazine announced that immorality existed in Washington's day. Because men spoke a purer language
in 1889 than in 1789, it proved America's progress to *Collier's.*

Among the last appeals in behalf of a cherished past was an
1891 address before Minnesota veterans of the Civil War. It
urged the wisdom of following tradition. If the Republic was
"to progress to that high destiny of which its past career gives
promise, its citizens must join in patriotic consecration, to foster
and perpetuate a spirit of reverence for the institutions under
which its proud position has been reached." But now "the tyro
and the demagogue," eager to undo the conservative forces of
society, "approach with unhallowed steps that sacred rock of
liberty." The orator, Hiram E. Stevens, called for prayer and a
new spirit of heroism "versed in the chronicle of gallant deeds."
In short, American fulfillment needed a stewardship of emulation.

This doctrine was used in 1898 by those refusing to escape the
old Trust through imperialism. For them America's model obedience to ancient injunction remained the only means of overcoming the weakness long inherent in man and society. At
Thanksgiving 1898, one of America's most admired speakers,
Henry Van Dyke, made such affirmations. He warned against
the philosophy of inevitability used by the advocates of a new
duty. In one sentence Van Dyke summarized the old Trust's
cause: "There is one thing that can happen to the American flag
worse than to be hauled down. This is to have its meaning and
its message changed." Meanwhile the more waggish admirers of
the past were quipping: "Dewey took Manila with the loss of
one man—and all our institutions."

More Americans, however, felt that with God at Dewey's side,
America had been shown how gloriously to break from the past
with its record of national inadequacy. They argued that the
war had brought into sight America's elusive goal, the future
which contained both triumph and a superior group of Stewards. Throughout this era, as in earlier time, men affirmed that
national agony was a thing of the moment, owing to unwholesome leadership. This would pass. America had to survive until
a new and purer generation could establish a righteous course.

As one commentator put it, peering into the gloom: "the misfortunes of the time are of the time only." These were "maladministration" and the "accidental ascendency for a time of bad men." Samuel J. Tilden believed that America was momentarily "a betrayed, wronged, and sacrificed people." The nation's being "a good example to mankind" rested on the coming Stewards. Henry Ward Beecher died championing the next generation as America's hope. With it must come "a future vastly greater and more glorious than the present—a future such as never was developed in any other age or nation." [5]

By the 1890's the future dominated national doctrine. Even members of the Grand Army of the Republic customarily were encouraged to turn from the heroic past to contemplate the approaching age when "we are going to demonstrate the right and power of man to govern himself." Accompanied by references to "the grand destiny God has in store for this people," Americans began incessant calls for "a revival of patriotism." This seemed especially necessary during the depression after 1893, which many persons agreed showed that "when self-seeking and avarice possess themselves of men, patriotism is abandoned." America must turn "anew to the work of fitting the nation more and more for its grand destiny of leading and lighting the other nations of the world toward man's highest goal." This renewal was evident for much of America in the Spanish-American War. With a "moral exaltation," the Republic was at last "true to itself." Its new direction "points to duty above temptation." "That dear old flag" could wave gladly, for it carried "all the hope and promise of the future." Indeed, "It is the banner of dawn. It is the flag of the morning."

A masterful explanation of how the future overtook the present was made by Assistant Secretary of State David J. Hill. "A great crisis, bravely met and victoriously passed, lifts a country, as an individual, to a prouder elevation than before." The American ascent was truly impressive. Said Hill in 1898: "My country —with what patriotic pride I call it mine!—never seemed so great, its people so noble." The nation had at last entered fully into service for humanity, with no regard "but to vindicate their principles." A Napoleon might have pushed America further into passion and greed; a McKinley had taken America into a triumph of selflessness. Hill believed America had entered with confidence a new age, one a man like Jefferson would not have comprehended.

It had been the place of men like Jefferson, Hill argued, "to prepare the seed." At last a new generation was trained and ready "to scatter it." All this was the wondrous result of the mysterious development at work in the universe. America had initially been deposited in the individual, said Hill. But now the composite nation was significant. According to Secretary Hill, "one of the most precious fruits of the late war is the evidence that the nation has a truer instinct than the individual." Under the old nationality, kernels of righteousness had come from the toil of individuals. According to Hill's interpretation, the planting would be done henceforth by a corporate people guided by the "unseen force" which had freed America in 1898. Hill invited "a nation rising to the full splendor of its responsibilities" to join in reverence for "the august and imperative law of universal development." [6]

There were skeptics, of course. Chauncey Depew, an inveterate orator, led in replying from the ancient scripture. "The political mission of the United States is purely internal." America's duty was to produce by individual example a "moral effect" satisfied with "inspiring the hopes of the patriots of every country of the world." Not only was it said that a divine design had been shattered, but dissenters contended that America had not fulfilled its first assignment. Public and private corruption still defiled the American garden. The defenders of an inner responsibility talked of final desecration if the Stewards put aside "our national postulate" in order to create "a missionary-industrial nursery" far beyond God's limits. Critics called the new Trust a crass and self-seeking venture. They scoffed at the argument that it would bring spiritual and material blessings to benighted souls throughout the globe. William Jennings Bryan made the ultimate indictment of the revised doctrine. It was, the Great Commoner said, "a foreign idea" and "directly antagonistic to the idea and ideals which have been cherished by the American people since the signing of the Declaration of Independence."

An immutable and edifying course of events was the concept sustaining those whom Bryan assailed. Nationality had long sought to confine the Republic's purpose within each citizen's heart. Here was the traditional source for a vital impulse to make freedom and republicanism thrive. This energy had been embarrassingly inhibited, making welcome a new explanation. Such reinterpretation of the Trust was attempted before the Hawaii and Cuba episodes. A speaker at Columbia University in 1887 had said that America's "thirst for gain" would diminish. The nation was in "a period of transition, a period of preparation." It was a season of "questioning" as Americans sought the "law of progression," whose discovery would show the nation "a grand new life" with dimensions at least of the Western world. Signs of this discovery were evident in doctrine after 1894. While America had been God's theater for the proving of human nature, now there was "a grand process of development going on to establish mankind more firmly in material comfort, morality, and a spiritual religion." This process increasingly was cited in calls for broader statesmanship and a new role as brother's keeper. Advocates began saying that "no oppressed people should turn to us in vain. Every germ of republican liberty must be nurtured." To shirk "so plain a duty" would bring upon America the retribution "always added for national delinquency."

Evidence of the changing doctrine after 1894 included declarations of virtue triumphant over evil and of pleasure with the rise of Anglo-Americanism. Affirmations of an "instinct of solidarity" accompanied insistences that a universal tide swept America to a new place in history. Generally, the religious press sounded amen. God, instinct, and history soon permitted the new doctrine of universal duty to abuse tradition. America's old introspective attitude, said one advocate, "if not a myth or a humbug, [was] at least an archaism, with no place in the dawn of the twentieth century." The new duty would, said a Kansas newspaper, lift the country out of sordid political discussions that revolved interminably around the "American dollar." Realizing that the Fathers mandate no longer applied, America could move into "the future with stout hearts and faith in Providence." It was widely asserted that the American people at last "feel the influence of national glory. They are full-ripe for the beginning of a new career by their mighty republic." [7]

A more thoughtful exposition of the new Trust came from Washington Gladden, expounder of the social gospel. Gladden confessed in 1898 that indifference and imperialist greed possessed many American minds. He anticipated that these evils would be overcome by the same emerging conscience which had prompted America to heed suffering humanity's call. "There is a jingoism and anti-jingoism both of which are purely egoistic," said Gladden, adding, "let us have neither of them." Now, he felt, "the Nation can be trusted to distinguish between philanthropy and piracy." This new capacity would at last lift America beyond the "hateful power [of] the bad politicians." Gladden believed that great new "responsibilities" had awakened nationality to the crucial inner need. With justice and honor at home and abroad, Gladden predicted the stars and stripes would become "the emblem of a Nation that is brave to help and strong to suffer in the service of mankind." The editor of *Northwest Magazine* put the expectation more simply: "The most wholesome influence upon our home politics will be exerted by getting interested in questions that concern the whole world."

By autumn 1898 it was generally asserted that in sacrificing for Cuba, America had found her own soul. "We have risen to a new conception of our national possibilities and our national greatness." This was the usual refrain, followed by the affirmation: "We are all prouder to be Americans, and have a broader and truer understanding of the greatness of our country and of the grander destiny which lies before the American people." In this way, America's prevailing outlook put aside the old Trust. The escape was accompanied by many claims to broader and deeper vision, making the previous century of ideological struggle seem immature and myopic. Americans took pride in the newly discovered racial assurance coming from deep in the Teutonic past. One person observed: "It is impossible to fitly nourish the soul of a powerful people unless you give it something to do for the general progress of mankind." At last the truth was out. America's nationality had faltered because of an enfeebling diet for a hundred years.

The president of Oberlin College, John Henry Barrows, made one of the ablest summations of the new doctrine. He called events of 1898 a miracle. "God spake in his providence," leaving "the destinies of the greatest of republics . . . indissolubly united to the moral and material fortunes of eight hundred millions of human beings on the other side of the world." It was a fitting end to a century wherein Barrows said America had sought self-knowledge. Now both Europe and the United States had been shown, after decades of misconception, what America meant. For Barrows, this itself was fulfillment, since the nation's "true glory" was found to be "the future of the race." In fact, "it means toleration, education, freedom, justice, equality, and opportunity for vast areas that have been desolated or underdeveloped." All previous American nationality Barrows dismissed as "selfish." Forgotten were the difficulties which men like Jefferson and Lincoln had pondered. There was now a prime new fact about America: "God has made us a world power."

The new doctrine centered on Barrow's discovery. The Republic had a noble ministry in and among the world's cares. No longer needed were the sylvan glades which Frederick Jackson Turner had recently interpreted. In fact, one of the most vigorous endorsements of the new Trust was the report issued in 1898 by the American Historical Association. It urged that as a world power America must learn world history. Scholars like Andrew C. McLaughlin, Herbert Baxter Adams, Albert Bushnell Hart, and Charles H. Haskins predicted that through broader understanding America would see "the history of their own country in its proper perspective . . . and may be relieved of a temptation to a narrow intolerance which resembles patriotism only as bigotry resembles faith."

These historians urged "a study of the centuries in which Englishmen were struggling for representation, free government, free speech, and due process of law." From such perspective would come "a sense of duty and responsibility, and an acquaintance with . . . human obligations." Adequate nationality required nothing less than an emancipated mind. "The genius of American civilization," said William McKinley, would now be "both original and creative." It would thereby sustain "all the great interests which shall be confided to our keeping." [8]

2

McKinley's invocation of a new outlook carried a spirit which overwhelmed finally the other elements of nationality. Old doubts about the citizen and society serving as Stewards were greatly affected. From John Adams' time, stewardship had implied a personal burden for citizens. With the events of 1898 came an impersonal setting where men could lose their painful immediacy in a historical-racial pursuit of universal good. Instinct succeeded virtue, leaving the labors of nationality at last endurable.

Most of this era, of course, heard further testimony of how man's weakness betrayed the nation. Only gradually was this superseded by the reassurance of racial instinct and timeless determinism. The obvious paradox attracted the attention of Charles Dudley Warner soon after he settled into the "Editor's Study" at *Harper's Magazine* in 1894. Have faith, was his suggestion. He cited the beauty of lofty principles which overarched American national purpose. "Considering what human nature is, and, above all, what an assortment of perverted human nature we have been trying to assimilate, we have been doing very well. Have a little patience, and have a little more private virtue!" Meanwhile biology, philosophy, and economics were helping to redesign the Steward. Ironically, the effort drew upon the integral nationalism which had threaded its way through nineteenth-century American thought. As Clay and Webster had contended late in life, in the evolving national state alone could the individual realize inner good. Hegelianism, Anglo-Saxonism, and organic design joined late in the century to help enlarge this doctrine.[9]

An aged Democratic leader, Horatio Seymour, showed how gently a more comfortable view could emerge. Speaking in 1877, Seymour reviewed the nation's bloody baptism, after which "our country has become great beyond the wildest dreams of our fathers." Such success was due to the Founders being animated "by common views, feelings, and purposes." It was the Republic's need which then had shaped the national outlook. Americans submitted to national purpose, said Seymour, adding that this example of united motive "should give us new faith in the lasting nature of our government."

Seymour's view was comforting in the troubled days after 1877 when men wondered if the polity, the economy, or the society in America could hold intact. National need, it was often said, must again grip the minds of faithful citizens. Like the Founders, men should once more look first for "the good of the nation." This concept of a submissive stewardship was linked to the cult of the people. Henry Ward Beecher preached similarly in 1877. It was not noble men who guided the American pilgrimage, "it was the sound moral instincts of the great thinking mass of the common people." Like most observers at this time, Beecher combined fear and hope in trumpeting the message of stewardship's corporate nature. He spoke with horror of the possibility that domestic strife in America meant that the nation's Trust would be "thus betrayed by miscreant men" and that America would end as "a scoffing and a byword all over the world to the end of time." Such deepening uneasiness made it conventional to say that individuals were morally obligated to accept the dictates of what Wendell Phillips in 1881 called "a distinctive American character and purpose." An innate popular instinct seemed for many the intellectual antidote to the old belief in individual responsibility for national fulfillment. Wendell Phillips took the outlook to its extreme. "Trust the people—the wise and the ignorant, the good and the bad—with the gravest questions, and in the end you educate the race." The Founders were said to have embraced this view, giving them what Phillips called "a serene faith." Now, as the nation was "afloat on the current of Niagara," let it turn to the composite instinct of "the masses."

The slain Garfield reposed in this rising sense of stewardship. As he eulogized a second murdered President, Richard Storrs called Garfield "the most conspicuous representative, in his generation, of a complete and genuine American manhood. In his blood he represented the commingled and powerful life of the people." Storrs acclaimed the "vital genius of the expanding American people," the "American spirit," and the "immense and religious enthusiasm born of the past history of the nation." Neither Washington nor Lincoln could reflect such character, Storrs said, for in those days a corporate stewardship had not emerged. Now there was "an American manhood" which Garfield personified. Storrs' eulogy became a tribute to a mystical popular instinct. Garfield's significance was in his having been absorbed by this idea.

The public spirit reacted to Garfield's death with such lament as to give John Greenleaf Whittier "a new hope for the republic." It disclosed deep in the nation a "great heart" which Whittier said had become basically "sound." This became a favorite theme at Memorial Day gatherings. Such occasions began explaining the Civil War as a stirring of a mutual national spirit which would soon begin pursuit of "the one common destiny of the American republic." Scholarly feast days said much the same, even denouncing the concept that man's learning or wisdom could be relied upon to carry the national purpose. Edward Everett Hale in 1885 joined those announcing the uselessness of individual knowledge in American endeavor. For sixty years, he said, American leadership had been "generally so bad." Any progress was due entirely to "the people." The learned man must bow to this innate popular wisdom about American purpose. The Republic's blunders "have all been the mistakes of theorists. The great successes have been wrought when the people took their own affair in hand, and pushed it through." Hale called for a great public mind in the future. Duty and destiny required no less.[10]

This ideological soil brought the flowering of Anglo-Saxonism. Leaving popular wisdom alone to battle late nineteenth century conditions was cruel. Many people found sustenance in knowing that America's public shared a limitless evolution toward triumph. While this affirmation cost America much of its traditional delight in uniqueness, such difference had proven a bleak existence. Being separate from time had afforded little reward for the Republic. Henry James shared the emerging nationality when he indicated in 1888: "I can't look at the English-American world, or feel about them, any more, save as a big Anglo-Saxon total, destined to such an amount of melting together that an insistence upon their differences becomes more and more idle and pedantic." Much of the emerging doctrine accepted John W. Burgess' popular advocacy of an evolving "Teutonic political genius." Generally, these affirmations sought the same goal. As Boston's John F. Fitzgerald said, there must develop a broad accord ready "to sacrifice private interest for the public good." The ultimate and only consideration for revamped stewardship should be "the welfare of the community."

Much of the jubilance in 1898 chose to insist that America's acceptance of duty indicated surrender to national purpose. Addresses by the widely popular George R. Peck, a Chicago attorney, included characteristic uses of this new affirmation. America had demonstrated that the citizenry "can be trusted to keep unsullied their heritage from our fathers." Indeed, said Peck, "History has been busy in these last eventful months, interfusing

all the elements of our national life, so that the parts forget that
they are parts," remembering only the presence of one indestruc-
tible nationhood. Fruitfulness came only through remembrance
that all individuals were part of "a greater nation." America's
outlook would at last be guided by a "logic of events" beyond
any individual. This composite and irresistible endeavor would
carry America triumphantly through what Peck called "new conditions." [11]

3

The revised attitude about the Stewards affected the modest attention this era paid to the once compelling doctrine of the
Vineyard. Talk about the unique setting and an inspired polity
faltered under circumstances vexing late nineteenth century
America. When traditional concepts gave little sustenance, the
notion of a world as America's theater easily won attention. Just
as enlistment in Anglo-Saxon development promised to free the
nation from individual frailty and temporary exasperations, so
the acknowledgment of a universal plan released America from
being limited to native cities and countryside where tribulation
could not be disguised.

This expectant turning to a world-wide field did not end the
debate. Some voices insisted to the century's end that national
vigor and success came from "the ancestral cottage which stood
on the New England hillside," or that patriotism arose from "the
village green." However, the general inclination was that taken
by Frederick Jackson Turner. He was evidently impatient with
the insistence of the California historian, Hubert Howe Bancroft,
that the Pacific coastal Vineyard would inspire the ultimate,
Aryan civilization. Here the new Republic would "unlearn" the
erroneous outlook of the older America and thence permit the
national "diathesis" to be fulfilled. Bancroft was among the few
remaining persons who saw a miraculous contribution to American nationality from the untouched richness of surrounding
grandeur. Turner gently suggested in 1893, while the nation rejoiced in the vision and courage of Christopher Columbus, that
America prepare itself for a wider field, as yet unseen. Now, "the
first period of American history" was closed.

A year earlier Turner had stated in *Ægis* that American nationality was essentially the flourishing of germs whose origin

was far back in the Old World. But he also urged that Americans
learn how influential for their endeavors had been the natural
Vineyard in which they toiled. This confusion between an organic process and its natural host had always been difficult for
American nationality. At the close of its first century the nation
was left to speculate over geographical inspiration for what
Turner now acclaimed as America's "composite nationality." It
seemed clear that the familiar natural Vineyard was no longer a
sustenance for troubled America. A larger harvest land had been
sighted by such prophets as Alfred T. Mahan.

Like a natural Vineyard, ideas about an inspired polity as the
Trust's setting had deepening difficulty. With a President slain
by a disappointed spoils-seeker, the nation was challenged to
reform both the political system and the citizen. Typical was the
relentless exposure by such journals as *Harper's Weekly* of the
humiliating breakdown in America's polity. The marvel was that
America stumbled on, despite the awful aberrations of the governing process. Events in this era made it necessary to establish
America's setting beyond the routine of democracy. The politics
of America, it began to be said, had no bearing upon the morals
of the nation. By the close of the nineteenth century, the doctrine
of nationality stressed duties considered well above the unspeak-
able level of governance. *Harper's Weekly* regularly noted that
Americans could have only contempt for what passed as republicanism at local, state, and federal levels. The nation moved
forward in spite of political folly.

In due time even the polity would be altered. First, however,
the nation must master the broad reality of its work. Until then,
the nation would remain, as one observer put it, "in a transition
period." It was enough now to know that the original "simple
rural republic, indeed, is lost." [12]

II: Anxieties   The transformation of the
old Republic and of its affirmations made more imperative the
need for new answers to old anxieties about being American.
Some observers found larger justification after 1876 for uneasiness over such issues as the nature of American experience, the
threat to it from flesh and emotion, and the distressing contributions from partisanship. Urbanism, immigration, industrialism,
labor organization, proposals for social and economic transforma-

tion, all these intruded upon America's traditional view of its struggle for fulfillment. Consequently, the arrival of new duty with more comfortable assumptions was gratefully received by many persons worried over the discrepancy between expectation and attainment. Most relief came through defining American endeavor as a vast, even mystical process. Claims that America's duty meant the preservation of an inspired design retired rapidly as the century closed, lingering mostly in apologias for the old Trust. Since upheaval seemed the order of things, the temptation increasingly was to see the nation's endeavor bound in a benign universal unfolding.[13]

4

Cause for anxiety was abundant in this era. The slaying of President Garfield was widely considered retribution for the nation's inadequate struggle. America's penitent mourning in the autumn of 1881 considered the surrender of Garfield to heaven as a sacrifice in exchange for a cleansed national spirit. One lamentation, "His First Sabbath in Heaven," included the lines:

> But, chastened and sorrowing nation, oh learn
> > The lessons our Father would give;
> From the ways that have grieved his good spirit return;
> > Repent, seek His mercy and live.

Another theme, from "At the Grave," was popular:

> . . . . a nation's tears
> Must mourn a nation's guilt
> And factious strife must plunge the knife
> > Of murder to the hilt.
>
> God pity and forgive us all
> > For bitter thoughts and speech;
> God in His love look from above
> > And heal his people's breach.

This spirit pervaded national expressions. Garfield's death pained America more than Lincoln's tragedy, which was seen as culminating the purification of a renewed nation. Lincoln's martyrdom was to have closed a struggle between good and evil

whose combatants had proportions far beyond human nature
and individual relevance. However, Garfield's murder was generally interpreted as God's punishment upon each citizen's greed
and unreason, as well as upon collective sin. Paul Hamilton
Hayne wrote a long poem which caught all the themes the nation
was endlessly repeating:

> I see the Nation, as in antique ages
> Crouched with rent robes, and ashes on her head,
> Her mournful eyes are deep with dark presages
> Her soul is haunted by a formless dread!
>
> "O God!" she cries, "why hast Thou left me bleeding
> Wounded and quivering to the heart's hot core?
>   Can fervid faith, winged prayer, and
>   anguished pleading
> Win balm and pity from Thy heavans no more?"

Hayne's poem told of America's faltering behavior in the postwar era which brought this judgment "in awful fashion." God
had "stripped our midnight of its last pale star." The poet
yearned to see among the Stewards "a holier faith" coming
through "the spell of one vast grief." Now the nation could only
wait:

> Today is dark; vague darkness clouds tomorrow,—
> Ah! in God's hand the Nations are but—dust!

Darkness indeed seemed to shroud the land as toilers struggled
in what many called fields of "lawlessness." Public expression
often mentioned such devastations for the Republic as "the vor-
tex of popular license," "conflagration," or "fires." The most
satisfying response sought to combine talk of benign evolution
with individual regeneration. Man in America must transcend
the frail flesh to attain both individual nobility and accord with
his fellows through some mystical social blend. The Trust
thereby appealed again that man reject the claims of being and
the lure of mammon and passion.

Here Garfield remained an inspiration, illustrating that Stewards might rise to this calling. Typical of a lingering view of
Garfield was a Wisconsin supporter's jubilation over the Ohioan's

nomination. *"Now* I can with my whole heart cast my ballot next fall for the one man who . . . has been raised up by God to save us from death by fraud, as Lincoln did from force." This theme persisted, leaving Garfield the nation's chance granted by "the hand of God stretched forth to save us from dangers" most citizens saw at hand.[14]

5

The need for reinterpreting national purpose grew with the recognition that with God's withdrawal of the heroic Garfield, America was being let drift from the mooring of the Founders' philosophy. The worship of success was newly assailed as an ir-religion enticing a chosen people beyond their duty. It warped "the moral vision," denying America its only escape from the be-witchment of self. E. L. Godkin wrote in the *Princeton Review* during 1887 that the national character faced destruction. A Michigan student called mammon's grip "this latest and most corrupting form of tyranny," one which citizens must escape through God's word. The nation could attain its purpose "serving not the god of paltry gold, but the God of Love and Right-eousness." Until then, another realist said, the "Dollar Devil" would drive America "till nothing is left but dust and ashes."

Once more the realities of national existence seemed to con-demn the present generation. It was an old complaint when, in 1894, a writer in *McClure's Magazine* asserted that "to preach to the present generation" was futile, like "the voice of one crying in the wilderness." If the future Republic was to inherit "some-thing more than piles of white or yellow metal," America must "bind the Dollar Devil with chains," destroying his role as a "cruel and remorseless tyrant." Much of William Jennings Bryan's appeal was as a noble Steward destroying what one person called "this dreadful Moloch." Admirers hoped that through Bryan the last spark of patriotism would flame up once again "for honor, for right, for liberty and justice." Without such restora-tion, America would enter the "dreadful abyss of ruin and deg-radation." When human rehabilitation and the powers of men like Bryan seemed unavailing, the appeal grew of powerful abstractions like destiny, process, and evolution. Some observers were quick to denounce this as a dismaying new form of un-steadying emotion. Charles Eliot Norton said the Venezuelan alarum had gravely injured "the national character" by loosing the worst of the wolves of passion, "the war-spirit." Norton asserted: "It makes a miserable end for this century."

Nevertheless, with destiny in view, passion entered a holier league with patriotism. Here was an elevated outlook which might yet spare America the final agony from greed. In 1897 John Bach McMaster heard from the Grand Army of the Republic's Textbook Committee that "the time is right for a real patriotic loyal history of the rebellion" which would recognize that triumph came because the North's cause "was right." Both McMaster's correspondence and his publications disclose the new succor American affirmation drew from war and bloodshed's memory and prospect, as well as from the sense of monumental progression in which the Republic's future rested. As another historian conceded, there was relief in "a brilliant spirited" American outlook on foreign affairs. It was too late, when, in 1898, the American Historical Association cautioned of the dangers from factitious patriotism. The realities of man's struggle brought a warning in the A.H.A.'s 1898 report that the rising nationality "is more or less a spurious one, a patriotism that would seek to present distorted ideas of the past with the idea of glorifying our country at the possible expense of truth." [15]

6

Many who felt stewardship required honesty about America were more preoccupied than ever with the evils of partisanship. Here as always lay the paradox of American nationalist ideology. The democratic process had consistently exhibited the waxing strength of the malevolent side of human nature. Garfield's assassination was an especially shocking revelation of how tragic a miscarriage the party system had been. "Tweedism" in America was said to disrupt the trials of national endeavor. William Tecumseh Sherman announced that to war for good might bring forward in each man the transcendent view vital for "a noble patriotism." Military strife became an antidote for party strife. The former was selfless and dedicated, the latter had proven greedy and debasing. Sherman said, ". . . 'tis well that every young man should, at least once in life, feel that glorious impulse which leads to deeds of heroic action, if not of self-sacrifice."

Sherman's uneasiness was part of the nation's mood through-out this final era. A citizen wrote to James Garfield before Gar-field's nomination reflecting the poignant melancholy still dogging American nationality: "I have ever looked upon the bright side of our history and hoped for a grand future for our country." Now, amid party shabbiness, the writer confessed to "a feeling of distrust for that future." He foresaw the irony of "revolution and anarchy" because of America's captivity by partisan scoundrels. The struggle was between national interest and party interest, which might produce such "a moment of pas-sion" as to "demolish the hopes of the republic." There was much of this realism in the era's consciousness. It conceded that America deteriorated in "a saturnalia of corruption," and foresaw "a day of reckoning."

With passion, mammon, and partisanship seeming to move at will in *fin de siècle* America, the events of 1898 brought blessed relief. For many they testified that God had not turned from his chosen nation. The impact upon American national expectation was broadly evident, even in the observations of the distant Henry James. In 1896 James saw "American national feeling" rapidly dividing between civilization and barbarism. The former had a chance "only on condition of its fighting hard." By 1898 James acknowledged that while war was loathsome, America's battle with Spain might ultimately be different. It could bring "some vision of how much the bigger complexity we are landed in." This new setting, James hoped, might at last force America "to produce people of capacity."

Henry James joined an assorted company of believers that the war had rescued the nation by altering citizen perspective. John B. McMaster asserted that "if the Spanish war has no other result than in awakening a love of country, it will be a great benefit to to us as a nation." Without war, there would continue "a laxity of national cohesions" far more evil than any unpleasantness ac-companying warfare. Iowa's Congressman Dolliver expressed the wide belief that the war took "the poison out of partisan strife." Consequently, battle "brought in the better era of American patriotism." Dolliver announced that "in the life of nations" there were times gripped by "impulses so pure that the appro-bation of the national conscience is a full reward for all sacrifice."

America's resurrection in 1898 was said "to silence the passion of party politics." A spiritual surge had elevated "the whole nation above the care of stocks and bonds."

The sense of relief overwhelming American nationality was conveyed by an Iowa congressman, Robert G. Cousins, to the Chicago Hamilton Club in November 1898. He called the war's outcome "the marvel of all the centuries." More than a triumph of arms, it permitted the completion of American virtue. "There was a moral fitness in the war with Spain." It had proved the Republic ready for its new tasks as foe of barbarism. For others the miraculous year brought more practical rewards. Henry Cabot Lodge was told that the new imperial trust was good both for America and for the Republican party. The revamped steward-ship, said George H. Lyman, "would give vent . . . to that rest-less spirit of our race which of late years has found its expression only in a desire for a change of government, institutions, and policies. From a political standpoint, always provided the thing is started right, it is bound to ensure the welfare of the Repub-lican party for another generation."

One of the best explanations of how the new nationality elevated America beyond the old distractions was Washington Gladden's little volume, *Our Nation and Her Neighbors,* written during the war. He recalled sympathizing with the widespread doubt at the war's outset that America's "moral elevation" could ever display the "righteousness" needed for world leadership. At that point it was not clear whether this new Trust was under-taken from the promptings of mammon or altruism. Now, Glad-den asserted, it was evident that America had accepted revised responsibility with a proper outlook which recognized that "we have got to free our minds of a good deal of cant, and stop chas-ing rainbows." After all, these new responsibilities had been "thrust into our hands." While it would be difficult to keep America worthy of "this high purpose," to pull away meant to lose the nation's soul. Accepting the new charge would prove at last that America stood for more than the "almighty dollar." It was a stance likely "to consume the iniquities of our own national politics."

Gladden closed with an apotheosis of the new Trust. Now the blights of the past could be escaped. "This sublime idea that the nation lives not for itself alone, lifted up and glorified, ought to throw a revealing light into all our caucuses and council chambers. What place has the self-seeker in the service of such a nation?" Gladden claimed that most Americans had at last faced the painful reality of national shortcoming, thereby seeing that "salvation could come" but only through "some high and pure passion in the national heart." Thus, "in saving others we may save ourselves." [16]

On this hopeful note, America's outlook in 1898 generally settled down with a new national doctrine. However, other spokesmen besides Washington Gladden could not assume a revised nationality without some lingering consciousness of human frailty. The new aggregate stewardship was unable to allay completely an anxious feeling that selfishness and emotion might again undo the American and his Republic. In discharging one debt to God and the world in 1898, the nation accepted another obligation. Men could only hope that America's new Trust would be borne more comfortably and successfully.

SPOKESMEN

The dramatic shift in America's meaning variously affected the era's spokesmen. Some voices loyally defended the original Trust, with its expectation of a symbolic victory of righteousness within the citizen. Reforming the individual as means for building a model republic was a deeply rooted idea. However, the flourishing antics of mammon and passion encouraged new interpretations of American significance. For some commentators none of the major interpretations adequately explained America at the century's end.

Behind every affirmation of American meaning there was a struggle between hope and despair. Even in entering a new sphere of moral expectation, warnings lingered that the new Adam could be as frail as the old. The hope of escaping history seemed more than anything else to encourage those advocating a new Trust. From the globe, from technology, and from evolution many spokesmen created a Vineyard and a national calling advertised as impervious to the traditional hazards. However, this revised outlook tried to convert many of the old affirmations to the new doctrine. Consequently, the escape to a new nationality created future anguish by bequeathing to a new century both a cause and a rhetoric which would trouble the modern American.

III: Advocates   In the final years of the nineteenth century, three viewpoints about nationality prevailed among representative voices grouped around the outlook of the presidents. One insisted upon the original Trust; another was baffled by the contradictory qualities between old ideas and new circumstances; while a third approach happily accepted America's new trusteeship. For traditional nationality, Carl Schurz, Grover Cleveland, and Woodrow Wilson made eloquent cases. Uneasiness with both the old and the new views enveloped Andrew Carnegie, Theodore Roosevelt, and John Fiske. Persuasive for the new Trust were Walt Whitman, John Hay, and Albert J. Beveridge.

7

The final advocacy for American nationality in the nineteenth century began with President Grant's comments on tabulating the votes in 1876's disputed presidential election. After pleading for order over citizen passion and for "a cheerful adherence" to any outcome, Grant surrendered the presidency by conceding the nation to doubt and anxiety. In such a setting, Rutherford B. Hayes seemed preoccupied with proving America was more than parties and greed. He was concerned that the role of a model republic be sustained, making his general outlook stoutly traditional. Consequently, Hayes found America's difficulty was man's frailty. God repeatedly made it clear that he was on America's side, so Hayes urged Americans to respond appropriately. His public pronouncements were conventional exhortations of the nation's Trust, accompanied by pleas for public pursuit of fulfillment. The annual message to Congress in December 1880 would have been more appropriate for 1800. Hayes pointed proudly to the recent election as evidence that republican institutions did have merit after all.

Hayes' successor, James A. Garfield, had barely time to pursue this familiar theme before his violent death illumined America's dubious performance. His inaugural message was tranquil, seeing in history evidence that time would complete the nation's destiny. While a century had passed "crowded with perils," it had also been "crowned with triumphs of liberty and law." This meant for Garfield that America was still "facing to the front, resolved to employ its best energies in developing the great possibilities of the future." He advised America no longer to debate the existence of a true national will. This will had to be enlightened and strengthened if it was to create a nation at peace with its purpose for the next generation.

A grieving nation received little spiritual solace from Chester A. Arthur. His public statements acclaimed material progress. For Arthur faith in the Founders' farsightedness and in national prosperity sustained belief that America would succeed. Arthur was left in 1884 acclaiming the public's calm welcome of a new Chief Executive as proof that Americans still loved order and were loyal to law. Said he: "Nothing could more signally demonstrate the strength and wisdom of our political institutions." [17]

However, the new President, Grover Cleveland, was unmoved by such modest testimony. In his administrations, Cleveland watched closely the final agony of a century of nationality. He never escaped to a new Trust, preferring to demand that the individual American awaken to his responsibilities. Cleveland saw a vast assortment of temptation and danger in American life which created a desperate struggle between good and evil. It was a setting in which man alone could not secure the nation's fulfillment. In the face of God and inspired Founders, Cleveland was outraged that man should be distracted by social controversies which were for him the latest form of mammon and passion. Class conflicts were impieties. Whether as economic strife or as polygamy, Cleveland roundly denounced all human impulses threatening the ancient cottage bliss which was the Republic's well-being.

Cleveland saw America as basically a sentiment, one which accepted social diversity as source for "the general good." To disturb this variety was beyond "true American sympathy and kindly feeling." The more difficult the hour seemed, the more Cleveland asked for stout reverence in citizen hearts. He rejected, for instance, a congressional proposal to aid drouth-stricken Texas on the premise that such paternalism "weakens the sturdiness of our national character, while it prevents the indulgence among our people of that kindly sentiment and conduct which strengthens the bonds of a common brotherhood."

Whether as emergency aid or support for manufacturing, Cleveland solemnly assailed all devices which could diminish the vital flame of inspired individualism which he saw as the only hope for America's success. Noting in 1888 that the centennials were about to end, Cleveland warned that a century of survival was not enough "to assure us that we no longer have dangers to fear." He called for further self-scrutiny to see whether indeed the nation was pursuing the way which "leads to happiness and perpetuity." Constitutional rectitude was, for Cleveland, the only measure of national health.

Cleveland's final admonition during his first term revealed what appeal the traditional outlines of the old Republic retained. He spoke wistfully of the nation's early days when frugality and equality were supreme. Then there was no pomp, no glitter, and no aggregation of wealth to delude a plain people. The Fathers had labored amid friendship toward "the grand destiny awaiting the land which God had given them." Alas, said Cleveland, the century so recently celebrated had transformed the Americans into a people "madly striving in the race for riches." This plight showed how distant was national fulfillment for now men sought to use the nation for greedy ends. Cleveland sternly insisted that American realization rested with individual impulse in an atomistic system bound by fraternity. The crux of nationality thus was a sense of fellowship within a simple, passive government. Cleveland renewed the Jeffersonian outlook, stating that the fruitful Steward expected little from government. Where two Stewards combined, there was potential harm to national endeavor.[18]

Cleveland's pleas in a time of suspicion and unease seemed to chant in a forgotten tongue. His successor as President, Benjamin Harrison, provided a more benign version of America's original promise. Rather than scold a frail humanity, Harrison led a litany of praise. Where Cleveland was loath to enter another century, Harrison was willing to accept the facts of America as evidence of present and future well-being. "I do not mistrust the future," Harrison announced while contending that a protective tariff program embodied lofty patriotism. He seemed to find only good where Cleveland saw cause for alarm. While regretting excesses of partisan zeal, Harrison simply called for moderation. America had been granted the best government in the finest setting. "God has placed upon our head a diadem," he said, adding, "we must not forget that we take these gifts upon the condition that justice and mercy shall hold the reins of power and that the upward avenues of hope shall be free to all the people."

This was as close as Harrison came to hinting at an ambiguous national future. Quickly changing tune, the President proclaimed that good arose from evil. Embracing a simplistic determinism, Harrison announced that America was moving with progress, vanquishing all hazards. "Passion has swept some of our communities, but only to give us a new demonstration that the great body of our people are stable, patriotic, and law-abiding." God was important. In re-enacting Washington's first inauguration, Harrison agreed that God again should be sought, as he was in 1789. His hand was needed to "lead us in the paths of righteousness and good deeds." In giving thanks in 1891, Harrison asserted that national well-being was so extensive as to prove that America's triumph was due to more than human effort.

However, late in 1891 Harrison's tone became more strident, his euphoria wavered. He looked for signs of a reviving national spirit, and he spoke earnestly of the "trust momentous in its influence" which rested upon the United States. Warning against a "faithless" people, he recommended flag-flying and stern efforts to "impress upon our youth the patriotic duties of American citizenship." Was it not "time that we should come together on the high plane of patriotism"? he asked rhetorically. What confidence Harrison retained rested on the conviction that America would keep growing. So long as there was a physical dynamism, Harrison was convinced the nation would carry forward her "great impulses." [19]

Cleveland easily resumed the threads of thought dropped four years before. While conceding that material growth and enterprise did justify national pride, he hastily added, "it behooves us to constantly watch for every symptom of insidious infirmity that threatens our national vigor." Even strong men could have disease lurking within, announced the President. Cleveland's aversion to phenomonology kept him warning that the nation's "stupendous achievements" encouraged "heedlessness of those laws governing our national health which we can no more evade than human life can escape the laws of God and nature." Folly accompanied the "exaggerated confidence in our country's greatness." The first indication of evil was when men looked to the nation for aid and advantage. Such expectation was perverting, degrading, and weakening. For Cleveland, the nation and the citizen must be separate, lest both be ruined. His second inaugural remarks talked soberly of the self-reliant Steward as the only capable embodiment of "the spirit of true Americanism." The aggressive polity was one which "stifles the spirit of true Americanism and stupefies every ennobling trait of American citizenship."

Grover Cleveland knew the nation was falling short of preserving the simple Republic. But his only advice was that Stewards somehow return to their ancestors' life. Contempt for the frugal, simple ways which were the true American virtues, as Cleveland tirelessly said, menaced "the strength and sturdiness of our national character." When a new temptation appeared in the form of expansion overseas, Cleveland responded by reciting his creed. With the moralism appropriate for an absolute view, he said of the temptation of annexing Hawaii: "If national honesty is to be disregarded and a desire for territorial extension or dissatisfaction with a form of government not our own ought to regulate our conduct, I have entirely misapprehended the mission and character of our Government and the behaviour which the conscience of our people demand of their public servants."

The old ways were God's ways in Cleveland's mind, as they had always tended to be for the preservationists. He was comfortable with the language of a nationality built on religion. In 1894 he prayed for the enhancement of American virtue so that "our national conscience may be quickened to a better recognition of the power and goodness of God, and that in our national life we may clearer see and closer follow the path of righteousness." Cleveland made unusually vigorous use of the traditional Thanksgiving proclamation to acknowledge all national progress as due to God's intervention. It was a divine mandate which Cleveland invoked against those who trifled with America's monometalism. To turn from the gold standard would bring "a self-invited struggle through darkness," leading only to national "humiliation." Ancient national policy was always morality incarnate, imbued with "integrity and rectitude" and to be "devoutly cherished as one of the traits of true Americanism." Cleveland suggested that the silver faction review its stance "in the light of patriotic reason." His nationality of moral absolutes did, however, take an ironical quality in his last message. There Cleveland said the nation could step into the Cuban crisis when "our obligations to the sovereignty of Spain will be superseded by higher obligations." [20]

President William McKinley seemed to have outdistanced Grover Cleveland in pursuing reverence for God, the national morality, and the past. The Ohioan was also remarkably blunt about the incomplete pilgrimage toward national fulfillment. Incomplete that is, until 1898. Before then, McKinley stressed the preciousness of the inspiring past and the importance of preserving the legacy from that history. Thus far had America "exalted mankind and advanced the cause of freedom throughout the world." The present generation could do no more, but this would require "that we adhere to the principles upon which the Government was established and insist upon their faithful observance." These admonitions in McKinley's first inaugural message concluded that recent events showed the need "of inculcating even a greater love of law and order in the future."

During 1897 McKinley pressed the theme of America's unfulfilled nationality, although he acclaimed the signs of an ever-increasing spirit of patriotism. However, by the close of 1898, McKinley led rejoicing in the rich benefit to nationality brought by the war. The military involvement, of course, had been a labor for such things as humanity and civilization. From it came not only the cementing of "the national spirit," but an enlarged awareness of "our obligations to the Divine Master." Happy that America and God were now in harmony and with the nation under "His safe guidance," McKinley accepted the new Trust that came with the heavenly partnership. It was stewardship with an eye on China, Turkey, and Hawaii.[21]

8

Cleveland and McKinley showed how the burden of being an American endured. For both men preservation had been the strategy for a trust not yet discharged. McKinley, however, discovered in the invitation to an expanded America deliverance from one national mission by another's beginning. On the other hand, Cleveland kept to the original Trust. For him, American nationality started and ended with the nurture of certain principles woven around a perfectly designed government.

Consequently, Grover Cleveland deserves to lead a trio of representative advocates faithful to the old nationality. Sharing Cleveland's valor were Carl Schurz and Woodrow Wilson. Each sought a larger public awareness of the awesome expectation still leveled upon citizen and nation by God and history. Grover Cleveland never lost sight of how sacred was America's Trust. His viewpoint remained direct and simple. If America ever completed a model of successful republicanism, it must be in the citizen's soul. It entailed the eventual transcendence of man's spirit over his carnal self. Cleveland stressed the traditional essence of nationality, leaving Wilson and Schurz to embroider around this theme. His advocacy showed the ravaging effects of Western civilization's insistence that man's better self must master the evil side. Cleveland spoke for a nationality believing both America and Americans were prisoners of absolute values. Upon these traditions men could lean; from them they could draw inspiration enough to triumph over sordidness. Danger came when man did not use his ability to appreciate and use these immutable values. An aroused public was the only hope for America. Cleveland gambled his ideology on the anticipation that the righteous impulses in each Steward's bosom would remain awake. He saw that the American experiment rested within the citizen as John Adams had seen. However, Adams expected more meager results.

According to Cleveland, honesty and frugality in public as in private affairs were the sustenance of the Republic. An active conscience, eagerly obeyed, was the essential for national fulfillment. Preaching to Harvard faculty members in 1886, Cleveland used this simple interpretation with great effect. Men should be as comfortable in political works as they were in scholarly ways. Said the President: "The people of the United States have one and all a sacred mission to perform." Citizens and presidents all must join in showing "to the world . . . the success of popular government." In celebrating the Constitutional Convention's centennial, Cleveland made the legacy more awesome. From God into "our hands" was "committed this ark of the people's covenant." Men of 1887 had "the duty" to guard the legacy "from impious hands. We receive it sealed with the tests of a century. It has been found sufficient, if the American people are true to their sacred trust." Sight of this role was never lost in simple lives. For Cleveland, "the plain people of the land" best perceived the meaning of America, ever mindful it was "a sacred Trust" which must "never be tarnished or neglected."

By 1888, however, Cleveland found the people asleep and, when awakened, too readily led astray A pause was needed, a time when the people might "reason together." After his defeat, Cleveland talked of the "combined selfishness" which had deluded the plain Stewards. A new emancipation was in order. Distracted and seduced though the people might be, "they will return to duty in good time." Misled, "they will discover the true landmarks none too late for safety." The errant stewardship, Cleveland predicted in 1889, "will speedily be found seeking with peace-offerings their country's holy altar."

Cleveland was fascinated with the hazards assailing the Republic in 1890, especially "selfishness," "unsavory forms," "corruption," and "debauched suffrage." All threatened to betray the Trust. Only the mysterious spiritual resources of the simple man offered the sustenance needed to avert America's disgrace. While these resources slumbered, "they will not always sleep." Wakefulness, watchfulness, fidelity to truth were admonitions constantly issued by Cleveland as he labored between his terms in office. He advocated more strenuous efforts in the home and school to indoctrinate the children with American meaning. Each generation was part of a chain which held the American purpose "in trust for those who shall come after them." Cleveland seemed never to weary of all the ancient admonitions. "If we permit grasping selfishness to influence us in the case of our Trust, we are untrue to our obligations and our covenants as Americans." For all Americans, "let us remember that it will be our blame if it is not made greater." Let any "boasting" about America be tempered with the thought that being an American meant being "charged with a sacred Trust." The nation "belongs to the world" and "in its blessed mission, belongs to humanity."

Finding an "un-American tendency" everywhere, Cleveland chose Washington's Birthday 1892 to make one of the last great apologias for the original Trust. He told students at the University of Michigan that the source of successful American living was in moral awareness, for "sentiment is the very lifeblood of our nation." This spirit was more vital than ever, for there was "stern labor" facing the Stewards "before we reach our determined destiny." Consequently, Cleveland undertook to illumine the nature of this vital spirit. It was nothing short of nationality itself, with its twin verities of freedom and equality, which must be cherished anew, as the Fathers had done. This required the fundamentals—God, morality, honesty, universal education. With these, Americans might "work out our destiny unaided and alone in full view of the truth that nowhere, so directly and surely as here, does the destruction or degeneracy of the people's sentiment undermine the foundations of governmental rule." Value was in emulating great lives, so that "during our stewardship no harm shall come to the political gifts we hold in trust from the fathers of the Republic."

For Cleveland and many other Americans, these old truths, deposited for safekeeping with the present generation, were as valuable as ever. The guardians would somehow be awakened, even though they were now "deluded, mistaken, and wickedly duped." Yet the waywardness seemed more depressing than ever. Cleveland called plans for annexing Hawaii "a perversion of our national mission." In 1898 he saw the "old landmarks" being forgotten. Only "our original designs and purposes" would sustain the American character. So quickly did the national spirit move in 1898 that this stouthearted defender of the old Trust confessed: "I despair of catching up with the procession." Sadly, he acknowledged no longer knowing "where we are tending." All around him was "a general cutting loose." 22

Cleveland represented an almost fanatical devotion to the Founders' ways and legacy. To cut loose or to seek escape from these was for him tantamount to national suicide. Woodrow Wilson, however, spoke with more moderate affection for the original Trust. He stood with Cleveland in lamenting America's indifference to the Founders' priceless truths. The distance between Wilson and Cleveland was the former's ability to translate ancient ways and values for new circumstances. To accept a changed America was beyond Cleveland. Wilson, however, began his 1879 treatise on cabinet government by saying: "Our patriotism seems of late to have been exchanging its wonted tone of confident hope for one of desponding solicitude. Anxiety about the future of our institutions seems to be daily becoming stronger in the minds of thoughtful Americans. A feeling of uneasiness is undoubtedly prevalent." While Wilson conceded that "statesmanship has been steadily dying out in the United States," he said it was owing to "want of unifying and utilizing principles." Without such changes as adopting a cabinet system, "our dangers may overwhelm us, our political maladies may prove incurable."

In arguing for moral emancipation in America, Wilson talked of altering a still infirm polity. But he did not concentrate on the mechanics of polities. A revived morality alone would "set our faces towards the accomplishment of that exalted destiny which has been the happiest, brightest dream of generations lately passed away." National morals came from a knowledge of history. "Our liberties are safe until the memories and experiences of the past are blotted out and the *Mayflower* with its band of pilgrims forgotten, until our public school system has fallen into decay and the nation into ignorance." But now this was occurring. Wilson wrote in 1884: "When grave, thoughtful, perspicacious and trusted men all around us agree in deriding those Fourth of July sentiments which were once thought to hallow the lips of our greatest orators," defenders of true nationality must do more than "flap wing and scream incoherent disapproval."

Wilson had a remedy. "If we are to hold to the old faith, we must be ready with stout reasons wherewith to withstand its assailants." Since men of great ability were taunting "these sacred institutions of ours," it would take positive improvement to preserve them. The nation momentarily might be nonchalant, "but presently there will come a time when she will be surprised to find herself grown old." Then, perplexed and strained, America would have to fall back "upon her conservatism . . . sober her views, restrict her vagaries. . . . That will be the time of change." America would finally realize that she actually was "living an old life under new conditions." The Republic's fulfillment needed this matured "nationality of our thought and habit."

In a setting of vigorous ancestry with inspired precepts and practices, Wilson insisted America could move toward completion if she willed to do so. This required confidence in the deep-seated

principles on which the nation was established. America had
not been born in revolution; it had come from adapting treasured old ways. The good Stewards would preserve the "old-time
originative force in the face of growth and imported change."
Joining the Cleveland refrain, Wilson said: "There is plenty
of the old vitality in our national character to tell, if we will but
give it leave."

Wilson warned repeatedly in the 1890's that America's headlong growth amid abundance was over. Momentum no longer
could be relied upon, and the mere phenomenon of America
was insufficient evidence of national security and fulfillment. The
nineteenth century was an interval of instinct and physical exhilaration, an era "at times so tragical, so swept by passion." By
1896 America had lost "the secluded vales of a virgin continent."
Facing realities, the nation must renew its respect for the messages of the past. "The peril," said Wilson, was that for many
Americans "the past is discredited among them, because they
played no part in it. It was their enemy, they say, and they will
not learn of it." Boasts of newness no longer were sustenance
when America faced the fact of maturity. Just as the Founders
had worked conscious of the past, Wilson contended that new
Stewards must accept the wise precepts of an earlier nationality.
Writing in *Forum* in 1896, he warned: "The days of glad expansion are gone, our life grows tense and difficult."

In *Atlantic* in 1897 Wilson urged recognition that America
was still unfinished. Only the foolish would believe "the making
of the republic had hastened to complete itself within a single
hundred years." From the wisdom and expectations of the Founders could come guidance for America's continued struggle. "It
is one thing to fill a fertile continent with a vigorous people and
take first possession of its treasures," said Wilson. But more was
expected from the nation: national fulfillment was far from complete. It would require "leadership of a much higher order to
teach us the triumphs of cooperation, the self-possession and calm
choices of maturity." Wilson refused to join the believers in
grand process. He expected America to finish with its responsibilities to the world some day, but this was far from certain.
It would take many generations, but if the sagacity of men like
Madison and Washington could be renewed, America would find
"a way out of chaos." [23]

The awesome wisdom from the past seemed to Wilson sufficient to restore America to worthiness. However, not every advocate of the original nationality could accept so simple a solution. Wilson believed that history-conscious men and appropriate mechanical changes would see the nation safely on its way, leaving a moral and intellectual elite with the burdens of steward-ship. Where Cleveland anticipated restoration through a mystical popular impulse, Wilson foresaw the rescue of nationality when impulse surrendered to reason. Carl Schurz, another devoted ad-herent to the old Trust, had views notably more earthy than either Wilson's or Cleveland's. Schurz seemed morbidly fascinated by the nation's rush away from virtue. He was quite willing to announce that the citizenry could no longer be defended as faithful Stewards. The heart of the matter was avarice. Schurz joined Wilson in urging emulation of the Fathers. The latter had perfected a "political morality" whose disregard meant na-tional decline.

Extolling ancient ways, Schurz insisted for a time that the cit-izenry at least was closer to past wisdom than were the nation's leaders. But when a new Trust appeared likely, Schurz grew alarmed. Disregarding the "limits of human possibility," the na-tion seemed about to ignore its basic problem by fancying triumph simply through more growth. Writing in *Harper's Mag-azine* in 1893, Schurz attacked Alfred T. Mahan's doctrine. "The United States will better fulfill their mission and more exalt their position in the family of nations by indoctrinating their navy officers in the teachings of Washington's farewell address than by flaunting in the face of the world the destructive power of rams and artillery." The American "fate" rested in strengthen-ing the popular wisdom and will. From this would come "a vigorous nationality." The lure of "aggrandizement" meant "de-terioration in the character of the people and . . . turbulence, demoralization and final decay."

Schurz struggled to preserve an old-fashioned stewardship from seduction. The rising outlook was a "mendicancy" willing to use the "guise of patriotism." It was indeed a strange teaching, Schurz said, to have war described as healthy. It was a crazed outlook. He scoffed at Theodore Roosevelt's fear of national effeminacy. There was simply too much "loose speech about 'Americanism,' " Schurz lamented in 1896. The nation was entrusted with a role of dignified, peaceful exemplarship. Schurz predicted the fulfillment of these original expectations, despite "hysterical cries of the alarmist" who saw world dangers. He promised joyful results if America continued its ancient, peaceful ways. There remained much yet to do for the traditional goals.

During the excitement in 1898 Schurz never wavered. Reason, peace, and dignity all would be lost, and with it America's true role, if "the reckless passions and ambitions of unruly spirits" captured the national outlook. Expansion, he told McKinley, meant "a stain of disgrace upon the American name." At Saratoga, New York, Schurz made his most eloquent defense of the original Trust. Speaking in mid-August, he said America faced the choice between two roles or images. In choosing, it would affect her future and fate. "It may be somewhat old-fashioned," said Schurz, "but I still believe that a nation, no less than an individual man, is in honor bound to keep its word." In professions of service to freedom, in affirmations of peace in Washington's treasured words, America had undertaken her career. To shrug this off meant a dreadful metamorphosis. Once the change occurred and America was misled by "vulgar ambition," nothing would stay her plunge. With the descent went "the moral ruin of the Anglo-Saxon republic."

Through the wisdom of men like Washington the nation might again find its way. These venerable ideas were more than old-foggish notions, Schurz stressed, adding: "it will be an evil day for the American people when they cease to appreciate the inestimable value of the treasure they possess in George Washington's counsel and example." By September 1898, Schurz talked sadly of America's casting away the stewardship of a century. All that now remained was to repeat "the old tale of a free people seduced by false ambitions and running headlong after riches and luxury and military glory, and then down the fatal slope into vice, corruption, decay, and disgrace." America's tragedy was especially wretched since she had been given so magnificent an opportunity to serve. The American bankruptcy would be "more shameful and discouraging than ever before in history."

Schurz considered the "catchwords" about a new call from Providence and destiny a snare and delusion. American fulfillment still required the old virtues and self-denials. When Americans conquered self, "there will be no prouder title than that of being an American—far prouder than the most powerful and costly armaments and the largest conquests can make it." The nation's primary responsibility was still unmet. With its discharge came endurance; abandoning it meant decay. This was Schurz's message to a nation he saw being swindled by false belief. No matter "how glossed over by high-sounding cant about destiny and duty and what not," to follow the "hot impulses" of the jingoes meant national destruction. "Have we sunk so low?" he asked at the close of 1898.[24]

The century ended with advocates like Schurz in despair. A dreadful new departure was under way, with a sacred obligation casually abandoned. Other observers, however, seemed suspended between impatience with the old national character and uneasiness over a new role. Three such cautious spokesmen were John Fiske, Andrew Carnegie, and Theodore Roosevelt. As a popularizer of Teutonism, John Fiske believed that English racial triumph was itself an ordered process. American meaning was steadfastness to an Anglo-Saxon role. Fiske preached the paradoxical comforts of a natural process whose outcome was pleasantly fixed. He believed that America's purpose was to be a wondrous example of the aim of history. Since the outcome was plain, evils like immigration and imperialism were unexpected. Fiske's inspired plan was threatened by an unkind series of events.

Unlike most thoughtful Americans, John Fiske was once untroubled about the nation's role. The latter was assigned by the great political evolution, it was "not the result of special creation." Washington and Lincoln could be understood only as "the fruition of the various works of de Montfort and Cromwell and Chatham." Their goal had been an admirable political order. Superior men in communion with the soil made possible America's completion of the English pilgrimage toward the known. For Fiske, the American Trust was to avert any danger to the maturing of the lovely republic. The Fathers were "a body of *picked* men," whose choice "was unquestionably the most prodigious event in the political annals of mankind." Thanks to them, the *"two Englands"* now labored together "toward the political regeneration of mankind." This fulfillment stemmed from being "an example of priceless value to other ages and to other lands." Here was Fiske's version of Manifest Destiny.

By 1898 Fiske talked like a preservationist. He became president of the Immigration Restriction League as a means of conserving the American design. Growth and evolution now needed significant qualification. Fiske saw the American model being threatened by "base human material." Change could even produce "a lower and more degraded way of regarding things." When expansion into the Pacific overcame the American venture, Fiske said he could no longer "feel sure of my ground. . . . I find my judgment hesitating between opposing considerations." For Fiske there was no escaping the unpleasant fact that the glorious process of things had taken an unanticipated, perhaps an unnatural turn. His sense of America's Trust was being ground between the rock of design and the rock of process.[25]

The same plight befell Andrew Carnegie. He was perhaps the most ardent phenomenologist among leading commentators in this era. For him physical growth was the assurance of completed nationality. It was growth according to a simple, well-established formula, which Carnegie eulogized in his 1886 volume, *Triumphant Democracy*. This widely acclaimed book spoke of the approaching American fulfillment. However, in 1898 Carnegie found himself stymied. He could only insist that the public somehow not permit passions roused by drumtap to destroy its earlier outlook.

Readers had written in delight to the author of *Triumphant Democracy*. Its pages had assured them that astounding development indicated the nation could be confident of eternal life. Carnegie's praise for the conservative quality of both existence and thought in America suggested that fulfillment came through cautious accumulation. George Pullman praised the timeliness of the book since, thanks "to the excesses of our turbulent population, so many are uttering doubts just now as to whether democracy has been a triumph in America." From Philadelphia came the confession: "Never, until now, have I realized truly the superiority and greatness of our republican institutions." These promised "an unshackled race marching to God in the sunshine of brotherly love." Another found the sight of America's greatness dizzying. One said the testimony from Carnegie was especially welcome "in these days of carping criticism, and hyper-criticism." It revealed fitly the "rich blessings" accompanying the national pilgrimage. "One rises from the book with the question, 'Who would not be an American citizen?'"

The point basic in all of these letters was best expressed by the reader who said that *Triumphant Democracy* "almost restores even my faith in democratic humanity." Carnegie's advocacy was said to give "a great and lasting impulse to the American idea," which was "that next to God, there is nothing so strong, so capable, so helpful, so inspiring, as the good successful man." For many sharing Carnegie's view this was the gospel of America. The nation was a wondrous Vineyard wherein ardent Stewards, willing to toil, could exhibit the good life possible for Anglo-Saxon brethren. Events after 1890 challenged Carnegie's gospel of nationality. In articles and commentaries he kept insisting "we have only to be prudent" and violent changes would not diminish American development. Disciples like Minnesota's Henry Fairchild pleaded that Carnegie's message somehow reach the masses of Americans who were "misguided" and "dupes" in a season of enormous corruption and class conflict. Fairchild argued in 1892 that the enemy in America was its rising self-distrust which in turn inspired "dangerous political as well as social doctrines." The nation's mood was, at least, to Fairchild, "a revelation."

In 1896, Carnegie published two articles in *North American Review*. The contrast between them discloses something of the division afflicting some national consciousness. On the one hand, Carnegie rejoiced in the sturdiness of America's international posture. "The republic has become of age and entered into the possession of his heritage." Yet he considered the nation capable of self-destruction and condemned the comforting delusions of evolution. He saw McKinley as called with the same trumpet which had sounded for Lincoln. Both were to preserve the nation amidst awful conflict. "The strife is mortal; one or the other must perish, for law and license cannot co-exist." While America might become great without material success, she could never attain her role in civilization without law and order.

Looking for the end of aimless drifting, Carnegie took hope in 1896, for "all hands are aroused; new men are about to take command." While he insisted that the Republic still had its future before it, national fulfillment had come to mean stability. This made the extraordinary turn of events in 1898 very disconcerting. Carnegie hid in the old Vineyard. Let the Republic develop "her vast continent until it holds a population as great as that of Europe." This was America's destiny, a growth clearly conditioned and guided. "It has hitherto been the glorious mission of the Republic to establish upon secure foundations Triumphant Democracy." This was an unmet challenge, and America was faltering. Carnegie asked: "Tires the Republic so soon of its mission that it must, perforce, discard it to undertake the impossible task of establishing Triumphant Despotism?"

Claiming he was no "Little American," Carnegie's doubts about human and national capacity forced him to argue that while America must grow, it could safely do so only under "past policy." The good republic could be established with dependable Americans only. Deeply distressed with the nation's casual escape into new darkness, Andrew Carnegie threw himself upon the teachings of a century before. America, he cried, "stands apart, pursuing her own great mission, and teaching all nations by example." [26]

Carnegie's distinction between prudent and imprudent stewardship was as simple as Theodore Roosevelt's view was confused and vehement. Torn among concepts of nationality, Roosevelt could not be content with Carnegie's belief that majestic physical achievement was itself national fulfillment. For Roosevelt, the spiritual outlook was fundamental. Doubting that the traditional phenomena of expanding farms, factories, railroads, and cities would sustain a new century's outlook, Roosevelt campaigned for a nationality comprised of passionate attraction. For him the faithful Steward was one whose heart and mind yielded joyously to whatever the nation might demand. Properly inspired, the citizen would withstand the temptations and torments of a changing world. Consequently, Theodore Roosevelt was eager for spiritual renewal. He was neither a guardian of an old Republic nor an advocate of a new Trust. For him, as for many, the challenge was to retain an inner Americanism when neither past, present, nor future circumstances were wholly satisfying. As he saw it, strengthening the energetic reverence of Americans for being American was the only necessity for continued national fruitfulness. This was in the face of a rising sentiment for a less personal and more distant sense of nationality.

Roosevelt believed in the nation's capacity to succeed despite frequent fumbling and even momentary failure. Despondent in 1884 over Blaine's nomination, Roosevelt observed that the nation "has stood a great deal in the past and can stand a great deal more in the future. It is not the first time that a vast popular majority has been on the side of wrong." By 1892 Roosevelt thought often about creating a proper perspective in this majority. There was an increasing zest for flying the flag and patriotic ceremonies in the schools and it pleased him. Increasingly, his commentary stressed emotion as the important ingredient in the American national outlook. Native or foreign-born, all Americans, according to Roosevelt, had to unite in affirming that being an American was superior to any other status. After such dedication, citizens could examine shortcomings in the Republic's progress. There were some problems and "we ought steadily to try to correct them." Crucial for such loving improvement was "a firm and ardent Americanism at the bottom of everything." Not to have this feeling meant a "fatal defect" in the national character.

Roosevelt endorsed the Founders' view that America should ignore mankind. "Our business is with our own nation, with our own people." The challenge within the American calling was of such magnitude that Roosevelt sounded his favorite call for all "the robuster virtues." American stewardship had no need of "milk and water philanthropy" and certainly none for the "denationalized" person who failed to regard America "in a different way." Beginning with an 1894 article, "True Americanism," Roosevelt regularly admonished the literate public. This group, he feared, would bring nationality's enervation.

In "True Americanism," Roosevelt renewed an appeal heard often in the previous hundred years. The nation had "many grave problems to solve, many threatening evils to fight, and many deeds to do. . . . We must neither surrender to a foolish optimism, nor succumb to a timid and ignoble pessimism. Our nation is that one among all the nations of the earth which holds in its hands the fate of the coming years." A difficult Trust and a familiar one, but Roosevelt's corollary here was unique. Let the Stewards move to their calling with "an intense and fervid Americanism." Roosevelt warned, "We shall never be successful . . . we shall never achieve true greatness, nor reach the lofty ideal which the founders and preservers of our mighty Federal Republic have set before us, unless we are Americans in heart and soul, in spirit and purpose, keenly alive to the responsibility implied in the very name of American." The upshot of this seemed to be a stewardship of introverted fervency, one that did not seek salvation for "the whole human race and all the world."

Roosevelt was outraged by men like Henry James whose outlook he considered at best flaccid and explainable only as an "organic weakness." Fortunately, most Americans were "robustly patriotic" and had "sound, healthy minds." Even so, Roosevelt's talk of commitment first and thoughtful analysis second became frantic. In many different ways he defined Americanism as a matter of spirit, then of conviction, and finally of purpose. This biological-emotional seedbed for a proper stewardship was stressed in another 1894 article, "The Manly Virtues and Practical Politics." Roosevelt here announced purity as an important quality for real Americanism. Soon he wrote again to plead that educated men be "heartily American in instinct and feeling and taste and sympathy." Roosevelt said the gravest threats to national endeavor were the "dim-colored mists that surround the preachers of pessimism." He did condemn "careless optimism."

In 1895 Roosevelt clearly separated his philosophy of nationality from that proclaimed by phenomenologists like Andrew Carnegie. He called for a stewardship aimed "toward things higher and nobler which can never be bestowed by the enjoyment of mere material prosperity." Roosevelt insisted that Americans had "nobler capacities" not yet displayed. He agreed with the venerable charge that pursuing demeaning goals had usually commanded the national outlook. Said he: "There is not in the world a more ignoble character than the ignoble American, insensible to duty . . . bent only on amassing a fortune." At the other extreme were men like John Peter Altgeld who incited the evil passions among Americans. Neither the materialist nor the dangerous reformer would lead America toward the "great thoughts and lofty emotions which alone make a nation mighty."

Throughout his advocacy, Roosevelt was no more explicit. In placing an exultant national consciousness above mere "thrift and industry," Roosevelt spoke simply of "nobler grounds than those of mere business expediency." The indescribable "elemental virtues" were apparently to be known by their impact, which was across America a thorough "saturation . . . with the national idea."

Until 1898 Roosevelt remained both uneasy and displeased with America's response to its calling. Neither morality nor manliness seemed sufficiently present for a proper entry into the new century. He continued to trace such morals and manhood to a visceral origin. Here Roosevelt's view of nationality lingered until the international adventure. He admitted that his incessant writing was meant to arouse "our wretched fellow countrymen who lack patriotism." Dismissing the sentimentalists who followed Charles Eliot and Carl Schurz, Roosevelt called for a Steward willing to fight. Yet the more Roosevelt talked, the vaguer his doctrine became. While his plea for strenuous patriotism hinted at universal values and their attainment, Roosevelt's goal never seemed to move beyond the citizen's predisposition. That is, he was often concerned with a topic familiar to American introspection, human capacity. Whereas, a hundred years earlier, men like Jefferson had hoped for the rise of deliberateness and reason over passion as the means of delivering America's responsibility, Theodore Roosevelt advocated a return to instinct.

As assistant secretary of the navy, he preached daring, valor, and especially an eagerness to battle as proof of the dedicated Steward. The thinkers, "timid souls," were to be swept aside. Such "craven" beings, along with the materialists, would produce only "utter decadence" in America. Thus Roosevelt saw war with Spain as more than the simple escape from a century of internal bumbling that war had proved to be for many thwarted Stewards. Not only would war free America from European dominance, but Roosevelt claimed that at last Americans would have "something to think of which isn't material gain." Although proud of being a jingo, Roosevelt's purpose was more complex than most ardent brethren. He hoped martial experience would lead to a finer breed of Stewards for America. They could prune the Vineyard of its old problems. Roosevelt anticipated a new virility hastening the nation toward a mysterious destiny once the Americas had been left to the Americans.[27]

Ardent loyalty, strenuous faithfulness, these were matters of deepest concern to Theodore Roosevelt, whose outlook was perhaps the most poignant of all the attitudes comprising the muddled American nationality at the end of the nineteenth century. More than any other leading spokesman, he saw the battle for American fulfillment still in the souls of men. Unwilling to rely on reason or guidance, Roosevelt could urge only a mystical dynamism. For him nationality was an intensely personal thing. However, advocates of the new Trust had something else in mind. Their capitulation to the sweep of phenomenalism was complete. Mammon and passion came to be guardedly held as allies in answering a revised American calling, and pragmatism also became a favorite philosophy. The Republic had moved far beyond the original Trust's stress upon design and principle.

Important advocates of a revamped nationality were John Hay, author and diplomat; Albert J. Beveridge, orator and statesman; and Walt Whitman, poet and essayist. Of these the pilgrimage of John Hay is most instructive. His outlook moved from deep misgiving over the nation's trusteeship to ecstasy over new propulsions discernible in national and universal events. Relief at a fresh national purpose was almost painfully evident in Hay's case. In the beginning, his attitude was simple: "We are in a bad way." He assailed politicians, marveled that mobs were so restrained, and generally conceded that America was disgraced. This was in 1877. Refusing to serve as President Garfield's private secretary, Hay described himself as unequipped for active public service in American democracy. He shrank from daily exposure to "envy, meanness, ignorance, and the swinish selfishness which ignorance breeds." For him American patriotism had a deplorable prospect.

The astounding change occurring in Hay's outlook during 1898 was evident when he told an audience in London: "We are bound by a tie which we did not forge and which we cannot break; we are joint ministers of the same sacred mission of liberty and progress, charged with duties which we cannot evade by the imposition of irresistible hands." The British and American flags were made to fly together, "carrying always in their shadow freedom and civilization." Hay surrendered completely to process. "Whether we will or not," English-speaking people labored jointly "by the very nature of things, and no man and no group of men can prevent it." This new venture was guided by "a sanction like that of religion." It was "the beneficent work of the world."

Hay recognized that 1898 was a juncture of great importance "not only for the present, but for all the future." The fresh Trust carried "the interests of civilization." He jubilantly told a Fourth of July audience, "this year all the omens are with us." For Hay, America's partnership with England was the most auspicious indication of a "triumphant march of progress." Although much remained within America "to be mended or ended," the great experiment of the Republic had at last resulted in "enormous good." Events proved that the nation's "keen pursuit of material gain" had not destroyed her spirit. Thus, Hay could tell Theodore Roosevelt: "It has been a splendid little war; begun with the highest motives, carried on with magnificent intelligence and spirit, favored by that Fortune which loves the brave." [28]

Walt Whitman, on the other hand, had begun earlier than Hay to seek a new American meaning. This he found in the far-off future. He was able to argue that the real American character was not yet evident. Consequently, Whitman made the story of America's first century a mere preface to national fulfillment. The slaying of Lincoln had marked the start of America's genuine career, Whitman contended. Such a great life and death brought a subtle cement "to the whole people." However, this was no more than a beginning. "Long, long are the processes of the development of a nationality. Only to the rapt vision does the seen become the prophecy of the unseen."

America's purpose, for Whitman, was to produce the American. Material now in hand was the "latent and silent bulk of America." From it would come the nation's contribution to civilization's "cosmic train." During 1881 Whitman commented on his notion of emergent nationality. America possessed two sets of "wills." One propelled things like greed and intelligence. The other, "deep, hidden, unsuspected . . . rising as it were out of abysses," would eventually goad the Republic toward its highest ideals. The paradox of national contradictions was thus explained, leaving Whitman to offer hope that in time this "great unconscious" would command American nationality.

Whitman set his expectation of American unfolding in the distance, believing that somehow it would occur within each American. The poet considered it too early for serious definition of the American Trust. The American identity and outcome were awarded to "sublime process," leaving America to think of "entire humanity and history." Whitman's view was clearly transcendent, putting meaning in the individual soul moved by the course of affairs to a point far beyond time. American nationality properly conceived, then, would lose itself in the emergence of the true American with the universe. The Republic would eventually surpass itself. For Whitman, the first century "of our national experiment, from its inchoate movement down to the present day" was to launch America "fairly forth, consistently with the entirety of civilization and humanity." The "real history" of the United States "is only to be written at the remove of hundreds, perhaps a thousand, years hence." America's Trust was, therefore, "custodian of the future of humanity." [29]

There were few complications in the viewpoint of Albert J. Beveridge. His acceptance of Saxon instinct as fundamental to an inevitable national development made other spokesmen cautious by comparison. Greed and demagoguery would be dangerous, according to Beveridge, only until America's character emerged. This was a biological event, for "we must obey our blood." Beveridge declared obsolete the outlook of a century before. America's nationality was not to be the "echo of the past." He was among the first to describe the new Trust as carrying "American law, American order, American civilization, and the American flag [to] shores hitherto bloody and benighted," where the American influence would make them "beautiful and bright."

Popularity as an orator brought Beveridge leadership in America's movement toward a new self. The Indiana statesman proclaimed, for instance, that America's new role required an "English-speaking people's league of God for the permanent peace of this war-torn world." For this glorious Trust, he said, "the stars in their courses will fight for us and countless centuries will applaud." Now indeed was "the golden dawn of the Republic's full-grown manhood." There was no reason for caution, so Beveridge was coldly impatient with shirkers. He insisted, "I would rather map out and advocate the imperial policy of the Republic than to have been the leading statesman of the late [Civil] war. It means more for humanity, more for our country, and a larger place in history."

Critics of expansion were told by Beveridge that such development was mandatory in the awesome energy of the American people. "So there you are, and what are you going to do about it?" he asked smugly. In his famous "March of the Flag" speech in September 1898, Beveridge rhetorically inquired whether the American people would indeed accept the course of events, and "rise as fits their soaring destiny." Or would they hesitate and "prove apostate to the spirit of their race." If England could be courageous, so could America, Beveridge announced in reply. He suggested to a delighted audience that what Britain could do, the United States could do better. Indeed, all the elements, including the ocean, "are in league with our destiny."

Beveridge's advocacy represented the clearest call for the new stewardship. Its assurance contrasted with the uneasiness which Jefferson, a Saxon whom Beveridge was fond of citing, had displayed. It required a century for the fear and doubt which produced the Washington Farewell decree and the Alien and Sedition gestures to subside enough so that Beveridge and those like him would gain a wide following. Affirmations of the new nationality used familiar words. Their qualities of assurance and detachment were new. But then these made all the difference. As Beveridge said, "It is God's great purpose made manifest in the instincts of our race, whose present phase is our personal profit, but whose far-off end is the redemption of the world and the christianization of mankind." [30]

9

As advocacy of American nationality changed at the close of the nineteenth century, the advantage of a new purpose was especially useful for magazine literature. The leading advocate of the old Trust was *Nation*. Those who hurried to embrace the new duty were not numerous. Among them were *Overland Monthly*, *Outlook*, and *Review of Reviews*. Other prominent journals responded cautiously, while showing how weary American thought

had become with the old Trust. Burdened by the traditional expectation, most magazines were relieved by developments at the
century's close. They accepted America's dramatically altered
prospects and circumstances as sufficient evidence of a new Trust.
Representative of the periodicals advocating the new Americanism were *Atlantic, Forum, Scribner's* which later became *Century, Arena, North American Review, Leslie's, Independent,* and
Youth's Companion.

Steadfast in reminding America of its original and ineluctable
responsibility was *Nation.* It said the jingo outlook showed the
damage venality had done to the American character. In sorrow,
Nation watched a fickle Republic abandon the Founders' precepts. As early as 1880, the magazine had scolded hypocrisy, although it did suggest that through education America might still
elude the grasp of materialism. This way of escape was especially
important when the public mind was being goaded by agitators.
Meaningful national growth could come only with reform. And
this, said *Nation,* must await "a return to the practice of the
fathers."

Little evidence of such a return was apparent to *Nation* in
1893. It saw instead more success for the diabolical appeals to
passion by the "Americanistic" tactics of men like James G.
Blaine. The barbaric zest for grabbing Hawaii was called tragic.
Nation insisted that such zeal could properly be addressed only
to the fearful domestic shortcomings haunting America. Ignorance, corruption, crime, education, drunkenness, and the city
were areas where Stewards must realize how much "might be
done for genuine national glory, how much for the salvation of
democracy and the elevation of the human race." Instead, the
sudden lusting after foreign growth "makes us seem the great
failure of modern civilization."

After 1893, *Nation* became preoccupied with the cheapening
of nationality. It deplored the casual manner in which titles like
"good American" were brandished. "We are the only nation
which indulges in this protestation," said *Nation,* adding: "Americans ought not to have to go about the world proclaiming their
patriotism, and ought not to have to address each other on the
beauty of this particular virtue." In *Nation's* opinion, America
desperately needed "self-respect and self-improvement." Inner

regeneration "would do more for the national fame, and command more foreign deference, than a thousand battle-ships." Venality and degeneracy were terms familiar to readers of *Nation*.

The magazine rejected any contention of America's proven superiority. "There has been no special creation either of men or things for the benefit of America. Human reason and human experience work here in just the same way as elsewhere." In 1898, *Nation* rebuked the joyful insistence that America was gripped by benign momentum. "People should think less of destiny and more of righteousness." Faced by America's drastic departure from cherished precepts, *Nation* suggested, "Revolution, rather than evolution, seems the appropriate word to describe it."

In desperation, *Nation* made a final plea to Stewards who talked of a new Trust: "Let them not lay the soothing unction to their souls that they must accept the decree of destiny and submit to the irresistible form of evolution." America had been "trying the greatest experiment" ever seen, "and we cannot yet say that the work of our hands is finally established." Late in 1898, *Nation* announced that the Republic had abandoned her soul to a new outlook, which "will prove beyond question that the original American ideals have utterly perished." A final defense of the old America must be mounted by the faithful. Those continuing to fight for restoring the original Trust, said *Nation*, "will hold as high a place in American history as those who became immortal by founding it." [31]

At *Nation*'s opposite were journals believing that America's metamorphosis would avoid calamity, not bring it. One of these preachers of a new Trust was *Outlook*. Its expressions captured the essential transformation of nationality. As editor after 1878, Lyman Abbott brought *Outlook*'s circulation by 1898 to 100,000. In that year, Abbott resigned from the pulpit at Plymouth Church, where Henry Ward Beecher had served before him, to devote himself to the journal. His special concern was to explain the challenge of the new day dawning upon America. In doing so, *Outlook* substituted one sense of nationality for another with no hesitancy or ambiguity. At the start of 1897, Abbott foresaw at hand no really basic change. One could embrace the old religion and the new theology, the old patriotism and the new politics, the old philanthropy and new institutions, and the old brotherhood within the new social order. Real patriotism would "talk less about Old Glory," preferring "to make children understand what it is that gives glory to a flag."

Rescuing the American people from a state of indifference, and worse yet, a "moral distrust," was the important point. The journal called for a new independence of perception so that both citizenry and leadership could be free of passion. Mobs and demagogues remained a serious danger to America while havoc spread from corruption, selfishness, and indifference. *Outlook* told every genuine American to feel humiliated, since America now faced greater danger than in 1861. The "dangerous feeling of pessimism and distrust" was warranted. *Outlook* kept talking of "mobocracy and plutocracy," and urged the Republic to be more concerned with "righteousness" than "greatness." This perspective might save "the experiment."

Then, in March 1898, Lyman Abbott and *Outlook* discovered the new Trust. With one of the most revealing statements in the final phase of traditional nationality, *Outlook* put America into a global family, with universal responsibilities. Conceding a noble war might be necessary, *Outlook* said America had become "a Trustee" in a new and broader fashion. Once "we were a feeble folk, scarce able to assure ourselves of our own maintenance on the edge of this great wilderness." Now, "whether we will or no we are part of the great world." Joining "the comradeship of nations" carried responsibility for "maintaining the peace and honor of the globe."

Discarding its recent sorrow at the sordid, weak character of America, *Outlook* pronounced the nation ready for its revamped role and with it a fine new "duty," war for humanity. Battle became the source of ennoblement and strength for a new national career. *Outlook* called the crusade against Spain "more righteous than the War for Independence, which was fought for our own liberties, more righteous than the Civil War, which was fought for the liberty of those whom we had ourselves helped to enslave." With this crusade, America had finally answered the call to be her brother's keeper.

Outlook discovered that the Republic's career was part of an implacable flow of events. This was "the final outcome of a great historic conflict. . . . it is the final act in the great drama" in which America "is simply the hand of Providence." The maga-

zine was no longer cautious. "The Nation has come to a consciousness of manhood, and with that consciousness to a sense of
the responsibilities which manhood brings with it." War's travail
was needed to awaken men to proper deeds and convictions, said
Abbott. Battle now brought a new "healthfulness" in America's
self-awareness. Momentarily hesitant when overseas expansion
became an issue, *Outlook* quickly accepted this as part of a loftier
Trust. America now replaced England as "head steward in the
household of the world." This duty was "a summons from the
God of nations." The new call came, however, after the United
States had first confirmed the meaning of freedom. The initial
labor expected of America had thus been grandly concluded.

All of this, according to *Outlook,* was a "moral miracle." A
great purpose had come anew to America, and America was
"accepting the trust in a spirit of exhilarant courage which au-
gurs well for its final achievement." A new readiness to dare and
do put to rest at last the lamentations over national decay. "We
thank God, then, not because he is on our side, but because he
has inspired America to be on his side, because he has thought
her worthy to execute his commissions of justice and liberty; because he has quickened in her heart a love for suffering humanity in all lands, which is more than patriotism." Increasingly for
Outlook, the war became a mystical experience. American Stewards "had lost their way, but suddenly, in the fierce light of battle, they found it again."

By Autumn 1898, *Outlook*'s acclaim of metamorphosis settled
into talk about methods for novel times. The "new position of
responsibility" meant final inner reformation springing from the
"quickened sense of the power of nationality" and the "deeper
love of country." With the new mission, it would be folly to
bind America "to the mere traditions of the past, and compel it
to follow in 1900 counsels which were wise in 1800." *Outlook*
decisively pointed toward a new world with faith and hope.
Memory and custom succeeded passion and greed as cause for
anxiety. *Outlook* believed America could turn to its new role
without misgiving for man or mission.[32]

Sharing *Outlook*'s conviction were *Overland Monthly* and *Review of Reviews.* The San Francisco-based *Overland* became one
of the most ardent expansionists. Its contributors generally con-
curred that "it is clearly our duty to take all proper measures to

insure a continuation of our blessings, and to avoid the short-sighted policy which takes no account of the coming morrow." That day could bring war, a challenge which would wrest Americans from their "venal and selfish motives," one author wrote in 1890. Only such an event would produce the "statesmanlike moral character which Jefferson supposed would come of itself." Until then, a "debased" national outlook would remain "the radical public evil in America."

Overland Monthly eagerly looked for this regenerate nationality. Such anticipations dominated its editorial on Lowell's death. Though Lowell was gone, and with him a generation of humane hope, he was seen as emblematic of the future unity of the English-speaking race "which ardent dreamers prophesy, a citizen of their sometime-to-be 'Anglo-Saxon' federation." The magazine kept insisting that America would escape "the merciless greed" with its "sheer destructiveness." A saving, innate altruism would finally intervene, taking Americans beyond themselves. In short, *Overland* expected circumstance to challenge the reluctant greatness in American character. For a time the magazine was not certain that the Spanish-American War represented this circumstance. It was content to say that "by the mysterious law of compensations, may good come out of evil." In July 1898, the magazine's patience was apparently rewarded. It announced: "Our destiny is growing more manifest every day."

Thereafter, *Overland* authors delineated the new nationality with a rare intensity. "The evolutionary force to which the trend of our history has responded, and must respond, is the racial aspiration to be a great nation, in all the attributes of greatness." This had brought America to world dominion. "Hereafter this great Republic is to be a factor in the meaningful movement of nations." It was a Trust which "cannot be interpreted by the vanity, the hypocrisy of eloquence, or the bigotry of mere sentimental patriotism." Stewards must realize that forces beyond their control or understanding had crowned "our country with a higher mission and a broader responsibility." The new moment brought "nobler aspirations, augmented possibilities, and the achievement of a higher place in the upward and onward pathway of destiny." [33]

On the other side of the continent, Albert Shaw's *Review of Reviews* shared in announcing a revamped nationality. It had been grieved at the torpor in America's thought, which was evidence of "the incompleteness of our development." Not to recognize a new Trust, including Pacific domain, would be "a confession of intellectual feebleness akin to real imbecility." It would mean abdication of "a duty as well as an opportunity." *Review* insisted that America's internal venture was no longer an experiment "and it is well-nigh treasonable for an American thus to refer to it." By contending that it was wrong to dispute "the fundamental soundness of our American body politic," *Review of Reviews* significantly advanced the advocacy of a completed American nationality.[34]

Generally, however, most of the major periodicals had struggled too long with the anxieties of nationality to embrace hurriedly a new Trust. Magazines like *North American Review, Century, Arena,* and *Forum* could not forget the much discussed shortcomings of American stewardship. Consequently, their pleasure in a new duty's suggestion of an old Trust's fulfillment developed slowly. After all, the glories of 1898 were close to the darkness of 1892 and 1896. There were clear memories of such dreadful moments as the slaying of Garfield.

The venerable *North American Review* had witnessed most of the distressing efforts of nineteenth-century America to fulfill itself. The veteran journal's uneasiness over national capacity persisted until the thunderclap of 1898. Until then, the old hazards stalked *North American Review*'s pages. Contributors like Francis Parkman, R. H. Dana, Jr., and George W. Julian worried over the "moral felonies" which scarred the nation. David Dudley Field, Albion Tourgee, and other commentators were obviously fretful. Talking about America became increasingly joyless for *North American Review*. Centennial drum-beating was little inspiration.

The first mention of a possible new nationality came in 1881. Congressman John Kasson wrote in *North American Review* that America ought now to forego its "interior struggles" and to think of the future in which expansion would be important. "We must turn our eyes abroad, or they will soon look inward upon discontent." However, such a view continued to be outdone by lamentation over the Republic's demoralization, especially among the youth. An article asking "Are We a Nation of Rascals?" answered itself affirmatively. The only modest comfort was offered by Julian Hawthorne, who took America's meaning into process and universal import. Men did not yet fully perceive this, said Hawthorne, so the impression persisted that America was "a series of episodes, of experiments." As if in proof, most contributors to *North American Review* stayed with the traditional outlook of misgiving. Typical was the magazine's dedication of the June 1891 issue to discussing national character, with a prominent theme entitled "Brutality and Avarice Triumphant."

By 1895, however, *North American Review* had published an article on the purifying effects of war and was noticing the vast natural momentum across the world of which American endeavor might be part. David A. Wells wrote in 1896, "The United States now stands at the parting of the ways." While for Wells this meant isolation or internationalism, others stressed anarchy and socialism as twin horrors facing an errant nation. Despite some of its contributors' dedicated alarm over human nature and republicanism, gradually *North American Review* seemed drawn to what one of its 1897 articles called the "New Epoch." The magazine began to stress how circumstances in the present were vastly different from those existing when the Republic was born. Included were affirmations that "the time has certainly arrived" when America "must either discharge its duty to itself and to humanity, or it must abdicate the high office with which destiny has clothed it."

This rising preoccupation with transition after "a changeful century" was behind George W. Melville's 1898 remark: "But a little more than a century has gone by since, on the winter wind at Valley Forge, there streamed a ragged flag. . . ." Now a nobler destiny beckoned that same banner, asking those who bore it "to follow the pathway of the stars" and "to win a new glory" beyond the continent. Bishop William C. Doane explained why resisting this new call would be selfishness and even sin, even though America still had "great evils to contend with." By June 1898, contributors to *North American Review* had accepted "the duty we owe to Christian civilization." It was time now to consider "what will be expected of the greater American citizen that is to be." [35]

This expectation troubled *Century* magazine, briefly called *Scribner's Monthly*. Although *Century* early foresaw world leadership as an American role, it was especially fearful that the

Republic would fail. To the end of 1898, *Century* called for stewardship built on reason, not passion, and upon deliberateness, not impulse or process. This was evident as early as 1877, when an editorial was written which conceded that America's development was astounding, for "almost literally, the nation has been born in a day." The question was: "What are we going to do with all this, and with ourselves?" If the Republic could not master itself, no material attainment would preserve "the national honor."

Events seemed for *Century* to be producing a deeper self-awareness throughout the Republic. "We are beginning to realize that the task that is laid upon us is not going to be so easy as thoughtless American patriots have sometimes supposed." Meantime, "the political interest of the world is centered in America, and awaits the realization of our destiny." America's destiny required that able men embrace rather than shun political leadership. Partisan shoddiness was steadily assailed in *Century* through interminable commentaries upon the national humiliation and discouragements brought by such frailty. By 1894, *Century* was denouncing the rush toward militarism as new evidence of human weakness and a threat to American purpose. "We need to realize as a people that the way to make our country great and to win for it the respect of mankind is not to shout constantly that we are the greatest nation in the world, but to show that we are capable of self-government." Equally distressing was the rising false nationality which encouraged the American "to look for an international rather than a domestic field wherein to display his devotion." In failing to recognize the full implications of republican weakness, "the mass of Americans have yet to realize that patriotism is less an impulse than a duty."

This ambivalence over new national responsibility vexed *Century* through the war. It took comfort in the merger of England and America, seeing it as bolstering national rectitude through a "noble vision of race patriotism." Amid all the acclaim for a new role, *Century* continued to plead that domestic challenges not be forgotten. The journal was pleased, therefore, to present Whitelaw Reid's predication that the new American endeavor would exalt American life and "dignify and elevate the public service." Even so, it was not quite ready to believe that the burden of republican success no longer persisted.[36]

Century was not alone in hesitating. A magazine which first appeared in Boston in 1889, *Arena,* also kept eyeing the national soul in a season of change. Down to the war this journal considered America close to failure. "The impulses of the race favor another step in the slow ascent of the ages," said B. O. Flower, the editor, "but ancient thought lies across the pathway; while intrenched power, monopoly, and plutocracy, are clinging to her garment in the vain hope of checking the inevitable." Flower called in 1893 for serious men to discover and study "the root causes of the evils which menace the Republic." He urged facing "the real facts and hard questions of American civilization," letting no "casuistical patriotism" blind the nation.

As outlet for the American Institute of Civics in New York City, *Arena* filled its pages in 1897 and 1898 with reminders of the inner challenge to stewardship. Thus, "true Americanism" would carry patriotism from "the realm of mere sentiment into that of noble passion." Finally, in April 1898, *Arena* examined the presence of a new Trust while "from the upper air came the sound of the rush of eagle wings." Outmoded views of national purpose were to be set aside, the periodical conceded, but the old morals had to be revered. America must beware of jumping "heedlessly into the currents of a passing emotion." It must be cautious lest its revised Trust be simply greed in a new and vicious form tempting the bewildered Stewards.

Arena conceded that the fresh assignment could contain an exalting, larger responsibility likely to wrest new valor from American endeavor. *Arena* ended 1898 with a summation by the Reverend George A. Gordon. Denouncing the nation's persisting sin, he invoked "the ideal America in all its purity and majesty and power." This will-o'-the-wisp, elusive for a century, was now within sight. Pray, Gordon urged, "that the one America may pass, and that the other America may more and more take its vacant place; that the nation of ignorance and incapacity, selfishness and crime, wickedness and godlessness may go and the nation founded in faith and in hope and in love may come." Such was "the one great end of this society's existence." *Arena* thus completed its own escape by urging trustees everywhere to fall back upon the giver of the assignment. The divine power creating America's role was still the only source for its fulfillment.[37]

In New York City, *Forum* began in 1886 to sustain the old Trust. Its stance remained conservative to the point of stuffiness until 1898, when a sudden transformation occurred. Until then, *Forum*'s editor, L. S. Metcalf, used a distinguished group of authors to lecture a stumbling band of Stewards. *Forum* pages demanded a restoration of the old Republic, and predicted a "day of reckoning" should the call to preservation go unheeded. The message was passed by such contributors as Elizabeth Cady Stanton, Washington Gladden, F. D. Huntington, and A. Lawrence Lowell. Mammon and passion were made as vivid for readers in 1890 as they had been for Americans of Jefferson's time. "If America is to be ruined, it will be by materialism," which in turn "makes the nation a seething caldron of selfishness and unrest." These comments by Howard Crosby had many counterparts, including James Parton's reminder that human nature had to be confronted realistically. "We cannot escape the limitations of our lot, do what we will." The nation must recognize that "man would still be weak and prone to error."

Always aware of upheaval and revolution, *Forum* was especially vigorous in renewing the ante-bellum belief that proper values be indoctrinated through the schools. This would avert "the extirpation of the moral sense of the people," still a threat to the Republic despite a century of labor. By 1890 public corruption claimed most of *Forum* attention, with authors like Harvard's A. B. Hart bemoaning the meagerness of the people's will. Frederick A. P. Barnard was particularly blunt in his essay on national degradation. His remedy was old-fashioned preservationism. Let education bring reverence for national tradition. Only this might spare America the crimson sword of passion.

Every event seemed to confirm *Forum*'s misgiving. Discovery of an "incomparable inheritance" from Anglo-Saxon spirit and history was the only happy development. But even this vaster process was not yet wholly reassuring. A *Forum* poet said:

> Whose loins begat us? Let tomorrow show
> If their stern acts hereditary grow.

As if to help, *Forum* published Thomas Davidson's 1894 essay, "The Ideal Training of an American Boy." The nation's greatest shortcoming, said Davidson, was that "we have not, thus far, arrived at any clear conception of the meaning and implications of freedom." Education must stress that American life could emerge "as the highest and inevitable outcome of the process of history." The American purpose was "universal and human." Consequently, "if America is to perform the part assigned to her in history, she must stand for ideal humanity and compel all partial ideals to converge and lose themselves in hers."

Other *Forum* authors began using evolution to argue that America was youthful, just begun, and forgivable. New inner strength and respect for the Constitution would be signs of benign process at work. Even Charles Eliot contributed modestly to this sense of hope in 1896: "It is on the minority of the people and on the individual effort of each member of it that the issue depends. . . . We must fight, each with his best strength. The fight will not be ended with our lives, but all good men are enlisted for the war." Until 1898, however, *Forum* evaded full meaning of a revamped national duty, talking instead about such old symptoms as the corruption of the United States Senate.

Forum hailed the war as a vital catalyst, one which "will stir the life-blood of the nation." With "our internecine quibbles" ended, America would discover "its importance as one of the great factors in the Anglo-Saxon civilization of the world." A few contributors, however, remained cautious. One conceded that while no "thinking person believes that the Republic can go back after the war to the place where it was before it," neither did anyone know "to what good" the "nation's feet" would move. By August 1898, everyone seemed more comfortable with process. Using an article by Brooks Adams which said "nations must float with the tide," *Forum* rejoiced in the new nationality. America was now in an "epoch-making" moment, one seen in few centuries. Suddenly there was "force and direction to hitherto apparently diverse and irreconcilable conditions." The Republic had been set on the way "toward a nobler and better existence for all men."

With astonishing swiftness, *Forum*'s authors began talk of the universal dependence on America and of how isolation had caused the inner tumult and weakness. Through an emancipated view, the latent goodness in Stewards would emerge. *Forum*'s November pages exulted in the "evident fitness in the happening of events" and in the "logical result of human action." All this brought revelation to America, as well as to *Forum*'s editors. "We are coming into our own. We are stretching out our hands for what nature meant should be ours. We are taking our proper rank among the nations of the world. . . . and humanity will bless us." [38]

The intellectual transformation of *Atlantic* was comparable to *Forum*'s. *Atlantic*'s discovery of a new Trust occurred in 1896. Before then, it too had belabored a faltering stewardship. *Atlantic* was quick to show delight with a freshened American meaning. It meant that the spirit of the Founders had reappeared. Events of the 1890's were said to lift America's outlook beyond "the mist of lower passion, sordid rivalries, eager greed." It was an awakening to what Gamaliel Bradford anticipated as "consciousness of the duties, as yet unfulfilled," which America owed "to the civilization of the century." Typical of *Atlantic*'s altered view was George Burton Adams' article, "The United States and the Anglo-Saxon Future," which appeared in July 1896. It said the entire world was entering "upon a new era of history" for which Washington's Farewell had no meaning. Adams later announced that the nineteenth century was merely preliminary to the great story of the twentieth century. Other pieces called for new ideas since "the power of senseless custom has been broken in America."

During 1898, these ideas were evident in *Atlantic*. Thanks to the war, "the real meaning of American civilization and ideals" would be more clearly understood everywhere. America entered the moment of transformation with "no more great enterprises awaiting us at home." Domestic stewardship had become "chiefly administrative," completing "the correction of past errors." In fact, said an *Atlantic* editorialist, "the decline in the character of our public life has been a natural result of the lack of large constructive opportunities." The real victory at hand "will not be over Spain, but over ourselves." James K. Hosmer expounded on the wonderful ordering of American development. The split among Anglo-Saxons in 1776 had been a healthy thing, just as the current renewal of interdependence was wise and timely. The world's evolution now handed a ready America a new duty, one that challenged Stewards beyond "the walled garden of our pleasant domesticity."

Even *Atlantic*'s poets took the new perspective. One of them confessed in August 1898:

> Our mighty bark, with masts that rake the sky
> Has lagged too long in port, and we have drowsed
> An idle crew or with wild mates caroused,
>   Forgetful of our past in Freedom's wars.
> But now, at last, with sail taut to the spars,
> For her whose rightful cause our sires espoused,
> Again our ship must steer where blow unhoused
> The winds of God, beyond the shoals and bars.
>   For still our orders hold, as in the past,
>   . . . to sail and search the sea
> Until we find a better world for man.

The editorial columns of *Atlantic* completed adoption of the new nationality through reconciliation with the old foe, mass emotion: "National feeling is a safer guide to national development than the mere reasoning process of critical minds." American transformation was considered almost miraculous. "Four months ago we were a great mass of people rather than a compact nation conscious of national strength and unity." Now, "with larger and further-reaching political duties, too, which appeal to the imagination rather than to the private greed of men, our public life will once more rise to the level of statesmanship." Equally astounding was the haste with which *Atlantic,* like the bulk of American thought, dismissed the ancient misgivings. In a new epoch, Americans realized that they were "the product of a thousand years of continuous effort to make brave and honest men." The culmination of that process now established America as trustee for inferior people. The course of events would control both passion and mammon.[39]

Many other periodicals in this era were caught up in the remodeling of nationality. Although their advocacy differed in tone and time, the relief from discovering a new call and a new labor was generally evident. For instance, in 1884, *Leslie's* magazine acknowledged the utterly shameful state of American affairs. It could only say that republicanism with stench was better than with lethargy. "The republic cannot perish until indifference seizes the mass of voters." The question of the moment was: "Are we becoming a nation of criminals?" However, the uncertainties were blown away by the winds of change. *Leslie's* talked of reading the book of fate and finding guarantees of republican progress. It discovered that Anglo-American fusion assured "not only our destiny and that of England, but also the destiny of nations just emerging from darkness into light." Now the message was: "We have outgrown the past. . . . We are marching onward. Woe to him who seeks to block the way!" As the Congregationalist *Independent* put it, God gave America "new responsibilities." [40]

Especially representative of the confusion and contradiction characterizing some outlooks was the argument in *Youth's Companion*. It wavered between brash self-confidence and abject sorrow and regret when speaking of American purpose and performance. It alternately scolded and praised the Stewards. For instance, in 1885, it urged that Americans "not pretend to ourselves that we are only working out the purpose of Providence, when we are actuated by greed to possess land that is not ours, and that we cannot obtain without committing a rational crime." A few weeks later, it announced: "The people have so learned the value of their institutions that they would regard any one who tried to teach them that revolution was expedient as a charlatan and a fraud, and would drive him from the field by ridicule." America's triumph was ensured because in "the hearts of the people" there was dedication to national form and purpose.

Generally given to preservation, *Youth's Companion* suggested that because America "fancies it has a mission to teach the world that all men are brothers," it ought not "give those brothers every advantage." Rather, the Republic was called to "the duty of preserving and improving the most magnificent estate that was ever transmitted as an inheritance to a younger generation." The magazine relied on indoctrination as means of building proper stewardship. The schools had one purpose—to make "good and true American citizens." Any newcomer should "become like the rest of us in the shortest possible space of time." Especially did *Youth's Companion* urge a mystical love of the flag. Young and old must "feel their patriotism swell at the sight of the banner." Inner evils "only interrupt, they cannot stop our national progress." However, "unwholesome masses" arriving from Europe must be repulsed.

With so many others, *Youth's Companion* began referring to a new Trust in 1896. It asserted that America had been "so engrossed" in establishing the nation that it gave little thought to "the form which our civilization will wear when it is complete." Now that "we have demonstrated our ability to cope with the material problems of nation-building," America must turn to a new "mission" which was "to develop, to illuminate, to civilize, to carry to the remotest quarters of the world the institutions of freedom, protection and just laws."

As a steady advocate, however, *Youth's Companion* made a poor example. In one issue it admitted America's failure to impress the world, and called for isolation. "If we go on our way unmoved by the criticisms of people who do not understand us, all will be all right in the end." Another time it shelved evolution to urge national self-criticism. "True patriotism is something more than blind instinct." Even during the war, *Youth's Companion* wavered between preservation and process; between racism and isolation; between breezy confidence and penance. One day the Trust had been discharged; the next it was still beyond the Stewards' reach. In this way, the magazine included most of the concepts persisting through 1898. Rarely, however, were other advocates found to be so confused. Most of American thought had somehow eluded the ambiguity and uncertainty so vexing since 1798. This was the release brought by escape.[41]

> *IV: Responses*   The transformation of America's nationality in its broadest sweep is best understood by recalling first the voices despairing over the national plight. These were overtaken late in the century by the exhortations of the hopeful, which soon merged with the final jubilation. Neither despair nor uncertainty kept most of America from the joy of apparent fulfillment and more reassuring duty.

10

While few Americans gave in completely to despondency in this era, there were significant avowals that the nation's struggle was no nearer success. As in previous times, hymns were an excellent setting for supplication as well as confession. In these God was asked again to pity an errant people who could offer only contrite hearts. A Congregational stanza of 1887 said: " 'Tis on Thy pardoning grace alone, Our failing hopes depend." If God "spares our guilty land" through His mercy, America might at least "live to pray." Presumably such prayer would be for the "impious members, bold in sin" who disgraced both the Christian and the American name. Usually the guilt described was vast and vague, America being simply "this polluted land" to which God's "sword might come, to drink our blood, and seal our doom." The hope was that those who recognized national sin might help spare the land. According to an 1889 Methodist song:

> Yet hast thou not a remnant here,
> Whose souls are filled with pious fear?
> O bring thy wonted mercy nigh,
> While prostrate at thy feet they lie!
>
> Behold their tears, attend their moan
> Nor turn away their secret groan:
> With these we join our humble prayer,
> Our nation shield, our country spare.

Religious indignation and regret ran a wide gamut. The letters received by William Jennings Bryan, for instance, show that his defeat caused redoubled self-scourging. The satanic forces commanding America's shameful captivity were often identified as "the idolatrous money men." When Bryan lost, his followers saw signs of national failure. Even during the war's glory some Americans said the nation was sinning, despite what others called God's clear charge.

Those expecting American disgrace, whether spiritual or secular, looked to a familiar reason, the indifference of the Stewards. The old enemies, mammon and passion, were not to be swept away by evolution. Hope still rested in the school's and the church's help through indoctrination. Representative of this concern was George T. Balch's remarkable book, *Methods of Teaching Patriotism in the Public Schools*. This 1890 volume assumed that the schools would determine whether the nation survived in the twentieth century. Educators still needed to plant American truth in young hearts. Youth must be inspired to transcend the self in worthiness of "high trusts." Balch's volume included elaborate school ceremonies designed to arouse an "ani-

mating force" within children. Once evoked, reverent young
people could be presented with "those great and distinctive political principles . . . those well-settled civic canons, that body
of original political doctrines, which have come to be known and
accepted as American institutions." These precepts had been
urged for a century on "the mass of the American people," said
Balch. But without their wider acceptance, the nation would
continue to lag. "There is an abundance of dormant patriotism
in the hearts of this people, but what is greatly wanted is something to thoroughly arouse it into vigorous life." For Balch's conservative view, the emotions rather than reason were required to
sustain a wayward America.[42]

Beyond these simplistic acknowledgments of national weakness was some sophisticated despair. It thrived on talk of "insidious forces that war upon the moral sentiment." Usually mammon was the culprit. Only "worthy sons of worthy sires" could
lead human nature to contain this inner "rot." A student orator
at the University of Wisconsin deplored that "in this electric century" America's pursuit of "an ideal freedom" had been stayed
while the nation loitered "in the realm of materialism." E. L.
Godkin predicted relief would come if the nation tried to see itself clearly. Through introspection the Republic might perceive
the weakness in "the popular idea of the American character, in
which individualism was the most marked trait." Self-interest
was no longer a reasonable guide for stewardship.

Privately, Godkin doubted that even education could sharpen
the perceptions of America's consciousness. "I am not sanguine
about the future. . . . I think we shall have a long period of decline like that which followed the fall of the Roman Empire."
He saw a "half-crazed public," cursed by a "great contempt for
history and experience," gradually losing the fight for republicanism which America had been called to wage. In a similar
vein, the courageous Booker T. Washington warned a jubilant
Chicago audience in 1898 that martial victories were not enough
to ensure American fulfillment. Speaking especially of racial
prejudice, he said: "Until we thus conquer ourselves, I make no
empty statement when I say that we shall have a cancer gnawing
at the heart of this Republic that shall one day prove as dangerous as an attack from an army from without or within." [43]

Men such as Godkin and Washington had hoped that the

Steward could rally his capacities so that American purpose could be renewed and properly guided. Other voices were much gloomier. Samuel Clemens, Robert Ingersoll, Edward Eggleston, and Henry Adams were four such professors of despair. In their varied ways, each represented the conclusion that neither man nor fate could carry out the national call. These opinions required courage since most Americans did not like to speak of more than momentary travail. Clemens concluded at the end of the century: "We have thrown away the most valuable asset we have—the individual right to oppose both flag and country . . . and with it all that was really respectable about that grotesque and laughable word, Patriotism." Robert Ingersoll simply announced: "The trouble is in the nature of men—the nature of things." In what was a rare moment of private candor, Ingersoll spoke for those who had dreamed futilely of a triumphant American stewardship: "I do not know what to do." Similarly repelled by the Republic, Edward Eggleston said: "In this tiresome time I don't seem to care much for American citizenship; it is a brand that covers a discouraging lot of claptrap."

A more profound gloom claimed Henry Adams. He kept trying to believe, as he wrote to Francis Parkman in 1884, that "in another generation psychology, physiology, and history will join in proving man to have as fixed and necessary development as that of a tree, and almost unconscious." Such organic improvement appeared less likely as the century ended. By 1894 Adams was sardonic: "Of late the century has amused me. It has become so rotten and bankrupt that I am quite curious to see what the next one will do about it. When I think of the formulas of our youth . . . I feel that somewhere there is the biggest kind of joke, if I could only see it." In 1898, Adams as less amused, seeing McKinley and Congress betraying "our true American policy." A revised role for the United States held no comfort. "The world has entered on a new phase of most far-reaching revolution." Even so, he added, "those who trembled and ran away two years ago, are now lightly taking risks and asserting rights that turn me peagreen." America as "a domineering tyrant" was a prospect sending "a cold chill down my back." [44]

11

Even in a season of exultancy, or of what Clemens and others called half-crazed passion, some persons responded to nationality by reiterating the doubts once predominant in America's outlook. Dwindling, these voices spoke only timidly about the quality of the American man. No amount of evolution or rising destiny seemed to guarantee relief. Others who were willing to consider the exchange of one Trust for another did so by accepting the appeal to surrender loyally to universal design. Much of American thought was still clearly uneasy. Given the trials in years after 1876, many observers needed some signal, some indication of how the labor progressed.

The results were varied admonitions. There were the familiar cautions. Others stressed preserving an ancient Trust. Still others delicately acknowledged a persuasive momentum in national development. Finally, some preached blind hope. A prominent Chicago clergyman, H. W. Bolton, gathered a wide audience by reminding the nation that physical progress was good in moderation but could produce vice, idleness, recklessness, and corruption if not carefully guarded. The most moderate course for America's frail undertaking was simply to avoid change, to cling to Christian doctrine, and to follow the testimony contained in the lives of noble Americans. Bolton said in 1890: "We propose to be American in all our thoughts, ways and institutions." The nation was yet in its "babyhood" and no prophet could foresee the time needed to reach maturity. Americanism therefore meant that we "hallow the memory of our ancestors, from whom we have inherited so much. Let us cherish with loving fidelity, and with unwavering patriotism, our inheritance!"

Bolton's monumental caution was frequently behind America's response in this era. It fostered an outlook requiring the revelations of 1898 to induce a joyful song. *Rocky Mountain News* in Denver was a good example of how uneasily Americans lived with their long record of shortcoming. Its editorials, especially in the late 1880's, suspected all events as contributing to incipient "un-American ideas." It urged the daily playing of the "Star-Spangled Banner." July 4 was for cherishing present circumstance. According to the *News*, good citizens could be recognized by their eager assertion that it was "a high privilege" to live in America. Those who felt otherwise "must be suppressed." In short, American survival now depended on an outlook of "intelligent selfishness."

As these instances suggest, a segment of American consciousness became grimly defensive in this era. Its praise for what America should be was mixed with chagrin over the public's bumbling. One person said the theory of America was "well-nigh perfect" whereas much of its practice would best be consumed by fire. Stewardship was too often "deviltry with a slight admixture of honor and honesty." Commenting in 1895 on this mistrust, Walter Hines Page observed that capable stewardship was ever more difficult in the Republic's deepening complexity. Consequently, the appearance of internationalism first produced a dubious spirit in many quarters. Jingoism was another threat to the conservatism on which republican survival relied.

For some who had hailed the original Trust, new responsibilities coming in 1898 proved discomfiting. The predicament of William McKinley was typical. Before his presidential election, the Ohioan had accepted the Trust's traditional doctrine. In 1887, he spoke of the "dangerous tendency of the times" growing from "the mad spirit for gain and riches which is so prevalent in American society." His remedy, repeated frequently, was characteristic of the public response: "Let us accept the advice of the fathers of the Republic, heed their patriotic counsels, walk steadfastly in their faith, preserve the mutual helpfulness and harmony of the industries, and maintain our independence, National, industrial, and individual, against all the world, and thus advance to the high destiny that devolves upon us and our posterity."

This was a decade before McKinley and much of American thought suddenly discovered the obsolescence of paternal admonition. The future President liked to bless the Civil War veterans for having fought a great battle for conservatism. There was no limit to "the future glory of the Republic," McKinley kept insisting, so long as "all of us practice the simple code of the fathers." It was, of course, the state of this stewardship which made McKinley and many others respond so apprehensively. "I am not so much troubled about how the thing is to be done as I am troubled that the living shall do what is right as the living see the right." It was all so simple. Americanism must be an unwavering devotion to the Founders. "What a debt we owe them!" The good Steward was, for McKinley, one who cherished, who preserved unimpaired, who kept pure, and who guarded the

Republic. With such deeds, "the future will be even more glorious than the past."

McKinley's simple appeal became the watchword as tribulation deepened in the United States. Henry George knew this and warned that the nation was in danger of cherishing the form of nationality and not the spirit. Petrification would surely accompany ancestor-worship, he said, for American republicanism had not yet produced abundance of both rights and possession. To such a dynamic concept, the answer was usually sharp and clear. Henry Cabot Lodge repeated it: "We must either maintain our system as it is, or plunge blindly forward. We have reached the last point of safe progress in government." America's "great secret [for success] lies in its conservatism," said Lodge. Danger was in being soft-headed. "We are too ready to admit that everything is open to argument, instead of adhering . . . to the practice of our ancestors." In hectic times, Lodge's response was commonplace: "Let us revert to the traditions of our race, and practice a little more wholesome conservatism. . . . Progress is a fine word, but it is not necessarily a good thing." Indeed, it could be "much worse than standing still."

In this way nationality's emphasis on preservation showed the impact of a material Vineyard of banks, factories, and farms. Socialism and anarchism, the feared embodiments of un-American forces, were simply extreme examples of how social aberration had become national heresy. The Trust was increasingly interpreted through economic orthodoxy, as America seemed more susceptible to corruption and unrest. Preachers of the original Trust in the 1890's interpreted the Fathers' legacy first as economics and second as political.

Also looming larger behind the uneasy response was the mob, whose destruction Hermann von Holst demanded in a vehement article of 1894. This essay illustrated the deepened relationship between the economic design, the Founders' achievement, and the nation's fulfillment. America must have the courage, preached this constitutional historian, to be "truthful toward itself." Admitting that the Vineyard was now ominously complicated, von Holst asserted: "Fearful is the responsibility that rests upon this people, not only for themselves and for their posterity, but for all mankind." To fail now in the presence of the "priceless heritage" would be the gravest moral crime of history. Fidelity to America's call meant hushing all social disturbance. The Trust's essence was "nothing less than the preservation of society." Smothering unrest should be "a matter of course" if the nation was to live in "the name of the great shades of the founders of the republic."

The strain brought by the widening gap between American promise and its actual condition grew excruciating. A Trust requiring massive social restraint stimulated fantastic interpretations of the traditional national dream of widened freedom, enlarged well-being, and improved manhood. Until the wondrous escape of 1898, responses droned on about unswerving acceptance of the Fathers' principles, which made duty a matter increasingly of obedience. The ubiquitous primers on patriotism in the 1890's carried to extreme Horace Mann's gentle talk of childhood as the season for surrender to an immutable polity and society. It was logical, therefore, that many persons suspected talk of a new Trust.

The war and its upshot were often assailed by familiar doctrine. William Jennings Bryan was especially eloquent, asking in June 1898: "Is our national character so weak that we cannot withstand the temptation to appropriate the first piece of land that comes within our reach?" America's changed role troubled the faithful disciples of preservation who pleaded for "our National character." Men were warned that the old enemy, mammon, hid in all the rejoicing over a new assignment. One spokesman said more than he realized by suggesting that the revised Trust would eliminate "the individual feeling of responsibility of the citizen for the welfare of his own Nation." [45]

For such hesitancy the saving answer was often to mention an unfolding of divine design. This was reassuring to many worshippers of the established order. The president of Harvard, Charles Eliot, conceded early that no one generation ever could fully appreciate its role in the revelation of national destiny. America was charged to strive "toward a progressive improvement of human condition, an amelioration of the average lot." Eliot predicted America would eventually mean "mutual dependence of man on man, and therewith a growing sense of brotherhood and unity." A national soul was the goal of American history. He often spoke of the heights to which the inspired human spirit might soar, and from which must come "a great uplifting of our country in dignity, strength and security."

President Eliot, however, was not confident enough to accept the jingoist appeal. He considered it a pernicious effort to corrupt the genuine Trust whose aim was to build and maintain a model Republic. "National impatience, combativeness, and successful self-seeking" would hinder the achievement of this goal. Nationality remained the need to prove that mammon and passion could be transcended. This threadbare viewpoint was refurbished by discovering a wonderful selflessness in the new American venture. Cushman K. Davis was one of those contending that America's new endeavors were preparation for the civilization of the twentieth century. War with Spain was meant to reveal American readiness for a larger leadership. According to men like Davis, America at last could rest on "the highest top of national pride."

Somewhere between Eliot and Davis' contrasting testimonies of faith was the remarkable observation made by Eliot's learned colleague at Harvard, Charles E. Norton. He advised contentment with what he considered to be the two Americas. One professed faith in noble ideals; the other struggled so futilely with life. Norton called America a success simply because of its ardent affection for such wondrous concepts as universal justice, education, free speech, and well-being. A kindly spirit "glows in the heart of the American, and inspires him with that patriotism which counts no cost." Norton's intellectual compromise was widely misunderstood. He was accused of saying that Stewards could not separate good from evil, so superficial was their dedication to abiding principle.

American sentiment generally resisted Norton's tempting logic. The national mind had lived too long with the need to believe that America could triumph over evil. Therefore, thoughts about nationality preferred to acknowledge what Abram Hewitt described as an achievement "beyond all legends of oriental treasure" in fulfilling humanity's hopes.[46]

12

A near-exhausted faith finally came into its inheritance simply by dismissing one national obligation and assuming another.

This was forecast in an 1897 essay by William Dean Howells which appeared in *Harper's Magazine*. Howells began with understatement: "The observant American whose memory runs back to the effulgent days following the close of the civil war must be aware of a signal change since then in the mood of his fellow citizens concerning themselves and the republic." It had come, in part at least, from healthful, unsparing self-scrutiny. Howells announced the presence of a deepening conscience, a calmer patriotism, and a more candid grasp of republicanism's capacity. All of which was basis for peace of mind. "I have no doubt that if we are tolerably faithful and honest we shall come out all right in the end, as every good American used to say we should."

For Howells it was impossible to think of "the end of the republic." He predicted Americans would devise a "more vital democracy, or equality, or fraternity to save us from the ruin into which our own recreancy may have plunged us." This was expected because Howells found America eager to know its weakness, to ask: "In what have we been false to ourselves? . . . What is the secret of our stupidity, our heedlessness, our blindness?" Stewards saw the folly of riches and vainglory. Consequently, Howells felt he could assert: "Our patriotism is not of the earlier passion and tenderness which the day of small things inspired. These would be out of keeping with our enormous prosperity, our irresistible power." Thus, for Howells, the old Trust was discharged. America had confirmed that the Fathers had established a good system. "We have really more faith in the republic than they had, for we found it works, and they could merely believe that it would work." Smugly, Howells closed the essay by charging that the future "be as true as the present to the ideals of the past."

Within a year, Howells was disconcerted. The most now to be said for national policy was that "we propose to do evil that good may come." He discovered that mammon was not chained after all, "and every good cause will be set back." In mid-1898 Howells was writing sorrowfully of unanticipated evils carried by a new national purpose in which so many rejoiced. It was not what Howells had intended. He and a few others had blundered in 1897 by misinterpreting the self-righteousness so recently arising in national consciousness. The expanding exultation was the nation's escape from a century of thwarted stewardship by accepting a new personality.[47]

A leader in the litany of American emancipation was Josiah Strong. By 1891 his enormously successful book, *Our Country,* had been reissued in an even more affirmative edition. Andover's Austin Phelps wrote an introduction, itself a revealing essay, which began by recalling that for over fifty years many Americans had accepted "the idea of *crisis* in the destiny of this country, and through it in the destiny of the world." With especially the menace of alien blood, "every day has been a day of crisis. Every hour has been an hour of splendid destiny." Since the nation's development had been "a succession of crises," Phelps argued that "the national salvation demands in supreme exercise certain military virtues." He called on all Stewards to show daring, force, persistence, and vigilance so that the final "moral conquest" of the nation could be carried out with the selflessness of the men at Gettysburg. Let the nation remember, Phelps said: "As goes America, so goes the world, in all that is vital to its moral welfare."

Through spokesmen like Strong, many Americans found moral regeneration, permitting them to move abroad in radiant righteousness to labor for the Lord. This response mingled familiar elements in American self-consciousness. While mammon and passion still skulked, men like Strong asserted there was both safety and righteousness in surrender to divinely called nationhood. Personal desires would be stifled by campaigns for rescuing the world. The new doctrine did not worry about being consistent. Strong mixed man's capacity to accept or spurn this Godly calling with the overwhelming forces of Anglo-Saxon impulse and destiny. These now afforded a gratifying immediacy. The nation's hour at last had come. According to such a view, the world would for centuries be affected by what American stewardship chose. Strong called the close of the nineteenth century a time second only in consequence to the moment of Christ's birth.

Our Country gave fervent reiteration to a theme fundamental in American intellectual history. The Republic had received and was itself a sacred Trust. As a century's pilgrimage ended, Strong proclaimed: "Our plea is not America for America's sake; but America for the world's sake." If men then alive were "faithful to its Trust," America would achieve its role as "God's right arm in his battle with the world's ignorance and oppression and sin." Strong was too much the cleric not to warn citizens against smugness or blindness as "a chosen people." He mentioned such evils as whiskey, urbanism, nature-worship, collectivism, labor restlessness, and above all "Mammonism." These could be overcome by right thinking which was the essence of Americanism. Men must be taught to believe that America was "the Gibraltar of the ages which commands the world's future." Further, citizens must know that "they are not proprietors, apportioning their own, but simply *trustees* or managers of God's property."

In this way Strong helped create the assured response which distinguished America's nationality at the century's close. His next book, *The New Era,* moved even more deeply into this new outlook. It stressed "the laws of progress," beneath which the nineteenth century had been an era of vast change, preparing for the grandeur of the twentieth century. America was the land of this future, because she was the seat of Anglo-Saxon influence. The Republic drew much of its new hope by believing in its triumph as a super race. Although doubt occasionally nagged even Strong, he closed the volume in rhapsody. "Surely, to be a Christian and an Anglo-Saxon and an American in this generation is to stand at the very mountaintop of privilege." [48]

It was this sense of a fresh charge which was the most significant feature of America's response to its meaning. The sudden trumpeting of 1898 cannot be explained except for the popular presentiment that American travail was ending. America escaped by using the long-awaited future. Well before 1898, exasperation had goaded many voices to speak of imminent change. William Cullen Bryant wrote in 1878 that there was a cleansing effect accompanying the shocking disclosures of national corruption. At last America was experiencing "a process of purgation" from which would emerge "the character of the nation at large." Only in this way would America be ready for what Bryant called "a new era with new responsibilities."

For others, the close of a hundred years of growth and maturation meant that "the century opening this hour will be one of moral and scientific growth," with "a loftier national life." To the stormy first century, "eventide has come," with time "to pray that the God of pilgrim and patriot will make the morrow of our republic even brighter and better." These widespread sentiments were familiar to Frederick Jackson Turner in 1891, when he wrote in an early essay: "To me it seems that we are approaching a pivotal point in our country's history." Linking the nation's life to the world required "a new statesmanship" and an enlarged view of history. With American destiny "interwoven" with Europe, Turner advised reappraising the human venture. "The story of the peopling of America has not yet been written. We do not understand ourselves."

To help clarify this, Cyrus Northrup from the University of Minnesota spoke on American progress. Northrup spread assurance that the western hemisphere was meant by the course of things for timely appearance as the home of the people called "to promote the development and happiness of mankind." He shamed those who considered America a failure "because everything is not yet perfect." America's story had necessarily been one of "striving" toward progress. This restlessness was the crucial quality which Northrup said would make the rising American an even finer thing. During the troubled 1890's, such announcements of final days for one age and the approach of the new became conventional rhetoric. Men like Northrup turned a moment of transition into a nation's confirmation.

The general response as spoken by Bryant, Turner, and Northrup was accepted by the Minneapolis *Times* in an 1896 editorial: "Now the whole face of America is being changed. We are passing through a great formative period. . . . Out of all of this a new Americanism is being born, whose meaning we do not know, and may not know for a generation or two to come. That it will be humane, generous, and great Americanism, who can doubt?" The *Times* considered the token for a new America would be a quieting of "the spirit of mere material progress."

Signs of America's new role and the triumph over mammon accumulated more quickly than the *Times* anticipated. Nationality in 1898 thrived on claims of a new day's arrival and of an old Trust discharged. Variations on the theme of new mandate and fruitful stewardship were endless. The glorious days in April were likened to those of 1787 and 1863 when freedom was triumphant. The happy intent of "irresistible forces" was saluted. The nation was advised it could now stand with pride. Edward

Everett Hale asserted that surely Americans had to agree that events showed the nation "is a Being." "The Lord God of nations has called it" and granted it "certain duties in defense of the civilization of the world." With God's companionship now assured, ex-President Benjamin Harrison predicted that America could not fail in its high commission.

One typical convert to the new ecstasy told President McKinley that he now recognized that Providence was moving the nation to a new circumstance. There was no turning back from "*the general evolution of our manifest destiny.*" In 1898, "a live McKinley is worth 100 dead Washingtons." This outlook generally agreed that in accepting "the changed order," Americans must look not to the Fathers' age but to the new world and new century. Repeatedly Stewards were told that the war's greatest blessing was in awakening "the consciousness of our larger mission in the affairs of the world, for the good of the world."

By mid-summer 1898, the rejoicing insisted that wherever its new call might take it, the United States was beyond defeat. Indeed, the purpose which the nation had embraced was no longer a Trust. It had become a holy crusade, with America's sword turned into a cross. The pervasiveness of triumph and relief was astonishing. The nation's ubiquitous after-dinner speaker, Chauncey M. Depew, saw in the marvelous experiences of 1898 "a new birth of liberty, a new era of civilization, a new development of the hidden treasures of the earth and a new and broader destiny for the United States." As in 1863, the "unexpected" had occurred in 1898. Depew confessed that not even "the wildest dream" of "the most optimistic believer in our destiny" had forseen the wondrous new America.

Even the somber atmosphere of the *Annals of the American Academy of Political and Social Science* nourished the new spirit by an essay which solemnly proclaimed an awakened nation. Exulting in the assurance of instinct and race, this response said that there would be no more agonizing over national fulfillment. Although Americans might not fully comprehend the workings about them, the nation's glory was ever growing and secure. Readers of the *Annals* were assured of hidden resources within the national character which would handle the world's and God's expectations. This was the great lesson of 1898. "The

war is a revelation rather than a revolution." The new nationality meant "an intelligent adaptation of ourselves to conditions
which transcend our power and our intelligence." [49]

The obvious relief felt by so many at escaping the uncertainties of an earlier Americanism was widely evident as 1898 ended.
Although doubt and dread were not everywhere dispelled by the
annunciation of the new role, the poem "Columbia!," published
in December 1898 by Ella Wheeler Wilcox, incorporated what
were for most persons the essentials of America's new sense of
being. The lines stressed that America had passed from a Trust
of proving to a task of leading. "Columbia, on you are fixed the
wide world's wondering eyes," to which at last America returned
"a holy light." The last stanza was the summing up, both for
the poem and of the rejoicing in a nation transcendent:

March on, march on, Columbia, the splendor of your day
Is but begun; you know the path, your feet will find the way.
The universal stumbling block of lands and men is greed,
Walk wide of it, and let Love be your watchword and your creed.

American thought in 1898 rarely bothered to recall the hazards
once considered so dangerous to national endeavor. However, in
the jubilance of escape, the specter of human frailty did not
vanish. It was assumed that destiny would see that newly inspired Americans eluded such old foes as greed. After a century
of stewardship, always distressing and often agonizing, Americans generally wanted to believe that their first account in God's
book had been satisfied. In accepting a new Trust, America muf-
fled lingering doubt and dread by dismissing her former self
with a resounding "well done!" [50]

EPILOGUE

Historians have been startled at America's changed mood in 1898. Many believe that new tactics and dimensions in American policy were meant to distract from the grimness overtaking life. Certainly this is plausible. However, a sense of futile national endeavor also made change agreeable. For one hundred years the Republic had sought to understand and attain its destiny. In being trustee for freedom and republicanism, nineteenth-century America had pledged to take man beyond a historical and theological perspective which deemed him frail, if not fallen. Each generation of Stewards struggled to harmonize lofty calling and meager attainment. Despite bloody rites of purification and intellectual sleights of hand, man's weakness persisted. Worldly things appeared as successful in America as elsewhere in misguiding human steps.

Pride at being American therefore was usually tempered by knowing that Americans were not behaving as required by their responsibility for mankind. Such knowledge could not be borne forever, so the Republic adopted a new stewardship in 1898. It was less personal in its responsibility and less immediate in its demands and setting. Talk of American uniqueness, of the nation as a lonely polity whose goal was the isolated preservation of an inspired design, diminished. In 1800 the citizen felt responsible for proving something. The United States would attempt to disclose the validity of ideals and practices of which man had dared to dream. By 1900, an exhausted and disappointed nation had accepted participation in a vast process, the values, purposes, and outcome of which were undoubted. Instead of there being a special contribution expected from each Steward, America found its duty remote from the lives of its citizens. The new nationality took comfort in believing the fullness of time would bring America's success.

For more than fifty years during the twentieth century America has carried its new identity, hardly realizing the fearful intellectual price paid to don this role. Yet the burden of being an American has grown no lighter. Four wars have resulted from the vaunted global responsibility and universal momentum. Only during the last of these, in Vietnam, have some Americans—especially young citizens—begun to wonder if national values and practices actually belong to God or progress. A century after the Civil War and Lincoln's martyrdom there is talk again of man's shortcoming. Time's unfolding had failed to bring America's fulfillment. Instead, it introduced fresh revelation of man's deficiency.

In approaching the 1976 bicentennial, some Americans have found reason to distrust both human nature and the course of events. Mammon had so dirtied the natural Vineyard as to menace healthy life. Passion had threatened to destroy the political Vineyard, as campus and city became centers of anguished upheaval. All this has suggested that the ancient issues of nationality are more lively and virulent than ever. Two hundred years after its career began, America is still a probing of man's nature and not an apotheosis of nature's man. Neither freedom nor republicanism has assured the peaceable kingdom. Neither racial superiority nor evolution has subdued violence and degradation.

With this knowledge America faces its bicentenary amid frantic reassertion and frank reappraisal. On the one hand are claims that Providence and human well-being called the Republic to such acts of stewardship as war in Indochina. Other men are insisting that righteousness demanded the erasure of America's disgraced self by riot, murder, and fire. These extremes of nationality are impelled by an anger and frustration that left flag-waver and Black Panther more nearly brothers in soul than anyone perceives. These senses of nationality, whether symbolized by a hard hat or by a clenched fist, share an anxiety and doubt which also gripped America in the nineteenth century. Thus, the first of nationality's concerns has been disinterred in the 1970's. Can the Republic survive?

Within this new agony a few voices speak differently to America. They say that the nation might yet fulfill itself if it trades pride and anger for humility. With this exchange, it is said, will come a transformed national consciousness. Such a contention believes that through candor about man himself, America can finally understand liberty and order, thereby confirming the Republic. These admonitions require that America re-examine considerations sensed by the Washingtons and Jeffersons, arguing that recognition of human limitation and social mandates must infuse the national consciousness.

The question remains whether enough Americans will discover the teachings of history and theology in time to help the Republic fulfill its Trust through humility.

NOTES

INTRODUCTION

1. Anyone who wishes to study nationalism and sectionalism must read David M. Potter, "The Historian's Use of Nationalism and Vice Versa," in Professor Potter's volume of essays, *The South and Sectional Conflict* (Baton Rouge, 1968), pp. 34–83. For helpful as well as revealing discussion of the problems in defining and using words such as "nationalism" and "nationality," see Carlton J. H. Hayes, *Essays on Nationalism* (New York, 1926), *passim*, esp. pp. 6–12, 248; Carlton J. H. Hayes, *Nationalism: A Religion* (New York, 1960), pp. 2–10, 164–65. Also valuable is Frederick Hertz, *Nationality in History and Politics* (New York, 1944), pp. 410–12. The years have enlarged my debt to the splendid work of the late Perry Miller. To know the American outlook, it is important to read Perry Miller, "The Shaping of the American Character," *New England Quarterly*, XXVIII (Dec. 1955), 435–54.

2. Beard's excellent questions were asked long before historians were prepared to find answers. Charles A. Beard, "Nationalism in American History," in Waldo G. Leland, *Nationalism* (Bloomington, Ind., 1934), pp. 39–51. The traditional assumptions about American confidence handicap even so fine a study as Louis Hartz, *The Liberal Tradition in America* (New York, 1955), pp. 58–59. An example of how even the simplistic interpretation of American nationality can persist is Louis L. Snyder, *The New Nationalism* (Ithaca, 1968). One of the first efforts to reappraise the American outlook was John H. Schaar, *Loyalty in America* (Berkeley, 1957). Schaar's volume is important for all students of American thought. Clinton Rossiter, *Conservatism in America* (New York, 1962), Chaps. III–V, should be consulted for early insights about American self-awareness. Another helpful beginning study is Eric Goldman, "Democratic Bifocalism," in George Boas, ed., *Romanticism in America* (Baltimore, 1940), pp. 1–11. The most successful recent efforts to grapple with concepts of America's meaning are led by the scholarship of Perry Miller. See, especially, Miller's *The Life of the Mind in America* (New York, 1965) and *Nature's Nation* (Cambridge, 1967). Valuable interpretation is in Bernard Wishy, *The Child and the Republic* (Philadelphia, 1968) and in Howard Mumford Jones, *Ideas in America* (Cambridge, 1944). See also Frederic I.

Carpenter, *American Literature and the Dream* (New York, 1955); Roger B. Salomon, *Twain and the Image of History* (New Haven, 1961); Marius Bewley, *The Eccentric Design* (New York, 1963); Howard Mumford Jones, *The Theory of American Literature* (Ithaca, 1948); and W. W. Rostow, "The National Style," in Elting E. Morison, ed., *The American Style* (New York, 1952), esp. p. 252. Outstanding instances of the insight offered by historians of American religion are: Sidney E. Mead, "The 'Nation with the Soul of a Church,' " *Church History*, XXXVI (Sept. 1967), 262–83; and James F. Maclear, " 'The True American Union' of Church and State: The Reconstruction of the Theocratic Tradition," *Church History*, XXVII (Mar. 1959), 41–62.

3. Purported hazards of intellectual history disturb David Donald, *Lincoln Reconsidered* (New York, 1966), p. 165. Some background for my interpretation may be found in Paul C. Nagel, *One Nation Indivisible: The Union in American Thought, 1776–1861* (New York, 1964). All students will profit from Merle Curti, *The Roots of American Loyalty* (New York, 1946); and also from Charles L. Sanford, *The Quest for Paradise* (Urbana, 1961), hereafter cited as Sanford, *Quest*. An important recent essay is Page Smith, "Anxiety and Despair in American History," *The William and Mary Quarterly*, Third Series, XXVI (July 1969), 416–24. I read Professor Smith's article at the time I was completing an early draft of this book. His findings were reassuring as well as helpful to me. Many of the sources cited in the following chapters are in the peerless collection of orations, sermons, and pamphlets found in the Rare Book Room of the Library of Congress whose staff I thank for its many courtesies. Also, splendid materials are in the Rare Book Collection in the Margaret I. King Library of The University of Kentucky. The unusually rich group of nineteenth-century American periodicals in the library of the University of Missouri-Columbia was of immense help. The chapter notes which follow try to acknowledge the scholarship which has aided or interested me.

CHAPTER ONE

1. The Farewell Address is in John C. Fitzpatrick, ed., *The Writings of George Washington*, XXXV (Washington, 1931–44), 214–38. Hereafter cited as *Washington*.

2. *Washington*, XXXVII, 192. To James McHenry, 17 Nov. 1799.

3. Howard Mumford Jones, *O Strange New World* (New York, 1964), p. 327; Max Savelle, *Seeds of Liberty* (New York, 1948), p. 575; Charles Francis Adams, *The Works of John Adams*, I (Boston, 1856), 66; useful is Cecelia M. Kenyon, "Republicanism and Radicalism in the American Revolution: An Old-Fashioned Interpretation," *The William and Mary Quarterly*, Third Series, XIX (Apr. 1962), 153–82. Also, see Perry Miller, "Covenant to Revival," in James Ward Smith and A. Leland Jamison, eds., *The Shaping of American Religion* (Princeton, 1961), pp. 322–66; Ralph N. Miller, "American Nationalism as a Theory of Nature," *The William and Mary Quarterly*, Third Series,

XII (Jan. 1955), 74–95; Hans Kohn, *The Idea of Nationalism* (New York, 1944), pp. 291–93.

4. For background, see John C. Miller, *Crisis in Freedom, The Alien and Sedition Acts* (Boston, 1951), esp. pp. 178–85, 225–30; James M. Smith, *Freedom's Fetters* (Ithaca, 1956); and Roger H. Brown, *The Republic in Peril: 1812* (New York and London, 1964), esp. pp. 3–9. While these and other works illumine the period around 1798, none seem to recognize the widespread misgiving over the nation's capacity to survive to carry out its Trust.

5. Keating Lewis Simons, *An Oration Delivered in . . . Charleston, South Carolina . . . the Fourth of July, 1806* (Charleston, 1806), esp. pp. 17–23. See also Robert Y. Hayne, *An Oration Delivered in . . . Charleston, South Carolina . . . the 4th of July, 1814* (Charleston, 1814), pp. 5–6; Ebenezer Mack, *An Oration Delivered Before the New York Typographical Society* (New York, 1813), esp. pp. 8–14.

6. Thomas Thompson, *An Oration Pronounced the 4th Day of July, 1799, at Salisbury, in the State of New-Hampshire* (Concord, 1799), esp. pp. 8–15; Luther Richardson, *An Oration Pronounced July 4, 1800 at . . . the Town of Roxbury . . .* (Roxbury, 1800); and Edward Bangs, *An Oration . . . at Worcester, July 4, 1800* (Worcester, 1800).

7. *Annals of the Congress of the United States,* 12 Cong., 2 Sess. (Washington, 1834), 812, 12 Jan. 1813, hereafter cited as *Annals.* See also Aaron Hale Putnam, *An Oration Pronounced July 4, 1805 at . . . the Town of Charlestown* (Charlestown, 1805); Abijah Bigelow. *An Oration Delivered at Bolton* (Leominster, Mass., 1808); *Annals,* 7 Cong., 1 Sess., 386, for a useful speech by John P. VanNess; Fisher Ames, "The Republican. No. I," Seth Ames, ed., *Works of Fisher Ames,* II (Boston, 1851), 251; Francis Blake, *An Oration Pronounced at Worcester (Mass.) On . . . July 4, 1812* (Worcester, 1812); Charles Paine, *An Oration Pronounced July 4, 1801 at . . . the Town of Boston* (Boston, 1801); John Foster, *An Oration Delivered in the White Meeting House, Stonington Borough* (Stonington, 1802); Adrian Hezeman, *An Oration Delivered . . . in the Township of Oyster Bay . . .* (New York, 1801); Oliver Cobb, *An Oration Delivered in . . . Rochester . . .* (New Bedford, 1803); Benjamin Greene, *Oration Pronounced at Lexington . . .* (Boston, 1809); John Lowell, Jr., *An Oration Pronounced July 4, 1799 at . . . Boston . . .* (Boston, 1799), esp. pp. 11–20; Hext McCall, *An Oration . . . Before the Inhabitants of Charleston, South Carolina* (Charleston, 1810).

8. Ruth Davis Stevens and David Harrison Stevens, *American Patriotic Prose and Verse* (Chicago, 1917), p. 54, hereafter cited as Stevens, *Patriotic;* George I. Eacker, *An Oration Delivered at . . . the City and County of New York . . .* (New York, 1801), pp. 22–23; John D. Gardiner, *An Oration Delivered in Roxbury, N.J. . . . .* (Morristown, 1807), esp. pp. 16–17, 22–29.

9. Representative of the sentiment discussed in the preceding paragraphs are: Nathanael Emmons, *A Discourse Delivered May 9, 1798 During the Day*

of Fasting and Prayer (Wrentham, Mass., 1798); Asa Messer, *Oration Deliv-ered at Providence* . . . (Providence, 1803); William W. Story, ed., *Life and Letters of Joseph Story*, II (Boston, 1851), 182, hereafter cited as *Story*; Spen-cer Pratt, *An Oration Pronounced at Norridgwock* . . . (Augusta, 1805); John Noyes, *An Oration, Delivered in Brattleborough* (Brattleborough, 1811); John Hubbard Church, *An Oration Pronounced at Pelham, New Hampshire* . . . (Haverhill, Mass., 1805); Stephen Thacker, *An Oration Pronounced at Ken-nebunk . . . Maine* . . . (Boston, 1803); Abraham Bishop, *Oration in Honor of the Election of President Jefferson* . . . (Hartford, 1804); George Gibbs, ed., *Memoirs of Washington and Adams Edited from the Papers of Oliver Wolcott*, II (New York, 1846), 312, hereafter cited as *Wolcott*; Andrew Bigelow, *An Oration Delivered . . . at Cambridge, July 4, 1815* (Cambridge, 1815); Christopher R. Greene, *An Oration Delivered in . . . Charleston, South Caro-lina* . . . (Charleston, 1815); *A Vindication of Captain Joseph Treat, Late of the Twenty-first Regiment* (Philadelphia, 1815).

10. Useful for these matters are Alan Heimert, *Religion and the American Mind* (Cambridge, 1966), esp. pp. 512–46; Sidney E. Mead, "Denominational-ism: The Shape of Protestantism in America," *Church History*, XXIII (Dec. 1954), 291–320; James F. Maclear, " 'The True American Union' of Church and State: The Reconstruction of the Theocratic Tradition," *Church History* XXVIII (Mar. 1959), 41–62; Manning J. Dauer, *The Adams Federalists* (Balti-more, 1953), esp. pp. 259–60; Jones, *Ideas in America*, p. 122; David Hackett Fisher, *The Revolution of American Conservatism* (New York, 1965); Smith, *Fetters*, pp. 10–11, 146–47.

11. For varied insights here, see Sidney E. Mead, *Nathaniel W. Taylor* (Chicago, 1942), esp. pp. vii–ix, 225–26; Shaw Livermore, *The Twilight of Federalism* (Princeton, 1962), pp. 262–65; Fischer, *Revolution of American Conservatism, passim*; Kenyon, "Republicanism and Radicalism," 174–76; and William Charvat, *The Origins of American Critical Thought* (Philadelphia, 1936), pp. 7–14; Ezekiel Bacon, *An Oration Delivered at Williamstown* . . . (Bennington, 1799); *Ames, Works*, I, 275; Eliphlet Nott, *A Discourse Deliv-ered . . . in Albany* . . . (Albany, 1801); Samuel L. Mitchell, *An Address to the Citizens of New York* (New York, 1800); Tristam Burges, *An Oration Delivered . . . in Providence* . . . (Providence, 1801); Lemuel Haynes, *The Nature and Importance of True Republicanism* . . . (Rutland, Vt., 1801); Bernard C. Steiner, *The Life and Correspondence of James McHenry* (Cleve-land, 1907), p. 522; Benjamin Whitman, *An Oration Pronounced at Hanover, Massachusetts* . . . (Boston, 1803); Samuel Willard, *An Oration Delivered at Topsham, District of Maine* (Portland, 1805).

12. John J. Pringle, *An Oration Delivered in . . . Charleston, South Caro-lina* . . . (Charleston, 1800); James Wilson, *An Oration Delivered at Provi-dence* . . . (Providence, 1804); Thomas Danforth, *An Oration . . . at . . . the Town of Boston* (Boston, 1804); Elias Glover, *An Oration Delivered at . . . Cincinnati* . . . (Cincinnati, 1806); James Bracket, *Oration, Pronounced*

in . . . Dartmouth College . . . (Hanover, N.H., 1805); *Order of the Washington Society* (Boston, 1823), pp. 9, 43; Selleck Osborn, *An Oration Delivered at . . . New Bedford . . .* (New Bedford, 1810); David Waldo Lincoln, *An Oration Pronounced at Boston . . .* (Boston, 1810); Benjamin F. Thompson, *Oration Delivered Before the Tammany Society . . .* (Brooklyn, 1811); Timothy Flint, *An Oration Delivered at Leominster . . .* (Worcester, 1815); Bessie Pierce, *Public Opinion and the Teaching of History in the United States* (New York, 1926), pp. 4–5; Charvat, *American Critical Thought*, pp. 2–6; Miller, *Crisis*, p. 92; Smith, *Fetters*, pp. 332–33; Salo W. Baron, *Modern Nationalism and Religion* (New York, 1947), p. 58.

13. *Annals*, 5 Cong., 2 Sess., House, 1761–64, 1826, 17 and 26 May 1798; William J. Hobby, *An Oration Delivered in . . . Augusta . . .* (Augusta, 1799); Edmund Mills, *An Oration . . . in Sutton . . .* (Sutton, Mass., 1809); John Lathrop, *An Oration Pronounced . . . at . . . Dedham . . .* (Dedham, 1798); Samuel Austin, *An Oration Pronounced at Worcester . . .* (Worcester, 1798); Leon Howard, *The Connecticut Wits* (Chicago, 1943), pp. 252–54; *Annals*, 7 Cong., 1 Sess., House, 965–66, 3 March 1802, John Clopton of Virginia; Henry Adams, ed., *The Writings of Albert Gallatin*, I (Philadelphia, 1879), 227, 12 Feb. 1805, hereafter cited as *Gallatin*; H. M. Wagstaff, ed., *The Papers of John Steele*, I (Raleigh, 1924), 258, Haywood wrote to Steele on 6 March 1802.

14. James Multimore, *An Address . . .* (Newburyport, R.I., 1808); Robert Sedgwick, *An Oration Delivered . . . in the City of New York* (New York, 1811); *Annals*, 12 Cong., 1 Sess., House, 1190; *Annals*, 13 Cong., 2 Sess., House, 841; Joseph L. Tillinghast, *An Oration Pronounced Before the Citizens of Pawtuxet . . .* (Providence, 1814); *Annals*, 13 Cong., 3 Sess., House, 805–6; Herman V. Ames, *State Documents on Federal Relations* (Philadelphia, 1900), pp. 21–22, 22–23, 37–38, hereafter cited as Ames, *Documents*; *Annals*, 13 Cong., 3 Sess., House, 865; Jothan Waterman, *An Oration Pronounced at Orleans* (Boston, 1809); William C. Jarvis, *An Oration Delivered at Pittsfield . . .* (Pittsfield, 1812); Edwin A. White, *An Oration Pronounced at Worcester . . .* (Worcester, 1814).

15. Manning J. Dauer, *The Adams Federalists* (Baltimore, 1953), has an interesting letter by Theodore Sedgwick, p. 199; Thomas W. P. Charlton, *Oration in . . . Savannah* (Savannah, 1802); Samuel Taggart, *An Oration Spoken at Colrain* (Greenfield, Mass., 1803); *Annals*, 7 Cong., 1 Sess., House, 74–77; *Annals*, 8 Cong., 1 Sess., Senate, 161–65; Henry Cabot Lodge, ed., *The Works of Alexander Hamilton*, X (New York, 1904), 458; Edmund Quincy, *Life of Josiah Quincy* (Boston, 1869), p. 206, hereafter Quincy, *Life*; Timothy Dwight, *Travels in New England and New York*, IV (London, 1823), 512–14; Chauncy Langdon, *An Oration . . . at Pawlet* (Salem, 1807); Jeremiah Bailey, *An Oration Pronounced at Wiscasset . . .* (Wiscasset, 1805); John Rodman, *An Oration . . . in the City of New York* (New York, 1813); for general helpful comment, see Smith, *Fetters*, pp. 23–34; Benjamin T. Spencer, *The Quest for Nationality, An American Literary Campaign* (Syracuse, 1957), *passim*, esp.

p. 72; interesting insights to be used cautiously are in Yehoshua Arieli, *Individualism and Nationalism in American Ideology* (Cambridge, 1964), pp. 128 ff.; Henry Ware, Jr., *Poem Pronounced at Cambridge, February 23, 1815, at the Celebration of Peace* (Cambridge, 1815); for similar aspirations for the Stewards, see John Holmes, *An Oration Pronounced at Alfred* . . . (Boston, 1815), Holmes tied pride to virtue as guardians of national honor.

16. There are helpful comments in Sanford, *Quest, passim,* esp. p. 134; see also P. Miller, "American Nationalism as Theory of Nature"; Jones, *Ideas in America,* pp. 128–38; Sanford, *Quest,* pp. 137–38; Roderick Nash, *Wilderness and the American Mind* (New Haven, 1967), pp. 67–83; Daniel J. Boorstin, *The Lost World of Thomas Jefferson* (New York, 1948), pp. 237 ff.; Spencer, *Quest for Nationality,* pp. 39 ff.; *Annals,* 5 Cong., Sess., House, 1142, 1 Mar. 1798; Jonathan Russell, *An Oration* . . . *in Providence* . . . (Providence, 1800); Samuel Taggart, *An Oration Delivered at Conway* . . . (Northampton, 1804); *Annals,* 11 Cong., 2 Sess., House, 387–88, and 12 Cong., 1 Sess., 712.

17. Samuel P. P. Fay, *An Oration Delivered at Concord* . . . (Cambridge, 1801); John Binns, *An Oration* . . . *Philadelphia* . . . (Philadelphia, 1810); John E. Anderson, *An Oration Delivered in* . . . *Augusta* . . . (Augusta, 1801); Joseph Chandler, *An Oration Delivered* . . . *in Monmouth* . . . (Portland, 1804); Benjamin Ames, *An Oration Pronounced at Bath* . . . (Portland, 1808); Enoch Lincoln, *An Oration Pronounced at Worcester* . . . (Worcester, Mass., 1812); James A. Winchell, *An Arrangement of the Psalms, Hymns, and Spiritual Songs* . . . (Boston, 1818), 579, hereafter cited as Winchell, *Hymns*; Heimert, *Religion and the American Mind* (Cambridge, 1966), pp. 548–52, has helpful insight; Perry Miller in Smith and Jamison, eds., *Shaping of American Religion,* pp. 351 ff.; John H. Schaar, *Loyalty in America* (Berkeley, 1957), p. 117; Gaillard Hunt, ed., *The Writings of James Madison,* VI (New York, 1900), 327, 330–31, hereafter cited as *Madison*; Jonathan Maxcy, *An Oration* . . . *in Providence* . . . (Providence, 1799); Cyprian Strong, *A Discourse Delivered at Hebron* . . . (Hartford, 1799); *Annals,* 8 Cong., 1 Sess., House, 461–62, 465; 9 Cong., 2 Sess., House, 144; Christopher Manwaring, *Individual and National Dependence and Independence Considered* . . . (Hartford, 1808); Joseph B. Caldwell, *An Oration Pronounced* . . . *at Barre, in the County of Worcester, July 4, 1808* (n.p., n.d.); Chauncy Langdon, *An Oration Pronounced at Poultney* . . . (Rutland, 1808); Chauncy Langdon, *An Oration Delivered in Castleton* . . . (Middlebury, 1812); Dwight, *Travels, IV,* 513; also Steele, I, 408, Steele wrote to Nathaniel Macon, 12 Sept. 1803; Samuel Cogswell, *An Oration Delivered Before the Republican Citizens of Newburyport* . . . (Newburyport, 1808).

18. Useful background may be found in Kenyon, "Republicanism and Radicalism," 181–82; Leonard Levy, *Freedom of Speech and Press in Early American History* (New York, 1963), *passim,* esp. p. 258; Leonard W. Levy, *Jefferson on Civil Liberties* (Cambridge, 1963), *passim,* esp. p. x; Stephen G. Kurtz, *The Presidency of John Adams* (Philadelphia, 1957), pp. 200–239;

Smith, *Fetters*, esp. p. 131; Charvat, p. 185; Jones, *Ideas in America*, pp. 123–24; Paul Allen, *An Oration . . . in . . . Rehoboth, Massachusetts* (Providence, 1806); Henry Wheaton, *An Oration Delivered . . . at . . . New York . . .* (New York, 1814).

19. Relevant comments by Perry Miller may be found in Smith and Jamison, *Shaping of American Religion*, pp. 362 ff.; Sanford, *Quest*, pp. 148–53; Miller, *Crisis, passim*; Dauer, *Adams Federalists*, pp. 150 ff.; Kurtz, *Adams*, pp. 404–7; Amos Stoddard, *An Oration Delivered Before the Citizens of Portland . . .* (Portland, 1799); Claudius Herrick, *An Oration Delivered at Deerfield . . .* (Greenfield, 1800); Gaius Conant, *An Oration Pronounced at Franklin . . .* (Providence, 1803); William Baylies, *An Oration Pronounced at Middleborough . . .* (Russell Cutler Press, 1808); Seth Ames, ed., *Works of Fisher Ames*, II (Boston, 1854), 255; Edward Durrell Smith, *An Oration Delivered . . . to the Citizens of Pendleton District* (Augusta, S.C., 1812).

20. These concerns have been variously noted by: Kurtz, *Adams*, pp. 303–16; Merle Curti, *Social Ideas of American Educators* (New York, 1935), pp. 47–63; Rush Welter, *Popular Education and Democratic Thought in America* (New York and London, 1962), pp. 29–40; Eugene Perry Link, *Democratic-Republican Societies, 1790–1800* (New York, 1942), p. 186; David Tyack, "Forming the National Character," *Harvard Educational Review*, XXXVI (1966), 29–41; Jones, *O Strange New World*, pp. 302–11. Many of these studies are impressed by the way in which uncertainty over both the times and the capacity of man prompted a wide eagerness to condition both the mind and impulse of men through education, handmaiden to religion. For Charles Carroll's comment, see Steiner, *James McHenry*, p. 473.

21. Theodore Dwight, *An Oration Spoken at Hartford* (Hartford, 1798); Richard Newcomb, *An Oration, Spoken at Greenfield . . .* (Greenfield, Mass., 1799); Timothy Dwight, *An Oration Delivered at New Haven . . .* (Hartford, 1801); Richard Furman, *A Sermon Preached . . . in Charleston, South Carolina . . .* (Charleston, 1802); Benjamin Silliman, *An Oration Delivered at Hartford . . .* (Hartford, 1802); E. Dean, *An Oration Pronounced at Tivertown . . .* (Dedham, 1804), p. 16.

22. Winchell, *Hymns*, #587, #576; Samuel C. Allen, *An Oration Delivered at Petersham . . .* (Boston, 1806).

23. Story, *Letters*, I, 229, 24 Aug. 1812; *Annals*, 7 Cong., 2 Sess., Senate, 133–34; 7 Cong., 1 Sess., Senate, 206; 13 Cong., 2 Sess., House, 1609; Charles Caldwell, M.D., *An Oration . . . Delivered Before the American Republican Society of Philadelphia . . .* (Philadelphia, 1810); *The Monthly Anthology and Boston Review*, VIII (Jan. 1810), 4–5; Howard, *Conn. Wits*, p. 383; Zebulon R. Shepherd, *An Oration Delivered . . . at Poultney . . .* (Middlebury, 1814); Edmund Foster, *An Oration Pronounced at Westford . . .* (Boston, 1804); Steiner, *McHenry*, p. 503; David Everett, *An Oration Pronounced at Am-*

herst, New Hampshire . . . (Amherst, 1804); for background, see Miller, *Crisis, passim*; Smith, *Fetters*, pp. 12–20; Kenyon, 177–78.

24. Gideon Starr, *An Oration Delivered in . . . the City of Schenectady . . .* (Albany, 1801); Richard Rush, *An Oration . . . at the Capitol in Washington* (Washington, 1812); quoted in Howard, *Conn. Wits*, p. 391; other interesting instances of the torment caused by the unfailing presence of party, see Joseph Story, *An Oration . . . at Salem . . .* (Salem, 1804); Ichabod Nichols, *An Oration . . . in Salem, Massachusetts* (Salem, 1805); Peter Thacker, *An Oration Delivered Before the Inhabitants of the Town of Boston . . .* (Boston, 1807).

25. For these sentiments, see James D. Richardson, ed., *A Compilation of the Messages and Papers of the Presidents*, I (New York, 1897), 258–59, 261–62, 266, 269, 270, 274–76, 282, 284, 295, hereafter cited as Richardson.

26. Richardson, I, 309–12, 315, 367–69, 443.

27. Richardson, I, 453, 460, 462, 470; II, 497–98, 505, 509, 511, 515, 518, 525, 546, 553.

28. For a good discussion of the views of John Adams, see Loren Baritz, *City on a Hill* (New York, 1964), pp. 91–156; Dauer, *Adams Federalists, passim*, esp. p. 161; Kurtz, pp. 297–305; John A. Schutz and Douglass Adair, eds., *The Spur of Fame, Dialogues of John Adams and Benjamin Ruch, 1805–1813* (San Marino, Calif., 1966), pp. 21, 108–11, 114, hereafter cited as Schutz, *Spur*; *Works of John Adams*, IX, 631; Lester J. Cappon, ed., *The Adams-Jefferson Letters*, II (Chapel Hill, 1959), 310, 352, 358, 397–98, 456–57.

29. Levy, *Jefferson and Civil Liberties*, pp. 167–68; Paul Leicester Ford, *The Works of Thomas Jefferson*, VIII (New York, 1904), 368, 430–33; IX, 76; X, 71, hereafter cited as *Jefferson*; Schutz, *Spur*, pp. 387–92, 458–59.

30. Lyman H. Butterfield, ed., *Letters of Benjamin Rush*, II (Princeton, 1951), 806–7, 812–13, 831–33, 886, 900–901, 919, 923, 966, 1001–2, 1054, 1095–96, 1154, 1158–59; Schutz, *Spur*, p. 133.

31. Like so many others, I am greatly indebted to Harry R. Warfel, *Noah Webster, Schoolmaster to America* (New York, 1936), esp. pp. 223–65, and to Harry R. Warfel, ed., *Letters of Noah Webster* (New York, 1953), hereafter cited as Warfel, *Webster*, and Warfel, *Letters*, respectively; Noah Webster, *An Oration Pronounced Before the Citizens of New Haven . . .* (New Haven, 1798); Noah Webster, *An Oration Pronounced . . . at Amherst . . .* (Northampton, 1814); Warfel, *Letters*, pp. 184–86, 187–94, 211–13, 213–15, 228, 235–37, 240–45, 265–66, 275–76, 292–94, 301–8; Warfel, *Webster*, pp. 278–79, 312–14.

32. Warfel, *Letters*, pp. 187–94; Charles Burr Todd, *Life and Letters of Joel Barlow, L.L.D.* (New York, 1886), pp. 207, 209, 235; Howard, *Conn. Wits*,

pp. 311–12, 331; Joel Barlow, *Oration Delivered at Washington* . . . (Washington, 1809).

33. *The Writings and Speeches of Daniel Webster,* XV (Boston, 1903), 475–84, 502, 505–21; XVII, 22; XV, 537–47; XVII, 225–26; XV, 578–82, hereafter cited as *Webster*; C. H. Van Tyne, ed., *The Letters of Daniel Webster* (New York, 1902), pp. 7, 11–13, 190, hereafter cited as Van Tyne; Daniel Webster, *Fourth of July Oration Delivered at Fryeburg, Maine in the Year 1802* (Boston, 1882).

34. James F. Hopkins, ed., *The Papers of Henry Clay,* I (Lexington, 1959), 216, 328–29, 450, 653, 769; II, 63, 70, 82, hereafter cited as *Clay Papers.*

35. John Spencer Bassett, *Correspondence of Andrew Jackson,* I (Washington, 1926–33), 43–44, 68, 165, 200, 220–21, 237, 241, 251, 263, 487, hereafter cited as *Jackson.*

36. Samuel W. Bridgham, *An Oration Delivered in* . . . *Providence* . . . (Providence, 1798); John F. Grimke, *An Oration Delivered in* . . . *Charleston* . . . (Charleston, 1807); *Annals,* 10 Cong., 2 Sess., House, 777; Harry Toulmin, *An Oration Delivered at* . . . *Frankfort* . . . (Lexington, 1804); Thomas Waterman, *An Address* . . . *Concord, N.H.* . . . (n.p., 1806); Nathaniel B. Boileau, *An Oration* . . . *at* . . . *Hatborough, Montgomery County, Pennsylvania* (n.p., 1814); Henry Rutledge, *An Oration Delivered in* . . . *Charleston* . . . (Charleston, 1804); Gulian C. Verplanck, *An Oration Delivered* . . . *Before the Washington Benevolent Society of the City of New York* (New York, 1809); Richard Bache, *Oration Delivered at Spring Garden* . . . (Philadelphia, 1813); Joseph E. Sprague, *An Oration Delivered in Salem* . . . (Salem, 1813); Timothy Fuller, *An Oration Pronounced at Lexington* . . . (Boston, 1814); Benton's letter is in *Clay Papers,* I, 805–6, 22 June 1813; David Waldo Lincoln, *An Oration Pronounced at Worcester* . . . (Worcester, 1805); Orasmus C. Merrill, *An Oration Delivered* . . . *in Bennington* . . . (Bennington, 1806); James T. Austin, *An Oration Pronounced at Lexington* . . . (Boston, 1815); Peleg Sprague, *An Oration Pronounced at Worcester* . . . (Worcester, 1815).

37. Barbara M. Cross, ed., *Autobiography of Lyman Beecher,* I (Cambridge, 1961), 194–95, hereafter *Beecher Autobiography*; Samuel E. Morison, *Harrison Gray Otis* (Boston, 1969), p. 90; *The American Review of History and Politics,* I (Philadelphia, 1811), 1–88, esp. 87; II, 75–76; Jeremiah Evarts, *An Oration Delivered in Charlestown* . . . (Charlestown, 1812); Barbara M. Cross in introduction, *Beecher Autobiography,* I, xxxv–xxxvi, and xxii–xxxiv, *passim*; Timothy Dwight, *The Duty of Americans* . . . (New Haven, 1798); John Crane, *An Oration Delivered at Douglass* . . . (Worcester, 1802); Samuel Swift, *An Oration Delivered in Middlebury* . . . (Middlebury, Vt., 1809); Thomas Snell, *An Oration, Pronounced at Brookfield* . . . (Brookfield, 1813); *Beecher Autobiography,* I, 109, 191–93.

38. *Jackson,* I, 53; Samuel E. Morison, *Life and Letters of Harrison Gray Otis,* I (Boston, 1913), 95, 280–81, hereafter cited as *Otis Letters*; Josiah

Quincy, *An Oration . . . at . . . the Town of Boston . . .* (Boston, 1798);
Isaac C. Bates, *An Oration Pronounced at Northampton . . .* (Northampton,
1805); *Otis Letters,* I, 319–20; *American Review,* I (Jan. 1811), ii–x; Ebenezer
Moseley, *An Oration Pronounced at Newburyport* (Boston, 1808); *Otis Letters,*
II, 48 ff.; Daniel A. Clark, *Independence Sermon* (Newark, 1814), see also
Cushing Otis, *An Oration Pronounced at Scituate . . .* (Boston, 1800).

CHAPTER TWO

1. Richard H. Dana, *An Oration Delivered . . .*
at Cambridge . . . (Cambridge, 1814).

2. Leo Marx, *The Machine in the Garden* (New York, 1964), p. 343; *Register
of Debates in Congress,* 20 Cong., 1 Sess., Senate, 645, hereafter cited as
Register; Edward H. Tatum, Jr., ed., "Ten Unpublished Letters of John
Quincy Adams, 1796–1837," *The Huntington Library Quarterly,* IV (No. 3,
April 1941), 379, to Richard Rush; Wishy, *The Child and the Republic,* pp.
3–5.

3. Albert Gallatin, *Inaugural Address . . . on Taking the Chair as President of the New-York Historical Society* (New York, 1843), pp. 14, 16, 18;
John William Ward, *Andrew Jackson, Symbol for an Age* (New York, 1955), p.
212; Charles G. Sellers, *James K. Polk, Continentalist, 1843–1846* (Princeton,
1966), p. 214; Hartz, *Liberal Tradition,* pp. 141–42; *Lord's Eulogy* is quoted in
John R. Bodo, *The Protestant Clergy and Public Issues, 1812–1848* (Princeton,
1954), p. 60.

4. Excerpt quoted in Perry Miller's essay in Smith and Jamison, I, 367;
Richard D. Mosier, ed., *McGuffy's Fourth Reader* (Cincinnati, 1838), pp. 36–39;
there is some interesting display of this approach in *The Youth's Companion,*
XVII (5 Oct. 1843), 86, where an effort is made to explain why Washington
was the world's finest human model. He was good, where men like Alexander
and Caesar were selfish and proud. Simple morality, argued the editor, was
the mandate of America's role.

5. Clark S, Northrup, William C. Lane, and John C. Schwab, eds., *Representative Phi Beta Kappa Orations,* II (Boston, 1925; New York, 1927), 10–35,
hereafter cited as *Phi Beta Kappa Orations;* Rufus Putnam Cutler, *Valedic-
tory Oration . . . Yale College . . .* (New Haven, 1839), esp. pp. 19–21, 31–32;
Psalms and Hymns . . . Arranged by Dr. Rippon . . . (Philadelphia, 1827),
pp. 333–34, hereafter cited as *Rippon Hymns;* Isaac Watts, *Psalms of David
. . .* (Albany, 1824), pp. 219–20, hereafter cited as *Watts, Psalms;* Wishy,
Child and Republic, p. 5; I have profited greatly from George W. Pierson,
"The Obstinate Concept of New England: A Study in Denudation," *The New
England Quarterly,* XXVIII (Mar. 1955), 3–17; *Address of the American So-
ciety for the Encouragement of Domestic Manufactures to the People of the
United States* (New York, 1817), the proceedings which prepared the address

were held on 31 Dec. 1816, with New York governor D. D. Tompkins in the chair; Nathaniel Hale Loring, *An Address . . . Charlestown, Mass.* (Boston, 1822); T. I. Wharton, *An Oration . . . in the City of Philadelphia* (Philadelphia, 1827).

6. Lewis Cass, *A Discourse . . . Before the American Historical Society, January 30, 1836* (Washington, 1836); see Nagel, *One Nation Indivisible, passim,* esp. Chap. 4, for discussion of the Union as an absolute in American ideology; Taylor's sermon quoted in Maclear, " 'True American Union,' " *Church History,* XXVIII, 51; Barbara M. Cross, *Horace Bushnell: Minister to a Changing America* (Chicago, 1958), pp. 15–20, 59–60, 72, 77–78, 81; Bodo, pp. 152–57; Beecher, *Autobiography,* II, 167, 321; Hooper Cumming, *An Oration Delivered at Newark, N.J. . . .* (Newark, 1823); Reuben Post, *A Discourse . . . in Washington, D.C.* (Washington, 1824); Samuel Austin, *An Address Pronounced in Worcester . . .* (n.p., n.d., [1825]); Caleb Cushing, *A Eulogy on John Adams and Thomas Jefferson . . .* (Cambridge, 1826); Benjamin A. Wisner, *Influence of Religion on Liberty . . .* (Washington, 1831), esp. p. 5; George W. Bethune, *Our Liberties: Their Danger* (Philadelphia, 1835), pp. 5–6.

7. Interesting comments are in Wesley F. Craven, *The Legend of the Founding Fathers* (New York, 1956), pp. 63–74; Albert K. Weinberg, *Manifest Destiny* (Baltimore, 1935; Chicago, 1963), esp. pp. 100–128; George S. Hilliard, ed., *Life, Letters, and Journals of George Ticknor,* II (Boston, 1878), 187–88, hereafter cited is *Ticknor*; Andrew Dunlap, *An Oration, Delivered at Salem . . .* (Salem, 1819, 2nd ed.); William D. Snodgrass, *An Address* (New York, 1845), delivered at Washington, Pa., 23 Sept. 1845; see esp. 25 Feb. 1824 issue of *New York Patriot*; another good illustration of the primitivism appeal is the 30 June 1823 issue of *Kentucky Reporter*; Calhoun's views are nicely summarized in J. Franklin Jameson, ed., *Correspondence of John C. Calhoun* (Washington, 1900), pp. 324–25, in a letter to Thomas Holland and Others, 2 July 1833; William Rawle, *A View of the Constitution of the United States* (Philadelphia, 1829), p. 295; George E. Baker, ed., *The Works of William H. Seward, III* (New York, 1853–61), 17–22, hereafter cited as *Seward*; Godwin's letter, from the Bryant-Godwin Collection, is quoted in Sellers, *Polk*, p. 420.

8. Marvin Meyers, *The Jacksonian Persuasion* (Stanford, 1957), pp. 164, 254, 274; Bessie L. Pierce, *Civic Attitudes in American School Textbooks* (Chicago, 1930), pp. 254–56; *Annals,* 16 Cong., 1 Sess., House, 1167; Robert J. Turnbull, *The Crisis* (Charleston, 1827), p. 148; *Congressional Globe,* 24 Cong., 1 Sess., Senate, Appendix, 226, hereafter cited as *Globe; Globe,* 29 Cong., 1 Sess., House, Appendix, 217, Davis' speech was on 6 Feb. 1846; see also *Globe,* 29 Cong., 2 Sess., House, 387–88; Thomas O. Elliott, *An Oration Delivered in . . . Charleston . . .* (Charleston, 1821); Thomas Fletcher, *An Oration Delivered . . . Before the . . . Citizens of . . . Natchez* (Natchez, 1841).

9. Edward T. Channing, *An Oration . . . Boston* (Boston, 1817); Matthew H. Smith, *A Sermon* (Boston, 1844); see the provocative comments in Robert

P. Hay, "The Glorious Departure of the American Patriarchs: Contemporary Reaction to the Deaths of Jefferson and Adams," *The Journal of Southern History*, XXXV (Nov. 1969), 543–55; Edgar E. Brandon, *A Pilgrimage of Liberty* (Athens, Ohio, 1944), contains numerous examples of the ideology evoked by Lafayette's visit, with Governor Coles' address of 30 Apr. 1825 being reprinted on pp. 221–22; *Niles' Weekly Register*, XII (7 June 1817), 228–30; XVI (3 Apr. 1819), 105–6; Roy F. Nichols quotes Goodrich in *Religion and American Democracy* (Baton Rouge, 1959), pp. 78–79; Charles R. King, ed., *The Life and Correspondence of Rufus King*, VI (New York, 1894–1900), 287, letter from Richard Peters, 29 Feb. 1820, hereafter cited as *King*; Westerlo Woodworth, *Oration* . . . (Albany, 1834); Gulian C. Verplanck, "The Advantages and Dangers of the American Scholar," in Joseph L. Blau, ed., *American Philosophic Addresses, 1700–1900* (New York, 1946), pp. 119–50, hereafter cited as *Blau*; Thomas S. Perry, *The Life and Letters of Francis Lieber* (Boston, 1882), p. 147, hereafter cited as Perry, *Lieber*; Sellers, *Polk*, quotes Baker on pp. 361–62.

10. Edward Everett, *An Oration* . . . (Boston, 1828); George Lunt, *An Oration Delivered in Newburyport* . . . (Newburyport, 1833); Miller, *Life of the Mind*, quotes the Home Mission Society statement, p. 58; excerpts from *The Home Missionary* and *The Missionary Enterprise* are quoted extensively in Bodo, esp. pp. 240–42 and p. 246; Mosier, ed., *McGuffy Fourth Reader; Register*, 22 Cong., 1 Sess., Senate, 367; Van Buren's statement was in the Washington *Globe*, as quoted in Sellers, *Polk*, pp. 60–61; *Globe*, 28 Cong., 1 Sess., Senate, Appendix, 318; Norman Graebner, ed., *Manifest Destiny* (Indianapolis, 1968), pp. 110, 217–18; R. C. Mallary, *An Oration* . . . (Rutland, 1826); Odell Shepard, ed., *The Journals of Bronson Alcott* (Boston, 1938), pp. 191–92, hereafter cited as *Alcott Journals*.

11. See Spencer, *Quest for Nationality*, pp. 60 ff.; Wishy, *Child and the Republic*, p. 6; David W. Noble, "Cooper, Leatherstocking and the Death of the American Adam," *American Quarterly*, XVI (fall 1964), 419–31; see helpful discussion in Wishy, *Child and the Republic*, pp. ix–x, 10; Edwin H. Cady, *The Gentleman in America* (Syracuse, 1949), pp. 101, 126, 183; Orestes Brownson, "Progress of Society," as quoted in Sherman Paul, *Emerson's Angle of Vision* (Cambridge, 1952), p. 266; *National Circular* (New York, n.d.), a pamphlet in the Marcoe Collection (Box 19), Rare Book Room, Library of Congress, internal evidence puts the publication clearly in the early 1830's; Edgar E. Brandon, *Lafayette, Guest of the Nation*, I (Oxford, Ohio, 1950–57), 164; Ruth Miller Elson, *Guardians of Tradition* (Lincoln, Neb., 1964), pp. 337–42; Francis Hodge, *Yankee Theatre* (Austin, 1964), pp. 42, 55–56; Perry, *Lieber*, pp. 69–70, 74–75, 118, 128; Mason Wade, ed., *The Journals of Francis Parkman*, I (New York, 1947), 178; II, 405, I, 277, hereafter cited as *Parkman Journals; Address of the State Convention of Teachers and Friends of Education, Held at Utica, January 12th, 13th, & 14th, 1831* (Utica, 1831), esp. pp. 5–6; Josiah Quincy, Jr., *An Oration* . . . (Boston, 1832); George M. Dallas, *An Address . . . the Evening Before the Annual Commencement of the College of New Jersey, September 27, 1831* (Princeton, 1831); Robert Rantoul, Jr.,

An Oration . . . (Salem, 1833); Edward N. Kirk, *Oration* . . . (Albany, 1836); Beecher, *Autobiography*, II, 342; Frederick Whittlesey, *An Address* . . . (Rochester, 1842); D. Macauley, *The Patriot's Catechism* . . . (Washington, 1843); John Quincy Adams, *An Oration* . . . (Newburyport, 1837); John Davis, *An Oration* . . . (Worcester, 1816); *Niles'*, XIV (16 May 1818), 199–200; Daniel Knight, *An Oration* . . . (Worcester, 1819); Anon., *Plain Sense on National Industry* (New York, 1820), pp. 3–5; William Wirt, *A Discourse on the Lives and Character of Thomas Jefferson and John Adams* (Washington, 1826); Warfel, *Webster*, pp. 362–64; William Price, *Address* . . . *Before the Alumni Association of Dickinson College* (Carlisle, 1830); Charles L. Woodbury, ed., *Writings of Levi Woodbury*, III (Boston, 1852), 191–95, hereafter cited as *Woodbury*; Frederic H. Hedge, *An Oration* . . . (Bangor, 1838); Alexis de Tocqueville, *Democracy in America*, I (New York, 1953, Philips Bradley edition), 405.

12. Rourke, pp. 392–93; *Annals*, 16 Cong., 1 Sess., House, 1583, Kinsey of N.J.; *American Watchman* (Wilmington, Del.), 26 June 1821, *Argus of Western America* (Frankfort, Ky.), 22 Sept. 1824; Robert Strange, *Oration* . . . *Delivered at Fayetteville, N.C.* . . . (Fayetteville, 1826); George Ticknor Curtis, *An Oration* . . . (Boston, 1841); Henry A. Miles, *Fidelity to the Political Idea* . . . (Boston, 1843); O. C. Hartley, *An Address* . . . (Chambersburg, Pa., 1844); Thomas F. Gossett, *Race, The History of an Idea in America* (Dallas, 1963), p. 311; Charles W. Cutter, *An Oration* . . . (Portsmouth, N.H., 1834); William Morris Meredith, *An Oration* . . . (Philadelphia, 1834); George W. Doane, *America and Great Britain* (Burlington, N.J., 1848), pp. 8–9.

13. Illumining discussions in this broad area are found in David W. Noble, *The Eternal Adam and the New World Garden* (New York, 1968); Perry Miller, *The Raven and the Whale* (New York, 1956), esp. pp. 310–11; Weinberg, *Manifest Destiny*, esp. pp. 130–45; Charvat, esp. pp. 59–71; Cushing Strout, *The American Image of the Old World* (New York, 1963), pp. 88–104; all historians of this period must of course be indebted to the writings of Leo Marx, especially his *Machine in the Garden*, pp. 203–8, 226; Charles G. Haines, *Considerations on the Great Western Canal: From the Hudson to Lake Erie* (Brooklyn, 1818), esp. pp. 7–9, 47 ff., 59.

14. Ticknor, I, 328; John Quincy Adams, *An Address* . . . *at the City of Washington* . . . (Cambridge, 1821), pp. 13–14, 23; Benjamin F. Hunt, *An Oration* . . . (Charleston, 1839); John Y. Simon, ed., *The Papers of Ulysses S. Grant*, I (Carbondale, 1967), 5; Parkman, *Journals*, I, 256–57; Calhoun's "Address on the Relation Which the States and General Government Bear Each Other," is in Richard K. Crallé, ed., *The Works of John C. Calhoun*, VI (New York, 1853–55), 60–66; Hayne's speech is in *Register*, 21 Cong., 1 Sess., Senate, 58, 27 Jan. 1830.

15. George Bancroft, *An Oration* . . . (Northampton, 1826); John G. Palfrey, *An Oration* . . . (Boston, 1831); Benjamin Drake, *A Public Oration* . . . (Cincinnati, 1826); Henry Wheaton, *Some Account of the Life, Writings, and*

Speeches of William Pinkney (New York, 1826), pp. 165–66; Alexander Dimitry, *Address . . .* (Washington, 1839), pp. 17 ff.; Francis A. Dyhers, *Oration . . .* (Washington, 1845), pp. 13–14.

16. Franklin Dexter, *An Oration . . .* (Boston, 1819); *Phi Beta Kappa Orations,* II, 63–97, for Story's Harvard address of 31 Aug. 1826; William W. Story, ed., *Life and Letters of Joseph Story,* I (Boston, 1851), 560–61; II, 49–50; Joseph Story, *Commentaries on the Constitution of the United States,* III (Boston, 1833), 759; *Phi Beta Kappa Orations,* I, 2–23; see also Cross, *Bushnell,* pp. 30–50, for helpful comments on Bushnell's Hartford ministry at this time.

17. C. S. Henry, *The Position and Duties of the Educated Men of the Country. A Discourse* (New York, 1840); George W. Benedict, *An Oration . . .* (Burlington, 1826); Ralph Lockwood, *Address Delivered Before the American Institute . . .* (New York, 1829); George Bancroft, *History of the United States,* I (Boston, 1837–60), vii, 4; VII, 21, 362; Alexander H. Everett, *An Address . . .* (Boston, 1836); Albert Barnes, *The Literature and Science of America . . .* (Utica, 1836); James Fenimore Cooper, *Home as Found* (New York, n.d., [1838]), p. 117; James F. Cooper, ed., *Correspondence of James Fenimore Cooper,* I (New Haven, 1922), 328, hereafter cited as *Cooper Corr.;* Gallatin, *Inaugural Address,* p. 11; *Globe,* Appendix, 28 Cong., 2 Sess., House, 277, 15 Jan. 1845; *Phi Beta Kappa Orations,* I, Job Durfee at Brown Univ., 6 Sept. 1843, esp. 74–75; II, Charles Sumner at Union College, 25 July 1848, 92; John Whipple, *A Discourse . . .* (Providence, 1838).

18. *Niles,* XVI (10 July 1819), 321; XLVI (23 Aug. 1834), 429; *Clay Papers,* III, 246; *King,* VI, 573; *The Ladies Magazine,* II (Aug. 1829), 372–78; Seward, III, 205; *Cooper Corr.,* I, 301–2, Cooper, *Home as Found,* pp. 10, 103; *Alcott Journals,* p. 59; Sellers, *Polk,* p. 364; Edward D. Barber, *An Oration . . .* (Montpelier, 1839); Henry S. Patterson, M.D., *An Oration . . .* (Philadelphia, 1841); Boston *Advertiser,* 29 Dec. 1845; Charles Eliot Norton, ed., *Letters of James Russell Lowell,* I (New York, 1894), 134, 12 May 1848, hereafter cited as *Lowell Letters.*

19. George Potts, *An Address . . .* (Philadelphia, 1826); Joseph Richardson, *An Oration . . .* (Hingham, 1828); William H. Fondey, *An Oration Before the Young Men's Association . . .* (Albany, 1838); Dana to J. F. Cooper, *Cooper Corr.,* II, 558, 10 Nov. 1845; Cooper, *Home as Found,* p. 240; George Bethune, *A Plea for Study* (Philadelphia, 1845); Peleg Chandler, *The Morals of Freedom* (Boston, 1844); Horace Mann, *An Oration . . .* (Boston, 1842); Lawrence Cremin, ed., *The Republic and the School* (New York, 1957), has Mann's 12th Report of 1848, pp. 79–112, see esp. pp. 92–100.

20. George S. Hilliard, *An Oration . . .* (Boston, 1835); M. M. Noah, *Oration . . .* (New York, 1817); *American State Papers, Misc.,* II, 573, 18 Jan. 1820, petition from Hartford citizens; *Amer. State Papers, Finance,* III, 537, 28 Apr. 1820, Memorial from Philadelphia Chamber of Commerce; *Clay Papers,* III, 412; J. Franklin Jameson, ed., *Correspondence of John C. Calhoun*

(Washington, 1900), p. 267; William Slade, *An Oration* . . . (Middlebury, 1829); *Ladies Magazine,* II (July 1829), 306–7; Calvin Colton, ed., *The Private Correspondence of Henry Clay* (Cincinnati, 1856), pp. 498, 512, hereafter cited as *Clay Corr.*; David Donald, *Charles Sumner and the Coming of the Civil War* (New York, 1960), pp. 103–4, quotes the Story letters of 1839 and 1842; *Psalms and Hymns . . . in the Presbyterian Church* . . . (Philadelphia, 1843), p. 381.

21. Samuel Lorenzo Knapp, *Lectures on American Literature* (New York, 1829), esp. pp. 11 ff., 36–38, 285; Samuel L. Knapp, *An Address* . . . (Boston, 1826), pp. 26 ff.; Cephas Brainerd and Eveline W. Brainerd, eds., *The New England Society Orations,* I (New York, 1901), 159–62, hereafter cited as *New England Society Orations.*

22. *Adams-Jefferson Corr.,* II, 461–63, 531, 569, 575, 614; Ford, *Works of Jefferson,* XII, 6, 159–60, 425–26.

23. Madison's remarks are in Richardson, II, 564–65; for Monroe's most illustrative comments, see Richardson, II, 574–76, 579, 615, 643–44, 662, 718–19, 746, 752, 787–89, 791–93, 831–32.

24. Richardson, II, 860–61, 862–65, 878, 882, 903.

25. Richardson, III, 1005–6, 1063, 1080, 1144, 1153–54, 1194–95, 1217, 1219, 1223, 1367, 1512–13, 1526–27.

26. Richardson, IV, 1530–32, 1536–37, 1771–72.

27. Richardson, IV, 1860 fl., for Harrison's Address; IV, 1921–22, 2110, 2187–88, 2189, for Tyler's observations.

28. Richardson, V, 2440, 2442–43, 2458–59, 2479, 2488 ff., 2503; VI, 2504, 2508–13.

29. Allan Nevins, ed., *The Diary of Philip Hone* (New York, 1936), pp. 38–39, 55–56, 64–65, 131, 157, 163, 167–68, 244, 267, 331, 367, 393, 568, 655, 719.

30. Warfel, *Letters,* pp. 449, 452–57, 501–3, 504–6, 513–15; Warfel, *Webster,* pp. 398–400, 424–25, 425–27, 432.

31. *Jackson Corr.,* II, 273, 275–76; III, 21, 156–57, 203–4, 227, 247, 250, 294, 412, 431; IV, 486, 492, 506; V, 19, 42, 46, 53, 56, 165, 261, 429, 462–63; VI, 78, 83–85, 235.

32. *Webster,* XV, 7–8; I, 181–82, 197–98; XVII, 318; Ticknor, I, 330; *Webster,* I, 249, 253, 323–24; C. H. Van Tyne, ed., *The Letters of Daniel Webster* (New York, 1902), p. 158; *Webster,* II, 43–44, 55–56, 64, 73; VI, 236–38; XIII,

55–56, 59–60; II, 180, 186, 249–50, 259; XIII, 87; II, 198–99, 230; III, 79–80; XVIII, 123; I, 259–83; XIII, 190–91, 233–34; III, 247; XIII, 339; IV, 144.

33. *Clay Papers*, II, 135, 141, 458–59, 658–59, 833–34, 838–39; III, 572–93, 624, 684, 711, 894; Calvin Colton, ed., *The Life, Correspondence, and Speeches of Henry Clay*, V (New York, 1864), 396, 440, 515, 543, 557, 561, 566, 577–78; VI, 70, 133, 162, 367–68, hereafter cited as Colton, *Clay*; Colton, *Clay Corr.*, pp. 347, 463–67, 517–18.

34. Roy P. Basler, ed., *The Collected Works of Abraham Lincoln*, I (New Brunswick, 1953), 108–15, 178–79, 278–79, hereafter cited as Basler, *Lincoln*.

35. Philip L. Nicoloff, *Emerson on Race and History* (New York, 1961), p. 12; Ralph L. Rusk, ed., *The Letters of Ralph Waldo Emerson*, I (New York, 1939), 120–21, 167–68, 245–47, 274; II, 357; IV, 115, hereafter cited as *Emerson Letters*; Edward W. Emerson and Waldo E. Forbes, eds., *Journals of Ralph Waldo Emerson*, IV (Boston, 1909–14), 109; V, 328–29, hereafter cited as *Emerson Journals; The Dial* (Boston), III (Oct. 1842), 194–95; (Jan. 1843), 312–13; IV (Apr. 1844), 484–507; *Emerson Letters*, III, 29 Aug. 1847, 413.

36. *North American Review*, I, 307–14; II, 33–40; VIII, 174–76; IX, 253–59; X, 113–14, 338–40; XI, 68, 84, 103; XII, 85–87, 303; XIII, 40–42; XV, 21–22, 250–54, 281–82; XVIII, 177, 314, 328–29; XIX, 336–37; XX, 420–21; XXI, 360 ff.; XXII, 177, 373–74, 400; XXIV, 23–24; XXV, 183; XXXI, 162, 166–67; XLI, 249–51; Samuel F. Bemis, *John Quincy Adams and the Union*, (New York, 1956), p. 230, from the Adams Mss; *North American Review*, XLIII, 190–91; XLV, 120–21, 126; L, 358–59; XLVII, 2, 52, 58; LXII, 251; LXIII, 376–78; LXVII, 321–22; XXXII, 128–29; XXXVII, 244, 248–49, 314; XXXVIII, 466; XL, 409–10, 411; XLII, 240–41; L, 12–14; LII, 301–38; LV, 261; LIII, 42–78; LVIII, 38–39; LIX, 44–53; LI, 90; LXVI, 446.

37. Some useful comment on *Knick* can be found in Perry Miller, *Raven and Whale*, p. 117, also pp. 31–35, 195–96; *The Knickerbocker, New York Monthly Magazine*, IX, 1–11; II, 1–13; XXXII, 347–52; VI, 304–9; VII, 72–77; VIII, 210–13; XIV, 1–15, 48, 112–21; XXII, 193–96; XXX, 399–407; II, 161–70; XIV, 39–52; XVII, 254–56; XXV, 95–102; XIV, 59–68.

38. *The New York Review* (1837–42), I, 430; II, 379, 404; III, 194; IV, 352–53; V, *passim*; X, 2–3, 176, 183, 331; VII, 378–403; VI, 145, 148, 152–67; X, 375–419.

39. *The New England Magazine*, I, 148–49, 249, 281 ff.; II, 65–71, 288–300, 302; III, 194 ff.; V, 124; VII, 265–76, 471–77, 499; VIII, 228; IX, 288–93, 480; VI, 318–24.

40. *The American Review: A Whig Journal* (New York, 1845–52), I, 4, 94–98, 275–79; II, 59–60, 99, 235–36, 577–78; III, 1–20, 268–89, 616–17, 623–24; IV, 30–32, 42; V, 231–39; VI, 55–59, 370–75; Perry Miller, *Raven and Whale*,

offers exciting commentary, only modestly diminished by an insistence upon traditional difference between the ideology of the *Whig Review* and *Democratic Review,* see esp. pp. 75–110, *passim;* also see John Stafford, *The Literary Criticism of Young America* (Berkeley and Los Angeles, 1952).

41. The material stressed above is found as follows: *The United States Magazine and Democratic Review* (Washington, 1837–52), I, 1–15; IX, 322–23, 374–91; XVI, 495, 532; XVII, 5–7; XVIII, 57, 59, 64, 91–94, 213–14, 243–56; XX, 391, 544; XXI, 285; XXII, 387–94. For additional glimpses of this journal's contribution to the search for nationality, see: I, 70–71, 108–22, 143 ff., 171–72, 257; II, 312–20; III, 51–57; V, 466, 523 ff.; VI, 127–42, 174, 208–17, 283–84, 309–19, 423, 426–30; IX, 23–44, 411–16; X, 107–21, 259–64, 364; XI, 56–57, 194–96, 200, 351, 373, 475–81, 620; XII, 3–12, 339–59; XIV, 335–43; XV, 219–33, 320; XVI, 112–20; XVII, 8–9; XIX, 3, 29; XX, 99, 264–72, 390; XXI, 102, 105–6.

42. *Boston Post,* 22 Feb., 4 July, 27 Nov. 1845; 17 June, 4 July 1846.

43. See especially *The Age,* 21 June, 6 Dec. 1844; 7 Feb., 4 July, 8 Aug., 5 Sept. 1845; 23 Apr., 4 June, 30 July, 3 Sept., 8 Oct. 1847; 14 Jan. 1848.

44. *The Union,* 29 May, 3 July, 2 Oct. 1845; 8 May, 28 Aug. 1847; 5 Feb., 10 June 1848.

45. For Rice's sermon, so representative of this deep vein of American thought, see *National Preacher,* III (Oct. 1828), 65–80; Halsey's sermon in *National Preacher,* III, #6 (20 Nov. 1828), 81–96; Beecher's sermon, *ibid.,* 145–60; for other sermons especially illumining the search for national meaning, see the following volumes: V, 33–48; I, 48 ff.; IV, 189–99; 313–20; V, 57–64; 145–60; X, 326 ff.; XIII, 49–64, 161–76; XVII, 217–39; XVIII, 36–37, 62 ff., 237 ff.

46. See these volumes of *Ladies' Companion* for instances of this cry for national achievement: V, 260; IX, 83–85; X, 41–42; XII, 141, 265; XIII, 245–56. Howard's article is in XVI (Jan. 1842), 156–58; *Ladies' Repository,* I (July 1841), 211–14 for Hamline's essay, "Christian Patriotism," see also I, 233–35; II, 5–7, 34–36, 147–49; VII, 89–94; VIII, 277–78; *Brownson's Quarterly Review,* I, 84–88, 104, 117; II, 77 ff.; III, 40–61, 493–94.

47. *The Merchant's Magazine and Commercial Review* (New York, 1839–69), I, 2–3, 370–75; II, 102–18, 369–72, 502–6; IV, 415–25; V, 37–50; VIII, 164–68, 301–13; XI, 217–23; XII, 421–32; XIII, 546–50; XIV, 499–515; XVIII, 256–69.

48. Brainerd, *New England Society Orations,* I, Cheever's oration is 289–320; Choate's is 325–53; Marsh's is 373–416; see also I, 11–48, 134–36, 172–205, 219–59, 263–85, 452–60; II, 3–79.

49. For illustrative viewpoints, see William Lance, *An Oration . . .* (Charleston, 1816); Ashur Ware, *An Oration . . .* (Portland, 1817); Eber Wheaton,

Oration . . . (New York, 1828); Niles, XII (5 July 1817), 300; Parke Godwin, ed., *The Political Works of William Cullen Bryant*, I (New York, 1883), 66–67; II, 17–19, hereafter cited as *Bryant Poetry*; Hugh S. Legare, *An Oration* . . . (Charleston, 1823); *Jackson Corr.*, III, 206–7; N. G. Pendleton, *Oration* . . . (Cincinnati, 1831); Samuel J. Wilkin, *An Address* . . . (Princeton, 1842).

50. Charles Sprague, *An Oration* . . . (Boston, 1825); F. W. P. Greenwood, *Character of the Puritans* (Boston, 1826), pp. 16, 20–21; John W. James, *An Address* . . . (Washington, 1826); Asher Robbins, *Oration* . . . (Providence, 1827); *Alcott Journals*, pp. 40–41; Caleb Cushing, *An Oration* . . . (Springfield, 1839); *Globe*, 30 Cong., 1 Sess., Senate, 157; *Annals*, 18 Cong., 1 Sess., House, 1016; *Register*, 19 Cong., 1 Sess., House, 1002, 1552; A. H. Everett, *An Address* . . . (Boston, 1836); James C. Cross, *An Oration* . . . (Danville, Ky., 1836), pp. 21–24; George W. Holley, *An Oration* . . . (Chicago, 1839); Theodore G. Hunt, *Oration* . . . (New Orleans, 1839); William Mason Giles, *An Oration* . . . (Natchez, 1843).

51. Robert H. Schauffler, ed., *Independence Day* (New York, 1927), pp. 203–5; William McCarty, *Songs, Odes, and Other Poems, On National Subjects* (Philadelphia, 1842), pp. 410–11, and *passim*; J. M. Peck, ed., *Dupuy's Hymns and Spiritual Songs* (Louisville, 1843), Appendix, p. 2, hereafter cited as *Dupuy's Hymns*; see also *Psalms and Hymns . . . in the Presbyterian Church* . . . (Philadelphia, 1843), pp. 574, 305–6; *Dupuy's Hymns*, Appendix, pp. 12–13; *Rippon's Watts,* pp. 406, 799–800.

52. James Haig, *An Oration* . . . (Charleston, 1820); Francis D. Quash, *An Oration* . . . (Charleston, 1820); David Ramsay, *An Address* . . . (Charleston, 1820); William Lance, *An Oration* . . . (Charleston, 1820).

53. C. J. Ingersoll, *A Discourse Concerning the Influence of America on the Mind* (Philadelphia, 1823), pp. 48, 64–67; for illustrations of the pledges and expectancies in the 1824 campaign, see *Argus of Western America*, 4 Aug. 1824; Boston *Patriot*, 23 Aug. 1823, 19 July 1824; Wilmington, Deleware, *Gazette*, 20 Aug. 1824; Kentucky *Reporter*, 7 June 1824 and 18 Aug. 1823; Mobile, Alabama *Mercantile Advertiser*, 8 Jan. 1824; and Richmond *Enquirer*, 7 Mar. 1823; Josiah Quincy, *An Oration* . . . (Boston, 1826); Solomon Lincoln, *An Oration* . . . (Hingham, 1835); George Robertson, *A Biographical Sketch of the Hon. John Boyle* (Frankfort, Ky., 1838), pp. 3–4; Orestes Brownson, *An Oration* . . . (Boston, 1840); Silas Mix, *An Oration* . . . (New Haven, 1830); James H. Wilder, *An Oration* . . . (Higham, 1832); John Addison, *An Oration* . . . (Baltimore, 1838); Silas Wright, *Address . . . 1839, At Canton, N.Y.* (n.p., n.d.).

54. A. B. Brown, *Address* . . . (Pittsburgh, 1842); Charles B. Boynton, *Oration* . . . (Cincinnati, 1847), pp. 8–24; *The New Englander*, I (Oct. 1843), 495; IV (July 1846), 381–84; V (Oct. 1847), 605, 612; see also William P. Lunt, *A Discourse* . . . (Boston, 1848), pp. 36, 42, 43–44.

55. *American Watchman*, 20 Feb., 26 May, 3 July, 8 Sept. 1819; 19 Apr. 1820; David Damon, *A Sermon . . . at the Annual Election, January 6, 1841* (Boston, 1841), pp. 18–20, 40–42, 48–49; for representative letters of "confession," see *Jackson Corr.*, III, 201; *Otis*, II, 303; Cooper, *Corr.*, 268–69; Clay, III, 848, Colton, *Clay Corr.*, p. 579; for hymns, see *Psalms and Hymns . . . in the Presbyterian Church . . .* (Philadelphia, 1843), pp. 398–99, 379, 382; Absolom Graves, *Hymns, Psalms, and Spiritual Songs* (Frankfort, Ky., 1825), pp. 252–53.

56. *DeBow's Commercial Review*, I (May 1846), 463–64; IV (July–Aug. 1847), 122; *American Literary Magazine*, I (July 1847), 48–53; II (Jan. 1848), 53–54.

CHAPTER THREE

1. Elias Peissner, *The American Question in Its National Aspect* (New York, 1861), p. 134; Miller, *Life of the Mind*, pp. 88 ff.; Henry Steele Commager, *The Search for a Usable Past* (New York, 1967), p. 284; students of this period must be grateful to the work of Professors David Donald and John Higham. Professor Donald's *Lincoln Reconsidered* (New York, 1966), esp. pp. 215–30, helps in understanding the mind of America on the eve of the Civil War. My conclusions are in part the reverse of Professor Donald's, who finds the American people eager to throw off precedent, to rebel from authority, and suffering from an excess of liberty. Professor Higham accepts the traditional notion of an overwhelming American optimism and confidence in its institutions. See John Higham, *Strangers in the Land* (New Brunswick, 1955), pp. 3–25.

2. Thomas Starr King, *Patriotism, and Other Papers* (Boston, 1864), pp. 32–54; Timothy Bigelow, *An Oration . . .* (Boston, 1853), pp. 12–80.

3. Barbara M. Cross, *Horace Bushnell: Minister to a Changing America* (Chicago, 1958), pp. 136–37, hereafter cited as Cross, *Bushnell*; Bodo, *Protestant Clergy*, p. 190; Bushnell's address is in Brainerd, *New England Society Orations*, II, 83–120; the society heard similar sentiments in 1852 and 1853 from William Adams and Mark Hopkins, both of whom stressed the importance of religion as the key to the process which was history, and thus to the importance of man's conformity to Divine Law, see *New England Society*, 165–231; typical expressions of this view of the Trust are in Hiram Ketchum, *An Oration . . .* (New Haven, 1851); Richard T. Merrich, *Oration . . .* (Baltimore, 1852); John Hull, *The Anniversary Oration . . .* (Trenton, 1859); George F. Gordon, *Oration . . .* (Philadelphia, 1858).

4. Henry W. Longfellow, *The Complete Poetical Works of Henry Wadsworth Longfellow* (Boston, 1893), p. 103; Charles Sumner, *Charles Sumner, His Complete Works*, III (Boston, 1900), 164, hereafter cited as *Sumner*; John Bassett Moore, ed., *The Works of James Buchanan*, VIII (Philadelphia, 1909), 390, hereafter cited as *Buchanan*; Samuel Gilman Brown, ed., *The Works of Rufus Choate*, II (Boston, 1862), 313–18, 326, hereafter cited as *Choate*;

George T. Curtis, *History of the Origin, Formation, and Adoption of the Constitution of the United States,* I (New York, 1854), 488; William H. Ryder, ed., *Our Country* (Boston, 1854), pp. 59, 128, 131; *Globe,* 35 Cong., 1 Sess., House, 260, 1339; Samuel L. Caldwell, *Oration* . . . (Providence, 1861).

5. Edward Everett, *Remarks* . . . (Boston, 1853); *Globe,* 34 Cong., 1 Sess., Appendix, Senate, 763, 2 July 1856; *Globe,* 36 Cong., 1 Sess., House, 1042–43, 7 Mar. 1860; Elias Peissner, *American Question,* p. 61; *Globe,* 37 Cong., 1 Sess., Appendix, House, 715, 5 June 1850; Bancroft wrote to Evert Duyckinck, 26 May 1855, and is quoted in Arthur A. Ekirch, *The Idea of Progress in America, 1815–1860* (New York, 1944), p. 263; *Alcott Journals,* pp. 280–81; Charles P. James, *Oration* . . . (Cincinnati, 1853); the Trinity College address was by Benjamin Apthorp Gould, Jr., on 15 July 1856, and was published in *The American Journal of Education,* edited by Henry Barnard, II (Sept. 1856), 265–93, see esp. 280–81, journal hereafter cited as *Barnard.*

6. *Alcott Journals,* p. 371, 15 Apr. 1865 entry; T. Sandford Doolittle, *A Sermon* . . . *on the National Thanksgiving Day, December 7, 1865* (Schenectady, 1866), esp. pp. 6, 16 ff., 21–22.

7. John Pierce, *Requisites to Our Country's Glory* (Boston, 1849); J. G. McClellan, *An Oration* . . . (Moundville, 1850); King, *Patriotism,* pp. 42–43; Anson Burlingame, *Oration* . . . (Salem, 1854); Edward Hartley, *An Oration Delivered Before the Irving Lyceum* . . . (Washington, 1855); *United States Magazine,* II (Mar. 1856), 305–6.

8. *Eighty-second Anniversary of American Independence* . . . (Boston, 1858), pp. 57–74; *New Hampshire Patriot,* 30 Nov. 1859; Selim H. Peabody, ed., *American Patriotism* . . . (New York, 1880), has Daniel Dickinson's Amherst College address, 11 June 1861, pp. 520–41, hereafter cited as Peabody, *Patriotism;* see Louis Snyder, ed., *Dynamics of Nationalism* (Princeton, 1964), for two speeches by Carl Schurz given in 1859 and 1864, pp. 268–70; Edward Everett, *The Great Issues* . . . *Before the Country* (New York, 1861), pp. 5–12, 42; J. Howard Pugh, *An Oration* . . . (Philadelphia, 1862).

9. Edward D. Mansfield, *The Political Grammar of the United States* (Cincinnati, 1848), pp. 231–33; *Globe,* 30 Cong., 2 Sess., Appendix, House, 106–7; William W. Greenough, *An Oration* . . . (Boston, 1849); Woodbury, I, 592–93; Mosier, *McDuffy Fourth Reader,* edition published in Cincinnati in 1853, p. 34; *Globe,* 33 Cong., 1 Sess., Appendix, House, 701.

10. Wendell Phillips, *Speeches, Lectures, and Letters* (Boston, 1863), pp. 375–76; from *Bibliotheca Sacra,* XIII, as quoted in Smith and Jamison, I, 201; Henry Reed, *Two Lectures on the History of the American Union* (Philadelphia, 1856), esp. pp. 3–12, 31–42, 65–68; Caleb Cushing, *Oration* . . . (New York, 1858); Edward Everett, *Orations,* IV (Boston, 1872), 237–38, 246; Edwin H. Tenney, *Oration* . . . (Rome, n.d.), p. 25; Joseph P. Bradley, *Progress— Its Grounds and Possibilities* (New Brunswick, 1849), pp. 14–15; Weinberg,

pp. 190–92; William Gilpin, *The Central Gold Region* (Philadelphia, 1860), pp. 18–22, 84, 133–34, 167, 194; a useful reflection of Gilpin's insistence on a physical inevitability about nationality is in Charles J. Ingersoll, *Recollections* (Philadelphia, 1861), pp. 19–21, 49, 55, 259, 394–95.

11. Caleb Cushing, *An Address . . .* (Newburyport, 1850), p. 10; for Sumner's observations, see letters reprinted in Henry James, *William Wetmore Story and His Friends,* II (Boston, 1903), 157, 158; Byron Sunderland, *An Oration . . .* (Syracuse, 1852), pp. 7–8; for helpful comments on the tendency to ally the organic and Augustan views, see Spencer, *Quest for Nationality,* pp. 162 ff. and 195 ff.; Harry H. Clark, "Nationalism in American Literature," *University of Toronto Quarterly,* II (July 1933), 509–16.

12. King, *Patriotism,* pp. 49–52; Thomas Starr King, *Oration Delivered Before the Municipal Authorities of the City of Boston . . . July 5, 1852* (Boston, 1892); *Globe,* 31 Cong., 2 Sess., Appendix, House, 256; Robert G. Gunderson, *Old Gentlemen's Convention* (Madison, 1961), pp. 46, 101; David A. Bokee, *Oration . . .* (Brooklyn, 1851); Brainerd, *New England Soc. Orations,* II, 137–62; Jerome B. Kimball, *An Oration . . .* (Providence, 1856); Thomas M. Clark, *Oration . . .* (Providence, 1860); E. H. Chapin, *An Oration Delivered in the New York Chrystal Palace* (Boston, 1854); Dr. Robert T. Hallock, *The Child and the Man . . .* (New York, 1856), pp. 6 ff.; *New Englander,* XIV (Nov. 1856), 527–42; Howard C. Perkins, ed., *Northern Editorials on Secession,* II (New York, 1942), 112.

13. For an excellent discussion, see William A. Clebsch, "Christian Interpretations of the Civil War," *Church History,* XXX (June 1961), 212–22; Morse, II, 414–15; Perry, *Lieber,* pp. 320, 340; *Parkman Letters,* I, 142–43, in *Boston Daily Advertiser,* 4 Sept. 1861; Oliver Wendell Holmes, *Oration . . .* (Boston, 1863), pp. 11–12, 30, 46–47, 63–64; George Barstow, *War, The Only Means of Preserving Our Nationality* (San Francisco, 1864), p. 11; Frederick Bancroft, ed., *Speeches, Correspondence and Political Papers of Carl Schurz,* I (New York, 1913), 225–30, speech at Brooklyn Academy of Music, 7 Oct. 1864, hereafter cited as *Schurz.*

14. Henry W. Bellows, *Unconditional Loyalty* (New York, 1863), pp. 15–16; *Proceedings at the Organization of the Loyal National League at the Cooper Institute, Friday Evening, March 20, 1863* (New York, 1863), pp. 3, 16; Buchanan, VIII, 403; *Globe,* 41 Cong., 1 Sess., Appendix, House, 1211–12; Brainerd, *New Eng. Soc. Orations,* II, 237–66, esp. 258, 264, 329–69; *New Englander,* XVII (May 1859), "Unchastity," 469–88; Rollo Ogden, ed., *Life and Letters of Edwin Lawrence Godkin,* I (New York, 1907), 173–76, 184–85, hereafter cited as *Godkin;* Perry, *Lieber,* 314–15; Walter Clark, *The State of the Country* (Buffalo, 1862), pp. 11 ff.; *Schurz,* I, 252.

15. Constance M. Rourke, *Trumpets of Jubilee* (New York, 1927), p. 413, hereafter cited as *Rourke;* Charles Eliot Norton, *Considerations on Some Recent Social Theories* (Boston, 1853), pp. 38, 44, 130–31; *Phi Beta Kappa*

Orations, II, 135–36, F. A. P. Barnard at the University of Alabama, 11 July 1854; *Journal of Education*, II (Aug–Sept. 1856), 139–47, 218–24; *Fourth of July in Boston, 1858*, pp. 13–14; *Leslies' Magazine*, II (14 Aug. and 6 Nov. 1858), 169, 360; F. O. Matthiessen, *The James Family* (New York, 1948), pp. 59–66.

16. *Globe*, 31 Cong., 1 Sess., Senate, 183–84; *United States Magazine*, I (1854), 86; Thomas K. King, *An Oration . . .* (Providence, 1854), pp. 26–29; George Washington Doane, *The Address at Burlington College, July 4, 1855* (Philadelphia, 1855); *Globe*, 34 Cong., 1 Sess., House, 37; E. D. MacMaster, *The True Life of a Nation* (New Albany, Ohio, 1856); *Parkman Letters*, I, 145–46, 163, letters to the *Boston Daily Advertiser*, 8 Jan. 1862 and 4 July 1863; John Bigelow, *The Writings and Speeches of Samuel J. Tilden*, I (New York, 1885), 337, hereafter cited as *Tilden*; *Alcott Journals*, p. 372, 4 July 1865.

17. Charles Eliot Norton, *Orations and Addresses of George William Curtis*, I (New York, 1894), 9–10, 40–59, 98–122, 125–48, hereafter cited as *Curtis*; Basler, *Lincoln*, VII, 412 for Curtis' letter of notification.

18. For passages illustrating these thoughts of Taylor, Fillmore, Pierce, and Buchanan, see Richardson, VI, 2542–44, 2547, 2614, 2701, 2715–16, 2717–18, 2730–31, 2732–33, 2734–36, 2750, 2825–26, 2883, 2950; VII, 3084, 3104, 3119, 3135, 3145, 3167–68.

19. Basler, *Lincoln*, IV, 264, 266, 270–71; Richardson, VII, 3229–31; Basler, *Lincoln*, IV, 426; Richardson, VII, 3237, 3334–36, 3343, 3365–66, 3371, 3373–74, 3383, 3392, 3405–6; Basler, *Lincoln*, VII, 512; VIII, 100–101; Richardson, VII, 3429–30, 3477–78. Helpful insights about Lincoln and nationality are in David Potter, *The South and Sectional Conflict*, p. 176; Sydney E. Ahlstrom, "History, Bushnell, and Lincoln," *Church History*, XXX (June 1961), 223–30; William J. Wolf, *The Almost Chosen People* (Garden City, N.Y., 1959), esp. pp. 163, 183–84, 189.

20. Webster's papers are filled with his obvious concern for nurturing a proper nationality. Some of the most revealing and important are found in: *Webster*, X, 57 ff., 93–98; XII, 221; X, 116–17; IV, 298, 308 ff.; X, 161, 167–70; XII, 249–50, 154–55; IV, 224–26; XVI, 586; XIII, 401–4, 406–7; IV, 267, 270, 281, 287; XII, 272–73; XIII, 444, 449, 466, 468, 487, 492–93, 498–99, 535; Van Tyne, pp. 406–7, 477–78; Choate's eulogy is in *Choate*, I, 555–56.

21. For some of Clay's representative statements, see Colton, *Clay*, VI, 418, 477, 513, 561, 563–64, 631. Douglas spoke about Clay at Cincinnati, 9 Sept. 1859, see Harry V. Jaffa and Robert W. Johannsen, eds., *In the Name of the People* (Columbus, 1959), p. 168.

22. Strong, *Diary*, II, 1, 26–27, 275, 348, 480; III, 93, 142–43, 162–63, 211, 271–72, 482–83.

23. Seward, III, 293; I, 58, 156; III, 105; IV, 99, 123, 334; *Globe*, 36 Cong., 2 Sess., Senate, 341–44.

24. *Emerson Journals*, VIII, 185–87, 203; *Emerson Letters*, IV, 461–62, 479, 501–2; V, 67, 249, 253; *Emerson Journals*, X, 82; *Emerson Letters*, V, 395–96. Some useful observations on Emerson's attitude toward the progress of nations and national character, are in Philip L. Nicoloff, *Emerson on Race and History* (New York, 1961), pp. 118–19, 128–30, 135, 155–57, 174, 236, 241.

25. Lowell's expressions are numerous and widely distributed. See esp. *North American Review*, LXIX (July 1849), 196–209; Lowell *Letters*, I, 261–62, 275; James Russell Lowell, *Political Essays* (New York, 1904, and VI of *Collected Works*), p. 12, hereafter cited as Lowell, *Essays*; Lowell, *Letters*, I, 296, 308–9; Lowell, *Essays*, pp. 58, 61–65, 80–81, 109–12, 116–17, 161, 182–85, 220–25, 260–66, 278–79, 285–86, 289, 299–301.

26. Many of Beecher's assertions are in Henry Ward Beecher, *Patriotic Addresses* (Boston, 1887), esp. pp. 217–23, 228–44, 248–66, 288–303, 334–41, 344–46, 384–97, 673–75, 687–89. For Beecher's speeches in England where he attempted to persuade often angry audiences that America fought for the universal advance of every man's liberty and progress, see *Patriotic Addresses*, pp. 451 ff., 518 ff., 570–71, 635.

27. Basler, *Lincoln*, II, 132, 272–73, 276, 318, 323, 364, 499–500; III, 95, 276, 311–12, 315, 375–76, 380, 435; IV, 169, 221, 226, 241–42. For Douglas' observations, see *Lincoln*, III, 9, 12, 54–55, 115–16, 224.

28. For illustrative passages, see *The United States Magazine and Democratic Review*, XXIV (Jan. 1849), 3; (Feb. 1849), 151–61; (Mar. 1849), 219–24, 257–58; XXV (July 1849), 5, 27; (Sept. 1849), 193–94, 506; XXVI (Jan. 1850), 44–49; (Feb. 1850), 156–57; XXVIII (Apr. 1851), 289–98; (June 1851), 500–511; XXIX (Sept. 1851), 257; XXX (Jan. 1852), 1–12; (Feb. 1852), 205–15; (Apr. 1852), 289–306, 375; (May 1852), 401, 423–24; (June 1852), 554–69; XXXI (July 1852), 33–43, 86–87, 96.

29. *Whig* began a new series in 1848, but the citations which follow use the continuous volume numbering. See *The American Review: A Whig Journal*, VII (Jan. 1848), 28–46; IX (Feb. 1849), 111–20; (Apr. 1849), 331–38, 399–406; X (Sept. 1849), 285–95; XI (Apr. 1850), 340–46; (May 1850), 523–28; (June 1850), 556–70; XIII (Jan. 1851), 60; (Feb. 1851), 149–56; (Mar. 1851), 210–12, 251–67; (Apr. 1851), 289–301; XIV (Sept. 1851), 187–93; (Nov. 1851), 359–67; XV (Feb. 1852), 1–10, 135, 176; XVI (Aug. 1852), 180; (Oct. 1852), 337–38.

30. *The Knickerbocker, New York Monthly Magazine*, XXXVI (Oct. 1850), 326–28, XLV (Feb. 1855), 148–50; LVIII (July 1861), 48–52, 65–69; (Oct.–Dec. 1861), 283–87, 377–83, 471–75; LX (Oct. 1862), 329–30; (Nov.–Dec. 1862), 436–41, 447–54, 511–17, 526–30; LXII (Nov. 1863), 408–14; LXIII (Jan. 1864), 1–6; (June 1864), 481–89; LXIV (July 1864), 102, 188; LXV (Jan. 1865), 10–11.

31. *The Merchants Magazine and Commercial Review*, XXI (Aug. 1849), 194–99; XXIV (June 1851), 689; XXVII (Sept. 1852), 275–88; (Nov. 1852), 579; XXVIII (Jan. 1853), 19–40; XXXV (Oct. 1856), 415–27; XXXVI (Feb. 1857), 198–202; (Mar. 1857), 316–17; XXXVIII (Apr. 1858), 403–6; XXXIX (Sept. 1858), 397; LI (Sept. 1864), 177–83; LII (Jan. 1865), 22–38.

32. *Ladies' Repository*, X (Mar. 1850), 85–92; XV (Dec. 1855), 715–16; XVI (Dec. 1856), 743–49; XVII (Feb. 1857), 97–102; (June 1857), 337–39; (July 1857), 420–23; XX (Oct. 1860), 588–92; XXII (Mar. 1862), 171–76; (Dec. 1862), 724; XXV (Apr. 1865), 220–21.

33. *The Country Gentleman*, I (6 Jan. 1853), 1; (20 Jan. 1853), 40; (12 May 1853), 296; (16 June 1853), 376; II (8 Sept. 1853), 156; IV (6 July 1854), 12–13; V (4 Jan. 1855), 12–13; VI (6 Sept. 1855), 160–61.

34. *North American Review*, LXVIII (Jan. 1849), 98–99; LXX (Apr. 1850), 421, 474–75; LXXI (July 1850), 267; LXXIII (July 1851), 35–43; LXXIV (Jan. 1852), 198–200; LXXXI (July 1855), 28–30; (Oct. 1855), 323–24; LXXXIV (Apr. 1857), 344–62; LXXXVIII (Jan. 1859), 52; LXXXIX (July 1859), 109–11; (Oct. 1859), 288–89, 301–2; XCI (Oct. 1860), 507–8; XCIV (Jan. 1862), 155–56; (Apr. 1862), 432; XCV (July 1862), 83–87; (Oct. 1862), 417; XCVIII (Jan. 1864), 105–7, 127; XCIX (July 1864), 117–19, 173–74; C (Jan. 1865), 328–29; (Apr. 1865), 331–34.

35. *Harper's Magazine*, XXII (Jan. 1861), 261–66; X (Jan. 1855), 259–63; XII (Mar. 1856), 554–58; (May 1856), 839–44; XIV (Jan. 1857), 207; (Feb. 1857), 409–14; (May 1857), 845; XV (June 1857), 121–25; (Oct. 1857), 692–98; XVI (Mar. 1858), 551–55; XVII (Oct. 1858), 694–700; XVIII (Dec. 1858), 119–24; XIX (Aug. 1859), 405–10; XX (Jan. 1860), 263–67; XXI (June 1860), 119–24; (July 1860), 262–66; XXII (Dec. 1860), 117–21; XXIII (Oct. 1861), 554; XXIV (Dec. 1861), 89; XXV (July 1862), 265–70; XXVI (Jan. 1863), 273–77; (Feb. 1863), 413–18; (May 1863), 809–16; XXX (Mar. 1865), 475–81.

36. *Harper's Weekly*, I, 1, 33, 81, 129, 177, 712–13; II, 98, 148, 384; III, 82, 163, 194; IV, 258, 306, 338; V, 258, 450, 482, 642; VI, 2, 130–31, 242, 318; VIII, 738.

37. *The Atlantic Monthly*, I (Dec. 1857), 239–49; (Apr. 1858), 755–60; II (Aug. 1858), 374–82; (Oct. 1858), 513–31; (Nov. 1858), 763; VII (Apr. 1861), 451–65; (May 1861), 613; VIII (July 1861), 89–90; (Oct. 1861), 506; XIII (Apr. 1864), 509; (June 1864), 763; XIV (Dec. 1864), 769–73.

38. For a good assortment of the lingering "Young America" outlook, see George Francis Train, *Spread-Eagleism* (New York, 1859), where on pp. xiii–xiv the author says, "Young America's platform is in a word—First—The eternal Union of the States. Second—Everlasting peace and friendship with England. Third—Free trade in commerce, finance, and literature. Fourth—The moral growth of spread-eagleism, which is only a modern word for the

Monroe doctrine." John P. Sanderson, *Oration* . . . (Jacksonville, 1856); Mildred Howells, ed., *Life in Letters of William Dean Howells*, I (Garden City, N.Y., 1928), 47, 58, hereafter cited as Howells, *Letters*; William B. Bradbury, *The Devotional Hymn and Tune Book for Social and Public Worship* (Philadelphia, 1864), p. 58; *The Psalmody* (Dover, N.H., 1853), p. 505; Bryant, *Poetry*, II, 94–95, 96–98.

39. Arthur McArthur, *Oration* . . . (Springfield, Mass., 1849); William M. Scott, *An Address Delivered at a Barbacue . . . at Danville, July 4th 1851* (Philadelphia, 1851); James Sheldon, *An Oration* . . . (Buffalo, 1852); Alonzo Ames Minor, *An Oration* . . . (Boston, 1855); *The Commercial Review*, XIV (May 1853), 461–70; XVII (Aug. 1854), 111–29; Malcolm Cowley, ed., *The Complete Poetry and Prose of Walt Whitman*, II (New York, 1948), 269–70, 280, hereafter cited as Cowley, *Whitman*. For useful comments, see Gene Bluestein, "The Advantages of Barbarism: Herder and Whitman's Nationalism," *Journal of The History of Ideas*, XXIV (Jan.–Mar. 1963), 115–26; and Edward K. Brown, "The National Idea in American Criticism," *Dalhousie Review*, XIV (July 1934), 133–47.

40. Isaiah Rynders, *Oration* . . . (New York, 1851); Isaac N. Shannon, *Divine Providence in American History and Politics* (New Brunswick, 1852), pp. 9–23; Rev. Andrew Leete Stone, *An Oration* . . . (Boston, 1854); *DeBow*, XVIII (June 1855), 741–44; Philip Schaff, *America* (New York, 1855; Belknap edition, Cambridge, 1961, ed. by Perry Miller), pp. 6–9, 16–20, 29–30, 37–38, 47, 52–53, 71.

41. Miss Peabody's essay appeared in the forerunner to Henry Barnard's great journal. See *American Journal of Education and College Review*, I (Mar. 1856), 269–78; (June 1856), 523–44; John Henry Hopkins, *The American Citizen: His Rights and Duties* (New York, 1857), pp. 19 ff., 65 ff., 76 ff., 179–80, 187–89, 443–44, 455–56, 457–59; Jefferson P. Safford, *A Discourse, Reverence for Law* . . . (Piqua, 1858); *Schurz*, I, 48–72.

42. Very helpful is Frank Freidel's two-volume edition, *Union Pamphlets of the Civil War* (Cambridge, Mass., 1967), and esp. I, 102–3, 135–39, 295–320, 381–403, 503–11, 551–64; II, 570, 581–82, 618–19, 697–738, 873–901; Benjamin F. Butler, *Character and Results of the War* (New York, n.d. [1863]), esp. p. 16; William Adams, *Christian Patriotism* (New York, 1863); John Greenleaf Adams, *Our Country and Its Claims Upon Us* (Providence, 1863) .

43. An excellent insight into this part of national feeling is in the collection of funeral sermons and orations, *Our Martyr President* (New York, 1865), esp. pp. 45–46, 55–60, 66–67, 73, 107–8, 205, 240, 359–81, 416–17, 419–20.

44. Worthington C. Ford, ed., *Letters of Henry Adams*, I (Boston, 1930), 12, 53; Perry, *Lieber*, pp. 315–16; David J. Baker to Lyman Trumbull, 22 Dec. 1860, Trumbull Manuscripts, Library of Congress, Vol. 27; Charles E. Fitch, *An Oration* . . . (Syracuse, 1861); David Magie, *Public Thanksgiving, A*

Sermon (New York, 1861); James W. Wall, *Address* . . . (Newark, 1863); *Wilkes' Spirit of the Times* (New York), VII (11 Oct. 1862), 88–89; The 1863 "Hymn" is in Robert H. Schauffler, ed., *Independence Day* (New York, 1927), p. 215; William B. Bradbury, *The Devotional Hymn and Tune Book* (Philadelphia, 1864), 95, 169. For an interesting analysis of some response to the Civil War, see George M. Frederickson, *The Inner Civil War* (New York, 1965).

CHAPTER FOUR

1. Two splendid studies marred by a view of the era following 1865 as one of complacency and given to recalling the antebellum period with admiration are Richard Hofstadter, *The Age of Reform* (New York, 1955), p. 60, and Wishy, *Child and the Republic*, p. 81; M. Russell Thayer, *An Address* . . . (Philadelphia, 1865), pp. 16–17; Ticknor, II, 485; P. T. Washburn, *An Oration Before the Re-Union Society of Vermont Officers 22 October 1868* (Montpelier, 1869).

2. Helpful comments on Lincoln are in Lloyd Lewis, *Myths After Lincoln* (New York, 1929), esp. pp. 402–3; hints about the intensification of old beliefs are in Barbara Miller Solomon, *Ancestors and Immigrants* (Cambridge, Mass., 1956), p. 13; other comments on the Civil War's general ideological impact are in Curti, *Roots*, pp. 151–72; and Spencer, *Quest*, pp. 316 ff. One of the best general interpretations of the agony of the American spirit during the late nineteenth century is in Rourke, *Trumpets of Jubilee*, pp. 429–32.

3. Ford, *Letters of Henry Adams*, I, 119–20; Perry, *Lieber*, p. 373; Henry A. Castle, *The Problem of American Destiny* (St. Paul, 1868); Miller, *Life of the Mind*, p. 94; there is much valuable insight in Sidney E. Mead, "American Protestantism Since the Civil War. I. From Denominationalism to Americanism," *The Journal of Religion*, XXXVI, No. 1 (Jan. 1956), 1–16. These views generally challenge John Higham's contention in *Strangers in the Land* that religious forces were weaker in American culture after the Civil War, p. 28.

4. Russel B. Nye, *George Bancroft: Brahmin Rebel* (New York, 1945), pp. 231–32, 286–90; Henry W. Adams, *An Oration* . . . (New York, 1865), pp. 8–9, 39, 44; J. Lewis Diman, *An Oration* . . . (Providence, 1866), pp. 5–8; Samuel K. Lathrop, *Oration* (Boston, 1866), pp. 21–32, 35–38, 60; *New Englander*, XXX (Apr. 1871), 175–202; instances of how divine or providential purpose was saluted by 1876 expressions are in Frederick M. Saunders, ed., *Addresses . . . Delivered in the Several States of the Union, July 4th, 1876–1883* (New York, 1893), pp. 422 ff., 433 ff., 466–67, 560–67, 610 ff., 650 ff., 695 ff., 782–84, 807–8, 815–23, 862–63, hereafter cited as Saunders, *Addresses, 1876; Celebration at Tammany Hall . . . July 4th 1866* (New York, 1866); Joseph M. Bailey, *Oration* . . . (Freeport, Ill., 1867), pp. 7–11; C. C. Norse, *Iowa and the Centennial* (Des Moines, 1876), pp. 29, 41–42; Saunders, *Addresses, 1876*, pp. 45–57, 654 ff.

5. See the commentary in Rush Welter, *Popular Education and Democratic Thought in America* (New York, 1962), pp. 239 ff.; James A. Garfield, *Oration*

. . . *Delivered at Arlington, Va., May 30, 1868* . . . (Cleveland, 1868), pp. 4–5; Joseph Leeds, *One Hundredth Anniversary of the Declaration of Independence* (Philadelphia, 1872), pp. 4, 14; Richard Frothingham, *Oration Delivered . . . in Music Hall, July 4, 1874* (Boston, 1874); Samuel A. Green, *An Historical Address* (Groton, Mass., 1876), pp. 7, 50–51; Charles H. Fiske, *Oration* . . . (Weston, 1876), pp. 37–38; Barbara M. Solomon, *Ancestors and Immigrants*, is very helpful here, esp. pp. vii–viii and 1–42; I cannot agree with B. T. Spencer that America's outlook in the years after 1865 was characterized by a sureness of direction, Spencer, *Quest for Nationality*, p. 292; see Saunders, *Addresses, 1876*, pp. 425 ff., 487 ff., 500 ff., 543–54, 575–90, 597–608, 640–46, for typical expressions of what the past meant.

6. Margaret Denny and William H. Gilman, eds., *The American Writer and the European Tradition* (Minneapolis, 1950), has relevant observations on Whitman and Melville by Willard Thorpe, pp. 99–103; Bryant, II, 167, 240; *Merchant's Magazine*, LX (June 1869), 428; William Everett, *An Oration* . . . (Boston, 1870), pp. 12–13; Bayard Taylor, II, 613–14; Charles H. Bell, *Discourse Delivered Before the New England Historic, Genealogical Society, Boston, March 18, 1871* (Boston, 1871), pp. 16–20; Champion S. Chase, *An Oration Delivered at Brownville, Nebraska, July 4th, 1872* (n.p., n.d.); Isaac S. Catlin, *Address . . . in Brooklyn, N.Y., July 3, 1876* (n.p., n.d.), pp. 4, 14; Saunders, *Addresses, 1876*, p. 591; Alexander W. Bradford, *An Oration* . . . (New York, 1866), pp. 6, 15, 42; *Lippincott's Magazine*, XVII and XVIII (1876), esp. XVII, 9–21.

7. For helpful general discussions, see Sanford, *Quest*, pp. 207–8; Spencer, *Quest for Nationality*, pp. 294–96; Arthur A. Ekirch, *The Decline of American Liberalism* (New York, 1955), pp. 116 ff., 130; Leon Howard, *Literature and the American Tradition* (Garden City, N.Y., 1960), pp. 170, 195–96, 206–7, 217; Solomon, *Ancestors and Immigrants*, pp. 67–68, 179–82, 191–93; *Youth's Companion*, XLIII (June 1870), 174 Charles A. L. Totten, *Oration* . . . (Hartford, 1872), pp. 11–13; Saunders, *Addresses, 1876*, pp. 618, 632; William Allan Neilson, ed., *Charles W. Eliot*, I (New York, 1926), 2–51, hereafter cited as *Eliot* (this was Eliot's inaugural address at Harvard).

8. Nathaniel P. Banks, *An Address Delivered . . . at the Customhouse, New Orleans, On the Fourth of July, 1865* (n.p., n.d.); Alonzo C. Paige, *Address Before the Common Council and Citizens of the City of Schenectady, July 4, 1865* (Albany, 1865), pp. 48–55; James T. Robinson, *National Anniversary Address* (North Adams, 1865); *Merchant's Magazine*, LIV (Jan. 1866), 52; Marius C. C. Church, *The American Republic* (Parkersburg, 1867), pp. 19, 31; Francis Lieber, *Fragments of Political Science on Nationalism and Inter-Nationalism* (New York, 1868), pp. 5–8, 13–23; David Gilman, ed., *The Miscellaneous Writings of Francis Lieber*, II (Philadelphia, 1880), 228, 233, 238; Charles Sumner, *The National Security and the National Faith* (Boston, 1865), pp. 5, 14; Beecher's remarks are in Saunders, *Addresses, 1876*, pp. 358, 370, 374; the ode is in Saunders, *Addresses, 1876*, p. 238.

9. Harry J. Brown and Frederick D. Williams, eds., *Diary of James A. Garfield*, II (East Lansing, 1967), 227–28, 29 Sept. 1873; *Alcott Journals*, pp. 387, 424; *Youth's Companion*, XLIII (12 May 1870), 149; Samuel Gilman Brown, *Oration* . . . (Claremont, N.H., 1865); *New Englander*, XXXIV (Jan. 1875), 160–74; *Phi Beta Kappa Orations*, I, 129–50; A. H. Bullock at Brown University, 15 June 1875; Indianapolis *Journal*, 15 Feb. 1876; A. H. Taisey, ed., *The Grand Centennial Parade at Philadelphia, September 20, 1876* (St. Paul, 1876), p. 35.

10. S. L. Caldwell and A. J. Gordon, *The Service of Song for Baptist Churches* (New York, 1871), p. 376; Saunders, *Addresses, 1876*, pp. 351, 753; Thomas N. McCarter, *Address* (Philadelphia, 1868), pp. 10–12, 30; *New Englander*, XXVIII (Jan. 1869), 19–46. For good discussions of the Anglo-Saxon cult, see Higham, pp. 32–34, Solomon, *Ancestors and Immigrants*, pp. 59–81; Curti, *Roots*, pp. 173–74.

11. *Memorial Ceremonies at the National Cemetery, Arlington, Virginia . . . 30 May 1868* (Washington, 1868), pp. 7–8; Emerson's remarks are in *New Englander*, L (Apr. 1871), 196–97; Cross, *Bushnell*, pp. 164–68; the powerfully conservative role of education in the face of the citizen's dilemma is described in Welter, pp. 141–59; Wishy, p. 137; Pierce, *Public Opinion and the Teaching of History in the United States*, pp. 13–33.

12. Wickersham's article is in Barnard's *American Journal of Education*, XVI (June 1866), 283–97; Eva Ingersoll Wakefield, *The Letters of Robert G. Ingersoll* (New York, 1951), pp. 143–44, hereafter cited as *Ingersoll Letters*; Henry Adams is quoted in Frank O. Gatell, *John Gorham Palfrey and the New England Conscience* (Cambridge, Mass., 1963), pp. 268–69; Charles F. Adams, Jr., *A Fourth of July Address* (Boston, 1869); *Phi Beta Kappa Orations*, II, 171–83; *Country Gentleman*, XXXV (15 Dec. 1870), 798; Bayard Taylor, II, 559; Horace Binney Sargent, *An Oration* . . . (Boston, 1871); Merle Curti, *The Learned Blacksmith* (New York, 1937), pp. 209–11; *Country Gentleman*, XXXVIII (3 Apr. 1873), 219–20; Strong, *Diary*, IV, 381–82, 386, 4 and 22 Sept. 1871; Clarkson N. Potter, *Address Delivered . . . at Tammany Hall* (New York, 1873), pp. 24–26; C. A. Bartol, *The War Cloud* (Boston, 1873), pp. 6–9, 12–14; Indianapolis *Journal*, 7 Feb. 1876; Boston *Post*, 2 May 1876; Newport *Mercury*, 29 July 1876; Charles Allen Sumner, *Oration* . . . (San Francisco, 1876), pp. 13–15. For illustrations of the concern over national corruption during the centennial, see esp. Saunders, *Addresses, 1876*, pp. 377 ff., 405 ff., 411–12, 471 ff., 512 ff., 567–71, 591 ff., 622 ff., 726 ff., 750 ff., 803 ff.

13. Franklin E. Felton, *An Oration Delivered at Vallejo* . . . (San Francisco, 1867), pp. 15 ff.; Mary R. Dearing, *Veterans in Politics* (Baton Rouge, 1952), pp. 165–66; Lieber, *Fragment*, p. 3; Perry, *Lieber*, pp. 389–90; E. Peck to Lyman Trumbull, 11 Nov. 1872, Trumbull Mss., Vol. 77, Library of Congress; Charles W. Eliot, *A National University* (Cambridge, 1874), pp. 9–10, 17–23; *Phi Beta Kappa Orations*, I, 165 ff., Charles K. Adams at the Univ. of Vermont,

27 June 1876; Benjamin A. Willis, *An Oration* . . . (Washington, 1876), pp. 20–21, Boston *Post*, 18 Dec. 1876.

14. For these and other insights about the developing view held by Henry James, Jr., see Leon Edel, *Henry James, The Untried Years* (New York, 1953), esp. pp. 264–66; Leon Edel, ed., *The Selected Letters of Henry James* (New York, 1955), esp. p. 37; Percy Lubbock, ed., *The Letters of Henry James,* I (New York, 1920), esp. 22–23, 30–31, 37; F. O. Matthiessen, *The James Family* (New York, 1948), pp. 289–91; Howells, *Letters,* I, 176.

15. Richardson, VIII, 3530, 3567–68, 3676–77, 3681, 3706–7, 3732–33, 3742–43, 3756–57, 3759–60, 3764, 3765–67, 3875–87.

16. Richardson, VIII, 3961–62, 4015–16; IX, 4050, 4074, 4158–59, 4175–76, 4286–88, 4310, 4345, 4346, 4351, 4353–54, 4364.

17. Henry Ward Beecher, *The Life of Christ Within and Without* (New York, 1906), pp. 50–55; Beecher, *Patriotism,* pp. 756–57, 769–71, 772–83, 787–88; Tilden, I, 411–12, 423, 448–49, 451–52, 484; II, 227, 358.

18. *Curtis,* I, 157–58, 168; III, 42, 51, 53–54, 87–121, 249; I, 246–49; *An Account of the Centennial Celebration . . . of the Town of Northfield, Richmond County, New York* (New York, 1876), Curtis oration is printed on pp. 18–23.

19. *Schurz,* I, 413–14, 416, 418–72; II, 56, 71–122, 122–76, 301, 355, 359; III, 4–5, 17, 62, 74–78, 151–53, 155, 219, 227, 229, 240–48, 296–98, 302, 337; *Atlantic,* XIX (Mar. 1867), 375.

20. Cowley, *Whitman,* II, 208–59; 282–91.

21. Lowell, *Essays,* pp. 326, 331–38, 368, 398; Lowell, *Letters,* I, 359–60, 361; *Atlantic,* XX (Nov. 1867), 618–32; Lowell, *Letters,* II, 93, 173; M. A. DeWolfe Howe, ed., *New Letters of James Russell Lowell* (New York, 1932), p. 220, hereafter cited as Lowell, *New Letters.*

22. *Harper's New Monthly Magazine,* XXXIII (June 1866), 64; XXXIV (May 1867), 793–800; XL (Mar. 1870), 546–56, 578–85; XLIII (July 1871), 231–38; L (Apr. 1875), 690–701; LI (Oct. 1875), 671–86; LII (Feb. 1876), 401–20. For more of the centennial papers, see L (1874–75) 67 ff., 212 ff., 371 ff., 518 ff., 880 ff.; *Harper's Weekly,* IX (8 July 1865), 418; (2 Sept. 1865), 546; (25 Nov. 1865), 738; (30 Dec. 1865), 818; XI (13 July 1867), 434; XII (4 Jan. 1868), 2; (8 Feb. 1868), 82; XIII (13 Feb. 1869), 98; XIV (16 Apr. 1870), 242; (21 May 1870), 322; (27 Aug. 1870), 546; XV (11 Feb. 1871), 122; (6 May 1871), 402; (25 Nov. 1871), 1098; XVI (24 Feb. 1872), 155; (2 Mar. 1872), 171; XVII (12 July 1873), 594–95; XIX (24 July 1875), 594; (31 July 1875), 614; XX (15 July 1876), 575–76, 578; (11 Nov. 1876), 914; (2 Dec. 1876), 966.

23. *The Overland Monthly,* III (Aug. 1869), 148–59; (Sept. 1869), 253–57; XI (Dec. 1873), 504–8; Mrs. Cooper's astonishing article is in VII (Dec. 1871), 535–44.

24. *Galaxy,* IX (Feb. 1870), 293–94; III (15 Jan. 1867), 224–25; V (Mar. 1868), 376–81; XIV (Nov. 1872), 700–701; XIX (June 1875), 846; XX (Sept. 1875), 432–34; IV (Dec. 1867), 919–37; VI (Nov. 1868), 661–65; VII (Apr. 1869), 486–92; XXI (June 1876), 733–37; XXII (July 1876), 5–6; (Nov. 1876), 618–23.

25. *Atlantic Monthly,* XIX (Apr. 1867), 478–83; XX (Sept. 1867), 275–306; XXII (Sept. 1868), 348–58; XXV (Jan. 1870), 56–63; XXVII (Jan. 1871), 105–20; XXVIII (Sept. 1871), 316–19; XXXVI (Sept. 1875), 298–315, 338–39; XXXV (May 1875), 561–67.

26. *North American Review,* CI (Oct. 1865), 313, 334, 385, 550–51, 563–64; CV (Oct. 1867), 490, 495; CVII (July 1868), 248, 252–53, 258, 266; CVIII (Apr. 1869), 541, 611; CIX (Oct. 1869), 443, 474–75; CX (Apr. 1870), 418–19; CXI (July 1870), 27–28; CXII (Jan. 1871), 82–83; CXIV (Jan. 1872), 87; CXV (Oct. 1872), 366–68; CXVIII (Jan. 1874), 88; CXIX (Oct. 1874), 255–62, 280–81, 284–85, 286, 307; CXX (Jan. 1875), 83; CXXI (July 1875), 1–36; CXXII (Jan. 1876) is the centennial issue, see esp. 46, 79–88, 119, 147–55, 196, 227; CXXIII (Oct. 1876), 326–27, 332, and 361 for gist of Adams and Lodge statement.

27. *Scribner's Monthly,* I (Nov. 1870), 106–7; (Dec. 1870), 212; (Mar. 1871), 562; II (Oct. 1871), 654–55; III (Nov. 1871), 111, (Dec. 1871), 234–35; IV (May 1872), 97, 106–7; (Sept. 1872), 627–28; VI (July 1873), 364–65; VII (Jan. 1874), 294–301; VIII (May 1874), 112–13; X (Aug. 1875), 381; (Sept. 1875), 509–10; XI (Nov. 1875), 123, 126–27; (Jan. 1876), 432–33; XII (July 1876), 360, 429.

28. *Hearth and Home,* I (27 Mar. 1869), 210; (10 Apr. 1869), 248; (9 Oct. 1869), 664; (13 Nov. 1869), 744; III (29 Apr. 1871), 322; (30 Sept. 1871), 762; (30 Dec. 1871), 1023; V (18 Jan. 1873), 34; (1 Feb. 1873), 67; (29 Mar. 1873), 194; (7 June 1873), 358; (5 July 1873), 423; (26 July 1873), 470–71; (8 Aug. 1873), 502; (23 Aug. 1873), 535; (27 Sept. 1873), 614; (4 Oct. 1873), 630; (6 Dec. 1873), 774; VI (21 Mar. 1874), 164–65; (6 June 1874), 360; (4 July 1874), 22; (8 Aug. 1874), 122; (29 Aug. 1874), 202; (28 Nov. 1874), 450.

29. *Ladies Repository,* XXV (July 1865), 391–94; (Sept. 1865), 559–60; XXVII (Mar. 1867), 164–69; XXVIII (Jan. 1868), 23–24; XXIX (July 1868), 10–14; XXX (Feb. 1870), 139–43; (Mar. 1870), 215–21; XXXI (May 1871), 321–25; XXXV (June 1876), 519–23; XXXVI (Dec. 1876), 522–33.

30. J. Howard Pugh, *Success and Promise of the American Union* (Philadelphia, 1865), pp. 16–22; Henry Winter Davis, *Oration* . . . (Chicago, 1865), pp. 14–15; Seymour L. Stebbins, *Oration* . . . (New York, 1865); Nathaniel Smith, *An Oration* . . . (Waterbury, 1865); Albert Webb Bishop, *An Oration Delivered at Fayetteville, Arkansas* (New York, 1865); *Nation,* I (13 July 1865), 38–39; Conrad Baker, *Address Delivered at Knightstown, Indiana, July 4th*

1867 (n.p., n.d.), p .7; *A Collection of Hymns* (Nashville, 1866), pp. 599–600; *Dedication of the Soldier's Monument at Worcester, Massachusetts, July 15, A.D., 1874* (Worcester, 1875), pp. 8–9; Marie Taylor-Hensen and Horace E. Scudder, eds., *Life and Letters of Bayard Taylor*, II (Boston and New York, 1884), 671; William P. Moore, *Centennial National Songs and Anthems* (Gabanna, Ohio, 1876), pp. 5–6, hereafter cited as *Centennial Songs; North American* (Philadelphia, see esp. issues of 1876: 12 Feb., 22 Feb., 24 Apr., 9 May, 10 May, 15 May, 5 July, 6 July, 7 July, 11 Aug., 14 Sept., 22 Sept., 2 Nov., 11 Nov.; Albany *Journal*, 10 June, 3 July, 5 July 1876; Indianapolis *Journal*, 1 Jan., 8 Mar., 13 May, 4 July, 1876; Saunders, *Addresses, 1876,* 59–61, 466–67; Hiram L. Richmond, *Centennial Oration* (n.p., n.d. [Meadeville, Pa., 1876]), Michael P. Nolan, *1876 Independence Day* (n.p., n.d. [Dayton, Ohio]), pp. 4–5.

31. *Nation*, I (13 July 1865), 43-44; *Phi Beta Kappa Orations*, I, 112–16, An address by Francis A. March; George Willard, *An Oration . . . at Vermontville, Michigan . . .* (Battle Creek, Mich., 1875), pp. 5–15; Allan Nevins, ed., *Selected Writings of Abram S. Hewitt* (New York, 1937), p. 152; Boston *Post*, 13 Mar., 18 May, 4 July 1876; William F. Phelps, *Centenary Address . . .* (Salem, Ohio, 1876); Richard S. Storrs, *An Oration Delivered Before the Citizens of New York . . . July 4th 1876* (New York, 1876), esp. p. 17; Saunders, *Addresses, 1876,* pp. 129–30, 184, 196; Smith M. Weed, *Centennial Oration . . . at Plattsburgh* (n.p., n.d. [4 July 1876]), pp. 7–8.

32. Perry, *Lieber*, p. 376; John M. Evans, *The Baptist Hymn and Tune Book for Public Worship* (Philadelphia, 1871), pp. 312, 344; John F. W. Ware, *An Oration . . .* (Boston, 1873), pp. 10–19; Strong, *Diary*, IV, 549; Ingersoll, *Letters*, pp. 160–61; *Phi Beta Kappa Orations*, II, 186–91, James W. Patterson at Dartmouth College, 23 June 1875; Zavarr Wilmshurst, *Liberty's Centennial; A Poem of 1876* (New York, 1876); *Nation*, XXII (6 Jan. 1876), 4–5; *New Orleans Times*, 3 Jan., 21 Feb., 18 Sept. 1876; Charles Wellington Stone, *An Oration Delivered in Templeton, Mass., July 4, 1876* (Boston, n.d.), p. 22.

CHAPTER FIVE

1. Students of this era have wonderful literature to aid them. Like any other person seeking a general grasp of the era, I owe thanks to many historians. The rise of imperialism and enhanced internationalism cannot be understood without using Ernest R. May, *Imperial Democracy, The Emergence of America as a World Power* (New York, 1961), esp. pp. 55–61, 261–68; and Ernest R. May, *American Imperialism* (New York, 1968), esp. pp. 202 ff. and 226 ff. May's excellent work does not oblige him to explore the background and extent of the psychological distress in the American outlook. Important background understanding is in Walter LaFeber, *The New Empire, An Interpretation of American Expansion 1860–1898* (Ithaca, 1963), esp. pp. 62–101. Also valuable are Julius W. Pratt, *Expansionists of 1898* (Baltimore, 1936), and Weinberg, *Manifest Destiny*, pp. 252 ff., 283 ff., 425–31, 453–61. Good insights are found in Bradford Perkins, *The Great Rapproch-*

ment (New York, 1968), and William E. Leuchtenburg, "Progressivism and Imperialism: The Progressive Movement and American Foreign Policy, 1898–1916," *Mississippi Valley Historical Review*, XXXIX (Dec. 1952), 483–504. See also Robert E. Osgood, *Ideals and Self-Interest in American Foreign Relations* (Chicago, 1953), pp. 27 ff., 42–57. The general scene has been thoughtfully treated in several studies by Richard Hofstadter. See his "Manifest Destiny and the Philippines," in Daniel Aaron, ed., *America in Crisis* (New York, 1952), pp. 172–200; *The Age of Reform* (New York, 1955); and *Anti-intellectualism in American Life* (New York, 1963), esp. pp. 368–69, 408–18. A helpful special study is Geoffrey Blodgett, *The Gentle Reformers* (Cambridge, Mass., 1966). John Higham's *Stranger in the Land* is very helpful for this era, esp. pp. 68–73, 106 ff., 161 ff. Racism and historical awareness were closely related. Material in the following is useful in this area: Edward N. Saveth, *American Historians and European Immigrants, 1875–1925* (New York, 1948); Edward N. Saveth, "Race and Nationalism in American Historiography: The Late Nineteenth Century," *Political Science Quarterly*, LIV (Sept. 1939), 421–41; Herman Ausubel, *Historians and Their Craft* (New York, 1950), pp. 20 ff.; Richard Hofstadter, *The Progressive Historians* (New York, 1968); H. M. Jones, *Theory of American Literature*, pp. 80–84, 90–104, 120–23, 131–35; and Arthur A. Ekirch, *The Decline of American Liberalism* (New York, 1955). The extraordinary insistence on patriotism and loyalty which accompanied this uneasy era has been analyzed in Wallace E. Davies, *Patriotism on Parade* (Cambridge, Mass., 1955); Mary R. Dearing, *Veterans in Politics* (Baton Rouge, 1952), pp. 402–96; and Bessie Louise Pierce, *Public Opinion and the Teaching of History in the United States* (New York, 1926), pp. 18–23.

2. Matthiessen, *James Family*, p. 296; Richard S. Storrs, Jr., *Martyr*, pp. 419–20; Robert L. Fulton and Thomas C. Trueblood, eds., *Patriotic Eloquence* (New York, 1900), has McKinley's speech, esp. pp. 218–19, hereafter cited as *Patriotic Eloquence*; May, *Imperial Democracy*, pp. 269–70; Watterson is quoted by Richard Hofstadter, "Manifest Destiny and the Philippines," from Grayson Kirk, *Philippine Independence* (New York, 1936), p. 25; Percy Lubbock, ed., *The Letters of Henry James*, I (New York, 1920), 309.

3. George Washington Warren, *Oration* . . . (Boston, 1881), pp. 36 ff., 52 ff.; Philip Schaff, *Church and State in the United States* (New York, 1888), pp. 54–55, 82–83.

4. Many excellent contemporary acknowledgments of God's charge are quoted in Julius W. Pratt, *Expansionists of 1898*, see esp. pp. 281, 287 ff., 291–95, 305, 314, 327 ff., 337, 348 ff.; Senator Platt's letters are reprinted in Louis A. Coolidge, *An Old-Fashioned Senator, Orville H. Platt of Connecticut* (New York, 1910), pp. 291–94, 287, hereafter cited as *Platt*; for a representation of this sentiment, see W. D. Washburn, Jr., *Cuba and Spain* (Minneapolis, 1898), pp. 3, 7–8; Tilden, II, 500; Putnam P. Bishop, *American Patriotism* (New York, 1887), pp. 4, 8, 11, 13.

5. *Nationalist*, I (June 1889), 33; II (May 1890), 180; *Collier's Once a Week*, III (Apr.–Oct. 1889), *passim*, esp. 2; George H. Peck, *An Oration* . . . (To-

peka, 1890), p. 12; Hiram F. Stevens, *Address* . . . (St. Paul, 1891), pp. 8–10, 13–16; helpful comments on the opposition to a new nationality are in Robert L. Beisner, *Twelve Against Empire* (New York, 1968), pp. 17, 220–25, 233; *Patriotic Eloquence* has Van Dyke's remarks, pp. 319–29, esp. 328; Norton quoted in Blodgett, *Gentle Reformers*, p. 267; William Wirt Warren, *Oration* . . . (Boston, 1877), pp. 30, 33, 40; Tilden, II, 492; Beecher, *Patriotism*, pp. 826–27.

6. Davies, pp. 319, 322–23; *Ingersoll Letters*, pp. 718–22; Eugene G. Hay, *Address* . . . *at Exposition Hall, Minneapolis, Minn.* (n.p., n.d. [30 May 1893]); *Patriotic Eloquence*, pp. 134, 136–37; David J. Hill, *Greater America* (Washington, 1898), pp. 3–4, 7–10.

7. Charles Sprague Smith, *The American University* (New York, 1887), pp. 6, 21–22, 25–26; Chauncey M. Depew, *Orations and After-Dinner Speeches* (New York, 1896), p. 51, hereafter cited as Depew, *Orations; Proceedings at the Dedication of the Soldiers and Sailors' Monument in Honor of Revolutionary Patriots at Sudbury, Massachusetts, June Seventeenth 1896* (South Framingham, 1897), pp. 35, 43–49, address by John L. Bates; *Patriotic Eloquence*, pp. 174–80, address by Rev. Charles E. Jefferson at the Broadway Tabernacle, New York City, 19 June 1898; Henry Strong, *Miscellanies* (Chicago, 1902), pp. 320 ff., 334–35, open letter to President McKinley; *Patriotic Eloquence*, pp. 42–43, has Bryan's December address at Savannah, Georgia; Hofstadter, *Age of Reform*, discusses the tie between democracy and aggression in America, pp. 272–73; Byron Sunderland, *A Sermon* . . . (Washington, 1885), pp. 10, 13; *Ingersoll Letters*, p. 651; *The Cosmopolitan*, XIX (Aug. 1895), 470–71; see the following instances in *The Literary Digest*, IX, 243, 278; XII, 32–33; XVI, 471, 693–94; XVII, 32–38.

8. Gladden's essay, "The Issues of the War," was published in *The Outlook*, LIX (16 July 1898), 673–75; *Northwest Magazine* quoted in May, *Imperial Democracy*, p. 257; *Patriotic Eloquence*, pp. 292, 293, 233, 236–37, 239; President Barrows' address is in *Patriotic Eloquence*, pp. 11–16; American Historical Association, *Annual Report, 1898* (Washington, 1899), pp. 429–564, see esp. 436, 446–47, 448, 468–69; McKinley spoke at the Atlantic Peace Jubilee, 15 December 1898, *Patriotic Eloquence*, pp. 221–23.

9. John L. Swift, *Oration* . . . (Boston, 1889), pp. 43–44, 46; Warner's statement in "Editor's Study," *Harper's Magazine*, LXXXIX (Aug. 1894), 475–76. For helpful comments on the growing appeal of integral nationalism and Hegelianism, see Weinberg, p. 411; Curti, *Roots*, pp. 178 ff.; Curti, *Social Ideas of American Educators*, pp. 336–43; Schaar, p. 86; racism is especially well treated in Higham, pp. 133–57. I find that the fearful quality in America's outlook goes back much earlier than Professor Higham seems to suggest, and also I find Anglo-Saxonism to be a conservative desire which repudiated the notion of America's unique mission.

10. Seymour's address is printed in Schauffler, ed., *Independence Day*, pp. 187–90; Newport *Mercury*, 13 October 1877; Beecher, *Patriotism*, pp. 789–91, 801, 805, 807–8, from 29 November 1877 sermon, "Past Perils and the Peril of Today," in which Beecher qualified his praise for the mass heart by suggesting that the mass mind needed instruction; *Phi Beta Kappa Orations*, II, 191–214, Phillips spoke at Harvard on 30 June 1881; *In Memorium, Gems of Poetry and Song on James A. Garfield* (Columbus, 1881), pp. 10–18 for Storr's address, and pp. 139–40 for Whittier's comment, hereafter cited as *Garfield Memorium*; typical of the Memorial Day appeal is an 1882 address by John D. Long in *After-Dinner and Other Speeches* (Boston, 1895), p. 79, hereafter cited as Long, *Speeches*; *Phi Beta Kappa Orations*, II, pp. 229–45.

11. Lubbock, *James Letters*, I, 141; John W. Burgess, *Political Science and Comparative Constitutional Law*, I (Boston, 1890), 38–39, 44–46; John F. Fitzgerald *Oration* . . . (Boston, 1897), p. 28; John Addison Porter, *Political Indifference* (Hartford, 1894), pp. 7 ff., 12, 15; Adolph A. Berle, *Oration* . . . (Boston, 1895); Peck's speech is in *Patriotic Eloquence*, pp. 243, 246, 248, 249.

12. *Platt*, pp. 134–35, Senate speech of 3 Mar. 1886; Nevins, *Hewitt*, pp. 211–12, House speech of 11 Feb. 1879; Hubert Howe Bancroft, *The Works of Hubert Howe Bancroft*, XXXVIII (San Francisco, 1890), 51–53, 203; Frederick Jackson Turner, *The Early Writings of Frederick Jackson Turner* (Madison, Wis., 1938), pp. 74–75, 82, 186, 188–89, 211, 219, 227–28, 229; for useful expressions, see *Harper's Weekly*, XXII, 126, 167, 267, 1006; XXV, 18, 226–27, 482, 547; XXVI, 434; XXVII, 418, 435; XXIX, 779, 810; XXX, 726, XXXI, 482–83, 518; XXXII, 846, 910; XXXV, 719; XXXVIII, 99; XLI, 482.

13. An interesting and helpful work is Frederic C. Jaher, *Doubters and Dissenters, Cataclysmic Thought in America, 1885–1918* (New York, 1964), esp. pp. 4–5.

14. Joseph Healy, *Oration* . . . (Boston, 1878), esp. pp. 6, 18 ff., 31; Long, *Speeches*, pp. 4–5; *Ingersoll Letters*, pp. 174, 210; *Garfield Memorium*, pp. 33, 42–44; Newport, *Mercury*, 6 Oct. 1877; Henry Strong, *Miscellanies* (Chicago, 1902), address before the Chicago Literary Club, 1886, p. 139; Irvin G. Wyllie, *The Self-Made Man in America* (New Brunswick, 1954), pp. 73–74, 133–50, 160–61, is very helpful; Edwin H. Abbott to Garfield, 8 June 1880, Garfield Mss., Book 72, Library of Congress.

15. *Phi Beta Kappa Orations*, I, 174 ff., 182, 188, 190; Godkin, II, 186–87; Davies, pp. 216, 242–43; Thomas C. Trueblood, William G. Caskey, and Henry E. Gordon, eds., *Winning Speeches in the Contests of the Northern Oratorical League* (New York, 1909), 1891 speech; *McClure's Magazine*, II (Feb. 1894), 302–3, 307; P. E. J. Martin to Bryan, 24 Oct. 1896, Bryan Mss., Box 4, Library of Congress; Arthur Hobson Quinn, *The Soul of America* (Philadelphia, 1932), recalls the sentiment of 1896, p. 119; *Platt*, pp. 265–66; Godkin, II, has Norton's views, 188; C.O'C. Hennessey to Bryan, 4 Nov. 1896, Bryan Mss., Box 6, Library of Congress; Eric F. Goldman, *John Bach Mc-*

Master, American Historian (Philadelphia, 1943), pp. 81–83, 96 ff.; AHA *Report,* 1898, p. 512.

16. General William T. Sherman, *Address . . . to the Graduating Class of the Michigan Military Academy* (n.p., n.d. [Orchard Lake, Mich., 19 June 1879]), pp. 3, 10; J. H. Atkinson to Garfield, 8 Mar. 1880, Garfield Mss., Vol. 69, Part 1, Library of Congress; *Phi Beta Kappa Orations,* II, CCNY address by Edward Morse Shepard, 27 Apr. 1882, 211–23; W. Stull Holt, ed., *Historical Scholarship in the United States, 1876–1901: As Revealed in the Correspondence of Herbert B. Adams* (Baltimore, 1938), pp. 61–62; Charles J. Bonaparte, *An Address . . . at . . . Yale Law School* (New Haven, 1890), pp. 9–15; Lubbock, *James Letters,* I, 243, 291–92; Goldman, *McMaster,* pp. 75, 76–78; *Patriotic Eloquence* has Dolliver's speech, pp. 123–24, and Cousin's, p. 89; Lyman's letter is printed in Blodgett, p. 266; Washington Gladden, *Our Nation and Her Neighbors* (Columbus, 1898), pp. 3–4, 8–9, 32–33, 38–39.

17. Richardson, IX, 4378–79; IX, 4395–96, 4398–99, 4409, 4411, 4431, 4440, 4442–43, 4446–47; X, 4553, 4556; X, 4597–98; X, 4620; X, 4735, 4822.

18. Richardson, X, 4885–86, 4888, 4895–96, 4944, 4946; XI, 5095, 5111–12, 5142, 5170, 5173–74, 5328–29, 5358–59, 5360, 5363.

19. Richardson, XI, 5440–49; XII, 5454, 5467, 5486, 5491, 5597, 5646, 5724, 5767.

20. Richardson, XII, 5821–23, 5893; XIII, 5943, 6025, 6065, 6085–86, 6090, 6091, 6146–47, 6151.

21. Richardson, XIII, 6236, 6239–40, 6243, 6251, 6292, 6307, 6320.

22. George F. Parker, *The Writings and Speeches of Grover Cleveland* (New York, 1892), pp. 13, 32, 114, 118–20, 121–22, 144, 147, 88, 99–101, 194, 122–24, 150–51, 155, 348, 291–92, 249–50, 167–68, 127–32, 238–41, 354–59; Allan Nevins, ed., *Letters of Grover Cleveland* (Boston, 1933), pp. 429–30, 443, 492, 505; *Literary Digest,* XVII (2 July 1898), 2–3; *Outlook,* LIX (2 July 1898), 502–3.

23. Ray Stannard Baker, *Woodrow Wilson, Life and Letters,* I (New York, 1927), 125, hereafter cited as *Wilson Letters;* Ray Stannard Baker and William E. Dodd, *The Public Papers of Woodrow Wilson,* I (New York, 1925–27), 19–42, 107, 354–70, 448–50, 171–77, hereafter cited as *Wilson Papers; Wilson Letters,* II, 125; *Atlantic,* LXIV (Nov. 1889), 577–88; *Forum,* XVI (Dec. 1893), 489–99; XVIII (Sept. 1894), 107–16; XIX (July 1895), 544–59; XXII (Dec. 1896), 447–66; *Atlantic,* LXXX (July 1897), 1–14; *Wilson Papers,* I, 336–37.

24. *Schurz,* V, 19–27, 76, 88, 93, 128, 143 ff., 191–214, 230, 250–59, 260–76, 399, 447, 452–57, 459–64, 465, 466 ff., 476, 477–94; *Century,* LVI (Sept. 1898), 781–88; *Schurz,* V, 513–14, 521 ff.; Carl Schurz, *A Review of the Year* (New York, 1898), pp. 22, 24.

25. John Fiske, *American Political Ideas* (New York, 1885), pp. 5–10, 18–30, 91 ff., 101 ff., 125, 129–30, 133–44, 148, 151–52; *Harper's Magazine*, LXX (Mar. 1885), 583–84; Ethel F. Fisk, ed., *The Letters of John Fiske* (New York, 1940), pp. 666–71, 673. For helpful comments on Fiske, see Milton Berman, *John Fiske* (Cambridge, 1961), pp. 211, 218–19, 250–52, 267–68, 270.

26. Andrew Carnegie, *Triumphant Democracy* (New York, 1886), *passim*, esp. pp. 471–509, see various letters of 1886 to Carnegie in Carnegie Mss., Vol. 9, Library of Congress; Burton J. Henrick, *Miscellaneous Writings of Andrew Carnegie*, I (Garden City, N.Y., 1933), 319, 349–50, hereafter cited as *Carnegie*; Henry S. Fairchild to Carnegie, 9 Jan. 1892, Carnegie Mss., Vol. 14, Library of Congress; *Carnegie*, I, 39–57; *North American Review*, CLXIII (Oct. 1896), 496–503; John Downing to Carnegie, 17 May 1897, Carnegie Mss., Vol. 42, Library of Congress; *Carnegie*, I, 65, 77; *North American Review*, CLXVII (Aug. 1898), 239–48.

27. Elting E. Morison, *The Letters of Theodore Roosevelt*, I (Cambridge, 1951), 71, 278–80, 379, hereafter cited as Roosevelt, *Letters*; Theodore Roosevelt, *The Works of Theodore Roosevelt*, XVIII (New York, 1906), 16–36, 38–39, 51; XIX, 92–98, 115; XVIII, 2, 7–10, 11–13; XIX, 51–63, hereafter cited as Roosevelt, *Works*; Roosevelt, *Letters*, I, 523, 630, 535–36, 554, 557–58, 566; Roosevelt, *Works*, XIX, 34, 42, 174–75, 184, 66 ff.; Roosevelt, *Letters*, I, 621–22, 637, 644–49, 655, 717, 724, 746–47, 764, 788; II, 803, 812–13, 817.

28. William Roscoe Thayer, *The Life and Letters of John Hay*, I (Boston, 1915), 429–30, hereafter cited as Hay; II, 1–6; I, 443–44, 471; II, 123; John Hay, *Addresses of John Hay* (New York, 1907), pp. 66–68, 77–80; Hay, II, 168; Hay, *Addresses*, pp. 70–74; Hay, II, 337.

29. Cowley, *Whitman*, II, 322–23, 305–6, 307–8, 309, 327–28, 402–3; *North American Review*, CLII (Mar. 1891), 332–38; Cowley, *Whitman*, II, 537, 339–40.

30. Claude G. Bowers, *Beveridge and the Progressive Era* (Cambridge, 1932), pp. 56–70; *Patriotic Eloquence*, pp. 24–26; Bowers, *Beveridge*, pp. 70–78.

31. *Nation*, XXX, 343–44; XXXI, 108–9, 336–37; XLV, 226; LVI, 136–37, LVII, 130–31, 365; LXII, 6–7, 46–47, 70, 190; LXIII, 398–99; LXVI, 22–23, 142, 218, 319, 454–55; LXVII, 306–7, 344, 404.

32. For 1897, see *The Outlook* as follows: LV, 15, 228; LVI, 197–98, 245, 290–91, 393–94, 431, 734–36, 928–29; LVII, 164, 944; LVIII, 309–10; 698, 708–9, 810, 903–5, 953, 961, 1058; LIX, 6, 11, 12, 14, 18–19, 105, 112–14, 156, 157–58, 161, 189–91, 211–12, 357–58, 362, 413–15, 454, 461–63, 492–93, 503, 510–14, 605, 623, 667, 765–67, 819–20, 923, 1004–5; LX, 215–16, 464–66, 527–29, 705–7, 791, 807–8, 998.

33. See, particularly *The Overland Monthly*, XIII (Apr. 1889), 423–29; XV (Feb. 1890), 134–41; XVIII (Sept. 1891), 333–34; XXV (June 1895), 684; XXVIII

(Oct. 1896), 428–35; XXX (Sept. 1897), 273–75; XXXI (May 1898), 472–73; XXXII (July 1898), 87–89; (Aug. 1898), 151; (Sept. 1898), 221, 291.

34. *Review of Reviews,* VII (May 1893), 387; IX (May 1894), 515–16; X (Aug. 1894), 131; XI (Apr. 1895), 415, 427; (June 1895), 622; XII (July 1895), 73; XIII (May 1896), 579–80.

35. Among the abundant material in the *North American Review,* see CXXIV (Jan. 1877), 1; (May 1877), 464; CXXVII (July–Aug. 1878), 4–16; (Sept–Oct. 1878), 237–60; CXXIX (Oct. 1879), 405–8; CXXXII (Jan. 1881), 30, 96–98; (Feb. 1881), 138–51; (May 1881), 407–26, 467–81; (June 1881), 537–45; CXXXIII (Sept. 1881), 241–54, 276–85; (Dec. 1881), 532–33; CXXXIV (Feb. 1882), 111–33; CXXXVI (Apr. 1883), 345–52; (May 1883), 454–66; CXXXVII (July 1883), 33–39; CXXXIX (Aug. 1884), 106–44, 164–78; CXL (Apr. 1885), 316–17; CXLII (June 1887), 583–95; CXLV (Oct. 1887), 435–50; CXLVI (Apr. 1888), 424–29; (May 1888), 548–57; CXLVII (Oct. 1888), 369–84; (Nov. 1888), 570–71; CXLVIII (Jan. 1889), 87; (Feb. 1889), 217, 224–25; CXLIX (Aug. 1889), 205–14; CL (Mar. 1890), 370–81; (May 1890), 547–62; (June 1890), 749–78; CLII (Apr. 1891), 423–30; (May 1891), 613–23; (June 1891), 656–81; CLIII (Dec. 1891), 672–83; CLIV (Mar. 1892), 304–18; CLXI (Sept. 1895), 297–312; CLXII (Apr. 1896), 385–405; CLXIII (July 1896), 1–16; (Aug. 1896), 175–82; (Nov. 1896), 587–94; CLXIV (Jan. 1897), 92–105; (Feb. 1897), 139–50; CLXV (Aug. 1897), 240–46; (Nov. 1897), 631–35; CLXVI (Mar. 1898), 257–67, 281–96, 310–23; (May 1898), 513–21, 585–94; (June 1898), 641–49; CLXVII (Aug. 1898), 223–58; (Dec. 1898), unnumbered, last page.

36. *Scribner's,* XIII (Feb. 1877), 559–60; *Century,* XXIII (Dec. 1881), 309–10; XXV (Mar. 1883), 787; XXVI (June 1883), 305–7; (July 1883), 362, 375, 950; XXVIII (Aug. 1884), 630; XXXIV (Sept. 1887), 791; XXXV (Dec. 1887), 325; (Mar. 1888), 807; XXXVI (June 1888), 313–14; (Oct. 1888), 854–55; XLI (Dec. 1890), 275–81; XLIV (Aug. 1892), 630–31; XLVII (Dec. 1893), 316–17; XLVIII (June 1894), 318–19; LI (Mar. 1896), 790–91; (Apr. 1896), 949–50; LII (June 1896), 315–16; LIII (Nov. 1896), 148–49; (Dec. 1896), 314–15; LIV (Oct. 1897), 951; LV (Jan. 1898), 476; LVI (July 1898), 314, 474–75; (Sept. 1898), 703–15, 788–94.

37. *The Arena,* I (Jan. 1890), 153–65; (May 1890), 700–709; II (Nov. 1890), 652, 763; V (Jan. 1892), 212–16; (Mar. 1892), 523–27; VII (Jan. 1893), 207; VIII (June 1893), 92–114; (Oct. 1893), 607–17; X (June 1894), 76–83; (July 1894), 260–62; XIII (June 1895), 26–30; XV (Mar. 1896), 654; (May 1896), 930–46; XVI (Aug. 1896), 512–13; XVII (Feb. 1897), 461–68; (Mar. 1897), 596–614; (May 1897), 975–79; XVIII (July 1897), 108–15, 126–27; (Aug. 1897), 245–53; (Oct. 1897), 562; (Nov. 1897), 577 ff.; (Dec. 1897), 827–33; XIX (Apr. 1898), 496 ff., 543–63; (June 1898), 740–51, 863–64; XX (Aug. 1898), 145–67, 223–38; (Sept. 1898), 344–63, 428; (Oct. 1898), 433–59; (Nov.–Dec. 1898), 558–68, esp. 567–68.

38. *The Forum,* I (Apr. 1886), 197; (May 1886), 216–17; (July 1886), 405–15, 468–75; (Aug. 1886), 507–17; II (Dec. 1886), 420–28; III (Aug. 1887), 622–30;

(Sept. 1887), 8–9, 443–57; (Oct. 1887), 133–42, 190–200; (Dec. 1887), 397–407; V (Mar. 1888), 16–26; (Apr. 1888), 156–65; (June 1888), 372, 444; (July 1888), 531; VI (Sept. 1888), 63–64; (Oct. 1888), 143, 204–5, 211; (Nov. 1888), 234; (Jan. 1889), 464; (Feb. 1889), 633; VII (June 1889), 358–59; (July 1889), 577–84; VIII (Sept. 1889), 27; (Feb. 1890), 612–16; (Mar. 1890), 56; (Apr. 1890), 125–30, 198–204; IX (June 1890), 430–35; X (Nov. 1890), 256–63; (Jan. 1891), 565; XI (Mar. 1891), 23–28; (May 1891), 342–43, 346; (June 1891), 408; XII (Sept. 1891), 2–8; (Nov. 1891), 399; (Jan. 1892), 667–74; XIII (Aug. 1892), 709, 710; XIV (Nov. 1892), 375; (Jan. 1893), 608–14; XV (Mar. 1893), 115; (July 1893), 521, 567–74; XVI (Nov. 1893), 315–24; (Dec. 1893), 518–19; (Jan. 1894), 563–67, 572, 587; XVII (July 1894), 514, 523, 571–72; XVIII (Sept. 1894), 1; XIX (Apr. 1895), 249–56; (June 1895), 385–89, 437; (Aug. 1895), 641–57; XX (Feb. 1896), 644, 651; XXI (Mar. 1896), 74–99; (June 1896), 438; (Aug. 1896), 673–74; (Oct. 1896), 234; XXII (Feb. 1897), 599, 600–606; XXIII (Apr. 1897), 144; (May 1897), 281; (Aug. 1897), 669–70, 719, 733–35; XXIV (Sept. 1897), 9, 45, 63–66; XXV (Mar. 1898), 11–24; (June 1898), 395, 403–25, 480; (Aug. 1898), 641–51, 723; XXVI (Sept. 1898), 14–26; (Oct. 1898), 167–68, 170, 177–87; (Nov. 1898), 279–81.

39. *Atlantic Monthly*, XL (July 1877), 49–64; XLI (Apr. 1878), 497–98; XLII (Oct. 1878), 385–86, 394–95, 397; XLIII (Jan. 1879), 2–9; (June 1879), 728; L (Sept. 1882), 309–11; LI (May 1883), 624–26; LIII (Jan. 1884), 129–30; (June 1884), 841; LX (July 1887), 3–9, 85–91; (Aug. 1887), 172; LXIII (Feb. 1889), 227–31; LXVII (Mar. 1891), 340–41; LXX (July 1892), 89–90; LXXI (May 1893), 579–80; LXXII (Dec. 1893), 814–19; LXXV (Jan. 1895), 16–28; LXXVIII (July 1896), 35–44; LXXIX (Apr. 1897), 443–50, 528–38, 569–73; LXXX (Dec. 1897), 745–52; LXXXI (Jan. 1898), 41–50; (June 1898), 721–27; LXXXII (July 1898), 29–36; (Aug. 1898), 145–53, 287; (Sept. 1898), 430–32; (Oct. 1898), 552–59.

40. *Leslie's Magazine,* esp. LVIII (9 Aug. 1884), 386; LIX (30 Aug. 1884), 18; (1 Nov. 1884), 162; LXX (1 Mar. 1890), 78; (29 Mar. 1890), 170; LXXXVI (31 Mar. 1898), 194; (2 June 1898), 350; (30 June 1898), 418; *The Independent,* esp. XXXII (4 Nov. 1880), 16; XXXIII (10 Mar. 1881), 16; (15 Sept. 1881), 16; (29 Sept. 1881), 16–17; XXXVIII (8 July 1886), 858–59; XXXIX (17 Nov. 1887), 1483; (24 Nov. 1887), 1516; (29 Dec. 1887), 1688; XLIV (20 Oct. 1892), 1479; (7 July 1892), 942; XLVIII (2 Jan. 1896), 20; (5 Nov. 1896), 1488; XLIX (29 July 1897), 972; (25 Nov. 1897), 1537; L (31 Mar. 1898); (19 May 1898), 652–53.

41. *The Youth's Companion,* LVIII (26 Feb. 1885), 76; (5 Mar. 1885), 58; (9 Apr. 1885), 140; (30 Apr. 1885), 172; LIX (15 Apr. 1886), 140; (3 June 1886), 212; (1 July 1886), 252; (29 July 1886), 288; LX (24 Nov. 1887), 526; LXI (1 Mar. 1888), 104; (30 Aug. 1888), 416; LXII (17 Jan. 1889), 32; (28 Feb. 1889), 104; (21 Mar. 1889), 144; (23 May 1889), 268; (27 June 1889), 328; (21 Nov. 1889), 604; LXIII (23 Jan. 1890), 48; (10 June 1890), 336; (4 July 1890), *passim;* (18 Sept. 1890), 484; LXIV (15 Jan. 1891), 36; (2 July 1891), 376; LXVI (16 Feb. 1893), 84; (17 Aug. 1893), 400; LXVII (18 Jan. 1894), 28; (8 Nov. 1894), 538; LXVIII (31 Jan. 1895), 52; (7 Feb. 1895), 64; (14 Nov. 1895), 584; LXX (2 Jan. 1896), 8; (6 Feb. 1896), 70; (5 Mar. 1896), 122; LXXI (21 Jan. 1897), 30;

(25 Feb. 1897), 90: (4 Mar. 1897), 102; (19 Aug. 1897), 386; (7 Oct. 1897), 466.

42. Characteristic hymns are: George Harris and William J. Tucker, *Hymns of the Faith* (New York, 1887), 595, 596; *Hymn and Tune Book* (Nashville, 1889), 367; see letter from Rev. F. B. Crunz to W. J. Bryan, 4 Nov. 1896, Bryan Mss., Box 6, Library of Congress; George T. Balch, *Methods of Teaching Patriotism in the Public Schools* (New York, 1890), pp. v–xxxiv, 1–8, 9 ff., 56–64, 75–77, 80–81, 97, 107–8.

43. Long, *Speeches*, pp. 158–59; *Northern Orations*, pp. 19–24; Godkin, II, 184–85; *Forum*, XVII (Mar. 1894), 48–51; Godkin, II, 199, to C. E. Norton, 202, to Norton; Washington's speech is in *Patriotic Eloquence*, p. 332.

44. Clemens is quoted in Roger B. Solomon, *Twain and the Image of History* (New Haven, 1961), pp. 136–37, and in Willard Thorpe's article in Denny and Gilman, eds., *The American Writer and the European Tradition*, esp. p. 104; *Ingersoll Letters*, pp. 624–25; Holt, ed., *Historical Scholarship,* has Eggleston's letter to H. B. Adams, p. 253; for Henry Adams' views, see esp. Harold D. Cater, *Henry Adams and His Friends* (Boston, 1947), pp. 134, 437–38, 442, 453; *Adams Letters*, II, 33, 47, 55–56, 103, 191, 194–95; for excellent discussion of Henry Adams, see Ernest Samuels, *Henry Adams, The Middle Years* (Cambridge, Mass., 1958), pp. 68–97, 349–50, 374, 385; Ernest Samuels, *Henry Adams, The Major Phase* (Cambridge, Mass., 1964), p. 209; and for Clemens, see Solomon, *Twain*, pp. 19, 42–43.

45. H. W. Bolton, *Patriotism* (Chicago, 1890), pp. 9 ff., 26–29, 181 ff., 193, 198–99, 203–10, 216, 220, 223, 245, 274, 285, 288; see the files of the *Rocky Mountain News* for 1887, notably 20 June, 4 July, 19 July, 30 Oct., 27 Nov., and 2 Dec.; *Literary Digest,* III (4 July 1891), 253; Page is quoted in Goldman, *McMaster*, pp. 71–72; *Northern Orations*, pp. 89–90, 92, 94; William McKinley, *Speeches and Addresses* (New York, 1893), pp. 218, 249, 360, 366, 431, 444, 485, 535–36, 538, 583 ff.; Henry George, *An Oration Delivered . . . in the California Theatre, San Francisco . . . 4th of July, 1877* (n.p., n.d.), pp. 3, 5, 7–11, 17, 19–20; Henry Cabot Lodge, *Oration . . .* (Boston, 1879), pp. 13 ff., 21–28, 37–40, 42, 44; Herman von Holst, "Are We Awakened?" *Journal of Political Economy,* II (Sept. 1894), 485–516; Alice M. Kellogg, ed., *Patriotic Quotations Relating to American History* (New York, 1898), *passim; Literary Digest,* XVII (2 July 1898), 2, 5, 6; *Outlook,* LX (24 Dec. 1898), 1031.

46. Charles W. Eliot, *American Contributions to Civilization* (New York, 1898), pp. 73–76, 80–100; Eliot, *Works,* I, 95, 361–62, 367; II, 752, 711–44; *Forum,* XVIII (Oct. 1894), 129–45; *Proceedings of the American Association for the Advancement of Science, 1898,* 587–615, esp. 615; *Northern Orations,* pp. 50–53; Cushman K. Davis, *An Address . . .* (St. Paul, 1898), *passim;* Cushman K. Davis, *Address Before the Society of the Army of the Tennessee,*

August 13, 1884 (St. Paul, n.d.), *passim;* Norton's talk is recorded and discussed in *Outlook*, LIX (6 Aug. 1898), 815–16; Nevins, *Hewitt*, p. 310.

47. Howells, *Letters*, I, 271, 413, 418–19, 429; II, 8–9, 52–53, 54–55; *Harper's Magazine*, XCV (July 1897), 199–204; Howells, *Letters*, II, 70, 95.

48. Josiah Strong, *Our Country* (Cambridge, 1963; edition of 1891 edited by Jurgen Herbst), esp. pp. 5–42, 102–6, 121, 132, 151–55, 160–86, 200–201, 212–25, 251–53; Josiah Strong, *The New Era* (New York, 1893), pp. 1–29, 64, 72, 80, 164–202, 296, 354; *North American Review*, CLXV (Sept. 1897), 343–49; *The Hymnal, Revised and Enlarged* (New York, 1892), 184.

49. Bryant, *Prose*, II, 414–19; Long, *Speeches*, pp. 206–23; Turner, *Early Writings*, pp. 60–64; Cyrus Northrop, *American Progress* (Madison, 1893), pp. 2–7, 12–13, 16–18; The Minneapolis *Times* is quoted in *Literary Digest*, XII (14 Mar. 1896), 583; Charles Henry Butler, *The Voice of the Nation* (New York, 1898), pp. 22, 124; *Literary Digest*, XVIII (2 July 1898), 4; *Outlook*, LIX (14 May 1898), 115; Spencer Borden to William McKinley, 10 June 1898, Series 1, Reel 3, McKinley Mss., Library of Congress; *Literary Digest*, XVII (2 July 1898), 3–4; Scott F. Hershey, *The Spanish-American War . . . Delivered . . . July 3rd, 1898, in The First Presbyterian Church, Boston* (n.p., n.d.), pp. 3, 12–16; *McClure's*, XI (July 1898), 287, 303–4; *Patriotic Eloquence*, pp. 115–16, 116–17; *Annals of the American Academy of Political and Social Science*, XII (Sept. 1898), 173–92, an essay by H. H. Powers.

50. *Harper's Magazine*, XCVII (Oct. 1898), 720–28; *McClure's*, XI (Oct. 1898), 553–58; *Patriotic Eloquence*, pp. 155–56; *Cosmopolitan*, XXVI (Dec. 1898), 212.

INDEX